The Days of Wine and Roses Are Over

*Governor Hugh Carey
and New York State*

Daniel C. Kramer

University Press of America, Inc.
Lanham • New York • London

Copyright © 1997 by
University Press of America, ® Inc.
4720 Boston Way
Lanham, Maryland 20706

3 Henrietta Street
London, WC2E 8LU England

Library of Congress Cataloging-in-Publication Data

Kramer, Daniel C.,
The days of wine and roses are over : Governor Hugh Carey and New
York State / Daniel C. Kramer.
p.   cm.
Includes bibliographical references and index.
l. Carey, Hugh L. 2. Governors--New York (State)--Biography
3. New York (State)--Politics and government--1951- I. Title
F125.3.C37K73   1996   974.7'043'092--dc20   96-41780   CIP
[B]
ISBN 0-7618-0562-1 (cloth: alk. ppr.)
ISBN 0-7618-0563-X (pbk. : alk. ppr.)

⊖™The paper used in this publication meets the minimum
requirements of American National Standard for information
Sciences—Permanence of Paper for Printed Library Materials,
ANSI Z39.48—1984

Dedication

THIS BOOK IS DEDICATED TO MY WIFE RICHENDA; MY CHILDREN BRUCE, TAMSYN AND ELSPETH; MY SON-IN-LAW HARRY RICHARDSON; MY MOTHER-IN-LAW MARJORIE LEE; MY MOTHER MILDRED; AND MY GRANDCHILDREN MARTHA, LEAH AND MADELINE RICHARDSON. MAY MARTHA, LEAH AND MADELINE LIVE TO SEE THE DAY WHEN A REASONABLE LEVEL OF TAXATION IS SEEN NOT AS A BURDEN BUT AS A PRECONDITION OF A CIVILIZED AND HUMANE SOCIETY

Contents

Preface and Acknowledgments

Biographies of Governors of American states have been appearing with some frequency over the past two decades. Limiting ourselves just to Chief Executives who never participated in a Presidential general election, there are David Kenney's *A Political Passage: The Career of Stratton of Illinois* (Carbondale: Southern University Press, 1990); Michael Kurtz's and Morgan Peoples' *Earl K. Long: The Saga of Uncle Earl and Louisiana Politics* (Baton Rouge: Louisiana State Univ. Press, 1990); Robert McElvaine's *Mario Cuomo: A Biography* (New York: Charles Scribner's Sons, 1988) and Robert Pack's *Jerry Brown: The Philosopher Prince* (New York: Stein and Day, 1978). Hugh Carey of New York, who was New York State's First Citizen from 1975 through 1982, had accomplishments that were at least as outstanding as those of the protagonists of these four works. The only book-length volume about his Administration that has appeared since he departed for private life, Gerald Benjamin and T. Norman Hurd (eds.) - *Making Experience Count: Managing Modern New York in the Carey Era* (Albany: The Nelson A. Rockefeller Institute of Government, 1985), **is** a valuable compendium of interviews with him and some of his aides. However, his policies and politics deserve more than a collection of essays. They warrant an in-depth study; and this book provides just that -- although space limitations prevent much if any discussion of how he dealt with certain areas, e.g., energy, the mentally ill.

Many contend that Carey's greatest accomplishment was keeping New York City out of bankruptcy in 1975. Several chapters of this volume are devoted to that topic and show how he exerted himself on the national, state and local levels to rescue the City and prevent the State itself from toppling over. They concentrate more on **his** role in saving the metropolis than do other works on the 1975 fiscal crisis. These chapters are preceded by two describing his pre-Congressional and Congressional careers, his stunning 1974 primary victory and his easy 1974 general election win. After he kept New York's head above water, he was at the peak of his prestige. However, as Chapter 7 indicates, his relations with some Democratic Party leaders and with the State Legislature were not as good as they could have been. Primary challenges and his vetoes of death penalty legislation helped make his 1978 reelection effort surprisingly dif-

The Days of Wine and Roses Are Over

ficult. Chapter 8 describes that campaign. Despite the tensions prevailing between Carey and the lawmakers, he was able to achieve important triumphs in many policy areas above and beyond rescuing New York City, victories discussed in my Chapters 9 through 13. These chapters sketch numerous problems American state governments now confront and indicate how one state coped with them. They thus should be of real interest to historians, political scientists and students of public policy. Had the book adopted the chronological format that is usual in biographies and discussed on one page how the Chief Executive reacted to this or that demand, on the second his personal problems, and on the third his dislike of this or that fellow politician, the analyses of the issues would have gotten lost in the shuffle. This would have been unfortunate, because it is how a leader approaches the troubles that confront her jurisdiction that is the most important factor making her a champion or a loser.

It is not that a politician's personality is without importance. In fact, Carey's prickly and detached nature did hamper his dealings with other governmental officials and lowered his reputation with the public. A horrendous series of stupid actions and statements, as well as an unlucky second marriage, further reduced his standing with the electorate; and this poor showing in the polls was one of the factors convincing him not to run for a third term in 1982. These blunders and his moodiness and inaccessibility are analyzed in Chapters 14 and 15. Chapter 16, the conclusion, shows that despite his remoteness and other personal flaws he was an outstanding Governor because of his many policy triumphs -- which were due in part to the fact that (as described in Chapter 15) he hired excellent people and let them get on with the job even though he was often insensitive in his dealings with them.

In writing this volume I have interviewed the Governor and over 125 people who had contact with him, e..g, legislators, political opponents, Commissioners and Press Secretaries. These individuals include, among others, William Abelow, Bella Abzug, Warren Anderson, T. Ludlow Ashley, Elinor Bachrach, Bruce Balle, Dominic Baranello, Abraham Beame, Stephen Berger, Peter Berle, Richard Berman, Barbara Blum, Richard Bonamo, David Burke, John Burns, Karen Burstein, Kevin Cahill, James Cannon, Hugh L. Carey, Stephen Chinlund, Barbara Collins, Elizabeth Connelly, Martin Connor, Thomas Coughlin III, Gerald Cummins, William

Preface

Cunningham, John Defiggos, Michael Del Giudice, Susan Dempsey, George Dempster, Fredric Dicker, Mortimer Downey, Perry Duryea, John Dyson, Peter Edelman, Julius Edelstein, John Egan, Eugene Eidenberg, Herman D. Farrell, Jr., Stanley Fink, Harold Fisher, Robert Flacke, Gerald Ford, Judith Frangos, Irving Freedman, Thomas Frey, Lester Gerhardt, Lois Gibbs, Martha Golden, Harrison J. Goldin, Peter Goldmark, Herbert Gordon, Victor Gotbaum, George Gould, Christopher Hansen, Raymond Harding, William D. Hassett, Jr., John Heimann, William Hennessy, Alan Hevesi, Thomas Hobart, Charles Holcomb, Judith Hope, Gedale Horowitz, James Introne, H. Graham Jones, Richard Kahan, Robert Kerker, Edward Koch, Lawrence Kolb, Stanley Kramer, Arthur Kremer, Mary Anne Krupsak, Robert Laird, James Larocca, Orin Lehman, Albert Lewis, Stanley Lundine, Frank Macchiarola, John Marchi, David Margolis, John Marino, Victor Marrero, Alton Marshall, Julio Martinez, Dick Netzer, Matthew Nimetz, Paul O'Dwyer, Manfred Ohrenstein, John Omicinski, Hugh O'Neill, Michael Patterson, Henry Peyrebrune, Richard Ravitch, Edward V. Regan, James Regan, Ogden Reid, W. Bernard Richland, Simon Rifkind, Felix Rohatyn, Alexander Rollo, Herbert Ryan, Jeffrey Sachs, Robert Schiffer, L. William Seidman, Donna Shalala, Albert Shanker, Menachem Shayovich, Clarence Sundram, John Tamagni, James Tully, Jr., Cyrus Vance, James Vlasto, Richard Wade, Robert F. Wagner, Robert F. Wagner, Jr., Benjamin Ward and Malcolm Wilson. I owe much to them all.

Additionally, I would like to thank Ms. Roxana Hnateyko, Ms. Szilvia Szmuk and Ms. Jean Wassong, in charge of the Carey Papers in the St. John's University Library, as I have spent many hours with -- and made extensive use of -- the documents in their custody. Likewise, I am pleased to express my gratitude to the men and women at the Gerald R. Ford Library at the University of Michigan in Ann Arbor, especially David Horrocks and William McNitt, for awarding me a grant to do research there; and for classifying and letting me leaf through its substantial collection on President Ford and the New York fiscal crisis. I also greatly appreciate the kindness of Ms. Diane Windham Shaw, Special Collections Librarian at the Lafayette College Library in Easton, Pa., in permitting me to peruse the William E. Simon Papers; and of Mr. James D. Folts, Head of the Research Services at the New

The Days of Wine and Roses Are Over

York State Archives, for allowing me to see the Carey materials in those Archives. I am once again in debt to the librarians at the College of Staten Island CUNY and at the New York Public Library at 42nd Street and Fifth Avenue in Manhattan for providing me with access to their newspaper, periodical and other collections.

Finally, let me acknowledge the permission granted by the following newspapers to allow me to quote from their respective publications: the *Boston Globe*, the *Democrat and Chronicle* of Rochester, the *New York Times* and the *Times Union* of Albany. I thank them warmly for their cooperation (as well as Rabbi Gunther W. Plaut of Toronto for letting me quote from his autobiography *Unfinished Business*).

Chapter 1
Carey: the Formative Years

BECAUSE New York with its 18 million people is one of the most populous of America's states and because the nation's leading newspaper (the *New York Times*) and the major radio/television networks have their headquarters within its borders, its Governor almost inevitably becomes one of America's leading political figures.(1) Since the Civil War, Grover Cleveland, Theodore Roosevelt and Franklin Delano Roosevelt all served in the White House after having been its Chief Executive. In addition, five of its Governors -- Horatio Seymour, Samuel Tilden, Charles Evans Hughes, Alfred E. Smith and Thomas E. Dewey -- contended unsuccessfully for the nation's highest office. Its First Citizen from 1983 through 1994, Mario Cuomo, probably would have obtained the Democratic nomination for the Presidency in 1988 and 1992 had he been willing to be tapped for this honor. To the list of the Empire State's Presidential possibilities must be added Nelson A. Rockefeller, Governor from 1959 through 1973. This liberal Republican was never the national-ticket nominee of his Party but everyone expected that he would be accorded that accolade one day. (He was, nonetheless, Gerald Ford's appointed Vice President from 1974 through 1976.)

Hugh Carey, whose Administration is the subject of this book, fits right into the New York mold of talented Chief Executives. Though still very much alive, this Democrat who was New York State's Governor from 1975 through 1982 is, unlike some of his predecessors, currently little more than a footnote in the writings of American historians and political scientists. Even to those men and women who remain aware of him, the mention of his name evokes one of two images, one positive and one negative. On the plus side, he is seen as the individual who saved New York City and State from collapse during fiscal crises that shook both jurisdictions during 1975 and 1976. In the words of an editorial in the *New York Times*, "The chief difference now [in a 1991 financial emergency faced by the metropolis] is the lack of leadership and help from higher levels of government. In the last fiscal crisis, Gov. Hugh Carey made it his historic mission to save the city. He was able to advance needed funds, created institutions to monitor and manage city finances, lobbied successfully for Federal help and

The Days of Wine and Roses Are Over

knocked heads to enlist labor and business in a rescue effort".(2) However, people also remember his disastrous marriage to a businesswoman of Greek ancestry, Evangeline Gouletas. (His first wife Helen had died of cancer in early 1974 just before he commenced his run at the governorship in earnest.) Ms. Gouletas had introduced herself to Carey and the press as a "widow": in the days immediately preceding and following their April, 1981 wedding it was revealed that she had been a spouse three times previously and that all three ex-husbands were alive and well in various parts of the globe. The Governor became a laughing stock. When I mention to colleagues, relatives and friends that I am writing a book on Hugh Carey, some smirk and retort "Oh, isn't he the sucker who married that woman with three husbands?".

In fact, he was an outstanding Governor. He not only kept the City and the State out of bankruptcy court but -- as will be one of the main theses of this book -- had many other significant accomplishments to his credit. Thus he is worthy of being mentioned in the same breath with Smith, Dewey and Rockefeller.

Furthermore, many of his victories had to run the gauntlet of a bicameral legislature whose lower house (the State Assembly) was controlled by his own Democratic Party but whose upper house (the State Senate) was Republican for his entire eight years in office. The Legislature mirrored, moreover, the many fissures in the State above and beyond the partisan. New York City and the rest of the State ("upstate") have for two centuries viewed one another as enemies. Within the metropolis of 8 million itself, blacks, Hispanics and many white ethnic groups live in wary proximity. The progressive, bohemian values of the City's Borough of Manhattan south of 96th Street are regarded with distaste by the churchgoing, family-centered residents of the outer boroughs of The Bronx, Brooklyn, Staten Island and Queens.(3) "Upstate" is split between the prosperous suburban counties of the New York metropolitan area such as Nassau, Suffolk and Westchester; aging cities large and small that are trying to rejuvenate themselves, e.g,. Buffalo, Syracuse and Newburgh; prosperous farm regions in the west; tourist destinations in the Catskills; and pockets of poverty in the spectacular Adirondack Mountains. Strong public employee unions and large employers whose departure would be disastrous have different visions of the State's future. New York's governors, to get anything important done, must fashion majorities out of these many powerful, clashing, and parochial factions. The difficulty of molding such coalitions makes even more impressive the triumph of the State's first-rate Governors such as Hugh Carey.

Carey was born on April 11, 1919 in South Brooklyn at 375 Douglass Street, between the Borough's Fourth and Fifth Avenues. This address no longer exists: it has been made part of a condo-minium that pompously calls itself "Park Slope Villas", since "Park Slope" is considered a fancier neighborhood than "South Brook-lyn". His parents, Margaret and Dennis, had been born in the United States; but the native land of his four grandparents was Ireland. His maternal grandparents were from County Tyrone, now part of Northern Ireland and thus of the United Kingdom; while his paternal set, Michael and Delia Carey, was from County Galway in what is presently the Republic of Ireland. Hugh was the third of six boys: of the other five, Edward, Dennis, John, Martin and George, Edward had the most impact on his political career. (Premature death has stricken his family too often; and in 1959 George, the youngest Carey sibling, was killed in a plane crash.)(4)

Margaret Carey, whose maiden name was Collins, was before her marriage secretary to journalist Nellie Bly, known for going around the world in 1889 and 1890 faster than Jules Verne's imaginary hero Phineas Fogg. When Margaret worked for Bly, the reporter had entered the more prosaic business of selling steel barrels to oil moguls. She appreciated her aide so much that she even named a barrel model after her. During World War I the oil drum business became more and more hectic and Margaret became busier and busier. One company that wanted this commodity was the Tidewater Oil Depot in Brooklyn. Dennis Carey was at the time an assistant there to a Mr. Murphy. When Murphy called the Bly company for barrels, Ms. Collins answered the phone. Since he did not want to haggle over business with a woman, he turned the negotiations over to his helper. The bargaining led to love, marriage and the future Governor of New York State.(5)

Though in the 1915 New York State census Hugh's paternal Grandfather Michael is listed simply as a "laborer-mason" and in the 1920 U.S. census as a "laborer for contractor", and though paternal Grandmother Delia is not described in either survey as having an outside source of income, the couple obviously were not living on the brink of starvation. In 1908, as records in the New York City Register's Brooklyn office indicate, they purchased the 375 Douglass Street residence where Hugh was born. Immediately after his arrival in 1919 they sold it and acquired a still-standing, three story brick rowhouse at 13 Park Place, a few blocks away but more clearly in Park Slope than was 375 Douglass. Thirteen Park Place is between Fifth and Sixth Avenues, but much closer to Fifth. When the Careys lived there, the area was mainly Irish. It is now predominantly Hispanic. Thus just across the street is the headquarters of the Ecuadorean Federation of Brooklyn, founded in 1981. When Delia and Michael moved to Park Place, they let a six-room flat on the second floor to Dennis, Margaret and their (eventually) six children. Hugh, his brothers and his parents lived in this apartment until the end of 1935. While residing there he nearly died of whooping cough, played stickball in the street, and was an altar boy at St. Augustine's Church at 6th Avenue and Park Place where he got into trouble for his pranks in that holy spot. He earned pocket money delivering goods for a neighborhood hardware store and answering phone calls for a local undertaker. (6)

Dennis may have had to lease an apartment from his parents but, buoyed by the American dream that anyone with talent who is willing to work hard can become successful, he declared his independence from Tidewater and started his own oil-and-kerosene distributing concern in Brooklyn. It flourished at first but when the large oil producers refused to grant it credit and the Great Depression hit, he had to neglect it and begin selling on behalf of the giants. It had fallen into debt and its creditors congregated in front of 13 Park Place offering Hugh and his brothers candy if they would just tell them where their father was. Dennis said they could take the sweets but must not retail any information. Once to avoid the horde outside his door he jumped over a fence in the back yard and dashed through a butcher shop to reach Fifth Avenue. The lenders were after Margaret, too; and on one occasion she left the house dressed as a "flapper" of dubious morality to avoid de-tection. This dismal period in his family's history helped convince Hugh when he became Governor that New York City must remain solvent. (7)

Once the end of the Depression was on the horizon, Dennis revivified his own company. The determined Margaret kept the books and the six boys helped out, partly for financial reasons and also partly because their mother wanted to develop their moral character.(8) Thus the business edged into the black, but barely; and actually did not start prospering until the 1940s and World War II. Oldest brother Edward labored hard to increase its sales and moved it to Long Island City.(9) Despite its problems, Margaret and Dennis were able in late 1935 to acquire an attached, still-handsome large brick house at 60 Rutland Road in the Lefferts Manor section of Brooklyn, a community near Flatbush just east of Prospect Park. Lefferts Manor, hit by white flight in the 1950s and 60s, is now predominantly African-American rather than Irish but whites and interracial couples have also been moving there recently and it remains middle class just as it was when it sheltered the Careys.

When Governor, Carey helped dish out billions of dollars in aid to the State's public schools. He himself, however, was entirely a product of his native borough's Roman Catholic educational system. He has always been a practicing Catholic who takes his faith seriously. Once his hands trembled when he was not allowed to take communion at a funeral because of his marriage to the divorced Ms. Gouletas.(10) He attended St. Augustine's Grammar School (11) and then entered St. Augustine's High at 64 Park Place. (Both institutions are now defunct.) St. Augustine's High was academically selective(12); but he had no difficulty being admitted since his 99.875 grade point average had put him academically at the top of his grammar school class.(13) He also had no trouble graduating from the High School. However, he obtained a lower average than in his younger years, since he not only helped his parents with the oil business but also joined the track team and worked in the shoe department of downtown Brooklyn's Abraham and Straus to earn change to support a rather full social life.(14). William Cunningham, his Deputy Appointments Secretary, is also an alumnus of St. Augustine's High. One of his instructors there who had previously had Carey told Cunningham to keep his eye on him, as he had a bright future.(15)

The Days of Wine and Roses Are Over

In 1939 Hugh entered St. John's University, a Catholic college then in downtown Brooklyn and attended almost entirely by the children of the Irish and Italian working and middle classes. To help pay tuition, he had to continue to work after school and also got a job in the College library through the New Deal's National Youth Administration. He still needed more cash, however, and so in 1939 he signed up as a private in Squadron C of the 101st Cavalry of the New York National Guard.(16)

As with millions of other young Americans, Carey's academic progress was interrupted by World War II. His unit was activated and he remained in the army until 1946. He soon became an officer and trained new draftees. Then his Division, the 104th Timberwolf, was sent to Europe where it and he engaged in heavy combat for a period of time so extensive that it came close to a U.S. Army record. In the midst of the fighting he had to have an appendix removed. The doctors who performed the operation told him to stay in the hospital a week; but he decamped.to join his troops almost immediately after leaving the recovery room.(17) He was among the officers who crossed the makeshift Remagen bridge across the Rhine, who participated in the capture of the City of Cologne, and who helped free a Nazi concentration camp in Nordhausen, a town right in the middle of Germany.(18) After his election as Governor, a "Fellow Timberwolf" from Greenville, South Carolina, sent him a letter saying:

> "Congratulations on the highest public office in the Great State of New York and loyal Democrat. Saw your little son's picture in our paper recently holding daddy's hat at the daughter's wedding. I have two radio programs from my office daily and one full hour TV farm program....[I would like] to help support your campaign for the greatest President [obviously Carey] we've had in a long time. I know demands are heavy on your time, but let me hear from you...."(19)

Similar in tone were notes from many other members of that Division.

Both the heavy fighting and the sight of the starving Nordhausen survivors made this product of a relatively sheltered Brooklyn boyhood realize how inhumane man could be toward man and bred in him a loathing of the use of violence and killing to solve political and social problems that has lasted to this day. A rabbi who was with the Carey unit when it entered the gulag says that the first thing that the soldiers saw was "....about 4000 dead lying around and 400 scarcely alive....Death for the others had come mostly through starvation, a fearful sight indeed".(20) Carey's role in the liberation of Nordhausen had one unanticipated political benefit. During a Congressional campaign in the 1960s, he was talking to some potential voters on 13th Avenue in the Orthodox Jewish quarter of Borough Park in Brooklyn. A baker and part-time rabbi named Moses Mandelbaum was in the audience. He could not believe his eyes. There in front of him was a man who was the carbon copy of the American major who had marched into Nordhausen to free it when he had been incarcerated there. A quick inquiry revealed that the Congress Member before him was indeed the soldier who had rescued him. Mandelbaum was so overcome that he kissed the hem of the legislator's suit jacket. Needless to say, he, his family and his community became stout political supporters of their Irish-American liberator.(21)

Carey was discharged in 1946, but not before receiving the Bronze Star and the Croix de Guerre with Silver Star. When he left, he had attained the rank of full Colonel.(22) He believes that his war experience was very valuable to him in his stint as Governor. As an army officer one has to develop strategy. Therefore he was, he claims, able to plan ahead during the 1975 New York City financial crisis and not simply react to day-to-day reversals. Also, an officer has to pick competent people to carry out his ideas. Thus when he arrived in Albany he already had had practice in choosing capable subordinates.(23) Most of his aides and Commissioners **were** top-notch individuals. They were men and women to whom he owes an incalculable debt for making a glorious success of an Administration that had to sail on turbulent seas.

Carey showed physical bravery in civilian as well as military life in addition to political courage as Governor. When still a Congress-man, he saw a mugging in progress at Prospect Park West and Second Street near his Park Slope home. He was with his 12 year old son Michael but ran over to catch the thief. A patrolman had also seen the incident and took over. After the police officer went for a wild ride in the comandeered cab of one

The Days of Wine and Roses Are Over

Jack Leon with the victim but without the Representative, the thug was finally apprehended.(24) On a more mundane note, Dennis and Margaret Carey because of Hugh's early sickness had in the 1920s acquired a summer home on East Pine Street in Long Beach, Nassau County (to which they ultimately retired). The Carey boys were wont to play with the other youths in the community. When a youngster named George made unwanted advances to a young lady, Hugh threw him off the dock. When he came up for air, the future public official told him to behave like a gentleman.(25)

After the Axis defeat, Carey returned to St. John's, thanks in part to the GI Bill of Rights that accorded so many working and lower-middle-class young men the opportunity for higher education. He majored in History but took some Chemistry courses.(26) He felt, logically, that knowing something about chemicals would make him more able to help his parents with Peerless Oil and Chemical, the sobriquet of their oil and gas business. However, any dreams he may have harbored of spending his life in a laboratory developing new polymers soon vanished; and he entered the evening/summer division of St. John's University Law School in 1947. Though any-thing but a rebellious child, he became an attorney in part as a reaction to his parents' demand that he devote his heart and soul to the business world, i.e., to their partnership.(27) In 1951 he got a joint B.A./LL.B from St. John's and was admitted to the New York State Bar. In law school he had worked hard and was near the top of his class academically as well its president.(28)

One reason that Carey could not attend law school during the day was that he had to support a family of his own. Before the War, he had met one Miss Helen Owen. By birth she was half Protestant and half Catholic but had been brought up a Catholic and had attended Marymount College. In 1945 she had married a young Navy Ensign named John Twohy, who soon afterward was killed in action in the Pacific. A daughter named Alexandria was born after her father died. In 1946 Hugh and Helen renewed their acquaintance and were wed in early 1947 in Manhattan's St. Patrick's Cathedral. He adopted Alexandria and eventually he and Helen had 13 other children. Four of these had been born by the time he graduated from law school.(29)

Carey: the Formative Years

To meet these demands on his wallet, he had to work daylight hours for Peerless. Despite the pressures of this job, law school and a child a year, Carey somehow found time in the late 1940s to join the New York State Young Democrats. He actually headed this group for a short while; and was offered the position of truant officer. He figured that rounding up customers for Mom's, Dad's and Ed's gas and oil concern had to be a better way of making a living than rounding up kids who were playing hooky from school, and so decided to remain in the private sector at least for the time being.(30) That he should have gone to the Young Dems rather than to the Young Republicans is hardly astounding. The Democratic Party was up until very recently the party of choice for the vast majority of New York City Irish Catholics. It was Manhattan's Democratic Tammany Hall and its Brooklyn and Bronx Democratic counterparts that not only welcomed them when they took their first steps in the New World; but also got them jobs, rehoused them when they were evicted from their flats by fire or landlord, sponsored glee clubs, baseball teams, picnic and dances for them and their children and gave them turkeys at Thanksgiving and Christmas when they came upon hard times. The Irish Catholic Carey family did not deviate from the tried and true Democratic path. Records of the New York City Board of Elections show Hugh's father Dennis joining the Democrats when living at 375 Douglass Street in 1915 and when residing at 60 Rutland Road in 1940; Hugh's mother Margaret registering the same way from 13 Park Place in 1929 and from 60 Rutland Road in 1940; Hugh's maternal grandfather Hugh Collins doing likewise from 60 Rutland Road the same year; and Hugh's brother Edward signing up with that Party in 1937 from the same address as soon as he reached his majority. (Helen's parents were Republicans(31); but then that particular family unit was half Protestant!)

Hugh's "natural" Democratic leanings were strengthened during his college years when his National Youth Administration job in the St. John's University Library further convinced him that the Democrats were fighting for the ordinary person.(32) Thus it is no surprise that the Board of Election's files show him enrolling in that Party in 1940, as soon as he was old enough to vote. The young Ronald Reagan also was a Democrat and a strong admirer of the New Deal, which had given jobs to his father and brother much as

10

it helped provide a college education to Dennis' and Margaret's third son.(33) Reagan converted to the other side; but Carey maintains his old allegiance.(34) Both of these veteran politicians, however, still deeply cherish the memory of Franklin Delano Roosevelt, the President under whose auspices were hatched the New Deal agencies that made life better for the Carey and Reagan families and for millions of other Americans.(35)

Notes to Chapter 1

1. Benjamin, Gerald - The Governorship in an Era of Limits and Changes at p. 125, 129 of Colby, Peter (ed.) - New York State Today: Politics, Government, Public Policy (Albany: SUNY Press, 1985).

2. New York Times, Oct. 13, 1991, Sec. 4, p. 14. (Copyright 1991 by the New York Times Co. Reprinted by Permission.) The New Yorker (May 15 1995, p. 36) praises him for having realized in the fiscal crisis that "....in hard times leaders depend upon the consent of the governed, and that that consent must be earned by a conscientious regard for everyone's welfare".

3. For a stimulating discussion of the differences between the social and political viewpoints of outer borough and Manhattan residents see Macchiarola, Frank - The Two New Yorks, City Journal, Spring 1993, pp. 57ff.

4. Public Papers of Governor Hugh L. Carey 1979 (Albany:State of New York Executive Chamber, 1992), p. xx; New York Daily News, Oct. 9, 1980, p. 9.

5. This paragraph is based on a two page history of the Peerless Oil and Chemical Corporation, issued in 1953 to celebrate its 30th anniversary. The history is entitled "Thank You....Miss Collins...." It is found in Special Collections. Library. St. John's University. Jamaica, NY 11439. Hugh L. Carey Collections. Gubernatorial Files 1975-82 (Personal Files 1975-82: Personal Subject Files M-T) file. (These collections will henceforth be referred to as "Hugh L. Carey Collection, St. John's Univ.(NY)".)

6. New York Daily News, Oct. 9, 1980, p. 9.

7. Remarks by Governor Hugh Carey at "Carey Years" Conference, Apr. 20, 1995, New York City.

8. Newsday, Oct. 16, 1978, p. 7. James Tully, Carey's Tax Commis-sioner and an old friend of his, refers to Margaret as a "strong" person. Interview, June 8, 1990, Albany, N.Y.

9. Some of the material in this and the preceding paragraph is based on Peerless Oil history, cited n.5 supra; New York Times, Nov. 6, 1974, p. 28.

10. Interview with Metropolitan Transportation Authority Chairman Rich-

The Days of Wine and Roses Are Over

ard Ravitch, Nov. 20, 1990, New York City.

11. Letter from Sister Annunciada Maria to Carey dated Nov. 6, 1978, Hugh L. Carey Collection, St. John's Univ.(NY), Gubernatorial Files 1975-82 (Governor's Personal Correspondence 1975-82: Inaugural/Reelection Correspondence 1974-75, 1978) file; New York Daily News, Oct. 9, 1980, p. 9.

12. Interview with Herbert Ryan, Carey's Congressional opponent in 1966 and later a Professor at John Jay College CUNY, Nov. 25, 1992, New York City.

13. New York Daily News, Oct. 9, 1980, p. 9.

14. Letter from Carey dated May 22, 1975 to Mr. James F. Meehan in response to a Meehan letter dated May 8, 1975, Hugh L. Carey Collection, St. John's Univ.(NY), Gubernatorial Files 1975-82 (Governor's Personal Correspondence 1975-78) file; Newsday, Oct. 16, 1978, p. 7.

15. Interview with Cunningham, Dec. 30, 1991, Albany, N.Y.

16. Carey, op. cit. n.4 supra, p. xx; New York Times, Nov. 6, 1974, p. 28.

17. Interview with Carey Superintendent of Insurance Albert Lewis, Dec. 6, 1994, New York City.

18. Carey, op. cit. n.4 supra, pp. xx-xxi.

19. Letter from Ben Leonard to Carey dated Feb. 11, 1975, Hugh L. Carey Collection, St. John's Univ.(NY), Gubernatorial Files 1975-82 (Governor's Personal Correspondence 1979-82 [sic]) file.

20. Plaut, Gunther W. - Unfinished Business (Toronto: Lester and Orpen Dennys, 1981), p. 128. Quote reprinted with the permission of Gunther W. Plaut.

21. Interviews with Lewis, cited n.17 supra; with Carey Assistant for New York City and Community Affairs Menachem Shayovich, Apr. 24, 1991, Brooklyn, N.Y.; Times Union (Albany), Nov. 11, 1979, Sec. 1, p. 1.

22. Carey, op. cit. n.4 supra, p. xxi; New York Times, Oct. 27, 1962, p. 13; Oct. 28, 1968, p. 41.

Carey: the Formative Years

23. Interview with Governor Hugh Carey, Nov. 30, 1991, Shelter Island, N.Y.

24. See correspondence between Leon and Carey dated Feb. 28, 1975 and Mar. 10, 1975, Hugh L. Carey Collection, St. John's Univ.(NY), Gubernatorial Files 1975-82 (Governor's Personal Correspondence 1975-78) file.

25. Letter from Mrs. William Kestenbaum to Carey Apr. 14, 1975, Hugh L. Carey Collection, St. John's Univ.(NY), Gubernatorial Files 1975-82 (Governor's Personal Correspondence 1975-78) file; speech by Carey dedicating a pavilion of the Long Beach Memorial Hospital on August 1, 1976, Long Beach Memorial Hospital News, Summer 1976, p. 1; New York Daily News, Oct. 9, 1980 p. 9; Newsday, Oct. 16, 1978, p. 7. Mrs. Kestenbaum was the young lady Carey had saved from George's obnoxious advances.

26. Carey, interview cited n.23 supra; Carey, material prepared for Current Biography and undated, Hugh L. Carey Collection, St. John's Univ.(NY), Congressional Files 1961-64 (Personal Files 1961-74: Miscellaneous Personal/Office Files) file.

27. Carey, interview cited n.23 supra.

28. Carey, biographical material cited n.26 supra; Newsday, Oct. 16, 1978, p. 7.

29. This paragraph is based on Carey, interview cited n.23 supra and op. cit. n.4 supra, p. xxi.

30. New York Times, Nov. 6, 1974, p. 28.

31. Carey, interview cited n.23 supra.

32. New York Times, Nov. 6, 1974, p. 28.

33. Cannon, Lou - President Reagan: The Role of a Lifetime (New York: Simon and Schuster, 1991), p. 43, 108.

34. Carey, interview cited n.23 supra.

The Days of Wine and Roses Are Over

35. Interview with Carey Commerce Commissioner John Dyson, Jan. 21, 1991, Millbrook, N.Y.; Cannon, <u>op. cit</u>. n.33 <u>supra</u>, p. 108.

Chapter 2
Carey Wins the Governorship

IN 1960 Hugh Carey, lawyer for Peerless and one of its executives, had become vaguely dissatisfied with the prospect of spending the next thirty years of his life hawking the energy products that New Yorkers have to buy to keep from freezing in the City's winters. During the late 1950s, as he was getting less and less of a thrill from the oil and gas trade, he developed an appetite for embarking on a career of public service and he broached the topic of his political ambitions to various friends. They were supportive; and so in 1960 he decided to run for United States Congress from Brooklyn's Irish-Italian-Jewish Twelfth District stretching from Brooklyn Heights through Flatbush to Canarsie. Since no one else wanted it and since he had come to know the head of the Flatbush Democratic Club, he had no trouble getting the Democratic nomination.(1)

His opponent in the general election was moderate Republican Francis Dorn, who had been in office since the Eisenhower landslide in 1952. Dorn and Carey had a lot in common. Both were lifelong residents of Brooklyn, in their forties, lawyers and veterans of World War II. Both had attended parochial schools. Carey had the edge in children -- then 11; but Dorn's five did not contribute to zero population growth either.(2) Most commentators predicted a fifth-straight Dorn win in this district that had been gerrymandered to make it safe for the GOP. However, the challenger had several factors going for him. His brother Edward, by now a wealthy businessman, gave him a large contribution. Hugh proved to be a marvellous campaigner.(3) He traveled throughout the District, shook thousands of hands, rang hundreds of doorbells, and brought his charming offspring to rallies. The older ones distributed campaign paraphernalia and were joined by teenage friends after school was out. He sent out a postcard showing the 11 children, including baby Brian in a stroller, on the steps of the Brooklyn Public Library. Shots of himself and wife Helen were superimposed on the background.(4) He also attached himself to the campaign of John F. Kennedy, running for President that year. He pointed out that both he and the Senator were young Irish Catholic Democrats and war veterans who espoused progressive social measures such as increasing federal aid to education and providing government-subsidized medical care for retirees. He emphasized everywhere that he stood "foursquare behind the program of Senator Kennedy".(5) And not only were his wife and children and Ed fully behind him but so was his mother. She saw an advertisement in a Brooklyn Heights newspaper attacking her son; bought up all the copies she could find; excised the offending blurb; and returned the paper to the newsstands!(6) Carey also convinced the local Liberal Party to nominate him.(7) It delivered 9000 votes, which when added to the 59,000 or so he received as a Democrat gave him 68,000 plus votes to Dorn's 67,000.(8) So Citizen Hugh Carey became Congressman Hugh Carey in January, 1961.

He was reelected six times from a Congressional District that beginning with 1962 was called the Fifteenth. (He made an unsuccessful run in 1969 for the Democratic nomination for the Presidency of the New York City Council. In that year, as well, two of his children were killed in a car crash.) In 1960 he had been living at 715 East 22nd Street, a single-family, three-story Flatbush home which he and Helen had purchased for $15,500 in 1948. The neighborhood, just north of Brooklyn College, is still handsome with well-tended lawns: more African-Americans and Orientals reside there now than in the 40s and 50s. In May of 1962 he acquired for $40,000 a magnificent 16 room-nine bedroom house, fairly close to the Park Place domicile of his childhood, at 61 Prospect Park West in Park Slope. "The Slope" always remained part of the Fifteenth while Carey represented it: other communities that were usually or always included in that District were liberal Brooklyn Heights, Orthodox Jewish Borough Park and conser-vative Irish-Italian Bay Ridge in the shadow of the Verrazano Bridge. In 1962 his edge over Dorn (whose "last hurrah" this was to be) was razor-thin. In 1964 he won by a slightly larger margin; and in 1966, 1968 and 1970 he breezed in. 1972 was a different story. The Republicans in the New York State Legislature had added several conservative communities to the District. What made matters even worse for him was that the Democratic Presidential nominee was Senator George McGovern, the candidate of the left of the Party who was viewed with extreme distaste in places such as Bay Ridge. So he basically ignored McGovern in those locales.(9) His literature there showed a picture of him with President Richard Nixon, then at the height of his popularity, as the latter signed the "general revenue sharing" bill

Carey Wins the Governorship

that New York's Governor Nelson Rockefeller desperately needed to balance his budget. When by accident the *New York Daily News* inserted an anti-Nixon ad containing Carey's name, he remembered what his mother had done during his first campaign and had his aides rush out to buy all the copies of the paper they could discover in the Bay Ridge neighborhood. They then carefully removed the piece from the *News* and returned the altered copy to the area's candy stores. He did not engage in the same ploy in the more liberal sections of the Fifteenth.(10)

The Republican choice in the District was a young, attractive former Assistant District Attorney named John Gangemi. His effort was well-financed and he did everything he could to link himself to Nixon.(11) However, Rockefeller was extremely grateful to Carey for the work the latter had done on the House Ways and Means Committee to get general revenue sharing enacted. So he and his aide James Cannon somehow persuaded Brooklyn Conservative leader William Wells not to back Gangemi but to put up his own candidate, Franklin Jones. Rumors circulated that Wells received $10,000 from either Carey or Rockefeller to place Jones on the ballot; but these were never proven.(12) In the event, the Congressman did not owe his victory to the Conservative snub of Gangemi for his vote total substantially exceeded the Gangemi and Jones support added together. In fact, the Orthodox Jewish community of Borough Park, to whom the "Liberator of Nordhausen" was a demigod, deserved credit for the victory. This politically-conservative neighborhood supported Nixon; but heeded their Congressman's admonition that they could by "splitting their ticket" vote for both the President and himself.(13)

In Congress, Carey usually took a "liberal" position, backing all the important measures comprising Lyndon Johnson's Great Society. He generally received ratings of substantially more than 50% from liberal interest groups such as the Committee on Political Education (COPE) of the AFL-CIO and of considerably less than 50% from conservative organizations such as Americans for Constitutional Action. However, as a member of the House Education and Labor Committee at the time, he departed from the liberal ranch by fighting hard to insure that the Elementary and Secondary Education Act (ESEA) of 1965 provided aid for the

The Days of Wine and Roses Are Over

pupils of parochial as well as public institutions. Many of his constituents sent their children to Orthodox Jewish or Catholic schools, and the majority of his children attended the latter. Thus his heart as well as politics pushed him to insure that the ESEA, the first program of federal assistance on a large scale basis to primary and secondary education, did not ignore pupils in schools operated by religious bodies.(14) Unlike most progressives, moreover, he was sympathetic to the problems of the oil industry, in which brother Ed was an important figure; and so received campaign contributions from some of its members.(15)

In 1970 House Speaker John McCormack announced his intention of resigning. He was succeeded in 1971 by Majority Lead-er Carl Albert of Oklahoma. Albert's ascension gave other ambit-ious House members a chance to rise. The Democratic caucus picked Hale Boggs of Louisiana as the new Majority Leader. It was then up to Albert and Boggs to select the Majority "Whip", whose duty it is "to make sure that members of his party are present for important votes, and that they vote the way the leadership wants".(16) The choice came down to Hugh Carey and Thomas P. "Tip" O'Neill of Massachusetts. They opted for O'Neill who, of course, eventually became Speaker. Carey admits that his rejection as Whip was one event that convinced him that he should seek the New York Governorship.(17)

However, this defeat was not the major reason he decided to leave the House. His beloved wife Helen had been diagnosed in 1969 as having cancer. For a while it was kept under control; but by 1973 she was so sick that she sometimes had to use oxygen and be ferried for treatment by her husband to the National Institutes of Health.(18) Later that year her condition significantly improved; in medical terms, she was in remission. So she, the Congressman and four of the children flew at Thanksgiving time to the Ireland of their ancestors. In Dublin she told him that she would very, very much like him to leave Washington, D.C. and run for Governor of New York State in 1974. Her reason was an intensely personal one; she strongly suspected that her days were numbered and so wanted her husband at her side as much as possible. As long as he was the Representative of the Fifteenth C.D., there was no way he could be with her all week. Were they to stay in the suburban Washington house that they had been

ing home since 1970, he would have to continue to make pilgrimages to Brooklyn almost every weekend to keep in touch with his constituents. On the other hand, were they to remove to Brooklyn, he would have to spend midweek in the nation's capital to attend committee meetings and vote. But as Governor, Helen thought, Hugh would be living in one spot, i.e., in the Executive Mansion on Eagle Street in Albany. It is clear, therefore, that the main reason why Carey desired to become Governor was that his wife wanted him to so they could be together more. Not only he but persons very close to him such as his daughter Susan Dempsey and his 1974 campaign manager Gerald Cummins confirm this point. Dempsey adds, however, that another factor involved in his decision to depart the nation's capital was that though he was well-respected in the House and socialized with some of its members, there was something in him that made him in part a loner who wanted to be his own boss.(19)

The Congressman may have coveted the Governorship; but he also knew that winning it would not be easy. Rockefeller was still Chief Executive in 1973 when the Careys were in Dublin. He had won the job in 1958 defeating Democrat incumbent W. Averell Harriman; and had been reelected three times. A breezy, outgoing campaigner with plenty of his own money to finance his campaign and with an almost 100% name recognition among adults, he would be extremely hard to top if he decided to run for a fifth term -- and as of the Careys' Irish jaunt it was still possible that he would. But in mid-December of 1973 he resigned and was succeeded by Lieutenant Governor Malcolm Wilson. Now any doubts Carey harbored about running for Governor vanished, as he knew that Wilson was quite vulnerable.(20)

With Rockefeller out of the way, Carey's initial obstacle was not Wilson but Democrat Howard Samuels. Samuels was well known throughout the State of New York as head of the Off Track Betting Corporation (OTB). Even prior to becoming OTB chief, he had had statewide exposure. He had run unsuccessfully for Lieutenant Governor in 1966 and had been beaten in the 1970 Democratic Gubernatorial primary by former United States Supreme Court Justice Arthur Goldberg. He had been Lyndon Johnson's Undersecretary of Commerce and Small Business Administration head in the late 1960s. Moreover, he was wealthy, having owned plastic factories upstate. Thus as of Spring, 1974, he was the clear favorite to win the Democratic nomination.(21)

There were other factors beside the fact that Samuels was a familiar face and had money that made Carey an underdog in the contest for the Democratic gubernatorial nod in 1974. In 1973 the Congressman had a minuscule three-person staff: himself, his fireman friend and campaign worker Tom Regan, and his son-in-law Hank McManus. As late as March of 1974 he had a piddling 6% name recognition statewide as opposed to Samuels' 91%. His initial campaign office was a hole in the wall right below Samuels' impressive headquarters: Regan used to race up to Samuels' office; pick up his position papers; and give them to Carey to critique.(22) A majority of the Democratic county chairpeople backed the OTB head.(23) Finally, Samuels was Jewish and Jews made up the largest bloc of Democratic primary voters.

But below the surface there were currents running in Carey's favor. At the time the Liberal Party was headed by an outstanding political operative named Alex Rose. Though the Liberals had stopped backing Carey in his Congressional races because of his advocacy of federal aid to parochial schools, Rose had never lost respect for him. Moreover, Carey had become very friendly with former Mayor Robert Wagner, still a power in Democratic circles. During Robert Morgenthau's campaign for District Attorney in Manhattan in 1973 Rose and Wagner had several polls taken and noted a strange phenomenon: though Samuels was very well known his share of the vote in the upcoming gubernatorial election was not increasing. A survey conducted by the reputable Peter Hart showed that he never received more than 40% of the vote and that his negatives were high. Carey was much, much less of a household word but fewer people voiced their dislike of him. So Rose and Wagner became certain that Samuels would lose the general election to Rockefeller or even to Wilson and decided (privately at first) to back the Congressman.(24) They secretly enlisted Patrick Cunningham, the powerful Democratic leader of The Bronx, to work with them. Richard Wade, a historian who had headed the 1972 campaign of George McGovern in New York and who had had a falling out with Samuels in the course of that contest, joined the Carey camp.(25)

The antagonism to Samuels was due to various personal and

Carey Wins the Governorship

political weaknesses of his. Puritans who believed that gambling was intrinsically wrong could not be expected to warm up to the President of OTB. His hair combed back sleekly gave some voters the impression that he was too slick.(26) Many figures in organized labor were suspicious of him because his plastics factories had been non-union.(27) But Carey's strongest card was neither the powerful figures who were turning to him nor Samuels' liabilities but brother Edward, in the 1970s the head of an energy conglomerate known as New England Petroleum Company (NEPCO) and a millionaire many times over who was very ready to put his considerable fortune to use in his brother's gubernatorial bid. And since the New York State election law in force at the start of 1974 limited campaign spending but not campaign contributions, Ed was not only willing but also able to help Hugh.

Energized by Rockefeller's departure from Albany, Hugh began campaigning in January of 1974 even before he had formally announced his candidacy. In addition to being on the stump then, he and his tiny campaign staff, armed with the expectation of financing from Ed, were assembling a professional crew to manage the race. By far the most important player they caught was media consultant David Garth, who had worked in various successful campaigns, including John Lindsay's second mayoral effort in 1969. Garth was worth every cent and more of the many dollars he cost the Carey race. But it was not only the money that led Garth to work for Carey; it was also the cajolery of Helen Carey, who convinced the television expert that the Congressman was a serious candidate for Governor who was not likely to abruptly pull out and announce that he was seeking reelection for an eighth term in the House of Representatives.(28)

The Hugh Carey of early 1974 was really three persons. Publicly, he carried out his "informal" gubernatorial campaign in his usual hearty, joking style as if he did not have a care in the world. Behind the scenes he and his closest aides such as Tom Regan were building up the campaign staff. In addition to getting Garth, Carey saw his old friend Harold Fisher, a power in Brooklyn politics, sign on. So did long-time political supporter and law partner Jim Tully, who had contacts upstate.(29) In his purely private life, tragedy was striking once again. Helen's malignant cancer came back and she had to have further surgery and chemotherapy. While she was being treated she contracted pneumonia and died on March 8th. All of a sudden, he was left a widower with 12 children: Alexandria, 29; Christopher, 26; Susan (Mrs. Martin Dempsey), 25; Michael, 20; Donald, 19; Marianne, 17; Nancy, 16; Helen, 15; Brian, 14; Paul, 11; Kevin, 10 and Thomas, 7. This tragedy could have led him to turn away from the gubernatorial race and return to Congress or perhaps leave public life altogether and embark on a full time legal career. But, ironically, it strengthened his resolve to reach Albany's Executive Mansion. Remember, to a considerable extent it had been Helen's urgings that had led him to consider a run for State office in the first place; and he sincerely and deeply felt that to continue the campaign was but to fulfill her wishes.(30)   Mrs. Carey's passing did, however, delay her husband's formal announcement of his gubernatorial candidacy until the end of March. In the interim both Samuels and Republican-turned-Democrat Ogden Reid, who represented Westchester County in the United States House of Repre-sentatives, had officially pro-claimed that they were going to enter the contest. Reid came from a wealthy family and, like Carey, had a pro-labor voting record in Congress; but, also like the Brooklynite, had a name that few in New York State recognized. (31) In March Carey got a campaign manager, Gerald Cummins, the owner of a printing shop in Man-hattan. Cummins had come to know him when as a Kennedy volunteer in 1960, he had been asked to keep an eye on promising Congressional candidates. Over the next few years they had become social friends. In 1974 the two met and Cummins outlined a strategy that he believed would make his fellow Irish-American Governor. Carey was so impressed that he put him in formal charge of the race.(32) In May, Garth began to roll the dice. Between the beginning of the month and mid-June, he spent $300,000 of Ed Carey's petrodollars on television commercials featuring the Congressman. The purpose of this blitz was not to put Carey "ahead" of Samuels -- it was universally admitted that the OTB chief would be in the lead for quite a while -- but to make the residents of New York State familiar with his name and achieve-ments in Congress. In this they were quite successful.(33)

    That Garth sought to make Carey's name known via a bunch of television bites should occasion absolutely no surprise: someone

Carey Wins the Governorship

almost a total stranger cannot attain political office. But there was a second and less obvious reason behind the May/June flurry of video clips. New York State's election laws are among the craziest in the country. The section (#6-104) governing party designation provides that the choices for statewide office (Governor, Lieutenant Governor, State Comptroller, Attorney General and U.S. Senator) of a majority of a Party's State Committee Convention shall automatically appear on the primary ballot. The statute also deals with those who were the losers at the State Committee conclaves. An also-ran who garners at least 25% of the vote on at least one ballot is ipso facto also a primary contestant. An aspirant who cannot reach the magic 25% figure may still enter the primary race; but in 1974 (Election Law Sec. 6-136) had to send his/her minions dashing throughout the State to gather 20,000 (the number is somewhat lower now) valid signatures on petitions backing his/her candidacy. Carey's operatives knew that Samuels would get the nod of a majority of the delegates at the Democratic State Committee Convention scheduled for Niagara Falls, N.Y., in mid-June; but they very much wanted their man to collect the 25%. Cummins felt that the petition route was too time-consuming and expensive.(34) One central Carey staffer believed that if Carey could not get the "twenty five" his candidacy would be viewed as dead in the water.(35) So, to return to the Garth offensive, enough people throughout New York State had to become aware of -- and favorable to -- Carey by mid-June to create a perception that he could give Samuels in the primary and Wilson in the general a run for their money. His aides assumed that only under this condition would at least a quarter of the delegates seriously consider voting for him in Niagara Falls.(36)

The Carey forces won a major victory in that resort community: a full 31% of the vote with Samuels receiving 68%. They had some luck in that Reid had dropped out of the running just before the Convention opened. But much of it was hard work. The Congressman's campaign aides personally contacted every delegate. They refused to take any individual for granted. For example, even after Cunningham had agreed to give them about half the Bronx vote, they still met with the Bronx delegates. They courted State Committee people who were identified with the Democratic Party's reform wing. (37) Crucial in the plans of the

The Days of Wine and Roses Are Over

Carey staffers was Suffolk County, Long Island, on whose Shelter Island he had his summer home. New York State's First Congressional District is located in that County and, accordingly, its State Committeepeople vote first at the State Convention. If the first county to vote would give a significant percentage of its yeas to Carey, enthusiasm for his candidacy would be bound to grow, or so his staff reasoned. Consequently the Congressman, Garth and others lobbied the Democratic Chairman of Suffolk, Dominic Baranello; and were rewarded by getting the support of about half the Suffolk delegation. They also convinced Baranello to make the speech nominating the Brooklynite. The Suffolk leader had never met the candidate before 1974 and did not even know that he had a vacation home in his county. But he was impressed by Carey's wit, intelligence and grasp of the issues and felt that the Party needed a new face. Though he was reluctant to come out against Samuels since he felt that the wishes of his Party's leaders should normally prevail; and though he wished that Carey had cleared his candidacy with Brooklyn Democratic head Meade Esposito; he finally resolved to back the Congressman on the very morning of the day he put his name in nomination.(38)

The order of voting at the Convention moves westward from Suffolk across Long Island. Next to choose were the Nassau and Queens delegations; and Carey did not have much support here. The fourth group scheduled to cast its ballots was Kings (Brooklyn), his home county; and here his troops were faced with a dilemma. If the Congressman got no help from this borough, not only he would look weak in the eyes of those delegates who were to vote later, but, as well, the momentum generated by his Suffolk success would dissipate. On the other hand, if he swept the Brooklyn delegates' votes, he would be seen as Esposito's pawn and could not pursue his plan of running not as but against "the candidate of the bosses".(39)

What ultimately happened was that he received the ayes of nearly half of the Brooklynites. Among their leaders who opted for him were Democratic district leader (later Kings County Surrogate) Bernard Bloom and his brother State Senator Jeremiah Bloom. His relationship with the brothers was soon to deteriorate. But all was love and roses between them and Carey in 1974; and the large number of votes he got from their mutual borough thanks in part

Carey Wins the Governorship

to their efforts and in part to some reform support, when added to his successes in courting the Suffolk, Bronx, Staten Island, Albany County, Erie County and other delegations, gave him his respectable 31%.(40)

Now that he had received that desired 25 plus percent, Carey sculpted a well-defined strategy to keep pushing his opponent down the slippery slope while simultaneously rising himself. It consisted of several elements, including most importantly personal campaigning and television. He continued to be masterful on the stump.(41) He knew how to tell jokes that humored his audience, how to make them feel wanted and liked, and how to address their needs and preferences. For example, campaigning in Hispanic areas of The Bronx, he praised Puerto Rico's legendary ex-governor Luis Munoz Marin.(42) By the end of August, he had expended almost $700,000 on television commercials to Samuels' $122,000. Garth's Carey blurbs were seen in May, June and August; Samuels was off the air during these three months. Carey's ads were extremely effective; they showed him (thinner than at the beginning of the campaign on Garth's orders) on location claiming credit for concrete accomplishments as a Congressman: e.g., getting funds to assist the National Technical Institute for the Deaf in Rochester and to rehabilitate a block in Brooklyn, pushing through federal general revenue sharing, and helping to keep the Brooklyn Navy Yard from becoming a wasteland. His feats were summed up on TV with the slogan "Before they tell you what they want to do...make them show you what they've done". Though on paper this maxim sounds banal, it "shrewdly puts the burden of proof on 'them' and forces 'them' to redirect their campaign to answer Garth's".(43) Some ads were more directly negative and blasted Samuels for not doing much more with his life than inventing a plastic clothes line.(44)

Another crucial part of the Garth/Cummins/Carey effort was to get prominent Democrats to endorse the Congressman seriatim. This created in potential voters' minds the impression that despite the summer's heat, the Carey campaign was snowballing to such a size that it had an excellent chance of winning in the face of the opposition's early lead.(45) Dr. Kevin Cahill, a great Carey family friend who had treated Mrs. Carey for cancer, had studied under a professor who was married to a Lehman. He asked his mentor

The Days of Wine and Roses Are Over

to urge Mrs. Edith Lehman, widow of the beloved Democratic Governor Herbert Lehman, to meet the Brooklynite. At first the professor refused; but he did make the plea after Cahill reminded him that this was the first time in decades he had ever asked him for a favor.(46) She and former Governor Harriman publicly and simultaneously joined the Carey camp: Mayor Wagner had taken the same step earlier. Lehman and Harriman were followed by Bronx Borough President Robert Abrams.(47) The Wagner/Lehman/Harriman/Abrams imprimaturs were of importance not only because many average New Yorkers knew their names but also because they were respected by Jews and by the liberals who made up the membership of the Democratic "reform" clubs. The New Democratic Coalition, the "umbrella" organization loosely uniting these groups, had backed Samuels but Carey had to woo away at least some of their members because they almost all voted in primaries. Reid further enhanced Carey's status with liberal Democrats by announcing in his favor.

Wagner had, as seen, been working for Carey behind the scenes for several months; and with his ties to the black community was able to improve the Brooklynite's standing with it. Many labor union leaders came over to him, both because of his pro-labor voting record in Congress and also because of Samuels' non-union plants.(48) And some figures in the "regular" wing of the Dem-ocratic Party, who were supposed to be on Samuels' side because he was the pick of the State Committee, showed themselves either pro-Carey or neutral. Thus Howard Golden, later Borough Pres-ident of Brooklyn and then head of a muscular political organ-ization called the Roosevelt Democratic Club, endorsed Carey even though Kings County Democratic chief Esposito remained loyal to the OTB head.(49) Bronx Democratic leader Patrick Cunningham and many of his district leaders exerted themselves sub rosa for Carey.(50) And Queens Democratic chief Matthew Troy, another supposedly fervent Samuels fan, quietly told his district leaders that they could labor in his opponent's vineyard if they wanted to.(51) All these maneuverings made the race very close. By the September Sunday before the primary it was considered a toss-up; while at the beginning of August Samuels had been up 20% in his own polls and about 10% in Carey's. (52) Garth's TV blips would not

Carey Wins the Governorship

have led to the Congressman's spurt had he shown himself ignorant on the issues: no one could have accused Samuels of this for he had published detailed position papers on many topics and his television commercials emphasized his stands on policy matters. But Carey could familiarize himself in a trice with policy problems and so was able to come out at least the equal of his rival in the television and radio debates.(53) The differences between the two on meaningful matters were rather minimal. Both favored better mass transit, more government assistance to increase the housing supply, and protecting social security.

Somewhat ironically, given Carey's proven record of getting federal funding for parochial schools, it was Samuels who courted the Catholic vote here by calling for the use of tax credits to aid these institutions; Carey asserted that this type of assistance would be unconstitutional.(54) The question of legalized abortions was surprisingly muted in the race. In 1973 the United States Supreme Court had decided the divisive case of *Roe v. Wade*(55), declaring essentially that the states cannot constitutionally ban abortions during the first six months of pregnancy. Samuels himself strongly supported the Supreme Court. Carey, as a very religious Roman Catholic, could have been expected to have taken a stance against it. However, though the decision did not please him, he refused to back a constitutional amendment to overturn it.(56) This kept him in the good graces of the "pro choice" forces.

Since there was only slight disagreement on substance and the race was close, the contestants had to resort to rather bitter personal attacks on one another. Samuels emphasized that Hugh's brother Ed had financed most of the Carey campaign and that Ed's NEPCO was a major supplier of oil to the hated Con Edison and Lilco utilities. Accordingly, in Samuel's words, Hugh's massive TV campaign was "involuntarily paid for by every New Yorker who pays a monthly Consolidated Edison or Long Island Lighting Company bill".(57) He added that he did not see how a candidate who was being funded by the oil industry could stand up against its lobbyists if he were elected. Carey did not take these challenges lying down. He and his aides charged that 13 full-time Samuels campaign workers had been employed by OTB; and pounded on the fact that his rival had paid no City taxes during

1971 and 1972 though he was making over $40,000. Samuels responded to this one that he had had so many deductions those years that he was entitled to a refund of all the City had withheld from his paycheck. (58)

Cummins was one of the few experts who refused to believe the race would be tight. The campaign manager's polling during the couple of days before the election had convinced him that his candidate was ripe for a big win; but he did not want to reveal his feelings to the press for fear of keeping some potential Carey supporters at home watching television.(59) His prediction proved right on target. On Primary Day, September 10, 1974, the Congressman absolutely wiped out the OTB President. He won about 60% of the vote to Samuels' 40% or close to 600,000 votes for under 400,000 for the original front runner. The victor took every one of New York State's 62 counties except Broome, the locale of Senate Majority Leader Warren Anderson's Binghamton. He carried New York City by about 120,000 votes, the Nassau/ Suffolk/ Westchester suburbs by about 15,000 and the rest of the State by approximately 70,000 or 2-1. It is hard to overstate the magnitude of Carey's win. Remember that Samuels came from the upstate that totally turned its back on him. By the time of the election he was living in Manhattan, and even that borough, the most liberal in the City and State, rejected this New Democratic Coalition candidate by several hundred votes.(60)

The obscure Brooklyn Congressman's stunning upset did not mean his task was over: he now had to win the November general election against Governor Wilson. As veteran political commentator Richard Reeves pointed out, that contest shaped up as a clash of like against like. Both men were religious Catholics from middle-class, New York City-area Irish families. (Actually, Wilson, from Yonkers in Westchester County just north of The Bronx, was only half Irish.) Both received all their education in Catholic schools, Wilson attending Fordham College and Fordham Law School. Both had seen active service in World War II. Both had had legislative experience: Wilson had been a State Assemblyman for 20 years until Nelson Rockefeller had tapped him to run for Lieutenant Governor in the 1958 election, when Rockefeller wrested the Governorship from Harriman. And Wilson as well as Carey had taken steps to insure that religious schools got public

Carey Wins the Governorship

funding.(61)

Wilson's gubernatorial race began to collapse right after the Democratic primary. The Brooklynite's win had left him with a strong, energized organization.(62) More importantly, Cummins points out, the press was so taken with his victory that they concentrated on it and essentially ignored the Wilson effort until the beginning of October, just slightly over a month before the general.(63) Also to Wilson's dismay, the State AFL-CIO endorsed the Congressman in mid-September. Rockefeller had received its support in 1970 over ex-union lawyer Goldberg; and the Governor expected a similar bounty in 1974. After all, the President of the Federation, Raymond Corbett, had as recently as March, 1974 referred to him as even "a little bit better" than the Rockefeller he had favored.(64) However, Wilson made a political blunder which led it to back his antagonist. One of the most powerful groups in the State AFL-CIO was and is the United Teachers of New York (NYSUT), whose constituent unions even in 1974 had a total of over 200,000 members. Its convention that year was held not in a New York locale but in Montreal. Wilson came to that meeting and won the hearts of many of the delegates when he said he would "review" the Taylor Law, which bars strikes by public employees. (65) However, later in the year at a private meeting between NYSUT head Thomas Hobart, Nassau County Republican Assemblyman Joseph Margiotta and Wilson, the Governor referred to striking teachers as "outlaws" whom decent instructors would shun. This so alienated Hobart that right after the Democratic primary he got the NYSUT Executive Council to back the winner of that fight.(66) NYSUT then took this endorsement of Carey to the State AFL-CIO Convention at Kiamesha Lake in early October of 1974. Though the building trades unions were firmly in Wilson's camp, New York City teachers' union leader Albert Shanker, aided by Victor Gotbaum, head of District Council 37 of the American Federation of State, County and Municipal Employees, was able to get the AFL-CIO's Executive Council to recommend Carey by 11-10 and the 1800 delegates as a whole to endorse the Democrat by 90% to 10%. Since there were 2 million members of unions adhering to the State AFL-CIO, its support was a major boost for the Congressman.(67)

The Days of Wine and Roses Are Over

Wilson's campaign was certainly not helped by polls taken showing his opponent far ahead.(68) Nor was it aided by a revelation about Wilson's former "boss", Nelson Rockefeller, while Congress was considering whether to approve him as Gerald Ford's Vice-President. During the 1970 New York State gubernatorial race, a book by conservative journalist Victor Lasky had appeared which lambasted Goldberg, Rockefeller's opponent. In October of 1974 it was disclosed that Nelson's brother Laurance had financed the publication of that volume and that the then Governor had been aware of the arrangement. He apologized to Goldberg in October of 1974; but the publicity about the episode did not help his successor.(69) Cropping up again in October was the story that Wilson during his 15 years as Rockefeller's #2 had practiced law in White Plains, Westchester County; and had made about $500,000 for cultivating that terrain. This first had been revealed in an answer he filed in a lawsuit brought against him in June of 1974 by Queens Borough President Donald Manes charging that he had been engaged as an attorney by some parties who wanted favorable treatment from the State.(70) Wilson himself feels that the play given the allegation by the *Daily News* hurt him. He adds bitterly that little coverage was provided about its quick dismissal by a federal judge.(71)

He is, however, a seasoned and decent politician who is wise enough to confess that the Goldberg story and the Manes lawsuit were not what really finished him off. As he himself admits(72), the worst roadblock in his way was the Watergate scandal, which forced President Nixon out of office in August of 1974 and which was compounded by President Ford's subsequent pardon of the Californian in early September for any crimes he might have committed while residing in the White House. As he sighed, 1974 was a bad year for Republicans all over the country; and he was not spared by the Democratic deluge.(73) Added to his woes was that he was a lackluster campaigner, especially as compared to the sprightly, witty Carey.(74)

Another problem faced by Wilson was that the normally factionalized Democratic Party was for once united behind Carey and the remainder of the statewide candidates -- Mary Anne Krupsak for Lieutenant Governor; Arthur Levitt for State Comptroller; Ramsey Clark for U.S. Senate and Robert Abrams for Attorney General.

Carey Wins the Governorship

Samuels himself quickly endorsed the man who had beaten him so badly. The campaign was managed by two highly competent professionals, Mayor Wagner and Cummins. They worked well together and were backed by new episodes of Garth's top-notch television commercials, as well as by Rose and his Liberals. A bevy of Carey's attractive children often appeared for him in towns and villages that he had no time to visit.(75)

The ideological differences between Wilson and Carey were somewhat greater than those separating Carey and Samuels. Wilson favored capital punishment; Carey, articulating a theme that was going to give him trouble during much of his stay in Albany, opposed it.(76) As always in New York, crime was an issue; and Wilson aired a 30 second TV ad depicting the funeral of a murdered policeman. The deceased was lying in a flag-draped coffin and the viewers then were treated to a retired police officer's emphasizing that the Governor backed the death penalty, and that Carey "laughed it off" while "his running mate voted against it...."(77) However, unfortunately for Wilson, crime was ranked only #3 by the voters among the problems facing the State: the poor state of the national economy and the high level of State and federal taxes were most on their minds.(78) Beside, who would believe that the squat, broad-shouldered Carey, who "looks like an Irish cop", was soft on crime even though he had called for the decriminalization of marijuana use?(79) And working class men and women more concerned with taxes than with law and order or the lack thereof were doubtlessly overjoyed by the challenger's pledge not to raise the income tax that low and middle income people had to pay Albany. Wilson brushed off this promise as "irresponsible".(80)

Carey also struck a chord in the hearts of Watergate-scarred voters tired of hearing about politicians being influenced by large contributors by advocating partial public financing of political campaigns through a state income tax checkoff; Wilson opposed it.(81) Wilson wanted to end legalized abortion; while Carey essentially stuck to his primary guns and said that while he personally disliked this practice, *Roe v. Wade*(82) constitutionalizing it was the law of the land.(83) As Wilson noted in his interview with me, however, his anti-abortion stance did not help him greatly with conservatives. The reason was that he had failed

The Days of Wine and Roses Are Over

to approve a 1972 act repealing the State's liberal 1970 abortion measure while functioning as Acting Governor when Rockefeller was on one of his trips outside the State. Upon his return, Rockefeller killed the repealer.(84)

Hugh O'Neill, a graduate student at New York City's Columbia University who entered Carey's Administration as Deputy Director of the Department of Social Services and then became head of his Office of Development Planning, did some campaigning for him in the 1974 primary and general elections. He also briefed him prior to his debates with Samuels. He believes that the major distinction between the candidates in the general was on crime, with Wilson taking a "harder" stance. What in retrospect strikes him most about the Carey-Wilson contest was that, to use his language, it was "disconnected" from the crucial problems that the State was facing: the looming bankruptcies of its Urban Development Corporation and of New York City.(85) The Brooklynite had no real idea until after the election about either crisis: even the Governor did not know that the investment community was about to pull the plug on the five boroughs. He had a clearer perception than did the challenger about the quagmire into which the Corporation (set up by Rockefeller) was sinking; but nonetheless he still was not fully aware of how bad things were.

The results in the November 5th election were as the polls had predicted, with Carey and Krupsak being selected as Governor and Lieutenant Governor over Wilson and his running mate Ralph Caso from Nassau County by a large margin. Statewide, Carey received about 2,880,000 while Wilson obtained about 2,100,000. In percentages, this translates into about 58% for Carey and 42% for the incumbent. The victor took New York City, upstate, and the suburban counties of Nassau, Suffolk and Rockland. He came in second in Wilson's native Westchester by only about 117,000 to 131,000 or 47% to 53%. His own Brooklyn gave him about 333,000 votes and Wilson 190,000, or 63.5% to 36.5%. Overall, New York City cast its ballots for him 1,200,000 to 532,000 or about 69% to 31%.(86) The next year was to show him more than reciprocating the help that his native metropolis had furnished him.

Neither candidate had a real edge in spending during the 1974 general election. In that struggle, the loser disbursed $2.7 million and the winner about the same.(87) Ed's assistance to his brother amounted to only about one fifth to one fourth of the new Governor's total primary/general payments of $5.2 million. The remaining millions were raised in good part from individuals and groups that traditionally give to Democratic candidates in New York State and/or which worry about legislation enacted by Albany. "Labor, real estate, waterfront and oil interests, which often have major stakes in state legislation and regulations, account for a large share of the Carey campaign contributions. Labor unions alone contributed at least $478,750 during the election and primary campaigns."(88) Some of the unions such as the Seafarers International Union with its gift of $43,000, had been long-time supporters of the Congressman because of his pro-labor record in the House and/or his work to keep the Navy Yard in operation. Joining the Seafarers in backing him were, e.g., the New York State United Teachers with $43,000, the Committee on Political Education of the AFL-CIO with $51,000 and Victor Gotbaum's District Council 37 with $50,000. Builder Christopher Boomis gave $30,000 and Fred Trump, founder of the Trump real estate empire now headed by the flamboyant Donald, $25,000. The New York Democratic State Committee donated $110,000 while Pat Cunningham's Bronx Democratic County Committee advanced the candidate $46,000.(89)

One problem with the Carey 1974 campaign financing effort was that so much of its cash arrived in the form of loans rather than gifts. Thus on his inauguration day in 1975, he still owed $2.4 million.(90) So one of his concerns during the next several years was to raise the dollars to pay off these obligations. They were not fully retired until 1978, when he ran for a second term.(91) Various fund-raisers were held to obtain the needed sums. One in April 1977, when the 1974 campaign was still $1.3 million in the red, brought in $369,000 in honor of his birthday. Givers here included Charles Dyson ($5000), father of Commerce Commissioner John Dyson, and Steven Ross ($10,000) of Warner Communications. (92) At another of these gatherings Frank Sinatra sang. The guests, for $500 a plate, ate and drank "(c)old poached salmon, sliced filet of beef, ice cream topped by New York strawberries and blueberries and Courvoisier cognac and New York State red and white wines and champagne...."(93) Nonetheless, reducing this debt burden remained a distraction for Carey throughout the New

Notes to Chapter 2

1. Interview with Carey's first Metropolitan Transportation Authority head Harold Fisher, June 13, 1990, Brooklyn, N.Y.;draft letter from Carey to Stanley Reiben dated Mar. 26, 1980, Hugh L. Carey Collection, St. John's Univ.(NY), Gubernatorial Files 1975-82 (Governor's Personal Correspendence 1979-82) file; Newsday, Oct. 16, 1978, p. 7.

2. New York Times, Oct. 22, 1960, p. 32; Oct. 27, 1962, p. 13.

3. Fisher, interview cited n.1 supra; Newsday, Oct. 16, 1978, p. 7.

4. Ibid.; New York Times, Oct. 22, 1960, p. 32. The postcard can be found in the Hugh L. Carey Collection, St. John's Univ.(NY), Guber-natorial Files 1975-82 (Governor's Personal Correspondence 1975-82: Miscellaneous Correspondence) file.

5. New York Times, Oct. 22, 1960, p. 32.

6. Interview with Governor Hugh Carey, Nov. 30, 1991, Shelter Island, N.Y.

7. New York Times, Oct. 22, 1960, p. 32.

8. New York Times, Nov. 10, 1960, p. 41.

9. New York Times, Oct. 18, 1972, p. 29.

10. Interview cited n.6 supra.

11. New York Times, Oct. 18, 1972, p. 29.

12. Interview with Carey Superintendent of Insurance Albert Lewis, Dec. 6, 1994, New York City; Reeves, Richard - Carey vs. Wilson: And in each corner - Nelson Rockefeller, New York Times Magazine, Oct. 27, 1974, p. 17, pp. 100-101; New York Times, Oct. 18, 1972, p. 29.

13. Lewis, interview cited n.12 supra.

14. Former Representative James Scheuer of Queens, also a member of the Education and Labor Committee, described Carey's role there as the "representative of the Catholic Church". But Scheuer admitted that without the pro-aid-to-parochial-school clauses that the Brooklynite wedged into the ESEA, it would never have received the needed support

The Days of Wine and Roses Are Over

of powerful House Catholics such as Speaker John McCormack. Scheuer added that Carey was very interested in education for the deaf and practically adopted Gallaudet, a college for the hard-of-hearing. Interview with Scheuer, Apr. 12, 1991, Queens, N.Y. Carey was one of the prime sponsors of the legislation setting up the National Technical Institute for the Deaf in Rochester, N.Y. See the brochure printed for the Institute's 1971 groundbreaking ceremony, Hugh L. Carey Collection, St. John's Univ.(NY), Congressional Files 1961-74 (Personal Files 1961-1974: Personal Office Miscellaneous Files: Carey - Biography Material 1966-1972) file.

The six children who accompanied him to Albany went to Roman Catholic parochial schools there. Interview with Carey Executive Assistant Martha Golden, Dec. 5, 1990, Washington.

15. See letter of July 12, 1966 from John K. Evans, Executive Director, Independent Fuel Oil Marketers of America, Inc. to Edward Carey, Hugh L. Carey Collection, St. John's Univ.(NY), Congressional Files 1961-74 (Personal Files 1961-1974: Campaign Files 1961-1974: 1964-69, 1966 Campaign) file.

16. O'Neill, Tip - Man of the House (New York: Random House, 1987), p. 219.

17. Carey, interview cited n.6 supra.

18. Golden, interview cited n.14 supra; New York Daily News, June 30, 1974, p. 71.

19. Interview with Carey, cited n.6 supra; with Cummins, Feb. 28, 1991, New York City; with Dempsey, Nov. 30, 1991, Shelter Island, N.Y.; New York Daily News, June 30, 1974, p. 31.

20. Dempsey, interview cited n.19 supra.

21. Kramer, Michael - The City Politic: Early Warnings, New York Magazine, Feb. 25, 1974, p. 5; New York Times, Mar. 31, 1974, Sec. 4, p. 6.

22. Interview with a Carey aide, June 5, 1992; New York Daily News, July 1, 1974, p. 5.

23. New York Times, Feb. 14, 1974, p. 45.

Carey Wins the Governorship

24. Interview with Carey Special Assistant (later State Liberal Party Chairman) Raymond Harding, July 2, 1990, New York City; with Professor Richard Wade, Mar. 11, 1991, New York City; with Mayor Robert Wagner, Dec. 11, 1990, New York City.

25. Harding and Wade, interviews cited n.24 supra.

26. Interview with Carey aide cited n.22 supra.

27. Kramer, op. cit. n.21 supra, p. 5.

28. Dempsey, interview cited n.19 supra.

29. Interview with Carey Tax Commissioner James Tully, June 8, 1990, Albany, N.Y.; New York Times, Jan. 18, 1974, p. 17.

30. New York Post, June 28, 1974, p. 3.

31. Kramer, op. cit. n.21 supra, p. 5; New York Times, Mar. 31, 1974, Sec. 4, p. 6.

32. Cummins, interview cited n.19 supra.

33. New York Daily News, July 1, 1974, p. 4; New York Times, Aug. 12, 1974, p. 1.

34. Interview cited n.19 supra.

35. Interview with the staffer, Nov. 30, 1991.

36. New York Times, Aug. 12, 1974, p. 1.

37. Interview with Carey staffer cited n.35 supra.

38. Interview with Baranello, July 29, 1994, Patchogue, N.Y.; Cummins, interview cited n.19 supra.

39. Ibid.

40. New York Times, June 14, 1974, p. 1.

41. Wagner, interview cited n.24 supra.

The Days of Wine and Roses Are Over

42. Remarks of Bronx Borough President Fernando Ferrer at "Carey Years" Conference, Apr. 20, 1995, New York City. For a description of Carey stumping, see New York Post, June 28, 1974, p. 3.

43. Blum, Howard - Have I got a governor for you..., Village Voice, Oct. 10, 1974, p. 5, 7.

44. Interview with Carey staffer cited n.35 supra.

45. Wade, interview cited n.24 supra.

46. Interview with Cahill, July 26, 1993, New York City.

47. New York Times, Aug. 1, 1974, p. 56 (Wagner); Aug. 9, 1974, p. 66 (Lehman/Harriman); Aug. 26, 1974, p. 1 (Abrams).

48. Wade, interview cited n.24 supra; New York Times, Aug. 2, 1974, p. 6 (Amalgamated Clothing Workers, Textile Workers); Aug. 3, 1974, p. 24 (Teamsters Local 237).

49. New York Times, Aug. 25, 1974, Sec. 4, p. 5.

50. Harding, interview cited n.24 supra.

51. Tracy, Phil - State Secrets, Village Voice, July 25, 1974, p. 3.

52. New York Times, Aug. 12, 1974, p. 1; Sept. 8, 1974, Sec. 1, p. 1.

53. Cummins, interview cited n.19 supra; Wagner, interview cited n.24 supra.

54. New York Times, July 19, 1974, p. 31; Staten Island Advance, Sept. 1, 1974, Sec. 1, p. 1.

55. 410 U.S. 113 (1973).

56. See The Evangelist, Aug. 15, 1974 (official publication of the Albany Roman Catholic diocese), p. 1.

57. Quoted New York Times, Sept. 1, 1974, Sec. 1, p. 38.

Carey Wins the Governorship

58. New York Times, Sept. 1, 1974, Sec. 1, p. 38; Staten Island Advance, Sept. 1, 1974, Sec. 1, p. 1.

59. Cummins, interview cited n.19 supra.

60. The figures in this paragraph come from New York Times, Sept. 12, 1974, p. 3.

61. Reeves, op. cit. n.12 supra, pp. 101-102.

62. Interview with Governor Malcolm Wilson, June 25, 1990, White Plains, N.Y.

63. Cummins, interview cited n.19 supra.

64. New York Times, Sept. 16, 1974, p. 25.

65. Ibid.

66. Ibid.; Interview with Hobart, Sept. 17, 1991, Albany, N.Y.

67. New York Times, Oct. 5, 1974, p. 1.

68. New York Times, Oct. 1, 1974, p. 43.

69. Wilson, interview cited n.62 supra. For stories about the Goldberg book episode, see New York Times, Oct. 12, 1974, p. 1; Oct. 13, 1974, Sec. 1, p. 1.

70. New York Times, June 8, 1974, p. 63; Oct. 18, 1974, p. 47.

71. Interview cited n.62 supra. The News article about the charges was a Page Five story appearing on June 8, 1974.

72. Interview cited n.62 supra.

73. Ibid.

74. Cummins, interview cited n.19 supra.

75. Interview with Carey Deputy Appointments Secretary William Cunningham, Dec. 30, 1991, Albany, N.Y.; New York Times, Oct. 18, 1974, p. 1.

76. New York Times, Oct. 30, 1974, p. 33.

77. New York Times, Oct. 24, 1974, p. 32.

78. New York Times, Oct. 28, 1974, p. 1.

79. Reeves, op. cit. n.12 supra, p. 104; New York Times, Nov. 6, 1974, p. 1; Wall St. Journal, Oct. 31, 1974, p. 18.

80. New York Times, Oct. 15, 1974, p. 1.

81. Ibid., p. 32; New York Times, Nov. 6, 1974, p. 1.

82. 410 U.S. 113 (1973).

83. New York Times, Nov. 1, 1974, p. 24; Wall St. Journal, Oct. 31, 1974, p. 18.

84. Interview cited n.62 supra; New York Times, May 14, 1972, Sec. 1, p. 1. Since leaving Albany, Carey has become "pro-life".

85. Interview with O'Neill, June 17, 1992, New York City.

86. These figures comes from New York Times, Nov. 7, 1974, p. 39.

87. New York Times, Oct. 31, 1974, p. 53; Nov. 27, 1974, p. 13; Jan. 2, 1975, p. 38. Carey's $2.7 million general election figure was calculated by subtracting the $2.5 million he spent in his primary from his total 1974 spending of $5.2 million.

88. New York Times, Jan. 2, 1975, p. 38.

89. These figures come from ibid.

90. Ibid.

91. Interview with Arthur Emil, Treasurer of Carey's 1978 election race, Nov. 12, 1991, New York City.

92. New York Times, May 29, 1977, Sec 1, p. 23.

93. New York Times, June 2, 1976, p. 18.

Carey Wins the Governorship

94. Ibid.

95. New York Times, Dec. 29, 1974, Sec. 1, p. 34.

96. Remarks by Governor Hugh Carey at "Carey Years" Conference, Apr. 20, 1995, New York City.

97. Public Papers of Governor Hugh L. Carey 1975 (Albany: State of New York Executive Chamber, 1982), p. 21.

Chapter 3
The Fiscal Crisis:
Prelude, Big Mac and the EFCB

THE 1960s and early 1970s were years of a sort that this country has not witnessed since. Despite the Vietnam War, urban rioting and student takeovers of university buildings, there was a feeling that the country could with the help of government solve its major problems. The hunger, poverty, ignorance, ill-health and racism that inexplicably continued to fester in the then-richest nation in the world could be cured by a few laws and some dollars. In Washington, the optimism was symbolized by Presidents John F. Kennedy and Lyndon Johnson, in Albany by Governor Nelson Rockefeller and in New York City by John Lindsay. Johnson initiated the Great Society programs such as Medicare, Medicaid and federal aid to primary and secondary education that Hugh Carey enthusiastically supported in the House of Representatives. Rockefeller set up a generous State Medicaid program to supplement the federal government's and greatly expanded the State University of New York. In acting this way, he was exemplifying New York State's tradition of being the "Empire State of public policy - a leader to be admired and emulated in the development and progressive implementation of successful programs to solve social problems and provide the means to a better life for all citizens".(1)

John Lindsay, elected as Mayor in 1965 as a Republican/Liberal and in 1969 as a Liberal/Independent, wanted the City to give its residents, especially the less-affluent, a helping hand. For example, he was very kind to the City University of New York (CUNY). Not only were new CUNY senior and community colleges opened under his aegis; but with his support it adopted an "open admissions" policy under which any high school graduate could get into one of its branches.(2) He continued the policy instituted by his predecessor, Mayor Robert Wagner, of spending more and more to upgrade the City's huge municipal hospital system.(3) Its Medicaid and welfare budgets burgeoned during his Administration; and he himself felt that it was right to treat these programs' clients decently.(4) Public employees received generous wage boosts during his tenure.(5) Their fringe benefits (e.g. health insurance, pensions) also significantly increased during his eight years.(6) By the end of this period, many City workers could retire at half pay after 20 years on the job; and for many the amount of their pension was based on their salary (including overtime) in their last and thus most highly paid year of service.(7) Some employees had to contribute nothing to fund their pensions. And the health benefits of its civil servants were borne 100% by the metropolis.(8)

New York City's expenditures on its social endeavors and its employees' remuneration kept increasing. Thus in fiscal year 1961 (i.e., the year ending June 30, 1961) its expense budget was $2.3 billion, in fiscal 1966 $7.8 billion and in fiscal 1975 $11.5 billion.(9) This growth would have been no problem had its economy been booming: in that event, the larger slice would simply have been taken from a larger pie. Unfortunately, both long-term and short-term economic trends were working against it. Manufacturing jobs started departing in the 1950s, though this decline was compensated for by a gain in office employment.(10) Real misery hit in 1969. Between that year and 1976 the metropolis lost a fantastic 616,000 jobs, even though the United States as a whole saw 13 million positions added during that period despite recessions in 1969-71 and 1974-75!(11)

The City's swelling expenditures when linked to a crumbling tax base had one obvious result: a budget deficit, i.e. an excess of outgo over inflow. "If the city had one endemic problem in the late 1960s and early 1970s, it was a recurring annual deficit".(12) To be able to pay its employees, its suppliers, and the beneficiaries of its programs as well as convince the world that it was solvent despite the red ink, it borrowed money by issuing "notes" (also called short-term debt, as the lenders to whom they are given have to be repaid within a year or less).(13) It made use of several types of short-term debt: Revenue Anticipation Notes (RANS); Tax Anticipation Notes (TANS); and Bond Anticipation Notes (BANS). "Tax anticipation notes....are short-term debt instruments issued in anticipation of tax receipts....Revenue anticipation notes can be issued in anticipation of other revenues, notably state and federal aid."(14) BANS were sold in the expectation that funds would soon be coming in from the sale of long-term bonds, which should be used to finance projects (e.g., road, school and subway construction) that will last many years and whose cost it is thus unfair for current taxpayers to shoulder entirely.(15)

The metropolis' short-term debt kept growing. On June 30, 1966, it had only $466 million of this type of obligation to pay; by March

The Fiscal Crisis: Prelude

31, 1975 this figure stood at $6.1 billion!(16) Added to almost $8 billion then owing on its long-term bonds (henceforth often referred to simply as bonds), it had a total of $14 billion in paper outstanding as of that latter date!(17) To put it starkly, as of that moment New York's liability to its creditors of $14 billion was a sum greater than its fiscal 1975 $11.5 billion expense budget.

By Fall, 1974 Mayor Abraham Beame, City Comptroller Harrison Goldin (both of whom had taken office in January of that year) and New York's major underwriters (the banks and brokerage houses that sell its notes and bonds to the public or to themselves) knew that it was in a fiscal bind. But, as seen, neither Hugh Carey nor Malcolm Wilson, the gubernatorial candidates that year, were really cognizant of this. As also noted, the Republican was more aware than his opponent that a state agency, the Urban Development Corporation (UDC), likewise had severe money worries. The UDC had been created by Rockefeller in 1968 to build low income housing throughout the State. He had hired Edward J. Logue, one of the best in the business of rebuilding cities, to become its President -- Logue had received high marks for leading the redevelopment of downtown New Haven, Connecticut. Where was the UDC to get its money? Since its projects would be designed to last for many, many years, it would obviously be impossible to finance them out of the State's expense budget. Therefore, they had to be funded largely by the proceeds from long-term bonds. But bonds backed by the "full faith and credit" of the State and that the State is thus under a constitutional obligation to repay have to be approved by the voters in referenda. And there is always a chance that they might be rejected in these exercises in direct democracy -- several of Carey's were.(18) And so it was decided that its paper should be backed not by the full faith and credit of the State but simply by the latter's "moral obligation" to pay the bondholders in case revenues from UDC projects were not enough to redeem these obligations.

The UDC looked to the federal government's "Section 236" program, enacted as part of Lyndon Johnson's Great Society and for which Congressman Carey had voted, to cover the difference between the low receipts from its rentals and the generous expenses involved in transforming its blueprints into reality. However, in 1973, President Richard Nixon, disturbed by financial irregularities in the program, froze "236" funds.(19) This put the UDC in an immediate financial bind. If the gap between the Corporation's expenses and income was large and if a kindly Uncle Sam were no longer willing to make up the difference, how could it satisfy its bondholders? It could not go to the State Legislature and tell them they **had** to provide the necessary cash, for, remember, this paper was simply a moral as opposed to a full faith and credit obligation of New York State. Rockefeller and Wilson admitted in 1975 that in 1973 and 1974 they knew of the problems created for UDC by the Nixon decision. In fact, Moody's rating service lowered the agency's credit rating in October, 1973; and Morgan Guaranty Trust in February, 1974 refused to act as an underwiter for its bonds because it feared it could not redeem them.(20) However, during the 1974 election campaign Wilson Administration officials put on a brave front about it. In October, 1974, Logue claimed, for example, that it was in strong financial shape.(21) It certainly was not; but Chase Manhattan (whose head was Nelson Rockefeller's brother David) and other banks provided it with enough cash to keep going through the election.(22)

By January 1, 1975, his inauguration day, Carey **was** fully aware of the UDC quicksand and its potential consequences. In his State of the State Message of January 8th to the Legislature, he told his listeners that they had to move immediately to meet the crisis faced by the Corporation. As he bluntly put it, "The UDC is facing an imminent exhaustion of funds. All of its ongoing projects will grind to a halt within four or five days unless we take immediate action".(23) Emergency legislation was needed to keep it from sinking before March 31, 1975, the end of the fiscal year. This bill would have to be a "first instance appropriation of $178 million dollars".(24) This was to go to pay off certain debts that became due on February 25, 1975 and to enable it to continue its construction operations until March 31st.(25) In January, the Governor, with the help of Republican Senate Majority Leader Warren Anderson, obtained a $30 million short-term loan from New York City banks to tide the agency over for a few more days until legislative assistance would, hopefully, be forthcoming.(26) This indebtedness would mature on February 28, 1975. New York builder Richard Ravitch was made the Corporation's Chairman and Logue quit his job as its President.

The Fiscal Crisis: Prelude

So the crucial dates in the UDC crisis were February 25th and February 28th. On the first, $105 million in UDC BANS were due; on the latter the $30 million January loan was payable. Had the Chief Executive's plan been accepted by the Legislature before February 25th all might have been well, not only for UDC but also for New York City; and he might have had an easier first year. But the lawmakers failed to act: both chambers wanted to test the mettle of the new resident of the Executive Mansion and thus were not willing to accede on the spot to any request of his.(27) The predictable happened: UDC did not repay either the BANs or the loan on time and banks and investors thus became even more leery of the New York City securities that had to be sold on a massive scale if the City were to avoid a similar fate. The Corporation was the first important government agency to default since the Depression of the 1930s. Therefore "Out-of-town investors, the key to the banks' underwriting function, got cold feet about all New York securities. 'Why should I buy the moral obligations of immoral politicians?' screamed one Wall Street bond trader".(28) And by mid-March of 1975 so many of his colleagues had joined this chorus that the City could not sell its paper even though this was "full faith and credit" and even though it needed a fortune in the way of additional funds by June 30th in order to be able to satisfy its workers, suppliers and lenders.(29)

What to do? The most pleasant course would have been to follow in the well-travelled ruts of the past and market more short-term notes to meet the cash needs of April, May and June. But this *modus operandi* was no longer open. One tried-and-true road that was taken was to ask the State for help. But the Governor's position was that Albany could be of only limited assistance; he maintained that it was faced with a $600 million budget gap itself for fiscal year 1976 ending March 31, 1976. In April of 1975 he did speed $400 million worth of welfare payments to the metropolis. This made it possible for Goldin to meet its April 11th payroll and its April 14th bond and note obligations without having to go begging in an unreceptive securities market that did not open again to its instruments until 1983. And the Governor advanced the City $200 million more of these welfare funds in May.(30)

If Beame could not get more than a cash advance from the

The Days of Wine and Roses Are Over

State's First Citizen, he hoped he could enlist him in his attempts to get help from Washington. Carey and President Gerald Ford had been fairly friendly when both had served in the House of Representatives.(31) The Governor and Mayor on May 13 did meet with the President and his aides but the results were disappointing. On May 14th, the next day, Beame received from Ford a "Dear Abe" letter.(32) This turned down the Mayor's request for a ninety day federal guarantee of loans to the City on the ground that it would provide no real solution to its problems. Ford pointed out that it had to come up with a plan to balance its budget, which would involve curtailing some nonessential services and transferring certain activities to the State. He continued that "Fiscal responsibility is essential for cities, states and the Federal Government. I know how hard it is to reduce or postpone worthy or desirable public programs. Every family which makes up a budget has to make painful choices. As we make these choices at home, so must we also make them in public office too. We must stop promising more and more services without knowing how we will cover their costs".(33)

The President's mid-May rejection of federal aid not only scared City officials but was a stage in the unravelling of the good relations that had previously prevailed between Beame and Carey. One reason not publicly mentioned for Washington's thumbs down was that it rightly or wrongly believed that the Big Apple's politicians had no clear idea of the extent of New York's fiscal problems.(34) In fact at the mid-May summit both Ford and Carey became annoyed at the Mayor because they had the impression that he could not tell them how much assistance he actually needed.(35)

The ex-Congressman may have been irked at Beame after the Washington trip but he knew as well as anyone else that this pique would not cure Gotham's very real financial problems. Above and beyond the personal commitment he felt to the City and its residents, there was no way he could let his State's major municipality fall flat on its face: if it did so, his reputation and any presidential ambitions he had would be totally shattered. Moreover, if he could work out a genuine solution for its fiscal woes his future political prospects would be greatly enhanced.(36) And its need for immediate funds was becoming worse and worse as it became clearer and clearer that it was not going to be able to sell any more bonds and notes for quite a while. The sum required by June 30th was $3 billion and it could only expect about $2 billion in taxes, fees, and federal and State grants-in-aid. It had by then to redeem $1500 million in various types of notes; $600 million in paychecks; and about a billion more for operating expenses and repayment of loans to the State.(37) Crossing his fingers, Carey appointed a "blue ribbon" panel consisting of Richard Shinn, head of Metropolitan Life Insurance Company, one of the City's major employers; Donald B. Smiley, chairman of Macy's, the department store chain; the lawyer Simon Rifkind and Felix Rohatyn, a partner in the investment banking firm of Lazard Freres. Rifkind had been a federal judge and his firm, Paul, Weiss, Rifkind, Wharton and Garrison, was famous not only because of its collective legal acumen but also because some of its partners handled liberal causes *pro bono*. The European-born Rohatyn had made his mark facilitating mergers between ITT and companies such as the car rental firm Avis and successfully pushing the federal government to save aircraft manfacturer Lockheed. Carey had never met Rohatyn until May, 1975, when Democratic National Chairman Robert Strauss set up a meeting between the two. The ex-Congressman was very impressed; and it was lucky that he was, for probably no one did more than Rohatyn to help the Chief Executive get New York out of the doldrums.(38)

The blue ribbon panel, less reverently referred to as the "gang of four", concluded over the Memorial Day weekend that the State should set up a body that would raise $3 billion by selling its own long-term bonds. It would then use these proceeds to pay off some of the City's short-term debt. Though the concept of such an agency was not new, Rohatyn in particular was attracted to it because, like the European Coal and Steel Community, the proposed financial entity could effect some political and economic changes.(39) The recommendation for creating the new unit was transformed into law with remarkable rapidity. The panel had been cobbled together in May, 1975; and on June 10th the Governor signed the act creating the Municipal Assistance Corporation. "MAC" or "Big MAC", as it is familiarly known, was not only given the power to vend the $3 billion in long-term bonds but also had the right to receive frequent reports on municipal finances and act-

The Days of Wine and Roses Are Over

ivities. If worst came to worst, it could refuse to hand over to the City the proceeds from the sale of MAC bonds, which would force it into default. However, it had no legal power to directly reject the budget of the metropolis as a whole or of one its its units. Nor could it scrap a City contract or impose a freeze on the wages of its workers.(40) The Governor appointed five members of the MAC Board and the Mayor four.

The measure passed so quickly because both the Governor and the banks were strongly behind it and working together. By Summer of 1975, their heads had come to respect him and were willing to listen to his suggestions as well as make recommendations to him. They had been distressed at the default of the Urban Development Corporation (UDC) and immediately after this episode had met with him to see what his plans were. (Their discomfort was largely self-inflicted, as they could have postponed demanding payment on the sums that had become due!) They had had relatively little contact with him before this because he had been squirreled away in Washington as a Congressman who was not chair of any committee and also because much of the cost of his gubernatorial primary had been financed by his brother Ed. But they were very impressed at this gathering by his grasp of the UDC's and the City's financial realities and worked well with him from then on. At first, he had to be prodded by his Secretary David Burke to talk with them regularly; but once the initial mutual reserve dissipated their relations reached a high plateau.(41)

The Republicans who controlled the State Senate also were advocates of MAC: in fact, Senate Majority Leader Warren Anderson wanted to go further than Carey's original recommend-ation in limiting the City's power. It was thanks to their efforts that the enabling legislation capped the amount of short-term debt it could incur. Carey himself had private chats with upstate Assembly Democrats who were worried as being perceived by their constituents as supporting a New York City "bailout" bill. Even though armtwisting of this sort was not to become a Carey trademark, on this occasion he pointed out to them, among other things, that they all had pet projects and that these were subject to his veto.(42) Eventually, MAC raced through the State Assembly by a vote of 93 to 47 and the State Senate by 50 to 6.(43)

The creation of MAC saved the metropolis from bankruptcy for

The Fiscal Crisis: Prelude

the fiscal year 1975, that ending June 30th of that year. The banks made an initial loan to the Corporation of $275 million and agreed to defer payment on $280 million in notes while Carey made another advance to the municipality, this time of $200 million in education funds.(44) This $200 million plus the $600 million in welfare dollars he had speeded to it in April and May made a total of $800 million in early assistance he had authorized in order to keep it from default. And the $200 million, plus the bankers' loan and deferral and a few other ploys, did enable it to redeem on time the $3 billion of its obligations due June 30th or earlier.

But New York was still deep in the woods. Thus for fiscal 1976, to run from July 1, 1975 through June 30, 1976, Beame had to propose a $12.7 billion "austerity" budget. This would cut 30,000 jobs and still feature a $641 million deficit that he declared should be made up by additional Albany aid plus its permitting about $400 million in increased City taxes.(45)(In New York State, most local levies cannot be increased without the imprimatur of State law.) After some sparring between the Governor and Senate Republicans over how much the State should give school districts above and beyond Carey's recommendations, and after a city garbage strike in early July to protest layoffs of sanitation workers led to "piles of stinky, smelly garbage strewn about the streets"(46), the Mayor was given about $300 million in new taxing powers. For a brief moment, all seemed well.

MAC had hoped to sell in three segments of a billion each the $3 billion in long-term bonds of its own that it was authorized to market. In this way, it would get the cash to satisfy the holders of the City's short-term debt.(47) $2.6 billion of that short-term indebtedness was to come due between August and December, 1975. Serious trouble cropped up very quickly, however. The first offering appeared in early July, 1975 and even it was not a big hit though its paper carried a high rate of interest and ultimately turned out to be an excellent investment for those who were cajoled or coerced into buying it.(48) The big reason for its unpopularity was the continued high level of municipal expenditures. Thus at MAC's meeting of July 14th, held in the offices of Rifkind's law firm, the atmosphere was ominous. Its Chairman Thomas Flynn noted that he had seen representatives of Morgan Guaranty Trust, Salomon Brothers, Chase Manhattan and Merrill

The Days of Wine and Roses Are Over

Lynch and that they had told him that there was no assurance that it could market any more of its bonds. Flynn continued that he and MAC Board members Donna Shalala and George Gould had met with Beame and Deputy Mayor James Cavanagh and told them bluntly that they had to come up with a "comprehensive plan for improvement in the administrative and financial areas of the City government, [or] any new debt would be in jeopardy".(49) Peter Goldmark, Carey's Budget Director, said prophetically that "the Corporation should set forth its own plan, including spending limits, with an option for the City to make any counter-proposals".(50)

Since the City needed $840 million just to meet its August cash requirements(51) and since investors were hardly thrilled about the strength of MAC's instruments, something in the way of reining in the metropolis' outgoes obviously had to be done to reassure them. And something was. First, Flynn was replaced on July 22th as MAC chairman by William Ellinghaus. Flynn had not charmed Rohatyn by comments at the July 14th meeting shedding doubt on the desirability of MAC's imposing a budget on the five boroughs against their will.(52) Then on July 31st, under considerable pressure from MAC, the Mayor said that "There will be a wage freeze [on City workers]-if not voluntary, then imposed".(53) And during the first half of August he signed into law a wage freeze measure passed by the Council.(54)

Initially, powerful municipal labor leaders such as Victor Gotbaum of District Council 37 had bitterly denounced proposals for a curb of this sort.(55) But the tune sung by him and his colleagues was privately and then publicly soon to change. A July 21st MAC meeting provided him with his first prolonged contact with Rohatyn. Up until then he had viewed the financier as a stooge of the bankers. However, Rohatyn almost immediately convinced him that he had the interests of City workers as well as those of the financial community at heart and won his trust. From then on, he functioned as a broker between the unions and Wall Street.(56) He was able to show Gotbaum that the municipality was really running out of money and that something drastic had to be done and fast. Union pension fund consultant Jack Bigel also speedily came to realize that New York was on the precipice.(57) Soon Bigel, Gotbaum, Ellinghaus, Rohatyn and City officials were secretly negotiating to see what concessions municipal workers might find acceptable. One product of these discussions was the wage freeze the Council enacted into law in early August (58). In September, the State increased its coverage.(59)

And where was Carey during this July when MAC was learning how to walk and Rohatyn was winning the confidence of Gotbaum and Jack Bigel? He attended few of the agency's meetings and, in fact, intentionally stayed in the background. Ford's Secretary of the Treasury William Simon accused him of not being "willing to take charge of the situation".(60) But behind the scenes the Governor was in constant contact with Gould, Rohatyn and others. Both before and after the meetings he would converse with the participants.(61) Shalala is quoted by Newfield and Du Brul as saying that "Even though I'm a member of MAC, I was only on the fringes of things. There were a lot of private meetings going on all the time, with Carey, Rohatyn, Ellinghaus, various bankers, and Shinn [of Metropolitan Life Insurance]".(62) Goldmark showed up regularly at MAC gatherings and one can assume that his comments (e.g., the one he uttered on July 14th to the effect that MAC should formulate its own plan to cut city spending leaving open the possibility of a counteroffer by the City) were made at the Governor's behest or with at least his *post hoc* approval.

Despite the wage freeze, the City during August appeared to be inevitably doomed to default within a month or two. The second issue of MAC bonds, that needed to get it through the month, was sold but only by extremely hard work on the part of the Corporation's officials.(63) The last MAC billion dollar bond fair was slated for September and some of its proceeds were needed to keep the city out of bankruptcy on the 11th of that month. However, August reports were very gloomy about the welcome these would receive. Thus Carey finally had to go public and openly demand that the Mayor make additional economies.(64) As Newfield and Du Brul put the matter, "Carey's undercover phase was to end [in mid August], when the bankers, who respected his intelligence and political adroitness, insisted he become a full, open participant, to help restore 'investor confidence'".(65) On August 21st he moved to front stage and on a bus tour of the Hudson Valley with reporters said that "The best intentions will do no good after Sept. 11"; that "we have to substitute drive for drift"; and that the City's "hospital corporation is not following a respon-

The Days of Wine and Roses Are Over

sible course...."(66) Upstate was intentionally picked as the locale for these barbs since this would show its voters that he also was concerned about what was happening outside the five boroughs. When Beame retorted by asserting that he was not going to cut vital services any more, Carey averred that he had not done enough to restore investor confidence and that further reductions had to be made.(67) In other words, by late August, 1975 the Governor had come to the conclusion that radical sugery was needed. He also had come to realize that he had to be the one to perform it. On Friday, August 22nd, he and MAC officials "broadly agreed that a 'state presence' in the city's fiscal affairs was necessary to reassure investors and that large state loans would again be necessary".(68)

So in early September he got through the State Legislature sitting in special session a "Financial Emergency Act" creating a panel originally known as the Emergency Financial Control Board (EFCB) and now called the Financial Control Board (FCB). It consists of seven persons: the Governor, Mayor and State and City Comptrollers ex officio and three individuals appointed by the Governor with the consent of the State Senate. Under the Act, the City had to develop a three year financial plan covering fiscal years 1976 (the ongoing one), 1977 and 1978 -- ending June 30, 1978. This plan was to provide for a balanced budget by that date. The EFCB could accept, reject or change any financial plan that the municipality handed to it and could approve or turn down any contract (including union contracts) it signed. The measure not only preserved the existing employee wage freeze for a year, but also expanded it and allowed the Board to extend it till that magic date of June 30, 1978.(69)

The statute was accompanied by a complex financing package to avoid default through November, 1975 involving, among other things a loan of $750 million from the State to the metropolis. This Albany contribution was contingent upon MAC's ability to dredge up a billion more to give the Big Apple. This billion was eventually culled from an agency called the State Insurance Fund, municipal employee pension funds and the banks.(70) As will be seen, unearthing it proved unexpectedly difficult. But in any event the measure had one immediate result: the City satisfied the $536 million in obligations due on September 11th.

The Fiscal Crisis: Prelude

The existence of the EFCB obviously diminished the power of the Mayor: his budgets and his contracts could now be nullified by a State body on which he had only one vote out of seven. Beame maintained in his interview with me that he did not object to the establishment of the Board(71): his memory here is essentially but not completely accurate. The Governor made the need for it clear to him in a face-to-face talk in a suite in the fancy Waldorf Astoria Hotel. He did agree to the basic EFCB idea but convinced Carey to make the Board an entity consisting only of himself, the Governor and the State Comptroller. Then because of pressure from the banks the Governor submitted to the Legislature a recommendation for a larger unit. Beame opposed this revision on the ground it gave the EFCB too much authority over the municipal budget.(72) During the next twenty-four hour period, however, the Governor had a couple of long conversations with the Mayor in Albany and Mr. Beame capitulated saying that "Basically we're seeing eye to eye".(73) As City Council President Paul O'Dwyer noted in my interview with him, Beame had no option but to surrender: in New York State, the Governor may remove any public official.(74) But it would be unfair to the Mayor to imply that he acceded to the creation of an EFCB that weakened him solely because he realized that objection would cost him his job. He loved and loves New York City; did not want to see it go into default; and, according to his bitter critic Ken Auletta, had the nobility of soul to accept his own humiliation as the price for avoiding bankruptcy.(75)

A bigger potential obstacle than Beame to the passage of the EFCB legislation was the Republican-controlled State Senate. In that chamber the result depended on the stance of Republican Senate Majority Leader Warren Anderson from Binghamton. Luckily, he was no raving reactionary out to bring New York City to its knees: he made it clear in my interview with him(76) that he feels himself more a "moderate" than a conservative. During the last couple of weeks of August when MAC realized that it could not sell its third $1 billion slice of bonds and knew that default was inevitable unless something were done quickly, the Majority Leader was escaping the heat at Cape Cod. This idyll ended in early September and he and his family started off for home. The way to Binghamton from Massachusetts that year led them through Albany. His wife was at the wheel when they approached the capital and he told her to leave him off and drive the automobile home with the children and the vacation gear. He then joined a meeting with Carey and his aides and agreed to support the creation of the EFCB.(77) Quite a few upstate Republican Senators wanted to see the City go into bankruptcy and thus opposed the Board; but Anderson's counsel Jack Haggerty and his staffer Richard Roth strongly urged the Republican chief to back the Carey proposal. (78) Thanks to Anderson's efforts, it passed the Senate by 33 to 26, with ten Republican Senators including Anderson voting for it. However, Assembly Republican Minority Leader Perry Duryea was of no help to the Governor in his bid to establish the EFCB. He convinced every Assembly Republican, including those from the metropolis, to oppose it; and as a result it scraped through the lower house by a surprisingly close vote of 80-70.(79)

There were Democrats as well as Republicans in the State Legislature who had qualms about the Control Board. Albert Lewis, later Superintendent of Insurance, was at this time a Democratic State Senator from Brooklyn whose district overlapped Carey's old Fifteenth Congressional District. He was worried that the creation of the new unit would unduly infringe upon the Mayor's pre-rogatives. At the same time, he felt that he ought to side with the new Democratic Chief Executive of the State. Caught between these conflicting pressures, he developed a psychological dread of receiving a Carey phone call. To avoid having to talk to him he paced up and down the hallway outside his office deliberating what position to take. His reveries were interrupted by the voice of an aide, who shouted "Your Congressman is calling". So he picked up his receiver and heard Carey imploring him to back the Board. He did not have the heart to brush aside this heartfelt plea and so acceded to it.(80)

One of the most important New York City municipal unions gave Carey and the Control Board an unexpected and serious scare soon after the agency's birth. Probably the closest the City ever came to defaulting on its obligations was on Friday, October 17, 1975. Under the EFCB legislation, various municipal pension funds were supposed to be in the ranks of the buyers of that $1 billion in MAC bonds that the Corporation had to sell. The New York City Teachers' Retirement System (TRS) was being relied on to acq-

The Fiscal Crisis: Prelude

uire $200 million of this paper but by mid-October had taken only $50 million worth. Without a TRS purchase of at least $150 million by October 17th, the City would be unable to redeem about $450 million in notes that would fall due on that date. TRS investments had to be approved by a majority of the System's six trustees. Though three of them voted on October 16th for the MAC purchase, the three representing the United Federation of Teachers (UFT) opposed it and thus the acquisition could not go through. As soon as he heard about this veto, Carey raced back to his office in tie and tails from the Waldorf Astoria where he was attending a political dinner. In that office MAC board members attempted without avail to change the minds of those who had voted con. Urban Development Corporation Chairman Richard Ravitch had arrived back in the City from Washington that day and was immediately phoned by the Governor to speak to Albert Shanker, the UFT head who controlled the votes of its three trustees. The Shankers and the Ravitches were personally close; and Ravitch spent much of the night of the 16th and the morning of the 17th attempting to persuade his friend to approve the MAC bond deal. Finally, in the early afternoon Shanker agreed that TRS should buy $150 million of MAC paper. He made this announce-ment with Carey at his side at 2:07 PM on Friday the 17th. The TRS trustees had been sequestered in the Governor's midtown office waiting for the word from the union leader. As soon as they heard "buy", they unanimously voted to do so. His last-minute timing seemed to make default unavoidable as Manufacturers Hanover Trust, which the metropolis used to redeem its notes, closed at 3PM. However, State Banking Commisisoner John Heimann ordered the bank to stay open past its normal closing time and enough was deposited there by the City on the afternoon of the 17th thanks to the UFT purchase to allow the noteholders to be paid before midnight.(81)

Why did Shanker prove so obdurate? In the first place, he had worked hard to get Carey the endorsement of the New York State AFL-CIO in the 1974 general election.(82) He felt that despite this aid Carey and his staff had often ignored his phone calls and that his teachers had suffered more layoffs, proportionately, than any other group of city workers. Moreover, he viewed a pension plan not as a vehicle for good works but as a means to provide public

Notes to Chapter 3

1. Colby, Peter and White, John - Introduction: Public Policy in New York State Today at p. 227 of Stonecash, Jeffrey, White, John and Colby, Peter (eds.) - Governing New York State, 3rd ed. (Albany: SUNY Press, 1994).

2. Morris, Charles R. - The Cost of Good Intentions: New York City And The Liberal Experiment, 1960-1975 (New York: W.W. Norton, 1980), pp. 43-46.

3. Ibid., pp. 38-42.

4. Ibid., pp. 188-91.

5. Ibid., pp. 172-75.

6. Ibid., pp. 177-82.

7. Newfield, Jack and Du Brul, Paul - The Abuse of Power (New York: Penguin Books, 1978), p. 240.

8. Auletta, Ken - The Streets Were Paved With Gold (New York: Random House, 1979), p. 206.

9. Morris, op. cit. n.2 supra, p. 129; Staten Island Advance, Mar. 20, 1975, p. 1.

10. Netzer, Dick - The Economy and the Governing of the City at p. 27, pp. 29-30 of Bellush, Jewel and Netzer, Dick (eds.) - Urban Politics New York Style (Armonk, N.Y.: M.E. Sharpe, 1990).

11. Ibid., p. 29, pp. 38-39.

12. McClelland, Peter and Magdovitz, Alan - Crisis in the Making: The political economy of New York State since 1945 (New York: Cambridge Univ. Press, 1981), p. 324.

13. Ibid., pp. 326-28, 379-80.

14. Ibid., p. 326.

15. Ibid., p. 326, 378.

16. U.S. Congress, House of Representatives, Committee on Banking, Finance and Urban Affairs, Subcommittee on Economic Stabilization, 95th Cong., 1st Sess. - Securities and Exchange Commission Staff Report on Transactions In Securities of the City of New York (Washington: Government Printing Office, 1977), Introduction, p. 2; Ferretti, Fred - The Year the Big Apple Went Bust (New York: G.P. Putnam's, 1976), p. 29.

17. SEC, op. cit. n.16 supra, Introduction, p. 2.

18. See Newfield and Du Brul, op. cit. n.7 supra, pp. 22-26.

19. Ibid., pp. 26-27; McClelland and Magdovitz, op. cit. n.12 supra, p. 237.

20. McClelland and Magdovitz, op. cit. n.12 supra, p. 237; New York Times, Mar. 23, 1975, Sec. 1, p. 42.

21. New York Times, Mar. 23, 1975, p. 42.

22. Newfield and Du Brul, op. cit. n.7 supra, p. 28.

23. Public Papers of Governor Hugh L. Carey 1975 (Albany: State of New York Executive Chamber 1982), p. 38.

24. Ibid., p. 39. A "first instance appropriation" is a short term loan from the Legislature that probably will never have to be repaid. McClelland and Magdovitz, op. cit. n.12 supra, p.134.

25. Carey, op. cit. n.23 supra, p. 38.

26. Interview with New York State Senate Majority Leader Warren Anderson, June 22, 1990, Binghamton, N.Y.; with Carey Banking Commissioner John Heimann, July 12, 1991, New York City.

27. Interview with Carey's Secretary David Burke, Aug. 28, 1992, New York City; Staten Island Advance, Feb. 6, 1975, p. 1.

28. Auletta, op. cit. n.8 supra, p. 88.

29. Ferretti, op. cit. n.16 supra, p. 168.

30. Ibid., p. 169; Staten Island Advance, May 30, 1975, p. 2.

The Fiscal Crisis: Prelude

31. Phone interviews with James Cannon, Executive Director, Ford's Domestic Council, May 21, 1992, Washington; with President Gerald Ford, Feb. 4, 1992, Malibu Beach, Cal; with William Seidman, Economic Adviser to Ford, Dec. 13, 1991, Washington.

32. This letter can be found New York Times, May 15, 1975, p. 38.

33. Ibid.

34. Phone interview with MAC Board Member Donna Shalala, July 25, 1991, Madison, Wisc. Shalala became President Bill Clinton's Secretary of Health and Human Services.

35. Interview with Ford's Assistant Treasury Secretary Robert Gerard, Mar. 6, 1992, New York City.

36. New York Times, Aug. 29, 1975, p. 1.

37. Staten Island Advance, May 13, 1975, p. 1.

38. Much of what precedes is based on Ferretti, op. cit. n.16 supra, pp. 194-95. In 1996, Senate Republicans prevented Bill Clinton from appointing Rohatyn as Vice-Chairman of the Federal Reserve Board. New York Times, Feb. 14, 1996, p. D6.

39. Phone interview with Rohatyn, Mar. 22, 1995, New York City; New York Times, June 10, 1975, p. 84.

40. Bailey, Robert W. - The Crisis Regime (Albany: SUNY Press, 1984) at pp. 27-29 gives a fine summary of MAC's powers. It was Carey who first called the new body "MAC" and then "Big MAC". Interview with his Press Secretary Robert Laird, May 18, 1993, New York City.

41. Burke, interview cited n.27 supra; interview with Governor Hugh Carey, Nov. 30, 1991, Shelter Island, N.Y.

42. New York Times, June 10, 1975, p. 1; Staten Island Advance, June 7, 1975, p. 1; June 10, 1975, p. 1.

43. Staten Island Advance, June 10, 1975, p. 1.

44. Municipal Assistance Corporation - Annual Report 1976 (New York: MAC, 1976), p. 11; Ferretti, op. cit. n.16 supra, p. 218.

45. See Ferretti, op. cit. n.16 supra, p. 193, 203; Staten Island Advance, June 22, 1975, Sec. 1, p. 5.

46. Staten Island Advance, July 6, 1975, Sec. 1, p. 8.

47. See New York Times, July 19, 1975, p. 9.

48. MAC Board member Dick Netzer (interview Feb. 7, 1991, New York City) and MAC adviser John Tamagni (interview Feb. 18, 1992, New York City) emphasize that MAC bonds proved to be an excellent investment.

49. MAC July 14, 1975 Minutes, p. 3.

50. Ibid., p. 6.

51. Municipal Assistance Corporation, op. cit. n.44 supra, p. 12.

52. Ferretti, op. cit. n.16 supra, pp. 240-41; New York Times, July 23, 1975, p. 1.

53. Quoted Ferretti, op. cit. n.16 supra, p. 275. See also MAC July 17, 1975 Minutes, p. 5.

54. Ferretti, op. cit. n.16 supra, p. 294.

55. See ibid., p. 237.

56. Interview with Victor Gotbaum, June 20, 1990, New York City.

57. Interview with MAC Board member George Gould, Feb. 7, 1992, New York City; Tamagni, interview cited n.48 supra.

58. Bailey, op. cit. n.40 supra, pp. 72-73; Ferretti, op. cit. n.16 supra, p. 268.

59. Bailey, op. cit. n.40 supra, pp. 73-74, p. 95.

60. Newfield and Du Brul, op. cit. n.7 supra, p. 184; Simon, Memorandum for the President: Report on New York City, Aug. 18, 1975, William E. Simon Papers, Lafayette College Library, box 24, folder 31.

61. Gould, interview cited n.57 supra; interview with Gedale Horowitz of Salomon Brothers, Jan. 14, 1992, New York City; Netzer and Tamagni,

The Fiscal Crisis: Prelude

interviews cited n.48 supra.

62. Newfield and Du Brul, op. cit. n.7 supra, p. 190.

63. Municipal Assistance Corporation, op. cit. n.44 supra, p. 12; Ferretti, op. cit. n.16 supra, p. 298.

64. New York Times, Aug. 22, 1975, p. 1.

65. Op. cit. n.7 supra, p. 184.

66. Quoted New York Times, Aug. 22, 1975, p. 1.

67. New York Times, Aug. 29, 1975, p. 1; Staten Island Advance, Aug. 23, 1975, p. 1.

68. New York Times, Aug. 29, 1975, p. 1.

69. Bailey, op. cit. n.40 supra, pp. 41-43, p. 50.

70. Municipal Assistance Corporation, op. cit. n.44 supra, pp. 12- 15; New York Times, Sept. 10, 1975, p. 1.

71. Interview with Beame, Dec. 27, 1990, New York City.

72. Ferretti, op. cit. n.16 supra, p. 310.

73. Quoted ibid., p. 312.

74. O'Dwyer interview, Feb. 14, 1991, New York City.

75. Auletta, Ken - Runnin' Scared, Village Voice, Sept. 15, 1975, p. 43.

76. Anderson, interview cited n.26 supra.

77. Ibid.

78. Interview with Haggerty, Aug. 9, 1990, Queens, N.Y.

79. Bailey, op. cit. n.40 supra, p. 41; New York Times, Sept. 9, 1975, p. 1.

80. Interview with Lewis, Dec. 6, 1994, New York City.

81. This paragraph is based on an interview with Urban Development Corporation Chairman, later Metropolitan Transportation Authority Chairman, Richard Ravitch, Nov. 20, 1990, New York City; on one with New York City Board of Education President (later Chairman of State Permanent Commission on Public Employee Pension and Retirement Systems) James Regan, Aug. 26, 1990, Staten Island, N.Y.; Ferretti, op. cit. n.16 supra, pp. 338-42; New York Times, Oct. 18, 1975, p. 1; Staten Island Advance, Oct. 17, 1975, p. 1; Oct. 18, 1975, p. 1.

82. Interview with United Federation of Teachers head Albert Shanker, Aug. 12, 1991, New York City; New York Times, Oct. 5, 1974, p. 1.

83. Shanker, interview cited n.82 supra.

84. Experienced political reporters Michael Azzara and Peter Harrigan took this position in Staten Island Advance, Oct. 18, 1975, p. 1.

85. Gould, interview cited n.57 supra.

86. Berger interview, Feb. 21, 1991, New York City.

Chapter 4
Washington to the Rescue

HUGH Carey and Felix Rohatyn were under no illusion that the Emergency Financial Control Board (EFCB)'s appearance on the scene would automatically make matters fine and dandy for New York City. Remember that the financing package that came along with the Board tided the City over only through November 1975. At the time he and his aides were putting pen to paper to sketch the structure of the new unit, the Governor said the chances of avoiding default were 50-50 even if everything went right -- unless the federal government agreed to warrant New York's loans or give it some other sort of assistance. In that event, he claimed, the odds that the metropolis would muddle through leaped to 90-10.(1)

When he enunciated these figures in late August of 1975 it looked as though the federal spigot would not be turned on even though he always harbored the hope that his "old pal Gerry Ford" would come through for him in the long run.(2) That month the President had gratuitously told the Mayor and City Council of Belgrade, Yugoslavia that the City does not "know how to handle money" and that "They have been pressing me to give the money, but everybody says no, until they get their management straightened out".(3) Throughout September and October, most members of the national Administration continued to be strongly opposed to aid to the metropolis; though, as ex-Ford aide Professor Charles Orlebeke insisted at a 1989 Hofstra University Conference on the Ford Administration, the tenant of the White House and his staff had always half-consciously realized that they might have to lend it a hand sometime in the future. As Ford's Secretary of the Treasury William Simon commented in a memorandum to the President dated July 25, 1975 referring to a meeting with MAC officials, "We did not say that under no circumstances would we consider action....but that until we saw a viable, concrete program of self-help, it would be counter-productive to discuss federal financial aid".(4)

By October, bills providing assistance to New York had been introduced in the U.S. Senate and House of Representatives. The main ones provided for federal "loan guarantees"; i.e., Washington would agree to pay off any City paper that it could not redeem itself. With the Federal Treasury as well as the City Hall vaults backing them, the Big Apple's bonds and notes would supposedly become marketable again. In the House the measure was intro-

The Days of Wine and Roses Are Over

duced at Carey's request by Democrat T. Ludlow ("Lud") Ashley, an old friend from his House days as well as an intimate of fellow Yalie George Bush. Ashley was head of the Subcommittee on Economic Stability of the Committee on Banking, Currency and Housing of the U.S. House of Representatives -- henceforth referred to as the House Banking Subcommittee! The crucial Senate Committee was its Committee on Banking, Housing and Urban Affairs (Senate Banking Committee), chaired by maverick Democratic Senator William Proxmire from Wisconsin.

Congressional as well as Executive Branch supporters of the loan backup legislation or any other form of boost to New York were in the minority until November of 1975. Carey's fine-tuned political antennae told him that as of September and October he would be a loser even in his old chamber.(5) Big cities have always been whipping boys in American culture as alleged hotbeds of vice and atheism. And of all American big cities New York is the most unpopular, viewed as a potpourri of radicals, Jews, blacks, Hispanics, sissified artists and dandified elites. Moreover, its 1975 "welfare state" of free colleges, low transit fares and a large system of public hospitals ran counter to the American Main Street, mainstream ideology that (unless you are a farmer receiving subsidies for not planting corn) you should pay for what you get. So Carey had a lot of work to do in a very short period of time: no federal aid by December, 1975, default then.

He and his aides, including Rohatyn, therefore contacted members of Congress themselves and organized a lobbying effort in which many others cooperated. Simon laments that Chase Manhattan Bank head David Rockefeller, the sibling of none other than the Vice President of the United States, "rushed about frantically warning financial leaders all over the world that the entire international financial system would disintegrate if New York defaulted".(6) One of the people Rockefeller and others spoke to was Helmut Schmidt, West Germany's Chancellor. And the respected Schmidt told Ford personally (and received Carey's thanks for doing so) that New York's insolvency could severely hurt banks in Frankfurt, Germany and Zurich, Switzerland.(7) The heads of the major New York City financial institutions testified in favor of the guarantee legislation. James Lebenthal of Lebenthal Securities, known for personally hawking "triple free tax bonds" over the radio(8); Brenton Harries, President of bond rating agency Standard and Poor's(9); Wallace Sellers of Merrill Lynch the stockbrokers(10); David Rockefeller; Walter Wriston of Citibank; Ellmore Patterson of Morgan Guaranty and Morris Crawford of The Bowery Savings Bank all came down to the nation's capital to push for it.(11) Perhaps more impressive to the legislators was the appearance on New York's side of such out-of-city bankers as A.W. Clausen of California's Bank of America(12) and R. Stewart Rauch of the Philadelphia Savings Fund Society.(13) Eugene Black, the former head of the World Bank, claimed that a default by New York City would hamper economic growth in the United States, Europe and Third World.(14)

A gaggle of city and county officials, perhaps visualizing that their jurisdictions might one day in the not-too-distant future be in the same mess as New York, backed Carey. Among these individuals were Moon Landrieu, Mayor of New Orleans and John Poelker, Chief Executive of St. Louis.(15) Also supportive were Lee Alexander, the Mayor of Syracuse who had been an unsuccessful candidate in the 1974 Democratic New York U.S. Senatorial primary, and Edwin Crawford, County Executive of Broome County where Warren Anderson's bailiwick of Binghamton is located.(16) So were S. Grady Fullerton, the auditor of Harris County (Houston), Texas and Joseph E. Torrence, Director of Finance for Nashville/Davidson County, Tennessee.(17) However, loan guarantees for New York did not play well in Peoria, Illinois, the town that is considered the embodiment of middle America. Its Mayor, Richard Carver, was one of the few city officials to oppose the loan guarantee legislation: his views were reported and backed by David Rodgers, Mayor of Spokane, Washington, a town located in the very conservative eastern part of that state.(18)

Carey himself spoke at length before both the Senate Banking Committee and the House Banking Subcommittee. In firm tones, he laid out before the Senators on October 10, 1975 many arguments in favor of assistance. He noted the various steps that had been taken to curb what he was willing to describe as the municipality's excesses. He pointed to MAC and the EFCB; the $750 million in State assistance furnished the metropolis in conjunction with the EFCB legislation; and the mandate imposed upon it to achieve a balanced budget by the end of fiscal year

The Days of Wine and Roses Are Over

1978. He described what the Control Board had been doing in its 33 days of existence, e.g., determining accurate revenue estimates for the City, perusing its proposed three year financial plan and starting a review of its contracts. He added that now the State had done all it could to help Gotham: Albany's resources were "stretched to the limit".(19) If the five boroughs defaulted, so would various state agencies that were in the midst of $1.6 billion worth of ongoing projects. This would mean that "Our State will be spotted with empty monuments to default, partially built class-rooms, dorm-itories, public and private hospitals, mental health facilities, and housing for low and middle income families....[They] will forever stand as only steel and concrete".(20) New York's school districts would find it impossible to borrow. Banks, businesses and individuals in every state had New York City paper; and they would be hurt by its bankruptcy. And a limited guaranty of its bonds would cost the federal government nothing. It would in fact provide it with revenue, since under the proposed legislation securities guaranteed by Uncle Sam would become taxable.(21)

After his presentation, he cleanly fielded questions from the assembled lawmakers. To queries from Proxmire and Republican Senator Edward Brooke of Massachusetts asking why Albany did not tax more, he pointed to the extra taxing authority given the City in July and his request for $600 million in additional State levies to close a State budget deficit. These steps were being taken or proposed, he added, even though New York had the highest imposts in the nation and businesses were fleeing.(22) After the quizzing was over and he was about to step down, he received congratulations from several Committee members. Harrison Williams of New Jersey, echoing Abraham Ribicoff of Connecticut, lauded the "clarity of your statement and its persuasive effect".(23) Alan Cranston from California at the end of the proceedings said that he wanted "to compliment you, Governor Carey, on your statement. I think it is a magnificently stated...presentation of the problems you as Governor face".(24) Elinor Bachrach, then a Proxmire aide and later a Financial Control Board staff member, believes that of all the lobbying before the Senate on behalf of the City in 1975, Carey's was the most impressive. He was articulate, especially in his extemporaneous remarks, and knew the details of the bill he was fighting for as well as the Upper Chamber's procedures and folkways.(25)

On October 21st he appeared before Ashley's House Banking Subcommittee. He emphasized there that the City had already fired 22,000 of its employees, had lost 9000 more positions via the attrition route, and had raised its subway fare and its taxes.(26) If the Big Apple should have to go into federal bankruptcy court, business people from all over the nation would be affected. Owners of citrus groves in Florida who had sold orange juice to its hospital system would not get paid immediately but would have to wait in a queue with other creditors.(27) And he revealed that Democratic Governor Marvin Mandel of Maryland had told him that his state was having to pay more interest because of the New York City fiscal crisis despite its AAA bond rating.(28) (He had already received the backing of many of the nation's Democratic Governors. Among those supporting his plea for help were Michael Dukakis of Massachusetts, Richard Lamm of Colorado and Mandel.(29))

Carey's performance before his former colleagues received high grades from them; just as his tour de force before Proxmire's group had greatly impressed the Wisconsinite's Committee. Democrat Leonor Sullivan from Missouri thanked him for his "excellent" statement.(30) Conservative Republican Richard Schulze of Pennsylvania congratulated him as being a "very articulate and intelligent spokesman for [his] point of view" though the Congressman still believed that the five boroughs were running wild.(31) Perhaps the praise that should have made the Governor happiest was that from Massachusetts Representative Paul Tsongas, a person of firm integrity given to understatement rather than gushes of emotion. This reserved man, who became known to the nation when he ran in the 1992 Democratic Presidential primaries, told Carey that he shared the feeling of other members that the City's testimony before the Committee the day before had been "sloppy and inadequate" in contrast "to your performance and to the people with you [Rohatyn, State Comptroller Arthur Levitt] that I find to be very persuasive".(32)

The Governor's activities in the House and Senate did not consist merely of speaking before committees. He made use of his network of friendships in the House among members of both par-

The Days of Wine and Roses Are Over

ties(33), and among conservatives as well as liberals, to try to develop a majority in that body for loan insurance. As Ford Economic Adviser L. William Seidman emphasized, both the President and Carey were from the old school that believed that you could disagree with someone politically and still get along with them personally.(34) Though while in Washington Carey was perhaps closest to other Irishmen in the New York delegation such as Brooklyn's Eugene Keogh, he had developed camaraderie with many House members and had never been nasty in his dealings with them.(35) He was at ease with them both in their lairs and on the Chamber floor, which, as an ex-member, he was entitled to traverse.(36) Martha Golden, who worked for him both in Washington and Albany, provides a fascinating insight into his relationships with other Congresspeople. During the 1974 gubernatorial primary, when he was still in the House, his opponent Howard Samuels charged that the Brooklynite did not have much to do with the passage of an education bill for which he was claiming credit. Carey then visited the office of a southern Congressman asking him to write a letter indicating that both he and the New Yorker had striven for the enactment of this measure. The Member said he would be happy to give this document to his House colleague; but asked that he use it only if he really needed to as he (the southerner) was involved in a close reelection bid. (Carey never disclosed its contents.) And during the fiscal crisis, Golden was told, some of the conservatives whose offices he entered promised not to vote against him if he needed their abstention even though they could not endorse his position. Carey knew why they could not affirmatively support him and did not complain to them about their stance.(37)

MAC Board member George Gould accompanied him on a visit to Washington. They went around the House and Senate office buildings to meet with some of his friends. Gould was astounded at just how effective a lobbyist the Chief Executive was. Before they entered a given office he gave him a precise rundown on the ideology of the Senator or Representative. They then went in and Carey talked with the lawmaker as an old friend. Within a few minutes, the Brooklynite and the solon were enjoying each other's company as they had done in the old days; and he was seen as a warm individual rather than as a spokesperson for the New York

City that so many in Congress disliked.(38) One of his comrades in Washington was Republican Representative from Wisconsin Melvin Laird. Laird was also close to Ford, having been instrumental in making him House Minority Leader. During the crisis, when the Governor was having trouble convincing some of the people around Ford to help the City, he phoned Laird. Laird insisted he come to Burning Tree golf course and play a round with him. The midwesterner won the match and a small bet on the result. He then told Carey that Chancellor Schmidt of Germany was coming to the United States to attend the International Monetary Fund Conference. He added that Schmidt would drop into the Carmel, New York, offices of the *Reader's Digest*, of which magazine the Wisconsinite was a director. During the chat with the Chancellor Laird obviously put in a good word for the City for, as seen, the German spoke to the President on its behalf.(39)

Decisions by Carey and his aides on whom to contact were not taken haphazardly. The New Yorker from his House era knew how to count the votes in the appropriate committees and subcommittees. At that time New York State's lobbyist in Washington was James Larocca, later State Energy Commissioner. Larocca, Carey and other Carey staffers gathered in strategy sessions to see who should touch base with which Senator or Representative. The Governor, Larocca and the others decided that former New York Governor W. Averell Harriman should lead the charge to Proxmire's office. Larocca also recommended that those who talked to him be both frank and firm. At the same time it was resolved that the Governor, Larocca, the Governor's Secretary David Burke and Rohatyn would chat with a staff member of the Banking Committee who was close to the Chairman. Carey knew very well that members of Congress cannot become instant experts on every issue before them and often rely on their personal and committee aides for advice on what stand to take. The tactics adopted to win the initially-sceptical Proxmire over worked to a "T".(40) Another victory was the conversion of Senator Adlai Stevenson III, an influential member of the Banking Committee. Chicago's Mayor Richard Daley, an old Carey friend, whispered in his ear; and John Tamagni of Rohatyn's Lazard Freres met with some of his staffers. He insisted to them that the City was "reforming"; they agreed, and were among those getting the Senator to cast his ballot in its favor.(41)

On October 29th Ford made a televised speech before the National Press Club in Washington that he wishes he had never delivered. In the most publicized lines he said that "I can tell you - and tell you now - that I am prepared to veto any bill that has as its purpose a Federal bailout of New York City to prevent a default".(42) Afterward, Rohatyn, who had just returned to New York from another lobbying trip with Carey, went to dinner at the 21 Club and bumped into *New York Daily News* Editor Michael O'Neill. Rohatyn ad-libbed to O'Neill that in essence Ford had told the City to "Drop Dead".(43) O'Neill relayed this bon mot back to his managing editor, who splashed all over page one of the October 30, 1975 issue of this widely-read tabloid the headline in capital letters: "FORD TO CITY: DROP DEAD".(44) In the opinion of some, this display cost Ford New York State's 41 votes in the 1976 election and thus made Jimmy Carter President of the United States.(45) Had Ford obtained these 41 votes he would have had 282 electoral votes, and it takes only 270 to win.

Carey referred to Ford's comments as a "kick in the groin" and scheduled a rally for Times Square in November to demand federal help(46), as the City's plight was getting worse and worse. Between December 1 and December 11, 1975 it had to have $644 million to meet its debt and payroll obligations and had no clue how it was going to get its hands on the money.(47) Ford's threat to veto a "bailout" bill was especially frustrating to its officials because on October 30th Proxmire's Senate Banking Committee had approved loan guarantee legislation by an 8 to 5 vote.(48) The House Banking Committee had followed suit a few days later.(49)

The Governor went on statewide radio on November 1st to announce that the City was close to bankruptcy. He began by pointing out that the Congress was about to pass a loan guarantee proposal that would avoid that tragedy but that the President had asserted that he would veto a "bailout" bill.(50) He continued by declaring that he agreed with the President: "Washington should **not** bail out New York".(51) But this loan guarantee measure is not a bailout: it "does not give New York City one red cent".(52) After admitting that Ford was right in declaring the City guilty of fiscal recklessness, he reemphasized that all the bill required was for Washington to stand behind the metropolis so investors would be comfortable again buying its notes. "**Washington need not put up a dime**."(53) New York will repay its paper itself and reimburse the federal government for any administrative costs involved in running the guarantee program.(54) Toward the end of the oration, he actually lauded the President. "I spent more than a decade with Gerald Ford in Congress. We disagree about many things. But I always found him a man ready to negotiate and compromise for a practical result."(55) Therefore, he said, he would again ask him to keep the metropolis from bankruptcy.(56)

The next several weeks were very hectic ones for both Governor and President. Carey on November 7th went to California to give a pitch for New York before the San Francisco Press Club.(57) On November 10th he was in St. Louis to address its Civic Progress Association.(58) He became very concrete here and pointed out that midwestern entrepeneurs who had been doing business with New York might have to wait a long time for payment if it defaulted. For example, in St. Louis itself the Car Division of General Steel Industries "is currently fulfilling a $72 million contract for subway cars".(59) And in neighboring Illinois the City owed $152 million for trains and communications equip-ment to companies in Chicago and elsewhere.(60)

After his National Press Club appearance, the President visited Jacksonville, Florida and on November 3rd insisted that he would veto any of the pre-default-aid bills then making their way through Congress. He focused the spotlight on a proposal he had made at the Club: i.e., that Congress should amend the federal bankruptcy law to permit cities such as New York to default and then undergo an orderly process of bankruptcy under which the Federal government would work in conjunction with the court to provide essential services, e.g., police, fire and ambulance.(61) On November 9th, just before a planned special session of the New York Legislature in Albany, a White House spokesperson said that the President "has not changed his position one iota".(62) But within a handful of days he was singing a kinder, gentler tune to the Governor's inner circle. On November 11th Rohatyn, Burke, Rifkind and Carey Counsel Judah Gribetz went to Washington to meet with Simon, Seidman and Arthur Burns, Chairman of the Federal Reserve Board. What Carey's contingent asked is whether Ford might support some sort of federal assistance without default

The Days of Wine and Roses Are Over

if at the special session new City and State taxes were imposed and the City's debt were "restructured". After listening to its report of the response of the President's aides, the Governor sounded optimistic, saying that "We are very near a possible change".(63)

His cheer proved well-founded. On November 12th he received word from Simon to the effect that if the Legislature enacted the reforms that Rohatyn and his confreres laid on the table, the President might support those loan guarantees after all! The special session was postponed briefly for a few more "signals from Ford".(64) A "beep" soon was heard. At a news conference on November 14th the President said that he would "take another look" at pre-default aid to the New York. But he mentioned certain legislation that had to be enacted by the State before he would even begin to reconsider his position. The first was a law that allowed the City to extend the maturity date on its paper. Another was a raise in State and City taxes. And others involved substantial reductions in the metropolis' expenditures and a renegotiation of the pension plans for its workers. Then in a November 19th statement he all but declared that he would provide pre-default assistance. He promised there that "if [New York continues]...to make progress, I will review the situation early next week to see if any legislation is appropriate at the Federal level".(65)

The midwesterner's change of heart thus appears to have taken place some time in the middle of November, 1975. However, at the 1989 Hofstra Conference on the Ford Presidency, Carey dropped a bombshell. First, he said that he had voted in 1976 for the Repubican over Democrat Jimmy Carter.(66) Second, he asserted that he had done so because on October 29th, when the President was delivering that disastrous National Press Club oration, he actually was already backing a measure to keep the metropolis out of bankruptcy court and was just giving his old friend time to round up enough votes in the House to insure that it would prevail.(67) Thus the Governor's current thinking is that the ex-Congressman from Michigan saw the light as early as sometime in October.

However, it is probable that the Governor is mistaken and that the President did not alter his position on pre-default support until mid-November. I asked Ford in my interview with him about the

Washington to the Rescue

accuracy of Carey's assertion that he was working behind the scenes for a pre-default rescue at the time of the Press Club talk. Instead of vouching for its correctness, as he certainly would have done had it been true, he merely replied that once the City followed his calls for greater fiscal responsibility, he felt a moral obligation to it.(68)

Moreover, all the documentary evidence indicates that at least for most of the first two weeks in November, the President was willing to do no more than follow through on his Press Club proposal to ease its suffering once it came within the jurisdiction of a federal judge. For example, at a November 4th "Economic and Energy Meeting" attended by himself and his chief aides, the first decision taken was that "he would accept no compromise with his previously stated [at the Club] public position on new Federal assistance for New York City".(69) On the same day, he met with the Republican Congressional leadership. Here too he asserted that he would help out only after default. When he told his audience to "Keep the pressure on to get the proper default procedure", Senator Roman Hruska of Nebraska commented that "those hoping for reversal by the President may tangle it up so much that default may result". Ford immediately interjected that "I have no inclination to change".(70) It is highly likely that if he had contemplated giving pre-default assistance on October 29th, he would have given some inkling of this to his closest aides and to the Congress members whose support he most needed. But even six days later he was telling them that he rejected Washington's furnishing this type of help.

On November 10th he spoke with five prominent Democratic Senators, including Proxmire and Stevenson, about the pre-default aid bill approved by the Senate Banking Committee. He was cordial; but he told his listeners that "if I had Bill's [Proxmire's] legislation here now, I would veto it. [The] Situation [is] so fluid, [it is] not wise to make commitments".(71) Even as late as November 18th, the day before the issuance of Ford's November 19th statement all but conceding that he would back pre-bankruptcy financing, a memorandum to Simon from his Deputy Assistant Secretary Robert Gerard said that "The situation is in limbo".(72) On the same day as Gerard's note was written, i.e., November 18th, the President informed the New York State Republican] Congressional delegation that "As of the moment, my [Press Club position has not changed. They [New York State] should act, and then we will consider what to do, if anything. I'm making no commitments. I have made no decisions".(73) In fact it was in the course of his conversation with these legislators that he resolved to issue the November 19th declaration! Press Secretary Ron Nessen's notes on that conclave with the lawmakers assert that "Well, he decided to issue the statement during the meeting with the New York Republican members of the State delegation and then the precise working [sic] of the statement has been worked on".(74) And on December 7th, when asked why he had not yet thanked the President for the lifejacket that ultimately was thrown, Carey responded that most of the credit for it should go to Congress.(75) This is a far cry from his present stance that Ford was so helpful.

Why, then, does the Governor now say that the Nation's Chief Executive favored pre-default aid as early as late October, 1975 even though he pretty certainly opposed it then? This problem is difficult to resolve but a reasonable stab at answering it can be made. Ford certainly did not **positively desire** a New York City default. He made this clear to the five Democratic Senators he met on November 10th(76), though he clearly favored default over a continuation of what he saw as the metropolis' profligacy.(77) In his autobiography, he indicates that he worried about the possible effects of severe service reductions on its residents. "Would the cutbacks leave them with adequate fire and police protection? Would they have enough doctors for their hospitals and teachers for their schools?"(78) It is more than likely that throughout Fall of 1975 he communicated to the Governor these concerns and his hopes that the City's problems could be solved without the intervention of a federal judge. And the latter, grateful for the aid eventually given, in retrospect over a decade later may well have mentally converted these anxieties and wishes into an early statement of support for the pre-default rescue.

What, in addition to his perception that New York had left its "spendthrift" course (because of, e.g., the EFCB legislation, Carey's willingness to raise State and City taxes), changed Ford's mind and got him and a hostile Congress to approve pre-bankruptcy aid to New York? Clearly, the immense lobbying effort coordinated by Carey as well as the superlative performances by himself and some of his aides in testifying before the crucial decision-makers were extremely influential. Tributes to their ex-colleague from various lawmakers have already been provided. Simon, probably the Ford Administration member most opposed to helping the City(79), unconsciously pays homage to the power of the Governor's campaign when he says in his autobiography that: "....[T]he pressure from all sides was enormous. The fear campaign and blackmail from all groups had their effect, and in a political forum, the result was inevitable: A compromise was sought. I discussed the situation at great length with President Ford and we agreed....The only possible compromise we could accede to was a short-term loan, with the most stringent conditions of repayment".(80)

Specific aspects of the Carey crusade for the City were especially effective. As noted, one point he made in his October 10th testimony before the Senate Banking Committee was that men, women, banks and businesses in every state of the nation held New York paper and would be hurt by default. This thesis as articulated by himself and others had a real impact on both Congress and the President. Ford aide James Cannon narrates an episode in which a Republican member of the House, a good friend of the Chief Executive from a Western state and at first opposed to helping the City, walked into the Oval Office one day and said "'Jerry, look, I just found out we have a problem. I just found out that the biggest Savings and Loan in my district has about 60% of its money in New York City paper. So I guess we have to do something'. Slowly, slowly, it [the anti-New York attitude] began to turn".(81) In my phone interview with him Cannon emphasized that a good number of conservative Republicans had a similar awakening.(82) MAC Board member Donna Shalala asserts that very important in changing the minds of Ford and some legislators was the publication of a document requested by a Congressman showing that banks and individuals from all over the country had City securities.(83)

Carey and others kept harping upon the notion that a New York City default would have baneful results for the national economy over and above hurting individuals and banks that had invested in City securities. His speech to St. Louis's Civic Progress Association has already been summarized. When he told the Senate Banking Committee that default would mean that states and municipalities throughout the country would have to pay higher interest rates, he added that this boost could cost them a total of $3 billion, negate the beneficial effects of the revenue sharing bill he himself had worked so hard on when in Congress and ultimately drive some of them into insolvency as well.(84) On November 7th he asserted in remarks delivered by Lieutenant Governor Mary Anne Krupsak -- he was speaking in San Francisco on the same day -- that economists were estimating that default would reduce the growth rate of the Gross National Product by 1%. This in turn would mean, e.g., a loss of $14 billion to business; 500,000 jobs not created and $3.5 billion in federal taxes not collected.(85)

Some of the President's top advisers became convinced that arguments like these had considerable validity. In October Burns started to fear, for example, that higher interest rates imposed upon city governments as a result of the five boroughs' collapse might lead to economic chaos. He also expressed to Rohatyn his appreciation of all the sacrifices New York City and State had made up to that point in time.(86) James Connor, a former Ford staff secretary and one of the speakers at the Hofstra Conference, admits that people like Burns, Alan Greenspan and other Ford braintrusters changed their minds and come to realize, as a result of the frequent statements by the Governor and others, that default posed a genuine threat to the economic health of the United States. He rightly continues that they are not to be criticized for their reversal. "People do make arguments; people do think that certain circumstances have changed. That Arthur Burns at one stage could say he doubted that the financial system would collapse as a result of the New York City problem, and then at a later date say 'well, maybe I'm not so sure', is perhaps less the wishy-washyness of Arthur Burns than....changing circumstances." (87)

In sum, the rigorous work of Carey and his colleagues played a major role in convincing Capitol Hill and the Executive Branch to support aid to New York, Ford, as seen, hinting in his November 14th news conference that this assistance might be accorded if State and City took certain steps. That very night in special session the State Legislature at Carey's behest followed through on the

President's call there for extending the maturity date on New York's paper. What they did was enact a "moratorium" under which the metropolis would suspend payments for three years on the principal of $1.6 billion of its short-term obligations, i.e., those whose period of maturity was a year or less. The owners of these notes were given the option of exchanging them for long-term MAC bonds, on which the principal would not be due for quite a few years. Those who decided to hold on to their short-term paper would receive interest but not principal until three years had gone by. About $1 billion of the short-term notes was not exchanged and thus remained subject to the freeze on the payment of principal.(88) Also, the municipal employee retirement systems, including the rambunctious Teachers Retirement System, agreed to buy about $2.5 billion of MAC bonds between December 1, 1975 and June 30, 1978. In a crucial but largely ignored "side-moratorium", they and the banks voluntarily agreed to defer the redemption of over $2.5 billion in City/MAC notes and to accept a lower interest rate on some of this paper.(89)

But was the legislatively-mandated moratorium not default? The average person might say so; but she and the law often inhabit two different worlds. Judge Rifkind, one of Carey's closest advisers in the fiscal crisis, was a man extremely learned in the law. Carey himself is an attorney. All lawyers have read a case known as *Home Building and Loan Association v. Blaisdell*.(90) Here the United States Supreme Court held that despite Article I, Section 9 of the United States Constitution prohibiting any State from "impairing the obligation of Contracts", a State may by law prevent a bank from seizing and selling ("foreclosing on") a private home on which it holds the mortgage even though the homeowner has not been able to make all her mortgage payments. This type of legislation is valid only during an "emergency": *Blaisdell* legitimated a mortgage moratorium statute passed by Minnesota during the Great Depression, which indubitably was an emergency. Often given as a footnote to *Blaisdell* is *East New York Savings Bank v. Hahn*(91), in which the Supreme Court upheld a measure passed by New York State, the last in a series of bills enacted during the Depression, that in essence allowed homebuyers to withhold the payment of principal on all or part of their mortgages as long as they satisfied their interest, tax and insurance liabilities. The lesson of *Blaisdell* and *Hahn* is that the the failure of a debtor promptly to repay some of her obligation (especially the principal) is **not** default when a law passed during a financial or other crisis permits her to temporarily hold back a portion of the payment and she continues to ante up at least part of what she owes.

The Carey/Rifkind moratorium was solidly based on that lesson. The weekend of November 1, 1975, these gentlemen were sitting around in the Judge's beautifully-paneled office tossing about ideas about what new steps could be taken to save the metropolis from default in December. Munching pastrami sandwiches the two men kept brainstorming. Carey took another bite and then mentioned to Rifkind that he remembered his father's telling him that a moratorium in the Great Depression shielded a family homestead from being sold to pay off the bank. Keeping on chewing, the Governor suggested to the Judge that the State should declare a financial emergency now and impose some sort of stop on the payment of the principal of New York City paper. Carey's comments rang the *Blaisdell-Hahn* bell in Rifkind's mind; Rifkind said the step seemed constitutionally okay; and so the Governor shouted "Let's do it". Rifkind and some other lawyers in his office worked out the details and they were part of the goodies on the tray that Rohatyn soon took to Simon. Thus when Ford said on November 14th that he wanted "legislation that permits cities...to extend maturity dates...on certain obligations", he was asking for a step that he already knew the State was willing to take.(92)

Rifkind was presented to the public as the originator of the freeze proposal. When asked why he had not propounded the idea earlier, he replied that "Nobody asked me".(93) It is almost certain that he had mulled over moratorium legislation in the quiet of his chambers prior to his working nosh with the Governor. Powerful figures in Washington had been supporting it. Senator Stevenson of the Banking Committee had said that a *Blaisdell*-type arrangement would be a good idea.(94) The President himself at an October 30th press interview explaining his National Press Club tirade took the (for him) strangely populist position that the bankers who had been recklessly financing New York's financial policy should have to suffer for their bad judgment by collecting the interest and principal on their notes later than they had expected.(95) Rifkind genuinely believed on the basis of *Blaisdell and*

Washington to the Rescue

Hahn that the moratorium legislation was constitutional though he also felt that the chances were about 50% that a court would disagree.(96) In any event, both he and the Governor knew that it would take at least a year for it to get to the New York Court of Appeals, the State's highest court; and that even if it were ultimately knocked down, the City would have at least twelve months of "breathing time" during which it would not have to disburse a large chunk of money that it currently did not have. At the end of that year, they hoped, New York's cash flow would be steadier so that even if the Court decided to overturn the freeze, it still could repay all its creditors.(97) As will be seen, the two men were prophetic.

In addition to the economic necessity for the moratorium, there were also political and philosophical justifications for it. The delay in repaying principal could have provided Ford with an excuse for giving aid on the ground that the moratorium was really a default. But the President himself never termed it such; someone in the White House even labelled it a "sham default".(98) Actually, Carey and Rifkind thought that it would give **Simon** an out. They hoped that once the plan was presented to him, he would say that it meant that the City has not met its obligations and now I'm free to advise the President to loosen up a little.(99) He did take the bait and felt -- not unreasonably -- that the City had defaulted.(100) He claimed, moreover, that because of the moratorium, an aid measure such as that which soon passed would not be the "bailout" that his chief had been opposing because the delay insured that "existing investors" would not be receiving "payment in full".(101)

The philosophical justification for the moratorium was that it would "spread the pain" that would inevitably result from putting the municipality on a firm financial footing.(102) It hardly needs showing how the crisis was hurting City workers and residents: firings, less police and fire protection, higher fares, etc. But, as just noted, the moratorium snared another group: the banks and private individuals who had purchased city notes and who because of it temporarily saw less cash in their vaults or wallets. Some of the public officials who backed budgets that were not in genuine balance or who allowed the City to sell notes without revealing its underlying fiscal illness suffered politically. To take just one case, Mayor Beame may have lost the 1977 mayoral primary because

The Days of Wine and Roses Are Over

of the Securities and Exchange Report's criticism of the metropolis' accounting techniques he approved while Comptroller under John Lindsay and of his refusal then and while Mayor to publicly reveal its budget problems while its bonds and notes were on the market.(103)

The enactment of the moratorium measure was one of the few things that came easily for Carey in 1975. Another condition that President Ford on November 14th imposed on New York before he would recommend pre-default assistance was the State Legislature's raising City taxes by about $200 million.(104) The Governor obtained the support of Republican Minority Leader Perry Duryea to have this passed in the Assembly, since that Chamber's minority members, all Democrats, opposed the hike.(105) The Black and Puerto Rican legislators were understandably angry: the five boroughs' budget cuts had severely affected their communities. Their poor and moderate income residents had to pay higher fares to take the subway; a good number of the discharged municipal employees were black or Hispanic since they had been hired last or occupied low level posts; and out-patient health clinics and day care centers were being locked.(106) In the Senate, helpful Majority Leader Warren Anderson brought 13 other Republicans with him to support the package and it slid through the upper Chamber by 31 to 27.(107) (The war over the Ford-ordered State tax boost will be described in the next chapter.)

On November 26, 1975, the day before Thanksgiving, the President said that he was proposing to Congress a scheme not of loan guarantees but of seasonal loans up to $2.3 billion through June 30, 1978. The purpose of these loans was to bridge the time gap between the dates the City had to pay its suppliers, employees and bondholders and those on which it received the revenue to do so from taxpayers and the State and federal governments. Normally, as Ford admitted, municipalities engage in short-term borrowing to bridge the gap; but, for reasons that certainly are clear by now, New York had been unable since March, 1975 to play that game. He also noted rather cheerfully that the members of the city unions would henceforce begin contributing again to their pension plans.(108) He suggested loans rather than loan guarantees for a couple of reasons. The former are cheaper, not

Washington to the Rescue

requiring a whole host of underwriters and lawyers. Moreover, the lending path enabled the federal government to exert more control over municipal spending. Once a loan warranty were given on a 15 year New York bond, it had to last as long as the life of the bond even if the City started disbursing money like water. But when the U.S. commenced doling out cash to New York at intervals throughout the year, it could (and in fact was obliged to) stop the flow of aid in case the recipient began wasting funds.(109) There was hardly any financial risk to Washington from Ford's loan recommendation. Not only would assistance to the metropolis have to be cut off if the Secretary of the Treasury determined that there was no reasonable prospect of the advance's being repaid, but it had to pay interest on some of the dollars it borrowed from Uncle Sam that was 1% higher than the sums which the U.S. Treasury had been charged for them.(110) And, in fact, the U.S. Government did make money on the loan transactions -- $30 million by early 1978.(111)

Upon their return from their holiday dinners, the Members of Congress received the President's seasonal loan bill. On December 2nd the House passed it 213-203, a close vote but perhaps not all that narrow because the legislative leaders had counted well and thus allowed some Representatives a "nay" vote for political reasons that would have been "ayes" had this been necessary to obtain a majority for the aid program. Of the 213 votes, only 38 were from Republicans and 12 of the 38 were the Republican delegation from New York State.(112) The Senate followed by a vote of 57-30 on December 6th: 16 of the 38 Republicans and 41 of the 62 Democrats supported the City.(113) Ford signed the measure on December 9th, just in time to enable the metropolis to avoid December 11th and later defaults.(114)

Notes to Chapter 4

1. New York Times, Aug. 25, 1975, p. 1.

2. Interview with Carey Secretary David Burke, Aug. 28, 1992, New York City.

3. New York Times, Aug. 5, 1975, p. 1.

4. Orlebeke, Charles, speech delivered Apr. 8, 1989, Hofstra College Conference on Ford Administration. Reprinted as Saving New York: The Ford Administration and the New York City Fiscal Crisis at p. 359, pp. 364-65 of Firestone, Bernard and Ugrinsky, Alexej (eds.) - Gerald R. Ford and the Politics of Post-Watergate America, Vol. 2 (Westport, Ct.: Greenwood Press, 1993). The quote is from Simon memorandum, William E. Simon Papers 1972-1977, Lafayette College Library, box 24, folder 31.

5. Carey, speech delivered at Hofstra College Conference on Ford Administration, Apr. 8, 1989. Reprinted at p. 390, 391 of Firestone and Ugrinsky (eds.), op. cit. n.4 supra.

6. Simon, William - A time for truth (New York: McGraw Hill, 1978), p. 161.

7. Ibid., p. 162; Carey, op. cit. n.5 supra, pp. 392-93; New York Times, Oct. 5, 1975, Sec. 1, p. 53.

8. U.S. Congress, Senate, Committee on Banking, Housing and Urban Affairs, 94th Cong., 1st Sess. - New York City Financial Crisis (Washington: Government Printing Office, 1975), p. 107. (Henceforth cited "Sen. Bank. Comm".)

9. Ibid., p. 302.

10. Ibid., pp. 323-24.

11. Ibid., pp. 640-59, 670-78; U.S. Congress, House of Representatives, Committee on Banking, Currency and Housing, Subcommittee on Economic Stabilization, 94th Cong., 1st Sess. - Debt Financing Problems of State and Local Government: The New York City Case (Washington: Government Printing Office, 1975), pp. 907-53. (Henceforth cited "House Bank. Subcomm".)

Washington to the Rescue

12. Sen. Bank. Comm., op. cit. n.8 supra, pp. 660-69.

13. Ibid., p. 679.

14. House Bank. Subcomm., op. cit. n.11 supra, pp. 1428-29.

15. Ibid., pp. 1478-96.

16. Ibid., pp. 1516-25.

17. Sen. Bank. Comm., op. cit. n.8 supra, pp. 352-55.

18. Ibid., pp. 557-58.

19. Ibid., p. 252.

20. Ibid., p. 253.

21. Ibid., pp. 253-55.

22. Ibid., p. 272, 278.

23. Ibid., p. 284.

24. Ibid., p. 293.

25. Interview with Bachrach, Aug. 16, 1991, New York City. Carey also testified on November 10th, 1975 before Congress' Joint Economic Committee. U.S. Congress, Joint Economic Committee, 94th Cong., 1st Sess. - Impact of New York City's Economic Crisis on the National Economy (Washington: Government Printing Office, 1976). Carey's testimony begins on p. 6. When he had finished, Senator Hubert H. Humphrey said (p. 35): "Thank you, Governor. Thank you very much. That was very powerful testimony and the Nation needed to hear it".

26. House Bank. Subcomm., op. cit. n.11 supra, pp. 980-82.

27. Ibid., p. 999.

28. Ibid., p. 1016.

29. New York Times, Oct. 10, 1975, p. 43.

The Days of Wine and Roses Are Over

30. House Bank. Subcomm., op. cit. n.11 supra, p. 1009.

31. Ibid., p. 1042.

32. Ibid., p. 1020.

33. Interview with ex-Congressman T. Ludlow Ashley, May 8, 1991, Washington.

34. Phone interview with Seidman, Dec. 13, 1991, Washington.

35. Ashley, interview cited n.33 supra.

36. Burke, interview cited n.2 supra.

37. Interview with Golden, Dec. 5, 1990, Washington.

38. Gould, interview Feb. 7, 1992, New York City.

39. Carey, op. cit. n.5 supra, pp. 392-93.

40. Interview with Larocca, May 29, 1990, Commack, N.Y.

41. Interview with Tamagni, Feb. 18, 1992, New York City; Carey, op. cit. n.5 supra, p. 392. Tamagni was a MAC adviser. Carey asked Adlai Stevenson, the Senator's father and Democratic Presidential candidate in 1952 and 1956, to urge his son to support New York. Comments by Mary Burke Nicholas, Director, Carey Women's Division, at "Carey Years" Conference, Apr. 20, 1995, New York City.

42. The speech is reprinted Ferretti, Fred - The Year the Big Apple Went Bust (New York: G.P. Putnam's, 1976), pp. 349-57; this quote is on p. 354.

43. Carey, op. cit. n.5 supra, p. 392.

44. See Ferretti, op. cit. n.42 supra, p. 358; New York Daily News, Oct. 30, 1975, p. 1.

45. Orlebeke, op. cit. n.4 supra, p. 381.

46. Ferretti, op. cit. n.42 supra, p. 361.

47. New York Times, Oct. 18, 1975, p. 16.

48. New York Times, Oct. 31, 1975, p. 1.

49. Ferretti, op. cit. n.42 supra, pp. 366-67.

50. Public Papers of Governor Hugh L. Carey 1975 (Albany: State of New York Executive Chamber, 1982), p. 1128. The speech can be found at pp. 1128-32 of ibid.

51. Ibid., p. 1128. Emphasis Carey's.

52. Ibid., p. 1129.

53. Ibid. Emphasis Carey's.

54. Ibid.

55. Ibid., p. 1132.

56. Ibid.

57. This address is excerpted ibid., pp. 1143ff.

58. This address is excerpted ibid., pp. 1154ff.

59. Ibid., p. 1155.

60. Ibid.

61. Ford made these comments at a television interview, excerpted at pp. 1933-36 of ibid.

62. New York Times, Nov. 10, 1975, p. 1.

63. New York Times, Nov. 12, 1975, p. 28.

64. New York Times, Nov. 13, 1975, p. 1.

65. This news conference is excerpted at pp. 1936-37 of Carey, op. cit. n.50 supra; this statement can be found Public Papers of the Presidents of the United States, Gerald R. Ford 1975 II (Washington: Government Printing Office, 1977) at p. 1886.

The Days of Wine and Roses Are Over

66. Interview with Governor Hugh Carey, Nov. 30, 1991, Shelter Island, N.Y.; Carey, op. cit. n.5 supra, p. 390.

67. Carey, interview cited n.66 supra; op. cit. n.5 supra, pp. 391-92.

68. Phone interview with President Gerald Ford, Feb. 4, 1992, Malibu Beach, Cal.

69. L. William Seidman - Memoranda of Decisions 1975, Memorandum, Nov. 5, 1975, Box 76 L. William Seidman files, Gerald R. Ford Library, Memoranda of Decisions file.

70. Minutes of GOP Leadership Meeting Nov. 4, 1975, Box 9 John O. Marsh files, Gerald R. Ford Library, Congress - Leadership Meetings/Republican 11-4-75 file.

71. Minutes of 11/10/75 Senators' Meeting on NYC, Box 4 John G. Carlson Files, Gerald R. Ford Library, New York City Financial Crisis (3) file.

72. William E. Simon Papers 1972-1977, Lafayette College Library, box 24, folder 35.

73. Minutes of Nov. 18, 1975 Meeting Between Gerald Ford and Republican Delegation, Box 296 Ron Nessen Papers, Gerald R. Ford Library, Handwritten Notes Nov. 18, 1975/N.Y. Republican Delegation file.

74. Press Secretary Ron Nessen's News Conference, Nov. 19, 1975, Box 15 Ron Nessen Papers, Gerald R. Ford Library, New York City/Nessen Briefings file. It is probable that a memorandum from Treasury Department staffer William Gorog dated Nov. 18, 1975 and headed "New York City Notes for Presidential Speech" was one of the drafts to which Nessen was referring. This memorandum is the earliest sketch I have seen of the federal aid-to-the-City plan that eventually was adopted, i.e., short-term seasonal loans as opposed to loan guarantees of New York securities. It can be found William E. Simon Papers 1972-1977, Lafayette College Library, box 24, folder 35.

75. Box 70 Ron Nessen Files, Gerald R. Ford Library, Meet the Press, 12/7/75 - Hugh Carey - file. On November 17th, Carey wrote a letter to a loyal constituent in Brooklyn thanking him for sending him a copy of the latter's daughter's epistle to President Ford asking for federal aid for the City. The Governor told his constituent that "I hope your daughter's tou-

ching letter.... will convince the President to extend to us....a guarantee for our securities so we may market them and continue to be able to help ourselves". Carey Materials, New York State Archives, Albany, N.Y., Fiscal (Budget, New York City) file. (Series 13682). Had Carey really thought as of the end of October, 1975 that Ford was backing rather than opposing pre-default aid, he almost certainly would have realized by the date of the letter to the constituent, i.e., November 17th, that the President was about to come out publicly in favor of pre-default assistance -- and thus that a letter of this type was inappropriate for him to write.

Likewise, had he genuinely believed that Ford favored pre-default aid when the President gave the National Press Club speech, he would not have smiled at Rohatyn when they first saw the News banner while having a late-night snack at Elaine's at 88th Street and Second Avenue and remarked "that does it". A phone interview with Rohatyn, Mar. 22, 1995, New York City, elicited this incident. Rohatyn himself does not think that Ford was quietly pushing for pre-default assistance at the end of October. Ibid.

76. Loc. cit. n.71 supra.

77. See, e.g., Nov. 19th statement cited n.65 supra.

78. Ford, Gerald - A time to heal (New York: Harper and Row, 1979), p. 317.

79. Ford, interview cited n.68 supra; Mayor Abraham Beame, speech delivered at Hofstra College Conference on Ford Administration, Apr. 8, 1989. Reprinted at p. 386, 388 of Firestone and Ugrinsky (eds.), op. cit. n.4 supra.

80. Simon, op. cit. n.6 supra, p. 167.

81. Cannon speech, Hofstra College Conference on Ford Administration, Apr. 8, 1989. Reprinted in Firestone and Ugrinsky (eds.), op. cit. n.4 supra, p. 395, 396; Sen. Banking Comm., op. cit. n.8 supra, p. 254.

82. Phone interview with James Cannon, Executive Director of Ford's Domestic Council, Dec. 13, 1991, Washington, D.C.

83. Phone interview with Shalala, July 25, 1991, Madison, Wisc.

84. Sen. Bank. Comm., op. cit. n.8 supra, pp. 254-55.

85. Carey, op. cit. n.50 supra, pp. 1149-50.

86. Rohatyn, interview cited n.75 supra; New York Times, Nov. 28, 1975, p. 1.

87. Connor, speech delivered at Hofstra College Conference on Ford Administration, Apr. 8, 1989.

88. Municipal Assistance Corporation - Annual Report 1976 (New York: MAC, 1976), p. 15; Annual Report 1977 (New York: MAC, 1977), p. 4; Ferretti, op. cit. n.42 supra, p. 389.

89. MAC, op. cit. n.88 (1976) supra, p. 15; Ferretti, op cit. n.42 supra, p. 15.

90. 290 U.S. 398 (1934).

91. 326 U.S. 230 (1945).

92. Carey, interview cited n.66 supra; op. cit. n. 50 supra, p. 1937; Ferretti, op. cit. n.42 supra, p. 388; Liebschutz, Sarah - Bargaining Under Federalism: Contemporary New York (Albany: SUNY Press, 1991), p. 91. It was not until Wednesday, November 5th or Thursday, November 6th that MAC (i.e., Carey and Rohatyn) definitely decided that the moratorium was the route to follow. See New York Times, Nov. 5, 1975, p. 1; Staten Island Advance, Nov. 7, 1975, p. 1.

93. New York Times, Nov. 28, 1975, p. 1.

94. New York Times, Oct. 26, 1975, p. 1.

95. See Carey, op. cit. n.50 supra, pp. 1928-33, especially p. 1929.

96. Rifkind, interview Feb. 28, 1991, New York City; Shalala, interview cited n.83 supra.

97. Carey and Rifkind, interviews cited n.66 and n.96 supra.

98. Ferretti, op. cit. n.42 supra, p. 388.

99. Interviews cited n.66 and n.96 supra.

100. Simon, op. cit. n.6 supra, p. 167.

101. See Simon letter to Tennessee State Senator Vernon Neal, Nov. 21, 1974, William E. Simon Papers 1972-1977, Lafayette College Library, General Correspondence Secretary of the Treasury (outgoing 1975 (Sept.) - 1976 (Feb.)) file, box 6.

102. Interview with MAC Board member Dick Netzer, Feb. 7, 1991, New York City; Shalala, interview cited n.83 <u>supra</u>.

103. Beame's Corporation Counsel W. Bernard Richland feels that the SEC Report hurt his chief in the primary. See Richland's remarks in <u>The Daily Bond Buyer</u>, Nov. 16, 1977, p. 1, 21.

104. Even before November 14th, the President had been calling for increases in New York State and City taxes. See, e.g., his news conference of Oct. 10, 1975, excerpted at p. 1920 of Carey, <u>op. cit.</u> n.50 <u>supra</u>; and his interview with reporters on Oct. 30th explaining his Oct. 29th National Press Club Speech, excerpted at p. 1928, 1931 of <u>ibid</u>.

105. See <u>New York Times</u>, Nov. 24, 1975, p. 56; Nov. 25, 1975, p. 36. Geoffrey Stokes - <u>City Bail Out: Carey's Big Win Is Our Loss</u>, <u>Village Voice</u>, Dec. 8, 1975, p. 32 criticizes Carey for failing to get much minority input when making the budget cuts. Stokes is right on target here. When particular policies disproportionately hurt a particular group, members of that group ought to be consulted at length before these policies are implemented. Carey certainly was no racist and usually was sensitive to minority concerns. However, that sensitivity was to some extent in abeyance during the financial crisis perhaps because, as one Carey aide told Stokes, the Governor was preoccupied with making and coordinating the complicated moves that were needed to keep the City out of bankruptcy. See the Stokes article at p. 34.

106. Newfield, Jack and Du Brul, Paul - <u>The Abuse of Power</u> (New York: Penguin Books, 1978), pp. 6-7.

107. <u>New York Times</u>, Nov. 26, 1975, p. 36.

108. <u>New York Times</u>, Nov. 25, 1975, p. 1.

109. Ford, interview cited n.68 <u>supra</u>; interview with Ford's Assistant Secretary of the Treasury Robert Gerard, Mar. 6, 1992, New York City; <u>New York Times</u>, Nov. 27, 1975, p. 42.

110. <u>New York Times</u>, Nov. 27, 1975, p. 1, 42.

111. Testimony of U.S. Secretary of the Treasury W. Michael Blumenthal at p. 277, pp. 280-81 of Pt. 1 of U.S. Congress, House of Representatives, Committee on Banking, Finance and Urban Affairs, Subcommittee on Economic Stabilization, 95th Cong., 2nd Sess - New York City's Fiscal and Financial Situation (Washington: Government Printing Office, 1978).

112. New York Times, Dec. 3, 1975, p. 1.

113. New York Times, Dec. 6, 1975, p. 39.

114. Carey, op. cit. n.50 supra, p. 1941; New York Times, Dec. 10, 1975, p. 1. On December 18th, Ford signed the crucial appropriations act putting meat on the December 9th authorizing law. The first $130 million given New York City under the appropriation arrived December 19th. This sum enabled it to meet its payroll due on that date and all its other obligations maturing on or before January 1, 1976. New York Times, Dec. 19, 1975, p. 77.

Chapter 5
The Goldmark Buildout
and the State Tax Hike

DURING 1975 not only New York City but various agencies of New York **State** and in fact the **State** itself were close to the brink and had to be defended by Carey and Company -- a struggle that Salomon Brothers bond expert Gedale Horowitz, a close observer of the New York City cash crisis, rightly insists was as important as how the City's fiscal bleeding was stanched.(1) The Governor's first Budget Director Peter Goldmark emphasized again and again how intertwined were the fiscal problems of City and State and that both had to be solved together.(2) That, as seen, the Urban Development Corporation's (UDC) default in late February, 1975 helped provoke the metropolis' near-catastrophe is but the first of many pieces of evidence in favor of his position.

Four other State construction agencies obtained their funds at least in part by selling moral obligation paper. The Housing Finance Agency (HFA) was set up to erect moderate income housing. The State Dormitory Authority (SDA) builds dormitories for SUNY units and private universities and facilities for CUNY colleges as well as hospitals.(3) The two other units were the Medical Care Facilities Financing Authority (MCFFA) and the Environmental Facilities Corporation (EFC). In 1975 both had a lot of non-full-faith-and-credit short-term notes outstanding.(4) The EFC aids municipalities in financing water pollution control plants and lends money at a low rate of interest to private companies for projects such as sewage treatment and solid waste management.(5) The MCFFA (now merged with the SDA) helps fund construction for non-profit hospitals, for nursing homes and for health maintenance organizations.(6) **If any one of the four during 1975 or 1976 had failed to redeem its bonds or notes or the UDC had flunked in this respect a second time, neither they nor the Municipal Assistance Corporation (MAC) nor the State itself would have been able to sell its paper and all of them plus New York City and State would have had to declare bankruptcy.**

Shortly after the UDC default the State pieced together a plan to bail it out.(7) This gave the Corporation temporary solace. However, the ripples from its default were felt not only by New York City but also by the other moral obligation agencies (hereafter referred to as "the agencies"): the HFA, the SDA, the MCFFA and the EFC. Because of the UDC's and the metropolis' financial problems, these by Fall of 1975 could not market any securities. They had over $2 billion worth of projects already underway and these would go down the drain if they could not get more cash.(8) To enable them to obtain this money Carey turned to his Budget Director, Peter Goldmark. Goldmark and a task force he set up worked day and night seven days a week for seven months and eventually came up with a solution (referred to as "the buildout") that was as complicated as the Carey measures (e.g., the creation of the Emergency Financial Control Board; the November, 1975 moratorium) taken to keep the City from bankruptcy.

Moreover, while working on the buildout, which had to be largely a done deed by the end of March 1976, i.e., before the start of the State's new fiscal year, the Budget Director and his staff had, of course, to insure that none of the agencies would fail to pay its debts before that safety net was in place. This was easier said than done, for each month at least one and usually two or three of them had short-term debt to redeem and no possibility of selling their own bonds and notes to get the necessary dollars. For example, mid-December was the turn of the HFA and the SDA. At this time Carey was in the midst of a battle with the Republicans controlling the State Senate about whether State taxes should be raised: Carey taking the affirmative position. Those of his aides worrying about the agencies had heart palpitations because the Governor was insisting on linking their rescue to the passage of his tax packet and Warren Anderson had expressed scepticism about the need for the hike. But, as will be seen, the Majority Leader finally signaled that he was willing to consider the increase and Goldmark and Carey squeezed about $200 million out of a recondite entity called the State Insurance Fund to keep the SDA and the HFA from insolvency. (This fund exists to guarantee that injured workers will be able to receive compensation from the State's workmen's compensation program.) The legislation permitting the Fund to buy the agencies' bonds was signed by the Governor at 11:20 PM on December 15th, 40 minutes before their repayments would have become overdue. At about this time, the City of Yonkers in Westchester County just north of The Bronx was getting

The Goldmark Buildout

about $4 million in state cash to enable it to avoid defaulting on notes due January 2, 1976.(9)

January 1976 was HFA on-the-precipice time again, the fourth straight month for it. Its partner in potential disaster on this occasion was the MCFFA. Goldmark propped up the wobbly duo by getting New York City's commercial banks to "roll over" $32 million in notes, i.e., take new ones in exchange for old. And the old reliable St. Bernard, the State Insurance Fund, was called on again, this time to the tune of $22 million.(10) February, 1976 arrived, bringing with it to Albany not only ice and snow but agencies on the edge -- this time all four.(11) The State Insurance Fund came through in the clutch again; the commercial banks did their "rollover" trick once more; and State Comptroller Arthur Levitt extended for three months the repayment of a loan made earlier.(12) The final monthly bailout took place in March: no more were necessary because Goldmark and his staff had by then completed most of the buildout.(13)

The fundamental aim of the buildout was to provide the agencies with $2.6 billion, much of which would come from new bonds issued in their names. This sum would enable them to finish their ongoing construction jobs. It would also make it unnecessary for Albany to throw them any more last-second life lines to avoid their defaulting.(14) The first component of the buildout strategy was similar to the activities of the Municipal Assistance Corporation on behalf of New York City. MAC was selling bonds in order to allow the City to retire its short-term paper. What Goldmark and staff had to do was locate all the holders of the agencies' short-term notes and convince them, to simplify somewhat, to convert them into bonds thus giving the quartet time to complete their facilities before they would have to worry about paying principal to their creditors -- they would always have to meet interest obligations, of course. Unfortunately for the Budget Division staff, the short-term debt was held by 150 banks, not just the 10 or 11 big New York City counting houses. Each institution had to be visited individually and asked to go along with the scheme. Goldmark felt that he would have little trouble winning over all of them: their sense of good citizenship could be appealed to while the stick was that if the agencies defaulted, the bankruptcy judge might force the holders of their paper to accept partial payment in full satisfaction of the

96

debt.(15)

The banks met Goldmark's expectations and proved receptive to his plea. However, he and his assistants at times had to use some elbow grease to get their way. Thus one aide flew to an upstate bank at the request of the directors only to be told that it would insist on the payment of its short-term debt. He angrily retorted that they shouldn't have asked him to come all this way just to be told no and began to walk out of the meeting. The embarrassed businessmen called him back and voted "aye". Another time Goldmark himself was putting his whole heart and soul into his presentation when he noticed that the chairman of the board was snoozing! Some institutions did demand high interest rates on their new paper, while many wanted assurances that other banks in their position were going along. To relieve their minds, he had each assenting bank sign a "pledge card" saying that it had agreed to his conversion plan on condition that its fellows would as well.(16)

Part two of the buildout plan involved seeking cash from private sources. Goldmark talked to large insurance companies, including the New Jersey based Prudential. Prudential moved quickly and made a favorable decision within 45 days after it was approached. Though some other insurance companies turned him down, eventually several decided to help out including New York's Equitable Life Assurance Society.(17) The buildout's third aspect involved getting the United States Department of Housing and Urban Development (HUD) to insure mortgages on various HFA projects. With such insurance, the mortgages could be sold to private investors and the proceeds used for the $2.6 billion kitty that Goldmark was trying to conjure into existence. Negotiations with HUD moved slowly but eventually it agreed to insure about $260 million worth of HFA mortgages, not as much as originally expected.(18) Fourth, certain agency projects were suspended; one was assumed by Westchester County; and yet others were (in 1990s' parlance) "privatized", i.e., given to private parties to complete. This fourth element brought in about $400 million. The buildout's fifth face involved receiving about $400 million as payment for the agencies' bonds from various State funds, including that goldmine the State Insurance Fund.(19)

Finally, Goldmark viewed State Comptroller Arthur Levitt in his capacity as sole trustee of two state pension systems, the State Policemen's and Firemen's Retirement System and the State Employees' Retirement System, as a big hope for the agency buildout. Levitt's two funds plus the State Teachers' Retirement System, which was not under his control but which usually followed his signals, had a cache of billions. However, the Comptroller had made it a firm policy never to acquire moral obligation bonds, feeling not unreasonably that they were unsound paper whose nonpayment could jeopardize the quality of life of his systems' present and future retirees. Thus initially he refused to contribute anything toward the buildout.(20) Goldmark was not happy with this stance, and referred to him as a tough nut to crack; at best passive and at worst obstructive.(21) However, it was necessary that he be won over; and therefore the Budget Director set up an informal "Committee to Manage Arthur Levitt". One of the members was Frank Smeal of Morgan Guranty Trust, a very active bank part-icipant in all the negotiations involving the New York City fiscal crisis. Goldmark and Smeal got Arthur Burns, Chairman of the Federal Reserve Board, to inform the Comptroller that the agencies had to be rescued and that he was the key to their salvation. If they sank, Burns told him, New York State itself might well go bankrupt. So eventually Levitt surrendered and bought about $400 million in bonds for Goldmark's pot. This was matched by $418 million from the Teachers' Retirement System, and the Budget Director now had the needed $2.6 billion in proceeds from the agencies' bonds and elsewhere.(22)

Goldmark and his helpers not only had to secure the $2.6 billion so that the agencies could complete their ongoing work and not default; but they also felt obliged to come up with a scheme that would convince investors **in the future** to buy SDA, HFA, etc. bonds and notes. When in doubt, create a new agency; and this is what Goldmark proposed and Carey and the Legislature accepted together with the buildout deal. The Governor's first Banking Com-missioner John Heimann had before his appointment participated in an investigation into what had gone wrong with the moral-obligation-bond Urban Development Corporation, and why it had defaulted in February of 1975. He concluded that one of its main weaknesses was that there had existed no group of persons with financial experience to oversee it to damp down the enthusiasm of its head, Edward Logue, for undertakings that were commercially risky.(23) Taking off from Heimann's critique, Goldmark recommended that the amount the four agencies that were salvaged by the buildout could borrow be limited and that a Public Authorities Control Board be set up to effect these caps and to stop them from working on too many projects.(24) The Legislature accepted this suggestion.(25) Thus later in 1976 we see the Board, e.g., considering whether to allow the HFA to issue more bonds to build the Amherst Campus of the State University of New York at Buffalo.(26) Of course, the Campus was eventually completed and is a major employer in the region. Like the Amherst Campus, the Public Authorities Control Board is still with us and its scrutiny of State construction projects doubtlessly helps the agencies sell their paper. Currently this paper does not consist of moral obligation bonds, however, but is backed by a state contract to pay the creditors.(27)

These pages have referred much more to Goldmark than to Carey. This is almost inevitable in any study of a political leader who was wont to delegate authority: much of the action will be undertaken by the delegee and therefore the analysis will have to spotlight his/her moves. Because of his lobbying effort for New York City, the Governor just did not have the time to participate much in the lengthy negotiations with the federal government, the insurance companies, the banks and State Comptroller Levitt that were the precondition of a successful State agency buildout. So Goldmark and his aides themselves had to bargain with the banks, etc., though the Chief Executive did meet with the trustees of the State Teachers' Retirement System to convince them to contribute a tad to the February, 1976 bailout.(28) Where they needed Carey was to support and sign the legislation that they proposed; and this he certainly did. Thus for two reasons he deserves praise for his role in saving the agencies: he handpicked the individual who so brilliantly headed the group that did this job and he worked to get their ideas enacted into law. Under the circumstances, more could not have been asked of him.

Carey himself did push his position vigorously in one conflict that bore a relationship to the agency crisis, among others. Having been told during the transition period after his win in the general election that the State was faced with a budget deficit in fiscal year

The Goldmark Buildout

1976, which began on April 1, 1975, his January, 1975 budget message asked for a hefty $800 million State tax increase. Income taxes on all taxpayers, especially the richest, were to go up and imposts on business were also to rise. Particularly controversial was a recommendation that the Legislature enact an boost of $.10 a gallon in the State gasoline tax. Legislators outside New York City reacted badly to that one. Their constituents relied on cars rather than mass transit not only for going to the mall to shop and for ferrying their children to Little League but also to get to work. Consequently, even Democrats from outside New York City balked at this idea and it died aborning. For example, liberal suburban Democratic State Senator Linda Winikow said that she would vote against it were it ever to come to the floor.(29)

Actually, the obstacle to the Governor's tax increase was more fundamental than mere opposition to one of its components. Republicans in the State Senate, including Majority Leader Anderson, made it clear that they wanted no hike at all.(30) However, by Fall matters were getting out of the Binghamtonian's control. It will be remembered that President Ford had sometime in November decided that he would recommend that aid be given to New York City to keep it out of bankruptcy but that this aid was conditional on the City and State doing even more to putting the former on an even financial keel. One publicly announced prerequisite articulated by the President was a rise in **State** levies. As he said in his November 14, 1975 news conference, "There are a number of other things that have to be done. They have to agree to raise their taxes-city and **State**".(31)

Having to bow to Ford's wishes was not the only reason a tax boost was needed. Because of the State's loan of $750 million to the City when the EFCB was created and because of other money the State had had to disburse to help UDC and the four other moral obligation agencies as well as Yonkers, the financial community in late 1975 and early 1976 was getting very dubious about buying any **State** paper. If the State could not in Spring, 1976 engage in what was then called "Spring borrowing" procedures, i.e., sell about $4 billion in short-term notes to tide over school districts and municipalities until their fiscal year began, New York City and many other jurisdictions in the State would collapse. Carey and Goldmark feared with justification that if the State did not come up

The Days of Wine and Roses Are Over

with a balanced budget for **both** the ongoing fiscal year (1976) and the subsequent one (1977, beginning April 1, 1976 and ending March 31, 1977), it would be unable to obtain the $4 billion -- and, as well, no bonds of Goldmark's four agencies could be sold.(32) And without tax hikes, the State's finances would be nowhere close to equilibrium.

What the Governor proposed on December 9, 1975, the same day that Ford signed the seasonal loan legislation, was a package to balance the budget for **both** fiscal 1976 and the upcoming fiscal 1977. Half of the bundle involved cuts in, e.g., welfare and Medicaid. The other half was a revival of the January, 1975 proposal to raise State taxes: this time, however, the suggested increments involved mainly taxes on businesses and banks.(33) Anderson and Republican Assembly Minority Leader Perry Duryea stuck to their position that these new revenues were unnecessary. But here a strange thing happened. There is no group more Republican than the heads of large financial institutions. But when they saw Anderson and Duryea persist in their anti-tax stance, the leaders of the major New York City banks, including Chase's David Rockefeller and Morgan Guaranty Trust's Ellmore Patterson, took a private jet to Albany on December 10th and laid it on the line to their fellow GOP stalwarts. They made it clear that "they wanted taxes and cuts to close the gap, and they wanted them fast".(34)

However, there still remained some tense moments between the articulation of the bankers' orders and their execution because even Democratic legislators had become angry at the Governor. One reason for this was that, following a good Albany tradition, the tax proposals were thrown on the lawmakers' desks with a ukase that they be enacted immediately.(35) On Saturday, December 20th at 4 in the morning the bills finally got through the State Senate and were signed by the Chief Executive. The vote was a squeaker, 31 to 24 in the Senate after a 76 to 59 split in the Assembly. Both chambers require an absolute majority for passage; and 31 and 76 were the lowest possible number of votes needed for Carey to be successful. In the Assembly all 53 Republicans voted con and were joined by six Democrats. After the Assembly had acted and while the result was still uncertain in the Senate, Speaker Stanley Steingut locked the doors of his body's meeting hall so that its members could not leave if they were needed for another ballot. In the Upper Chamber, 20 Democrats and 11 Republicans voted for the bill; two Democrats and 22 Republicans raised their hands nay. Now in favor on the Republican side were Anderson, who had proven so helpful in getting the EFCB through and in seeking federal aid, as well as Finance Committee Chairman John Marchi. Anderson became furious at Duryea when the latter persuaded the Suffolk (Long Island) County Republican Chairman to convince two Senators from that County (where Duryea also lives) to vote against the taxes after they had given the Senate Leader their word that they would cast their ballots in favor. So Anderson and Senate Minority leader Manfred Ohrenstein had to scramble to get two "substi-tutes", one a Democrat and one a Republican.(36)

This bank/business tax boost did not get the State out of deficit for fiscal 1976: in fact at the end of the fiscal year it still was almost $450 million in the red.(37) But the rise was a 15 month deal(38) and left hope that by the end of that period, i.e., March 31, 1977, the end of the **1977** fiscal year, New York State's receipts and expenditures would more or less cancel one another out. So securing the $4 billion in State Spring borrowing, which was needed to preserve the financial health of local jurisdictions and to keep the construction agencies operating, became more feasible. Clinching the acquisition of this sum was delegated to buildout hero Budget Director Peter Goldmark, and again he succeeded handsomely. First he got about $1.5 billion from "inside" sources: State funds and the State Teachers' Retirement System. In early March, the major City banks agreed to purchase $1 billion in State notes. He then urged the Bank of America, the California institution that was the most important bank in the nation after the New York City giants, to help out. Goldmark felt that if he could get this influential concern to invest, other banks would follow its lead. He spent a lot of time on the telephone during March of 1976 with Bank officials and by April 7th, only a few days after the beginning of the fiscal year, he received from it a pledge to buy $100 million in State paper, eventually to be upped to $200 million. Almost immediately after this savings banks and more commercial banks joined the parade. By the end of April, 1976, which he had set as his deadline, the entire $4 billion (well, just $3,890 billion!) was in the State's vaults for transfer to its cities and school districts.(39)

Notes to Chapter 5

1. Interview, Jan. 14, 1992, New York City.

2. Interview with Goldmark, Aug. 20, 1990, New York City.

3. Joseph, Ronald - The 1976 New York State Fiscal Crisis (Boston: Boston University, School of Management, Public Management Program, Curriculum Development Project, 1981) (Unpublished draft), p. 7; New York Times, Mar. 21, 1976, Sec. 1, p. 38.

4. Joseph, op. cit. n.3 supra, p. 7.

5. New York City - Greenbook 1991-92 (New York: Citybooks, nd), p. 299.

6. Walsh, Annmarie Hauck - Public Authorities and the Shape of Decision Making at p. 188, 193 of Bellush, Jewel and Netzer, Dick (eds.) - Urban Politics New York Style (Armonk, N.Y.: M.E. Sharpe, 1990).

7. New York State Moreland Act Commission on the Urban Development Corporation - Restoring Credit and Confidence: A Reform Program for New York State and its Public Authorities (Albany: The Commission, 1976), p. 202; New York Times, May 21, 1975, p. 41; Feb. 7, 1976, p. 24; Staten Island Advance, Feb 27, 1975, p. 2; Mar. 6, 1975, p. 1.

8. See Joseph, op. cit. n.3 supra, p. 3.

9. Ibid., p. 11, including Peter Goldmark's handwritten annotation on that page in the copy in my possession; New York Times, Dec. 14, 1975, p. 1; Staten Island Advance, Dec. 13, 1975, p. 1; Dec. 16, 1975, p. 1.

10. Joseph, op. cit. n.3 supra, p. 12; Staten Island Advance, Jan. 13, 1976, p. 8.

11. New York Times, Feb. 11, 1976, p. 32; Feb. 12, 1976, p. 62; Feb. 14, 1976, p. 52.

12. Joseph, op. cit. n.3 supra, pp. 12-13; New York Times, Feb. 11, 1976, p. 32.

13. Joseph, op. cit. n.3 supra, p.13; New York Times, Mar.14, 1976, p. 1.

14. Joseph, op. cit. n.3 supra, p. 58; New York Times, Mar. 21, 1976,

The Goldmark Buildout

Sec. 1, p. 38.

15. Joseph, op. cit. n.3 supra, pp. 15-16; New York Times, Mar. 21, 1976, Sec. 1, p. 38.

16. Joseph, op. cit. n.3 supra, p. 16; New York Times, Mar. 21, 1976, Sec. 1, p. 38.

17. Joseph, op. cit. n.3 supra, pp. 18-19; New York Times, Mar. 21, 1976, Sec. 1, p. 38.

18. Joseph, op. cit. n.3 supra, p. 19; New York Times, Mar. 21, 1976, Sec. 1, p. 38.

19. Joseph, op. cit. n.3 supra, p. 20, 58.

20. Joseph, op. cit. n.3 supra, p. 12; New York Times, Dec. 10, 1975, p. 70; Mar. 21, 1976, Sec. 1, p. 38.

21. Goldmark, interview cited n.2 supra.

22. Joseph, op. cit. n.3 supra, pp. 16-18, p. 58; New York Times, Mar. 21, 1976, Sec. 1, p. 38.

23. Interview with Carey Banking Commissioner John Heimann, July 7, 1991, New York City.

24. Public Papers of Governor Hugh L. Carey 1976 (Albany: State of New York Executive Chamber, 1986), pp. 489-92.

25. New York State Laws of 1976, Ch. 38, 39.

26. Carey, op. cit. n.24 supra, pp. 1677-78.

27. Interview with ex-New York State Division of the Budget aide Bruce Balle, June 3, 1992, Albany, N.Y.

28. New York Times, Feb. 14, 1976, p. 52.

29. Staten Island Advance, Mar. 19, 1975, p. 1.

30. Ibid., p. 2.

The Days of Wine and Roses Are Over

31. Public Papers of Governor Hugh L. Carey 1975 (Albany: State of New York Executive Chamber, 1982), p. 1937. Emphasis supplied. The news conference is excerpted ibid., pp. 1936-37.

32. Staten Island Advance, Dec. 9, 1975, p. 3. Had the City not repaid the $750 million loan, the State (and then the City, the agencies, etc.) might well have become insolvent. Phone interview with Felix Rohatyn, Mar. 22, 1995, New York City.

33. New York Times, Dec. 10, 1975, p. 1, 70.

34. Staten Island Advance, Dec. 14, 1975, Sec. 1, p. 5; also New York Times, Dec. 11, 1975, p. 1.

35. See New York Times, Dec. 19, 1975, p. 78.

36. New York Times, Dec. 21, 1975, Sec. 1, p. 1, 34.

37. Municipal Assistance Corporation - Exchange Offer $250 Million MAC 9 3\4% 1977 Series Bonds (New York: MAC, Mar. 22, 1977), p. 33.

38. New York Times, Dec. 21, 1975, Sec. 1, p. 1.

39. Joseph, op. cit. n.3 supra, pp. 22-27, p. 66; New York Times, Apr. 8, 1976, p. 1.

Chapter 6
Carey, the EFCB, and the CUNY and 1978 City Rescues

THE EFCB, with Carey as its ex officio chairman, began meeting on September 11, 1975, right after the passage of the Financial Emergency Act setting it up; and held frequent sessions through mid-1977. Its seven members were the Governor (Carey); the State Comptroller (Arthur Levitt, succeeded in 1979 by Republican Edward Regan); the Mayor of New York (Abraham Beame, followed in 1978 by Edward Koch); the New York City Comptroller (Harrison J. Goldin); and three private persons chosen with the consent of the State Senate. Carey's first three appointees were businessmen: William Ellinghaus, David Margolis and Albert Casey. In 1976 Casey resigned and was relieved by MAC Chairman Felix Rohatyn. Ellinghaus also left and was replaced by retailer J. C. Penney's Senior Vice President Kenneth Axelson, who had been "on loan" to the City for a year as Deputy Mayor for Finance.(1) In mid-1977 New York University President Dr. John Sawhill, Circle Line head Francis Barry and Stanley Shuman, Executive Vice President of Allen and Co., took over the seats of Rohatyn, Margolis and Axelson(2); but by then much of the Board's spade work was done and Rohatyn stayed on as MAC head anyway to give the Governor his invaluable recommendations.

The EFCB had an Executive Director and a professional staff. Though it had the right to reject or modify the metropolis' contracts and its financial plan (which had to produce a balanced budget by mid-1978), and also to order it to cut its total spending, it could not determine what specific agencies should be most harmed by the reductions (e.g., Sanitation Department, Police Department).(3) Observers from the labor unions and the federal government attended Board sessions. U.S. Secretary of the Treasury William Simon set up a staff of five to monitor the five boroughs' financial status. It reported to Assistant Treasury Secretary Robert Gerard, who was in constant touch with City and State officials.(4)

The financial plan was in essence a two and a half year superbudget to include the individual budgets for the rest of fiscal 1976 and for all of fiscal 1977 and 1978. New York quickly submitted a vague draft of one early in October, 1975 that had built-in assumptions that were overly optimistic (e.g., relief from its welfare and Medicaid burdens; more State aid for education).(5)

The Days of Wine and Roses Are Over

Carey became irritated: remember that at this time he was working to convince President Ford to assist the City. He phoned Beame and told him he wanted a detailed, realistic proposal on his desk soon. On October 15th the Mayor handed the Governor a modified blueprint that, e.g., cancelled plans to build housing for poor and moderate income New Yorkers and admitted that more layoffs might be necessary.(6)

It soon became evident that despite the fact that it was more in tune with the facts of life than the earlier effort, the October 15th document also was too hopeful. By the end of the year, the accounting firm of Arthur Anderson, advising Simon, noted that it was quite possible expenses would be more and revenues less than had been projected. On January 23, 1976 Carey himself made similar remarks at the Board and bemoaned the fact that there was **still** no solid and reliable information about the municipality's ability to repay its obligations.(7) At a special meeting on January 30th he groused that it was not meeting its planned budget cuts. At the February 13th session, he again said that the financial plan had to be revised.(8) At the March 12th gathering he continued to make this point, asserting that investor confidence in the City's paper would never be rekindled until a workable plan were on the table and being put into effect.(9) Clearly, the Mayor still had to take fairly drastic steps, even though he and his town had already raised transit fares, reduced its payroll greatly, cut health services, closed senior citizen and day care centers and compressed the hours libraries and museums were open.

In early March Carey replaced Herbert Elish with Stephen Berger as Executive Director of the Board. Berger had the reputation and looks of a person who was determined to cut fat in government. An extremely hard worker, he is a hard-nosed person who makes his goals known and abides no nonsense from those standing in the way of these aims. His brilliance and abrasiveness made many City officials queasy when the Governor tapped him.(10)

Their worries were not unfounded. In March the City had submitted to the Board yet another revision of its financial plan. In early June, Berger issued a letter sharply criticizing even this modified scheme. The letter tore into it for assuming, for example, that the State would take over the courts within the metropolis as well as the City University of New York (CUNY). At that moment, the Executive Director felt, Albany's assumption of the expenses of these systems was "extremely unlikely".(11) This blunt missive, which suggested among other things that Beame move about $200 million in cuts planned for fiscal 1978 into fiscal 1977 (whose start, July 1, 1976, was right around the corner), infuriated the Mayor. He fumed to reporters that it was "unfounded, arbitrary, conclusory and without facts".(12) The Governor openly backed up the EFCB head, though he took pains to contend that the accelerated reductions could be made without layoffs and in general his public tone was conciliatory.(13)

Back to the drawing board and calmed down, Beame and his aides came up in late June, 1976 with a new plan to accelerate $50 million in cuts into the first few months of the 1977 fiscal year. They also agreed to hold an extra $85 million "in reserve" for extra slashes if the $50 million in reductions failed to lower the fiscal 1977 deficit to the $686 million projected by the plan. Carey went along with this compromise; the Board accepted the Mayor's remodeled scheme(14); and the State's Chief Executive continued to insist that the City adhere to it.(15) When the Mayor showed himself less than enthusiastic about remaining on this path, the Governor retorted that New York had to show that it could manage its own financial affairs by achieving the goals of the modified plan. On this topic, no negotiation was possible.(16)

Rosy financial plans were not the EFCB's only worry. Carey was aware that if the metropolis were to have any chance of climbing out of the red by the end of fiscal 1978 as it was required to do by the statute creating the Board, it would have to be very niggardly granting wage hikes to its employees no matter how underpaid they were. The contracts of many of the major unions expired in 1976; and so the City and the Board were then faced with the reality of grasping the nettle of holding down labor costs so that the budget could come into equilibrium. As a first move in this direction, the EFCB extended the wage freeze embodied in the Financial Emergency Act through June 30, 1978 but noted that salary rises might be granted if based on productivity savings or compensated for by reductions in fringe benefits such as health and pension plan contributions.(17)

The Days of Wine and Roses Are Over

The first contract to expire was that of the Transport Workers Union (TWU). On April 1, 1976, just in time to avert a strike on subways and busses, the City's Transit Authority and the TWU had agreed on a new pact that provided the transit employees with a cost of living increase (COLA). It was hoped, but the document did not make this clear enough, that the boost would be funded from "improvements in worker productivity".(18) The Board, feeling that the linkage between the supplement and productivity was too loose, rejected the settlement and revised the contract on its own. During the Summer, agreements covering police officers, firefighters and Victor Gotbaum's District Council 37 were put in place under EFCB supervision. The 200,000 workers affected would get not an ordinary wage boost but simply a COLA to be financed by productivity savings and/or other revenues.(19) In fact the understandings provided the employees with small gains only: "There would be no major wage gains for city employees to June 1978 [when they expired]".(20)

Berger and Carey had potent allies in their crusade to prevent the new labor deals from thwarting their attempts to cut expenses. Since Senator William Proxmire was Chairman of the Senate Banking Committee that had considered the seasonal loan legislation and would deal with it again were its renewal necessary, his comments on the Big Apple's fiscal affairs had to be taken into account by the Governor, the Mayor and their staffs. Thus his April, 1976 denunciation of the original transit workers contract as excessively costly and as setting a bad precedent for the upcoming negotiations with the other unions was one reason the EFCB tightened that agreement.(21) Likewise under the federal seasonal loan legislation the Secretary of the Treasury (still Simon at this time) could cut off the flow of cash if he believed that there was little chance of its being repaid. Using this prerogative as a trump card, he demanded that all collective bargaining disagreements be settled by the beginning of July if the City still wanted the second slice of seasonal loans (due it on July 2). Gerard backed up his boss's remarks and insisted that any agreements entered into could produce no net cost to New York.(22) It was no wonder, then, that the negotiations in 1976 with the unions had an outcome that was largely a victory for Carey and the Board.

Carey and the EFCB

Another major problem the Governor faced in limiting municipal expenditures was that of the so-called non-mayoral (semi-autonomous) agencies. "Mayoral agencies" (e.g., Police, Fire, Sanitation) are headed by Commissioners whom the Mayor can discharge and thus they are under his direct control. But units like the public schools, CUNY and the Health and Hospitals Corporation (HHC) are headed by boards of trustees or directors who are primarily responsible for formulating their budgets and substantive policies. This is true even though the Mayor appoints some of the members of these panels and even though the City contributes to the funding of the programs they operate.(23) However, the Control Board made it clear as early as October, 1975 that it had jurisdiction over these non-mayoral (which it referred to as "covered") units, though it could not itself determine the specifics -- e.g., close this college or that hospital -- of the money-saving steps they would have to take.(24)

The two covered agencies that gave the Board and City most trouble were CUNY (including the Board of Higher Education (BHE) that controlled it) and the HHC, running the public hospital system. The CUNY problem will be analyzed later in this chapter. As for the HHC, the almost unanimous view among those who were intimately involved in trying to improve the metropolis' financial condition was that it was dreadfully inefficient. Margolis made this point vividly in my interview with him.(25) Rohatyn at an October 15, 1976 meeting of the EFCB said "that the management of the Health and Hospitals Corporation was generally recognized as inept...."(26) And the Governor asserted that there were 6000 unused hospital beds in the City; that both HHC and the private hospitals would have to economize; and that the City would have to take the lead in addressing HHC's management problems.(27)

Beame lent a helping hand here and set up a special committee to guide HHC toward fiscal stability. It was predicted in late 1976 that the Corporation's deficit (which New York had to make up) would swell to $150 million by the end of fiscal 1978, the midnight hour at which the City was supposed to have a balanced budget. The committee soon came up with a plan involving some service cutbacks at particular hospitals and job cuts through attrition rather than layoffs. In a fight that had bitter racial overtones, HHC head

John Holloman, a black, was ousted. But, most important from the EFCB's point of view, the HHC deficit was reduced to about $50 million.(28)

What role did Carey play on the Emergency Financial Control Board? As a glance at its minutes will show, he attended just about all of its meetings at least until mid-1978, when his reelection campaign began in earnest. Berger confirms that the Governor almost always put in an appearance at its gatherings as did Beame until he left office at the end of 1977.(29) The fact that the State's Chief Executive was not the most prolific speaker at Board get-togethers and that all decisions were made by consensus(30), disagreements having been thrashed out in private(31), does not mean that he exerted little influence on its deliberations. On the contrary, persons who worked closely with the EFCB all agree that he was its dominant figure. Gerard, who was the United States Treasury official responsible for keeping an eye on the City to insure that it continued to be eligible for the seasonal loans, emphasized that point in our interview. Carey made the decisions though he let, e.g., Rohatyn do much of the talking.(32) MAC member George Gould and Comptroller Goldin agree that the Governor really ran the Board. At informal conclaves prior to the formal sessions he laid out what he wanted and got it.(33) Carey's Secretary David Burke asserts that his chief called the shots at the EFCB: by the time it began operating, all the crucial players in the game of saving New York respected him.(34) It was not that he paid no heed to anyone else: Margolis feels that he listened most to the private members and Berger and not infrequently adopted their positions.(35) But, in the last analysis, Carey was the Board's real as well as legal master. As scrutiny of its minutes will show, he was also knowledgeable about the issues broad and narrow it was considering. Witness, for example, the specific figure he mentioned at the October 15, 1976 meeting about the number of empty hospital beds in the five boroughs.

However, he was not only a watchman making sure that New York City did not spend too much but also a politician who wanted to be reelected. As ex-Board staffer Frank Macchiarola stresses, Carey **was** interested in building up investor confidence and getting the City to stand on its own two feet; but he never forgot

Carey and the EFCB

that he would have to wage a hard gubernatorial campaign in 1978.(36) He had always received a lot of labor support and hoped for more in the future. Moreover, the municipal unions were big investors in MAC bonds, and in this way the City's financial future had become dependent on them just as their prosperity was conditioned on a good financial future for it. Thus he could not fully ignore their wishes. For example, one can assume that one reason that the EFCB's wage freeze could be thawed slightly via the COLA route was that the Governor did not desire to antagonize the unions too much or to make them feel totally excluded from the decision making process.(37) Berger told me that he wanted to institute significant reforms in the City's civil service system to make service delivery more effective but that the Governor vetoed this idea on the grounds that it would unnecessarily irritate labor.(38)

In short, Carey just could not use the Board as a tool for implementing all the economies in City spending that the "hawks" on the Board -- Berger and the private members(39) -- desired; but no one in her right mind could say that he allowed the unions, CUNY and the HHC anything close to what they wanted. As "boss" of the Board he **was** generally tightfisted -- witness his attacks on New York's financial plan and tardiness in budget cutting -- but he could not always play the role of Scrooge. His "tough on the City but not as tough as one could be" policy was manifested in the pattern of layoffs that resulted from the financial crisis. The metropolis lost about 61,000 jobs as a result of this emergency. (40) The Governor told the House Banking Subcommittee that, as far as could be ascertained from the City's then-sloppy method of keeping its books, by early October 1975 it had already shed 31,000 workers, 22,000 by discharge and 9000 by attrition.(41) Much of the "credit" or "blame" for this 31,000 figure must go to Beame rather than the Governor, for as of early October 1975 the EFCB had been functioning only for a month. The remaining 30,000 jobs vanishing by Spring, 1978 can be attributed to EFCB, i.e. Carey, pressure. However, assuming that the ratio of jobs disappearing by attrition to jobs lost by firing during the July 1, 1976 through Spring 1978 period was the same as the roughly one out of three ratio that prevailed throughout the entire crisis, the

The Days of Wine and Roses Are Over

number **given the pink slip** by the Governor's pushing for cuts was only two-thirds of 30,000 or 20,000. And an unascertained number of this 20,000 were soon rehired on a federally funded "CETA" line!(42) He and the Board did not object to this even though the possibility existed that CETA funding might be reduced and the City then pressured to put these men and women into locally-funded jobs.(43)

Carey's treatment of CUNY provides another fine example of how he as EFCB head eschewed partly for political reasons the course of maximum fiscal stringency. The system dates from 1847 when the voters created a "Free Academy". This is now City College, the oldest of its campuses and the one that educated Felix Frankfurter, a future U.S. Supreme Court Justice; literary critic Irving Howe; and Jonas Salk, who discovered the vaccine that helped rid the world of the polio scourge. By the 1950s, New York City operated four colleges: City, Brooklyn, Queens and Hunter. Admissions requirements for these schools were quite high and they had an excellent academic reputation.

During that decade the City started building community colleges. In 1961 CUNY was formally created and in the 1960s expanded from four to ten senior colleges. In addition, a Graduate Center offering master's and doctoral degrees in many subjects was established and the number of junior colleges grew to eight. By 1976, 275,000 men and women were enrolled in the University, up from 93,000 in 1960.(44) Tuition was free and the "open admissions" program inaugurated in 1970 allowed any high school graduate to enter the system.

Even many not viscerally antagonistic to the University were opposed to its policy of free tuition for undergraduates. (Graduate students already paid tuition.) This opposition could only become more strident when New York stared at bankruptcy in 1975 and had to seek help from bankers, the State Legislature and the federal government. Many of these potential angels were rich people whose children went to private colleges and who could not put themselves in the shoes of poor families for whom any sort of expenditure for the college education of their offspring would be an economic burden. Thus, according to Jack Newfield and Paul DeBrul, "[banker] Walter Wriston, in private....[became] irrational

Carey and the EFCB

in his fury against free higher education...."(45) Treasury Secretary Simon also detested free tuition(46); and President Ford could hardly be called supportive.(47) Of course, City politicians when running for office used to call for its retention: Carey himself had done so in the 1974 gubernatorial campaign.

The theoretical merits and demerits of free tuition can be debated from here to eternity: what was indubitable is that thanks to its expansion in the 1960s, the City University had become a very expensive proposition. Its budget was $45 million in fiscal year 1961 but a scheduled $587 million in fiscal 1976. Even when the last figure is reduced to take account of inflation, the jump is a striking one. Thanks to Governor Nelson Rockefeller, by 1975 Albany was bearing about 40% of CUNY's expenses.(48) None-the-less a bit of arithmetic will show that the University was promising to cost an indigent metropolis about $350 million ($587 million x 60%) in the fiscal year ending June, 1976.

As the fiscal year 1975-76 progressed, it soon became apparent that CUNY would get significantly less than the sum of $587 million that had been allocated for it. Under orders from the Emergency Financial Control Board to shrink its own spending for fiscal 1976, the City announced that it was reducing its contribution to CUNY by over $30 million -- a slash that automatically triggered a loss of State matching aid to the University and thus came to a total cut for the system of $55 million for that **ongoing** 1976 fiscal year.(49) In February, 1976 the University proposed closing or reducing the offerings of several of its colleges, but pressure from political leaders forced it to delete most of these plans. These cancellations left the Board continuing to wrestle with the conundrum of how to cut spending by millions right away. Its agony was compounded by the fact that the City and the EFCB had by April decreased the University's fiscal 1976 budget by more than the original $55 million slash -- to $481 million or $100 million less than it had expected to spend when that disastrous fiscal year commenced.(50) By that month the BHE had come up with schemes to reduce its expenditures for the ongoing fiscal year to $525 million. As it then had only $481 million to play with, it realized that it could run out of money before that year ended. And that is exactly what happened. At the end of May, during finals week for some units,

114

CUNY shut down operations. Its faculty did not receive their pay-checks; and senior students visualized a possible lengthy delay in their date of graduation and entry into graduate school or into the real world of work.

To make matters worse, the State's budget for its fiscal year 1977 (beginning April 1, 1976) had assumed that it would give CUNY $195 million for the latter's **1977** fiscal year, starting July 1, 1976. However, State law then provided that Albany could spend no more on the City University than the City did. The City's financial plan for fiscal 1977 provided that it would contribute only $160 million to CUNY. Under the law as it was at that time, therefore, the State contribution would have had to drop to $140 million.(51) This would have left the University with a fiscal 1977 budget of $348 million (from State, City and other sources). According it only this sum would have ruined the bulk of the system.(52) The situation cried out for redress; and it was here that Carey acted.

What the Governor proposed to do instead was, first, to "save harmless" the proposed $195 million in State aid to CUNY for fiscal 1977 despite the shrinking of the City contribution. This necessitated legislation to overturn the old rule that Albany could spend no more on CUNY than City Hall did: the appropriate measure (Chapters 345 and 365 of the 1976 Laws of New York) was signed into law on June 12, 1976. It maintained state funding at the $195 million level and also provided that $24 million of this sum was to be used to reopen CUNY for the rest of fiscal **1976**! Consequently, the colleges were unlocked, students took their finals, and professors started receiving their salaries again.

The Carey program for keeping the State aid at $195 million for fiscal 1977 made it crystal clear that even if it were passed, CUNY would still be in dire financial shape -- unless its under-graduates were forced to pay tuition.(53) The Governor had been hinting as early as December, 1975 that free tuition had to go(54); but did not make this position public until May, 1976.(55) Six members of the Board, including Chairman Alfred Giardino, felt that a vote for tuition would go against their consciences and so resigned and were replaced. Consequently, on June 1, 1976 the policy of free education at CUNY crumbled into dust. The amounts received from tuition plus State and City help allowed it to spend $470 million in fiscal 1977, **less** than its outgo in fiscal 1976 and requiring the sudden discharge of some faculty and staff, but enough to avert complete disaster.(56)

Despite these job losses, many felt that the CUNY crisis was over with the passage of the 1976 act allowing the State to bear more than half of the University's operating costs. However, what really had to be done to put it on a firm financial footing was to fulfill a non-binding promise in that law that the State would totally fund the senior colleges and to insure that this State aid would be adequate to meet their needs. In November of 1978 the respected Harold Howe 2d, the former United States Commissioner of Education, called for their full support by the State, pointing out that everywhere else in the country public four year colleges and graduate programs were the responsibility of the state rather than of local jurisdictions.(57) In 1979 the Governor signed a measure embodying this recommendation(58); and by CUNY's fiscal year 1983, starting Carey's last year in office, the State was paying over $350 million for senior college support and over $480 million in total CUNY aid -- including subsidies for CUNY's community colleges and for construction at the University.(59) Of course, increased Albany assistance to CUNY meant increased Albany control; and the Board of Higher Education was replaced under the 1979 senior college full-funding law by a "Board of Trustees", a majority of whose members are appointed by the State's Chief Executive.(60)

Thus Carey not only prevented the CUNY system from collapsing when it was tottering in 1976 but ultimately insured that the bulk of its cash would be provided by a jurisdiction more fiscally stable than New York City. The question remains: why did this Governor, himself neither a CUNY graduate nor parent, save it from becoming a wisp of its former self. The reasons are several. In addition to the voting power that the University's students and their parents could exercise in the 1978 gubernatorial election, many in the Assembly Democratic majority were from New York City. Thus this body viewed this University as its number one priority in the area of higher education.(61) For example, Assemblyman Mark Siegel was very supportive of it: its Hunter

College was located in his district.(62) Assembly Speaker Stanley Steingut from Brooklyn fought very hard on its behalf: he was one "unheralded hero" of the CUNY crisis.(63) CUNY Vice Chancellor Julius Edelstein as well as historian Richard Wade had been active in Carey's 1974 campaign; and their words to the Governor on behalf of the University were taken seriously.(64) Powerful Carey assistant (then Director of State Operations) Robert Morgado was a CUNY advocate though he was from out of town.(65) But the individual who was most instrumental in making Carey lean toward CUNY was his close political associate Robert Wagner. The former Mayor, whose father had graduated from City College in its free tuition days, was a firm believer in CUNY and succeeded in convincing the Governor of its importance to the metropolis and the State.(66) None of this is meant to belittle Carey's role as a godsend to CUNY: he did not have to listen to his advisers, friends and legislative leaders and could have let it dwindle down to four or five campuses. That he did not, but instead on this occasion followed what one aide referred to as his "egalitarian streak"(67), is a tribute to him. CUNY is a large, vital institution again; and, though he himself may not realize this, its ability to serve hundreds of thousands of students rather than just tens of thousands is as much a monument to his sojourn in the State capital as the State University of New York is to Nelson Rockefeller's.(68)

In November, 1976 New York's Court of Appeals tossed a bombshell that threatened to undo everything that federal, State and municipal public officials had accomplished to keep New York solvent. In the case of *Flushing National Bank v. Municipal Assistance Corporation* the State's top Court declared the three year moratorium on the payment of principal on $1.6 billion in short-term notes unconstitutional even though the imposition of this delay had been a condition of the City's receiving aid from the Ford Administration.(69) It seemed that a jurisdiction that was still running a deficit but that had to balance its books in slightly more than 18 months would just not be able to redeem the $1 billion of notes covered by the moratorium that were still in the public's hands.(70) It appeared, in other words, that the specter of a megalopolis hauled before a bankruptcy judge was as threatening in November, 1976 as it had been twelve months earlier. This was especially true because the November, 1975 side-moratorium that had been accepted by the New York banks and union pension funds, which included a deferral until 1986 of the payment on the principal of $816 million in notes, was in the banks' eyes no longer binding on them because of the Court of Appeals' action. Thus the City was faced with the horrifying prospect of having to dredge up $1.8 billion right away if it wanted to avoid the yoke of an insolvency tribunal.(71)

Not to worry -- at least not too much. Chief Judge Charles Breitel's majority opinion said that the noteholders who had been unconstitutionally deprived of their principal would nonetheless not be entitled to immediate satisfaction if the payment would be "unnecessarily disruptive of the city's delicate financial and economic balance".(72) More importantly, the City's economy was improving at the end of 1976 and the beginning of 1977: in fact because of inflation and expenditure caps the metropolis had a surprising amount of cash on hand then.(73) So fairly quickly Beame, Goldin(74) and Rohatyn were able to develop a package that enabled the $1 billion to be given the creditors. As is usual with financial rescues, the package was a complex one: suffice it to say that it included a large-scale exchange of high-interest MAC bonds for some of the $1 billion in notes and the unearthing of additional funds in the City's coffers.(75) By the end of June, 1977 only $200 million was still unpaid; and the banks and pension funds had proven to be amenable and had agreed to swap their $800 million or so of notes involved in the "side agreement" for MAC bonds bearing a moderate interest rate.(76) Again, therefore, the five boroughs nearly toppled into the abyss but managed to avert the fall. Though Carey did not participate in the drafting the details of this scheme, he backed it and the legwork was done by his *fidus Achates* Rohatyn as well as by local officials. With the settlement of the difficulties arising from the invalidation of the moratorium and with the dawning of better economic conditions for City, State and nation, the hard and unpleasant work that the EFCB had to accomplish (including successfully forcing New York to adopt a successful system of accounting(77)) was to a considerable extent behind it. Ironically Simon Rifkind, co-author with Carey of the moratorium, felt that *Flushing National Bank*, though

The Days of Wine and Roses Are Over

it invalidated his own handiwork, was a correct decision as of the date when it appeared for in the the long run it increased public acceptance of City bonds.(78)

The skirting of the collapse that could have resulted from the *Flushing National Bank* holding left New York with just one major obstacle between it and financial health: the ending of the federal seasonal loan program by the end of fiscal 1978, i.e., by June 30 of that year. Rohatyn as early as 1976 was pessimistic about the City's ability to reenter the credit markets by that date.(79) Other New York bankers shared his gloom and, as the Carter Administration assumed power in Washington in January of 1977, they asked for a five year extension of the seasonal loans. This go-round they had reason to hope for sympathy from the nation's capital, as Carter had said during his campaign that bankruptcy was not a viable alternative for New York(80), and as the Democrats, the Party of Carey and Beame, controlled both houses of Congress. What they had not reckoned with was that Proxmire was still in charge of the Senate Banking Committee; that all aid-to-New-York statutes had to be approved by this group; and that the Senator, albeit a Democrat and a supporter of the 1975 assistance package, was unshakably opposed to renewing it after its June 30, 1978 expiration date. His fundamental contention was that both New York State and the bankers could do a lot more to help the metropolis. Thus, he opined, it did not need federal subventions any more. He said, for example, that the holdings of banks such as Citibank in City and MAC securities were "really pretty pitiful" in quantity.(81) And the State was making only "a weak, feeble effort" to solve the fiscal problems of its major locality.(82)

So it was lobby-with-Washington time again. At Rohatyn's prodding(83), President Carter and Secretary of the Treasury W. Michael Blumenthal suggested to Congress not an extension of the Ford seasonal loans but a federal guarantee of City and MAC long-term paper.(84) To support this legislation, Carey attended the early March, 1978 hearings of the House Banking Subcommitte before which he had spoken so eloquently in 1975. Its chair was no longer his friend Ludlow Ashley but Democrat William S. Moorhead from Pennsylvania. The Governors testimony was again impressive; characterized by literacy and good organization. He emphasized that the State had indeed helped the City by assuming the costs of the courts and more of the expenses of CUNY. The loan guarantees that Blumenthal was proposing would cost federal taxpayers nothing: he was not asking for a "handout" from Washington.(85) His responses to questions Committee members put to him were convincing and showed a deep understanding of the details of State and City finances. Asked by Democrat Stanley Lundine of upstate New York about a proposed State tax cut that made Proxmire feel that Albany was doing little to help City Hall, Carey quickly responded that "....the tax reduction program of the State is one that is vital to the recovery of the economy of the State".(86) And to moderate Ohio Republican William Stanton's worry that the federal government was now giving the City more aid than was the State contrary to the situation prevailing in 1975-76, he pointed out immediately that much of the switch resulted from Washington's CETA program, which was active in New York "due to the inordinate level of unemployment, which was 11.7, now down to about 10.3".(87)

Carey's testimony was powerful in itself; but he made sure that he was not the only one arguing in favor of the continuation of federal assistance. At the same session speakers for this position included Senate Majority Leader Warren Anderson; Rohatyn; Assembly Minority Leader Perry Duryea; Rexford E. Tompkins, Chairman of the conservative New York City group known as the Citizens Budget Commission; and Mayor Ed Koch, who had just "graduated" from the House himself. Also backing the five boroughs were State Comptroller Levitt and Blumenthal himself.

Koch, Carey and others also appeared in early June before Proxmire's Senate Banking Committee. The Governor and the Mayor spoke to the Republicans as well as the Democrats on the Committee, including conservative Republicans Jake Garn of Utah and John Tower of Texas.(88) To the New Yorkers' surprise and joy, the initially hostile unit approved the guarantees by a lopsided 12-3 vote. Proxmire voted nay but Republicans Brooke of Massachusetts, Heinz of Pennsylvania, Lugar of Indiana and Schmitt of New Mexico all backed the assistance.(89) The Wisconsinite remained negative when the full Senate approved the measure in late June 53-27 with 18 Republicans joining 35 Demo-

The Days of Wine and Roses Are Over

crats in favor.(90) The House also cooperated, thanks to a considerable extent to House Speaker Tip O'Neill, who wished to insure that his old colleague Ed Koch became a successful Mayor. Koch himself probably lobbied for the bill even more vigorously than did Carey, though he admits that the latter's efforts in this regard were far from insignificant.(91) Thus President Carter, who also had fought hard for it, was able to sign it in New York City on August 8th in front of City Hall on a mahogany desk that had once belonged to George Washington. It provided $1.65 billion in guarantees for long-term loans; and the City would use this cash over the next four years to rebuild items of its infrastructure such as streets and bridges and to convert more short-term into long-term debt.(92) As its part of the bargain, all the State had to do was keep the EFCB alive.(93), It did so, renaming it the Financial Control Board (FCB). By now that unit has lost much of its power. However, it still monitors New York's finances and can reject a City budget whose deficit is $100,000,000 or more.(94) It will probably remain with us until 2008. By then all MAC bonds hopefully will have been paid off: thanks to Carey and others, the metropolis now can market its own paper!

Notes to Chapter 6

1. Public Papers of Governor Hugh L. Carey 1976 (Albany: State of New York Executive Chamber, 1986), p. 2153, pp. 2520-21.

2. Public Papers of Governor Hugh L. Carey 1977 (Albany: State of New York Executive Chamber, 1987), p. 1562.

3. Bailey, Robert W. - The Crisis Regime (Albany: SUNY Press, 1984), pp. 41-44.

4. New York Times, June 6, 1976, Sec. 4, p. 1.

5. Bailey, op. cit. n.3 supra, p. 60.

6. Ferretti, Fred - The Year the Big Apple Went Bust (New York: G.P. Putnam's, 1976), pp. 331-33, 335-37.

7. Emergency Financial Control Board Jan. 23, 1976 Minutes; Bailey, op. cit. n.3 supra, p. 64.

8. Emergency Financial Control Board Feb. 13, 1976 Minutes; Bailey, op. cit. n.3 supra, p. 64.

9. Emergency Financial Control Board Mar. 12, 1976 Minutes; Bailey, op. cit. n.3 supra, p. 64.

10. New York Times, Feb. 8, 1977, p. 40.

11. New York Times, June 5, 1976, p. 1, 50.

12. Ibid., p. 1.

13. Ibid.

14. New York Times, June 24, 1976, p. 29, 32; Oct. 15, 1976, p. A8.

15. Emergency Financial Control Board Aug. 16, 1976 Minutes.

16. Ibid. No such accelerated cuts were needed because revenue collections exceeded expectations. Thus the City's deficit for fiscal year 1977 was $375 million less than that projected in the financial plan approved by the EFCB. See Annual Report of the Comptroller of the City of New York for the Fiscal Year 1977, p. v, viii, xi.

The Days of Wine and Roses Are Over

17. Bailey, op. cit. n.3 supra, p. 76.

18. New York Times, May 1, 1975, p. 40.

19. Bailey, op. cit. n.3 supra, pp. 79-83; New York Times, May 19, 1976, p. 1; July 1, 1976, p. 1.

20. Bailey, op. cit. n.3 supra, p. 81.

21. New York Times, Apr. 7, 1976, p. 45; May 17, 1976, p. 1.

22. New York Times, June 6, 1976, Sec. 4, p. 1; June 16, 1976, p. 1.

23. See Bailey, op. cit. n.3 supra, pp. 91-94.

24. Ibid., pp. 95-98.

25. Interview with Margolis, Apr. 17, 1991, New York City.

26. Quoted Bailey, op. cit. n.3 supra, p. 108.

27. Emergency Financial Control Board Oct. 15, 1976 Minutes.

28. Interview with EFCB Secretary Barbara Collins, May 23, 1991, New York City; Bailey, op. cit. n.3 supra, pp. 104-11.

29. Interview with EFCB head Stephen Berger, Feb. 21, 1991, New York City.

30. Bailey, op. cit. n.3 supra, p. 119.

31. Ibid., pp. 120-2l; Collins, interview cited n.28 supra.

32. Interview with Gerard, Mar. 6, 1992, New York City.

33. Interview with Goldin, Sept. 18, 1992, New York City; with Gould, Feb. 7, 1992, New York City.

34. Interview with Burke, Aug. 28, 1992, New York City.

35. Margolis, interview cited n.25 supra.

36. Interview with Macchiarola, July 31, 1991, New York City.

37. Ibid.

38. Interview cited n.29 supra.

39. New York Times, May 27, 1977, Sec. 4, p. 6.

40. Auletta, Ken - The Streets Were Paved With Gold (New York: Random House, 1979), p. 295.

41. U.S. Congress, House of Representatives, Committee on Banking, Currency and Housing, Subcommittee on Economic Stabilization, 94th Cong., 1st Sess. - Debt Financing Problems of State and Local Government (Washington: Government Printing Office, 1975), pp. 979-82

42. See Auletta, op. cit. n.40 supra, pp. 295-96.

43. Ibid., p. 296.

44. Bailey, op. cit. n.3 supra, p. 94; Newfield, Jack and Du Brul, Paul - The Abuse of Power (New York: Viking, 1977), p. 191.

45. Newfield and Du Brul, op. cit. n.44 supra, p. 192.

46. See Simon, William - A time for truth (New York: McGraw Hill, 1978), pp. 140-41, p. 154.

47. See Ford, Gerald - A time to heal (New York: Harper and Row, 1979), p. 316.

48. Bailey, op. cit. n.3 supra, p. 94; New York Times, Nov. 15, 1975, p. 1; Dec. 9, 1975, p. 1.

49. See New York Times, Oct. 21, 1975, p. 1; Nov. 15, 1975, p. 1.

50. Public Papers of Governor Hugh L. Carey 1976 (Albany: State of New York Executive Chamber, 1986), p. 2629. (The data referred to here come from a document entitled The City University Crisis: The Governor's Program for Responsible Action, dated May 20, 1976 and found at pp. 2629-40 of ibid.)

51. Ibid., p. 2631, 2633.

52. Ibid., p. 2632.

53. Ibid.

54. New York Times, Dec. 20, 1975, p. 32.

55. Carey op. cit. n.50 supra, p. 1079; Newfield and DuBrul, op. cit. n.44 supra, p. 195.

56. Newfield and Du Brul, op. cit. n.44 supra, pp. 194-97; New York Times, June 2, 1976, p. 1; June 22, 1976, p. 31.

57. New York Times, Nov. 14, 1978, p. C6.

58. New York Times, June 28, 1979, p. B1.

59. See New York State Laws of 1982, Ch. 53, pp. 619-30.

60. New York Times, June 28, 1979, p. 1.

61. Interview with Herbert Gordon, ex-SUNY Vice Chancellor for Governmental Affairs, Mar. 24, 1992, New York City.

62. Interview with CUNY Vice Chancellor Julius Edelstein, July 18, 1991, New York City.

63. Interview with Carey aide Robert Schiffer, Apr. 27, 1991, New York City.

64. Edelstein, interview cited n.62 supra; Schiffer, interview cited n.63 supra; interview with Wade, Mar. 11, 1991, New York City.

65. Schiffer, interview cited n.63 supra.

66. Edelstein, interview cited n.62 supra.

67. Interview with Carey education aide Irving Freedman, phone call to Albany, May 7, 1992.

68. At times he did seem to be aware of this accomplishment of his. As he said in a speech given November 10, 1980, celebrating Brooklyn College's fiftieth anniversary, its creation was "an act of faith in the right of free men and women to educate themselves, in their ability to better themselves and to better the world....It is the same faith that motivated

my administration to have the State assume the full costs of [the CUNY] system and pledge itself to maintaining CUNY as the nation's finest urban university". Carey Materials, New York State Archives, Albany, N.Y., Governor's Speech Files, 1975-1982. (Series 13704).

69. The case is cited 40 N.Y.2d 731, 358 N.E.2d 848, 390 N.Y.S.2d 22 (1976). Excerpts from it appear New York Times, Nov. 20, 1976, p. 1.

70. Municipal Assistance Corporation - Annual Report 1977 (New York: MAC, 1977), p. 6.

71. Ibid.; Municipal Assistance Corporation - Annual Report 1976 (New York: MAC, 1976), p. 15.

72. Quoted New York Times, Nov. 20, 1976, p. 1. The decision did worry Rohatyn. Phone interview with him Mar. 22, 1995, New York City.

73. Goldin, interview cited n.33 supra; Macchiarola, interview cited n.36 supra.

74. Interview with Mayor Abraham Beame, Dec. 27, 1990, New York City.

75. MAC, op. cit. n.70 supra, pp. 6-8; New York Times, Mar. 11, 1977, p. A1.

76. MAC, op. cit. n.70 supra, p. 8, 10.

77. Collins, interview cited n.28 supra.

78. Interview with Judge Simon Rifkind, Feb. 28, 1991, New York City.

79. New York Times, Dec. 22, 1976, p. 1.

80. U.S. Congress, House of Representatives, Committee on Banking, Finance and Urban Affairs, Subcommittee on Economic Stabilization, 95th Cong., 2nd Sess. - New York City's Fiscal and Financial Situation (Washington: Government Printing Office, 1978), Pt. 1, p. 270.

81. New York Times, Dec. 17, 1977, p. 16.

82. New York Times, Dec. 16, 1977, p. A1.

The Days of Wine and Roses Are Over

83. Koch, Edward - <u>Mayor: An Autobiography</u> (New York: Warner Books Edition, 1985), p. 97.

84. House Bank. Subcomm., <u>op cit</u>. n.80 <u>supra</u>, Pt. 1, p. 291.

85. <u>Ibid</u>., Pt. 2, pp. 132-48.

86. <u>Ibid</u>., Pt. 2, p. 156.

87. <u>Ibid</u>., Pt. 2, pp. 159-60.

88. See <u>Public Papers of Governor Hugh L. Carey 1978</u> (Albany: State of New York Executive Chamber, 1988), pp. 910-14 for excerpts from the Governor's testimony on this occasion. See also Koch, <u>op. cit</u>. n.83 <u>supra</u>, pp. 101-102.

89. <u>New York Times</u>, June 16, 1978, p. A1.

90. <u>New York Times</u>, June 9, 1978, p. A1; June 30, 1978, p. A1.

91. Interview with Mayor Edward I. Koch, Nov. 11, 1994, New York City.

92. Gould, interview cited n.33 <u>supra</u>; <u>New York Times</u>, Aug. 8, 1978, p. A1.

93. <u>New York Times</u>, May 26, 1978, p. A1; <u>Staten Island Advance</u>, May 11, 1978, p. 2.

94. See, e.g., <u>Newsday</u>, Apr, 7, 1991, p. 4; <u>New York Times</u>, Dec. 9, 1994, p. B3. MAC still sells some bonds and exerts leverage over City officials through its ability to deny the metropolis the proceeds of these transactions if it fails to keep its spending at sensible levels. <u>New York Times</u>, May 15, 1991, p. A1; <u>Staten Island Advance</u>, Jan. 19, 1991, p. A9. The EFCB served as a model for a board to oversee the finances of a deficit-ridden Washington, D.C. <u>New York Times</u>, May 21, 1995, Sec. 1, p. 25.

Chapter 7
Carey, the Democratic Party, and the State Legislature

CAREY was extremely adroit as the fiscal savior of New York City, State and the public construction agencies and, as will be seen, scored impressive triumphs in other endeavors. His Administration was honest and efficient. However, when it came to functioning as the leader of New York State's Democratic Party and as a negotiator with the Legislature, he often had two left feet.

Very much on the plus side, his top-level choices were, to reiterate, first-rate. Party leaders had little say in their selection. And many of these appointees, e.g., his first Counsel Judah Gribetz, his first Secretary David Burke, his second Secretary Robert Morgado, his Urban Development Corporation and later Metropolitan Transportation head Richard Ravitch, and his close adviser Felix Rohaytn, were hardly old cronies: most of them had never even met him before he began campaigning for Governor in 1974. Burke, for example, was a former administrative aide to Senator Robert Kennedy. He had never talked to Carey before his election but he did know David Garth, the media whiz behind his 1974 campaign. Out of the blue, he received a phone call from Garth telling him the Governor-elect wanted to speak to him to get some advice. They chatted for a little while and then he offered him a job as his Secretary -- a New York Governor's most important adviser. Burke accepted even though he had no clear idea about the responsibilities of his new post and even though he had never set foot in Albany. Burke, in turn, recruited outstanding Youth Services Director Peter Edelman. The latter lived in Massachusetts and was familiar with Burke from the Kennedy era. He had never encountered Carey but received a phone call from the new Secretary asking him if he would like to join his team. Edelman felt he could make a difference and accepted.(1) Charles Hynes, who as Carey's Medicaid fraud prosecutor did so much to weed out dishonesty in that program, was also unacquainted with the new Chief Executive. He was, however, friendly with Secretary of State Mario Cuomo, who recommended him. He went to the Red Room in the Governor's second-floor Capitol Office, shook hands with him, and a few seconds later heard him announce that he was from then on in charge of cleaning up the Medicaid mess.(2)

It should have been fairly easy to predict that the new Adminis-

The Days of Wine and Roses Are Over

tration would not be a statewide Tammany Hall. Carey did not owe his jobs to Brooklyn Democratic Chairman Meade Esposito. As Howard Samuels' 1974 campaign manager Ken Auletta emphasized, "Though Governor Carey hails from Brooklyn, he has the same type of relationship with that borough's Democratic leader, Meade Esposito, as he does with his lieutenant governor, Mary Ann [sic] Krupsak: they make nice in public".(3) Thus the Governor had not been immersed in the "jobs and contracts for the boys" philosophy that guided the behavior of the Kings County Democratic Party. Furthermore, he knew that once he took up residence in the Executive Mansion, the eyes of the mass media would be focused on him. It might be easy for the Borough Presidents of Brooklyn, Queens or Staten Island to conceal a group of idlers in the corridors of their respective Borough Halls; it is much more difficult for the Governor of New York State to hide a bunch of drones in the Executive Office of the State Capitol. And this was especially true in an era when because of the Watergate scandal people's minds were very much on the problem of political corruption. Furthermore, he was very conscious that crooked Irish bosses such as Kansas City's Tom Pendergast, Jersey City's Frank Hague, Boston's James Michael Curley and Tammany's Richard Croker and Jimmy Walker had hurt his people's reputation; and he was very determined to show editors of papers such as the *New York Times* that he could run a government as principled and effective as those dominated by White Anglo Saxon Protestants Thomas E. Dewey, W. Averell Harriman and Nelson Rockefeller and by upper class, Jewish Herbert Lehman.(4)

An anecdote will show how far Carey (like many other modern governors) wanted to distance himself from traditional patronage politics. After Suffolk County Democratic leader Dominic Baranello had become State Democratic Chairman, some county Democratic chiefs asked to meet with the Governor. The latter agreed to see them on condition that they were not to mention anything about jobs for their loyalists -- the topic in which they were most interested. At the gathering, one Catskill leader asked whether one of his constituents could get a position with the State's highway repair crews. Carey's face darkened; and he could barely contain his displeasure.(5)

Carey the Democratic Party, and the State Legislature

However, no matter how much he/she may worship at the shrine of clean government, every chief executive will have some patronage to dole out. There will always be some openings in the executive branch which are not covered by civil service rules and which thus can be staffed on the basis of criteria other than doing well in a written or physical test or their "equivalents". No one is exactly certain how many "exempt", i.e., non-civil service, posts are at the disposal of the Governor of New York State. These certainly number in the thousands -- one 1975 estimate that seems high was 28,000. They range all the way from the individuals who are in personal contact with him (e.g. his Secretary and Counsel) and his Commissioners and Deputy Commissioners of Departments through part-time but well-paid Board or Authority positions down to summer employees clearing trails in State parks or sweeping lounges in State buildings maintained by the Office of General Services. They also include numerous unpaid or remunerated-for-expenses-only posts such as the Board of Visitors of a State psychiatric hospital or membership on the New York State Energy Research and Development Authority.(6)

Most State patronage in New York is handled by a body under the Governor known as the Appointments Office (headed by an Appointments Officer). The processing of most hirings for State positions not protected by civil service takes place here, though Carey, of course, personally tapped people to occupy high-level policy-making posts.(7) He desired persons immediately under him who would be loyal to his philosophy, do their jobs well, and not embarrass him.(8) These Commissioners and top assistants were in turn to select their non-civil-service aides by looking to merit as much as to political connections. In fact, in certain cases, the Carey subordinate was free to ignore the latter factor in making his/her choice. Stephen Berger when Social Services Commissioner was given carte blanche to choose his crucial adjutants. (9) Parks Commissioner Orin Lehman had considerable discretion in filling executive positions in the agency. The Governor never interfered for political or other reasons with Emergency Financial Control Board hiring. Richard Kahan, President of the Urban Development Corporation after it had been revived, remarked to me that he was never pressured to take on political timeservers.

The Days of Wine and Roses Are Over

Medicaid fraud prosecutor Hynes was never told by Carey whom to hire. Corrections Commissioner Benjamin Ward, chief of the State's prison system, was almost never subjected to patronage pressures. Superintendent of Insurance Albert Lewis did have as one of his aides a Carey boyhood friend whom he knew he could not fire even if he had wanted to. However, with this exception he was free to select his own staff and was even able to convince the Governor to rescind the appointment of a politically-connected nonentity who somehow had won the confidence of the Appointments Office.(10)

That Office was confronted with real difficulties when Carey went to Albany. Most importantly, the sheer volume of job ap-plications from Democrats confronting it in 1975 after the decade and a half of Republican rule was overwhelming.(11) Next, many potential appointees to non-salaried but "policy-making" positions (especial-ly to Boards of Visitors overseeing state institutions, State University of New York College Councils and historic site boards) objected to the financial disclosure forms required by a 1975 Carey document denominated Executive Order #10. They felt that these invaded their privacy without producing any revenue for them and so some turned down the berths they had been asked to occupy.(12) Also, many men and women who aspired to the posts, paid or unpaid, for which they had been tapped had to wait a long time, in some cases as long as six to nine months, before they could assume their duties. Even some high-level nominees remained on hold.(13) One reason was that the Carey Admin-istration, in its zeal for clean government, required all individuals being considered for an "exempt" job to complete a voluminous questionnaire in addition to the financial disclosure statement required by Executive Order #10.(14) In addition, they had to undergo a thorough background check by the State Police that consumed on average 48 hours of effort and that included a perusal of that questionnaire. Sometimes an officer had to return it to the candidate because she/he had left blank a line or two; and then she/he in turn would for several weeks forget to send it back.(15)

Ironically, one of Carey's few appointments of a "boss-type" individual impeded the smooth functioning of the patronage pro-cess during the Governor's early days in office. In 1974 he chose

Patrick Cunningham, Democratic leader of The Bronx and a man who believed in rewarding good Democrats with good jobs, as Chairman of the New York State Democratic Party. Though liberal groups such as the New Democratic Coalition resented this pick and Baranello thought that he would be selected(16), it was made because of the real help Cunningham behind the scenes had given Carey in his 1974 primary against Howard Samuels; because the chemistry between the two men at first was good; and because Cunningham was closer to Mayor Beame, with whom Carey would have to work, than was the Suffolk County Chair.(17) He had also introduced the Congressman to important Party figures in The Bronx and elsewhere. Selecting as head of the State Party someone who had been a county chairman was intended, moreover, to reassure other county chiefs that Carey had their interests at heart.(18)

The first few months of the Carey Administration saw the Bronx and Brooklyn Irishmen great friends, often socializing together.(19) However, the relationship began to pall even before State Special Prosecutor Maurice Nadjari in late 1975 named Cunningham as a seller of judgeships in his home borough. The main problem was that Cunningham had become so involved with taking over suspended owner George Steinbrenner's work for the New York Yankees baseball team that he often did not bother to return phone calls from Democratic county chairpeople about patronage and other matters.(20) In fact, by October, 1975, the Governor was so annoyed at his State leader that he ignored him in making some interim appointments to State Supreme Court. And even at the height of their friendship, the Bronx chief had had no impact on the framing of Carey's New York City-rescue and other policies.(21)

Accordingly, some Democratic county chairpeople became angry in the early Carey era. They felt that they were not getting enough of their supporters into State jobs and that Cunningham was never around to listen to their laments.(22) These chairpeople cannot deliver many votes, especially in a general election. However, if enough of them were angry at Carey they could deny him renomination at the next State gubernatorial convention or put on the ballot and work for a primary opponent. So they had to be placated soon. Ergo Judith Hope, who became head of the App-

The Days of Wine and Roses Are Over

ointments Office in 1976, had her deputy, John Marino, travel about the State in his white Chevrolet greeting them.(23) She also convinced the Administration that applicants for many non-salaried positions should no longer have to fill out the time-consuming questionnaire but could complete an abridged version.(24)

Of course, Carey could not satisfy all the county chairpeople all the time: not even Rockefeller had been able to do this with **his** contingent. Hope and her successor John Burns emphasized a point politicians and political scientists have been making for many years. There are always more seekers for public jobs than jobs available; thus each hire will create several ingrates and irritate the party potentates who have sponsored the losers. She often received sharp letters from chairpeople whose candidates had been passed over. But she felt obligated to seek patronage requests not only from them but also from the Black and Puerto Rican Caucus in the Legislature and women's groups -- she was a firm believer in bringing members of traditionally-underrepresented groups into State government. Moreover, she received quite a few suggestions about persons to appoint from strong Carey supporters ex-Mayor Robert Wagner and Liberal Party chairperson Alex Rose.(25) The county leaders had no love for Wagner, who had often called himself anti-organization though he had originally been elected Mayor with the support of New York City's regular Democrats.(26) And, naturally, they could not have been expected to cheer when jobs went to Liberals rather than to Democrats.

There was one patronage arrangement peculiar to the Carey Administration that was bound to displease the State's Democratic politicians. This was that at the Governor's insistence, all appointments to non-civil-service posts in the health/mental health sector (e.g. health planning bodies, Boards of Visitors for institutions for the mentally ill and mentally retarded) were to be made by his close friend and Special Assistant for Health Affairs Dr. Kevin Cahill. To insure that this would be the case, Patricia Cahill, his sister, was placed in the Appointments Office. The physician's picks for the honorary posts often left the county chairpeople unhappy, as they were usually nonpolitical people whom they did not know and sometimes had never heard of until the media were notified of the selection.(27)

The shadow of State Chairman Cunningham cast one more

cloud on the relationship between Carey and the county leaders during his first term. After Nadjari had accused Cunningham of auctioning off judgeships in The Bronx, the Governor decided to cut off personal contact with him until his legal problems had been solved. He appointed financier Arthur Krim as a liaison between the Chairman and himself.(28) Then in May 1976, a short time before Nadjari actually indicted Cunningham (the charges were dismissed by the end of the year), the Governor named ex-Mayor Wagner to the new post of Party "Executive Director". In essence this made Wagner head of the Party, with responsiblities for handling patronage (in conjunction with the Appointments Office) and legislative liaison. When Cunningham took a leave of absence from his Chairman's duties in early June, Wagner became even more powerful. This did not thrill the county chairpeople for, as seen, they were suspicious of this person who called himself "anti-boss". Some also grumbled, strangely in the light of Cunningham's lack of involvement with Party matters as Chairperson, that Carey was turning his back on a friend. As a result, Wagner was able to accomplish little.(29) On this matter of rejecting an intimate, the Chief Executive and his Secretary David Burke felt that as soon as Nadjari accused Cunningham, the latter ought to have resigned to protect the Governor. They made this known to him and the mutual resentment that developed persists to this day.(30) In early 1977, he did formally leave the State Chairmanship.

Patronage problems toward the end of Carey's first term and throughout his second were much less troublesome than in his early years. By his 1979 inauguration, any Rockefeller holdovers were out and replaced by Democrats, which in and of itself had reduced the number of members of his own Party clamoring for jobs. Baranello, whom Carey appointed State Chairperson in 1977 after Secretary of State Mario Cuomo had turned down the offer and who stayed throughout the remainder of his Administration, was a leader who treated his colleagues with respect and traveled throughout the State keeping in touch with them.(31) Hope did a fine job as Appointments Officer through 1978; while her personable replacement, John Burns from Binghamton, had himself been State Chairperson for six years, and there had become fully cognizant of the problems of his county counterparts. When it was desired that a non-political person get a paid or unpaid state job in

The Days of Wine and Roses Are Over

Cahill's domain or other areas, Burns took pains to explain the matter in advance to the affected county leader. Because of the shorter questionnaires used for some positions and because he continually pressured the State Police doing the checking to expedite matters, appointments were processed more rapidly than in the beginning of the Carey years. He personally would okay men and women under consideration for filling vacancies and then send the list to Morgado. The Secretary in some cases made the final decision himself and in some instances gave the name to his chief for formal approval. In all cases, persons appointed to civil service-exempt posts in a particular area (e.g. higher education) had to be approved by the member of the Governor's staff responsible for that field; as Carey continued to insist that incompetents not get a foothold in his Administration. (32)

1977 featured a contest that had the potential for driving a wedge between Carey and other powerful figures in the State Democratic Party so large that it might have led to their throwing him off the ticket in 1978 regardless of how many jobs he had been parceling out to them. Mayor Abe Beame had high hopes of reelection in 1977 since he could reasonably claim some credit for the fact that the metropolis had not gone under. Though the two Chief Executives had been sniping at each other since the investment community had closed its wallet to New York in Spring of 1975, by the end of 1976 things were looking up. Carey at this time remarked in a happy mood that both he and the Mayor should get "high marks" for their role in the crisis and that both merited reelection.(33) Though the Governor did not say outright that he would endorse his fellow Brooklynite, the latter was certainly within his rights in feeling that this benediction meant that it was very likely that he would back him for a second term. However, despite these words that seemed to speak to the contrary, Carey had by this time decided that someone else had to be at the City's helm. Why he blurted out this apparent imprimatur of Beame when he felt that the ex-City Comptroller had to go(34) is unclear. Maybe he was just in jolly holiday spirits and bellowed this praise without being able to control himself. Perhaps he really did not realize that his audience would take it as an endorsement of the Mayor. Or possibly he had had a drop too much of holiday cheer!

Carey, the Democratic Party, and the State Legislature

Even though because of this New Year's compliment Beame at the beginning of 1977 may have had good reason to expect Carey's backing, he knew very well that he would have opposition in the Democratic primary. Perhaps the strongest threat to the Mayor was progressive Congress Member Bella Abzug from Manhattan. Ed Koch, who was also from a Congress Member from Manhattan and was almost but not quite as liberal, had likewise made known his desire to move into Gracie Mansion; and there was talk about Secretary of State Mario Cuomo. However, by early 1977 Cuomo still had not made up his mind to run; which on the Democratic side left Beame and Abzug as the leading contenders. And Carey felt that the election of either "would make it all but impossible for the city to get back into the bond market and refinance its debts. That was essential both to saving the city from default and to aiding his own reelection effort in 1978".(35) Moreover, the Liberal Party, then and even today a force in City politics whose backing could make all the difference, would not accept the Mayor because he was in their eyes too close to the Brooklyn Democratic organization.(36) The Governor himself told me that he concluded that Beame did not deserve a second term because he had been out of touch with reality during the fiscal crisis believing, for example, that he could easily get a $750 million loan from Arthur Burns's Federal Reserve Bank to tide him over. Carey made this judgment even though Beame had been the honorary chairman of his Congressional campaign in 1972, and even though he would not have received the 25% of the vote at the 1974 Democratic State Convention needed to get on the ballot had the Mayor uttered the appropriate words.(37)

Not only did the likely Democratic Mayoral choices (Beame or Abzug) not seem very appetizing to Carey in early 1977, but there was a serious Republican candidate, liberal State Senator Roy Goodman from Manhattan. It looked quite possible that Goodman would get the Liberal Party nod as well, in which case he would be a good shot to win Gracie Mansion. The faithful Democrat in Carey shuddered at the thought, especially as Goodman then could use the Mayoralty as a springboard from which he could run for Governor in 1978. Strong Liberal leader and good Carey friend Alex Rose had recently died; and the Party was caught in the throes of a succession struggle. The two main contenders were Edward

The Days of Wine And Roses Are Over

Morrison and Raymond Harding. Morrison wanted Goodman; Harding did not but felt that he would have to go along with the Senator unless Carey and former Mayor Wagner could present him with Democratic alternatives acceptable to the Liberal chiefs. The Governor and the ex-Mayor finally gave him three names: Urban Development Corporation head Richard Ravitch, Secretary of State Mario Cuomo and Congressman Ed Koch. The Liberals would not back Koch; and so Carey settled on the Secretary of State as his Mayoral favorite.(38)

One of Cuomo's biggest negatives was that he was viewed as the Brooklynite's "puppet", a charge aided by the Governor's raising $150,000 for him at approximately the time he declared his candidacy.(39) Perhaps to rebut this accusation, Carey did not actively campaign for him until a fortnight before the primary.(40) Another big problem for the Secretary of State was that he, like the Chief Executive, opposed the death penalty. Koch supported it and Beame helped himself by announcing that he was changing his philosophy of a lifetime and backing it too. It became the main issue in the race even though it was irrelevant, as major criminal legislation in New York State is the province of the State rather than of local government.(41) Though at the end of August Carey finally rolled up his sleeves and openly worked for his friend, in the September 9th primary Koch got 19.8% of the vote, Cuomo 18.7%, Beame 17.9%, and Abzug 16.6%.(42) These results required a September 19th runoff between the two leaders.

If the Queens lawyer lost that contest, Carey knew he would be in trouble. If he backed Koch in the general, he would be breaking a promise he had made to Cuomo and the Liberal leaders to support him in November even if the Secretary of State had the okay of the Liberals only. On the other hand, his continued endorsement of Cuomo could alienate Democratic county chairpeople and office holders so much that they would toss the Governor aside in the 1978 race. Unfortunately for the Chief Executive, Koch won the runoff 55% to 45%. Carey decided to go with his Party's choice and backed Koch against Cuomo running on the Liberal line. "Freed" of Carey's seal of approval, Cuomo worked surprisingly hard in the general election and lost to the Democrat by only eight points, an amazing showing for one relying almost entirely on minor party backing. Though publicly he contended that he was not bitter over Carey's defection to Koch (43), in fact he was furious.(44) But his anger against him was nothing compared to that of Beame and his circle. In 1978 the dislike was so intense that when Mrs. Rosalynn Carter, President Jimmy Carter's wife, asked Beame at Carey's urging to get behind his bid for the Governorship, the ex-Mayor rejected her plea. He felt that if he went along with this request his wife would leave him and he would never be able to look at himself in the shaving mirror.(45)

Some aver that the relationship between Carey and the New York State Legislature was as bad as that prevailed between him and Beame in the late 1970s. At the end of his eight years in office he called the solons "small boys".(46) From their perspective, many members saw him as arrogant, remote and indifferent to their needs.(47) A Democratic Assemblyman to the cheers of his colleagues in that body labelled him a "no-good-son-of-a bitch". (48) One article even referred to the interactions between the executive and legislative branches in the Brooklynite's time as a "state of war" where the "trenches [were] dug deeply".(49)

The New York Legislature by and large features the practice of party discipline, that is, its rank and file members generally vote as the legislative leaders of their respective parties wish (which is often as the relevant "party conference" in the relevant chamber has decreed). Ergo the occupant of the Governor's Office on the State Capitol's second floor, to be able to achieve his goals, must at least win over the heads of the majority parties in both houses. For Carey's purposes, that meant being able to convert Republican State Senator Warren Anderson from Binghamton, the Senate Majority Leader during his entire Governorship, and also the Democratic Speakers of the Assembly, the late Stanley Steingut from Brooklyn during his first term and Stanley Fink from the same borough during his second. Since party discipline is not always 100%, most Governors need good rapport with the leaders of the minority party in each chamber, particularly that in which their own party is the minority. Thus the Chief Executive had to build up a positive relationship with State Senator Manfred Ohrenstein from Manhattan, Democratic (Minority) Leader of the Senate while Carey lived in the Executive Mansion on Eagle Street. Leaders of the minority Republicans in the Assembly were Perry Duryea from

1975 through 1978 and James Emery from upstate Geneseo from 1979 through 1982.

That Ohrenstein became Senate Minority Leader at all was due to a lack of care in dealing with that body that some would say characterized for eight years the way Carey and his staff treated both chambers. The favorite to win this post in 1975 to succeed the retiring Joseph Zaretzki was the ranking Democrat on the powerful Finance Committee, Jeremiah Bloom from Brooklyn. We first met Senator Bloom and district leader Bernard, his brother, breaking with Brooklyn Democratic leader Meade Esposito in the 1974 gubernatorial primary and backing Carey rather than Howard Samuels. The Blooms therefore with reason felt that he owed them something and that the very least he could do for them was to clinch the Senate Leadership election for Jeremiah. But the new Governor hardly lifted a finger. His aides who were supposed to count the votes did not strain themselves to do so. Neither he nor Pat Cunningham leaned on any Democratic Senators to back Bloom.(50) Ohrenstein waged a magnificent campaign going from Senator to Senator telling them why he was best qualified to lead their group and eventually he won a close race. Bloom, who was the favorite of New York City's county leaders and who felt at the start of the session that he would obtain the support of as many as 20 of the 26 Democrats, ended up with only half that many. He simply assumed that the trophy was his; and did not bother to dangle prizes, such as membership on important committees, to several Democratic lawmakers he wrongly assumed were in his back pocket.(51) After his rout, Bloom became irritated with Carey, though to some extent the fiasco was of his own making; and the annoyance turned into fury as the session wore on and the Governor did not bother to personally consult with him.(52)

There was no way that the rest of 1975 could have led to warmth between Legislature and Chief Executive. This was the year of the fiscal crises, and his thoughts and energies had to be concentrated on developing plans to keep New York City and State construction agencies such as the Dormitory Authority from insolvency. Major measures aimed at these ends such as providing a financial package for the Urban Development Corporation, creating the Municipal Assistance Corporation (MAC) and the Emergency Financial Control Board, and raising State and City taxes had to be

Carey, the Democratic Party, and the State Legislature

pushed through both houses. But there was no time to accomplish this via sweet talk and hand holding; what had to be done in essence was to tell the Senators and Assembly-people that these packages had to be passed because disaster would flow from inaction. Burke admits he antagonized the Legislature that year by hectoring it and ordering it to shape up and swiftly enact these and similar measures.(53)

As emphasized, the receipt of federal loans at the end of 1975 and the raising of City and State taxes then did not mark the end of these jurisdictions' fiscal emergencies. The 1976 legislative session thus was handed by the Executive Branch crucial proposals to put the construction agencies on a firm financial footing and to keep the City University of New York from collapse. Accordingly, the Governor and his staff could not relax and stop pressuring the Legislature. The only trouble was that the law-makers were intelligent, sensitive, proud human beings whose feathers became more and more ruffled by the lack of sympathy and understanding they felt continued to emanate from Carey's mansion on Eagle Street. Matters may have reached a low point in March when a vote had to be taken by a Friday to keep the Dormitory Authority from a default that would make impossible the sale of State and MAC bonds and notes. Assembly Members and Senators from New York City love to leave Albany on Thursdays to get back to their families and cultivate their constituencies. Consequently, by 11 PM Thursday March 11th, so many had fled that Speaker Steingut could not get the 76 votes he needed to pass the Dormitory Authority bailout. He had decided to adjourn until Monday, when the lawmakers would have returned from the Big Apple, when he heard the Governor's aides knocking at his door screaming that the Authority would go bankrupt if it were not propped up by Friday morning and begging him to send the State Police out to round up the errant members. A whole flock of them was found by the gendarmes and ordered to return to the Capitol. And it was not only lazy timeservers who were hauled back but hardworking members such as health expert Alan Hevesi (now New York City Comptroller) from Queens and future Speaker Mel Miller from Brooklyn. This pair were discovered "living it up" drinking coffee and eating pie about midnight in the unpre-possessing New Baltimore service station restaurant on the New

The Days of Wine and Roses Are Over

York State Thruway about 20 miles south of the capital. As an insurance policy, Steingut and the Governor's aides told the Capitol Police to lock the building's exits so no more sheep could stray. Eventually, enough of the members returned to the fold to enable "discussion" to resume: Duryea proved a big help by convincing some of his minions to support the aid bill. It passed by 78-2 early Friday morning, but the members' sense of outrage against the Chief Executive increased. And what it culminated in was the Spring, 1976 override of the Governor's veto of the Stavisky-Goodman bill protecting from cuts the education component of New York City's budget, the first time in 104 years that a Chief Executive had had a negative quashed.(54)

Even after the worries about default had vanished, there is considerable evidence that the Carey - Legislative Branch relationship remained tense. To take just one example, because of an OPEC oil embargo in 1979, the price of heating oil soared. One would have expected that the Governor would have jumped for joy when his own Legislature passed a trio of bills that would lighten some of the financial burden weighing on New York families who were being forced to pay a lot more for gas or oil to keep themselves and their families warm despite arctic blasts of Canadian air. The measures, approved in a special session in November, 1979 provided, respectively, for a repeal of the State's sales tax on home heating fuel beginning October 1st, 1980; a grant of a $35 tax credit to residents over 64 whose annual income did not exceed $14,000; and a subsidy to directly pay part of the home heating costs of moderate--income and indigent households. The first was signed, albeit grudgingly, with Carey lamenting that "I have repeatedly expressed serious reservations with respect to the wisdom of this legislation. The resulting benefit to the individual taxpayer is extremely modest --estimated at $25 to $30 per household--while the loss of revenue to the State is substantial".(55) However, on the same day, November 15th, he vetoed the other two. His veto message noted that the Federal government had already passed assistance legislation that covered many of the people benefited by the state subsidy. More importantly, "approval of these bills, in addition to the sales tax phaseout legislation which I have approved today, would be fiscally irresponsible".(56) The two rejected proposals together could, he continued cost the State as much as $165 million even though their sponsors had estimated that they would deprive its vaults of only $57 million.(57)

Assembly Speaker Stanley Fink, who had assumed this position when Steingut lost his Assembly seat in the 1978 election, saw red. The two vetoed bills had been sponsored by him personally; while the one that had been signed had originated in the Republican Senate. He and other Assembly Democrats were getting numerous phone calls and letters from their voters moaning about excessive home heating costs and demanding that their representatives do something about the situation. He thought that the measures would cost a lot less than the Executive believed they would; and was well aware that Governors traditionally underestimate revenues and overestimate expenses. As a Republican Assemblyman had pointed out, the State that supposedly would be bankrupted as a result of these proposals to aid the needy had agreed earlier in the year to help build the $375 million Javits Convention Center in New York City. And, to top it all off, Fink had difficulty getting to see Carey, who he believed would be receptive to his position; and had to deal with Morgado, who at times was more sensitive to economic rather than political necessities. Thus it was hardly surprising that the Assembly almost unanimously overrode the Chief Executive's veto. The Senate followed suit, not wanting to be accused of causing senior citizens and moderate income people to freeze because they could not afford to pay their neighborhood oil dealer. This was the first veto override since Stavisky-Goodman; but remember that no Governor in the hundred or so years preceding the Stavisky-Goodman debacle had suffered a similar fate.(58)

Thus there is no doubt that whatever the successes of the Carey Administration were, building up a great deal of trust and goodwill in his dealings with his legislative counterparts was not one of them. A college professor might give them a "C". Why not an "F", those who have read everything that has preceded might say? The answer is that the "state of war" referred to earlier was not continually in effect. We are not talking about eight years of continual battles between enemies each of whom has sworn to annihilate the other. The state of affairs was closer to medieval disputes between great lords where bloody skirmishes were suc-

The Days of Wine and Roses Are Over

ceded by frequent truces and where the rivals would occasionally fraternize. The main reason that the interface between Carey and the legislature cannot be deemed a total failure is a simple one: **cooperation** between the two branches made possible many of the accomplishments that this book describes, including the resolution of the State and City fiscal crises. Had the dealings between the ex-Congressman and the legislative branch continually been akin to those between, say, Protestants and Catholics in Northern Ireland, the State would have seen eight years of gridlock. No, it would probably have witnessed only four such years; for under these circumstances Carey would have certainly gone down to defeat in 1978 as a Chief Executive who was able to get nothing accomplished, who fiddled while Rome burned.

In fact, I was amazed in doing the research for this book that most of the Carey era legislators I spoke to liked him, or at least gave him good marks as Governor. Perhaps absence makes the heart grow fonder, but both Fink and Senate Minority Leader Ohrenstein say that, in retrospect, Carey had vision; that the State was spending too much and that the Governor saw that expenditures had to be curbed in order to reduce taxes and keep the middle class from moving to New Jersey or Connecticut in droves. At the same time, the Speaker continues, the Governor never discarded the position that the State did have a responsibility toward its poorest and most helpless citizens. As for that 1979 dispute involving State aid for low and moderate income citizens to help them pay home heating bills where Carey's veto of two measures sponsored by Fink was overriden, the latter now takes a more conciliatory tone. Though he still supports these acts the dispute there, he admits, was to a considerable extent about their cost to the State; and on this matter, reasonable people could differ. The Speaker also notes that during the financial crises of 1975-76, the Governor did give breakfasts, lunches and dinners for elected officials, business people and labor leaders trying to get them all to pull together. Though both he and Democratic State Senator Martin Connor (who also appreciates Carey) feel that the Governor could have done a lot more in the way of building up contacts with individual legislators, he points out that he did have all the lawmakers over to the Executive Mansion at least once a year and often turned the charm on then.(59)

Democratic Assembly Member and long-time Chairperson of its Mental Health Committee, Elizabeth Connelly from Staten Island, feuded with Carey over his proposal to build a coal-and-garbage-fueled power plant in the western section of the Island. Yet she is personally fond of him and calls him a good Governor. In the midst of their fight over the power plant she won reelection in 1980. At a reception he gave for the legislative victors he took her aside and said that on election night he had glanced at her results first and was overjoyed to see that she had won.(60) Assemblyman Arthur "Jerry" Kremer from Long Island, Chairman of its Ways and Means Committee in Carey's time, says that he always got along with the Governor and does not feel that he was "arrogant". Assemblyman Hevesi told me that the Chief Executive often treated him well and went to functions in his district. Both Kremer and Hevesi think, though, that he could have established better rapport with rank and file lawmakers.(61)

According to veteran observer of the Albany scene Professor Gerald Benjamin of the State University of New York at New Paltz, the relationship between Carey and Senate Majority leader Anderson "grew more and more acrimonious as time passed".(62) And there were specific occasions on which the Governor seemed to go out of his way to put the affable Binghamton Republican's back up. For example, during a late night Senate session Anderson wanted to talk to the Governor personally. But the Chief Executive was already in his pajamas and did not want to speak with him, who consequently had to settle for Morgado. The snub flew in the face of Albany tradition under which a legislative leader who wants to converse with the Governor rather than one of his aides has the prerogative of doing so.(63) According to Anderson's Counsel Jack Haggerty, the Brooklynite would sometimes set up meetings with the Majority Leader and then not show up himself but send Burke or Morgado. This would infuriate him, especially when it was a Friday and he wanted to drive back to Binghamton to meet with his constituents. In fact, Carey, unlike Rockefeller, considered the Executive Mansion his home and forgot that legislators are eager to leave the capital for their districts on the weekends. But, Haggerty continues, the Governor **for the most part** treated his chief decently.(64)

The Days of Wine and Roses Are Over

Maybe Anderson, now retired from the Senate and practicing law in Binghamton, is like Fink suffering from nostalgia for the good old days when he, the Speaker (Steingut before 1979) and Carey ruled the State; but he echoes his Counsel and seems to contradict Benjamin when he says that he (and Fink, for that matter) **usually** got along with the Chief Executive though at times there **was** serious friction between them. For example, most of the Governor's proposed health programs were enacted into law by virtue of close cooperation between himself, Kevin Cahill, Senate Health Committee Chairman Tarky Lombardi and others. In New York State, Anderson points out, the Governor has to work with the legislative leaders if he wants to get things done; and Carey, just like Thomas E. Dewey, W. Averell Harriman and Nelson Rockefeller before him -- these are the Governors that Anderson personally remembers -- accepted this philosophy of "getting things done" and thus dealt frequently and often pleasantly with the Legislature's bigwigs. Anderson recalls one episode with particular fondness. Both he and the Brooklynite are avid golfers and one day movie star Bob Hope came to Albany. Carey invited the Majority Leader, a big Hope fan, to join them on the links. Both on the course and in the clubhouse afterwards the three men got along famously and when the Hollywood celebrity was about to leave, the New Yorkers jointly presented him with a key to the City of Albany. We do not know what the actor thought of this gift; but the Republican solon was left with a glow in his heart.(65)

Chairman of the powerful Finance Committee (the Senate equivalent of the Assembly's Ways and Means but with the additional power to recommend the rejection of gubernatorial appointments as well as to enact or repeal taxes) throughout the Carey years was Staten Island's Republican Senator John Marchi. He admits that relations between the Legislature and Governor were often frayed and attributes this to some extent to the Chief Executive's habit of saying "outrageous" things. Nonetheless, he and Carey personally like and liked each other and he feels that Carey is a "brilliant" person who has an excellent grasp of economic problems.(66)

Marchi has been a Senator since 1956 and normally gets reelected with ease. However, in 1978 he was faced with serious opposition from Robert Gigante, a young pro-capital punishment

Democratic lawyer. Marchi was, and is, the one Republican State Senator who rejects the death penalty; and Gigante during the campaign took him to task for this. In the course of the 1978 race, Carey came to Staten Island and followed the time-hallowed ritual of meeting with commuters rushing to catch the Staten Island Ferry to get to their jobs in Manhattan. One would have expected that a Democratic Governor would praise a Democratic Senatorial candidate to the skies, particularly as wresting the Senate from Republican control would have put him in a better position to secure passage of his legislative agenda. Though at the ferry Carey did not exactly endorse Marchi, he referred to him as a "man of great courage" and a "man of public virtue" because of his stance on capital punishment and other issues.(67) In the late 1980s Marchi entered a Korean fruit store in Manhattan to buy some apples. Some watermelons fell to the floor and the Staten Islander and another customer spontaneously began picking them up. Who should that other patron turn out to be but Hugh Carey! The two men smiled broadly and each began singing the other's virtues to the amazed proprietor!(68)

Another Republican legislator surprisingly appreciative of Hugh Carey is Duryea, his gubernatorial opponent in 1978. He says that contrary to some press reports, he did not "despise" the Governor. In fact, he always got along quite well with him and "respects" and "has affection" for him. He did not think that Carey's plans for saving New York City in 1975 would work; but adds admiringly that they did. The Governor, he contends, did not shut the legislative leaders out but, on the contrary, met with them on a reasonably regular basis.(69) This is hardly a portrait of a Chief of State whose dealings with the legislative branch were continually marked by rancor.

On the surface, the Governor and Stanley Steingut, the Speaker his first term, seemed tailor-made for one another. Both were Democrats, both were moderately progressive and both were from Brooklyn. True, Carey did not come out of clubhouse politics while Steingut was a member of the powerful Madison Democratic Club that also produced his father Speaker Irwin, State Comptroller Arthur Levitt and Mayor Abe Beame; but the Chief Executive had rarely bucked the Kings County Democratic organization or its ancillaries. Yet right after the Stavisky-Goodman debacle in Spring

The Days of Wine and Roses Are Over

of 1976 the *New York Times* remarked that "Mr. Carey and Mr. Steingut do not appear to like or trust each other very much...."(70) My own interviews obtained some data to confirm this. A Carey aide who does not wish to be identified here recalls that the Governor deemed the Speaker inferior to Sam Rayburn, who had been Speaker of the U.S. House of Representatives for part of his chief's sojourn in the nation's capital. Kremer says that the Chief Executive's relations with Fink were better than they were with Steingut. The former was a negotiator and compromiser while his predecessor wanted to be his own man.(71)

However, the interaction between the two Brooklynites was not on balance unfriendly. Lieutenant Governor Many Anne Krupsak, who had once been employed by the Assembly herself and whose husband Edwin Margolis was a chief aide to Steingut, told me that the latter liked and helped Carey. There were disputes between the two when the legislator felt ignored; but basically he considered the new Governor "his boy". Director of State Operations Thomas Frey, who had been in the Assembly himself during 1975 and 1976, also insisted that the relations between the two were good and that the Brooklyn lawmaker exerted himself, albeit unsuccessfully, to prevent the override of the Stavisky-Goodman veto.(72) Steingut lost the Democratic Assembly primary in 1978 to one Murray Weinstein, whose platform emphasized bringing back the electric chair: the Speaker like the Governor was a strong opponent of capital punishment. He ran on the Liberal ticket in the general election, but came in second again. Out of gratitude for all his help as well as recognizing his bravery on the death penalty issue, Carey appointed the ex-Assemblyman to a patronage sinecure, membership on the New York State Sports Authority.

Those who argue that the Carey-Legislature interface was catastrophic could point to his frequent statements that he would be a "no deals" governor and not play the "Albany game".(73) He was referring here to Rockefeller techniques such as securing the passage of a ridiculously punitive drug measure by adding to it a section creating a gaggle of judgeships that the many legislators with a law degree could yearn for.(74) On one occasion Rockefeller, to get the 76 votes in the Assembly necessary for the passage of his budget, simply gave Democratic Assemblyman Charles Stockmeister a position on the State Civil Service Comm-

Carey, the Democratic Party, and the State Legislature

ission.(75) Carey never used a trick as unsubtle as this one to improve his dealings with the Legislature. But legislators did request that this or that constituent get this or that patronage position; and his Appointments Office seriously considered all pleas of this sort and sometimes acceded to them.(76) His Administration went relatively slowly in replacing Republican holdovers with Democrats: one probable motive for this was to induce Senate Republicans to cooperate with him in enacting the legislation necessary to solve the fiscal crisis.(77) He successfully pushed State aid for building a sports stadium in Syracuse while the bill providing for the construction of New York City's Convention Center was being considered by the Legislature; some concluded that the Syracuse facility was supported at least in part to get upstate votes for the downstate complex.(78) So he did strike bargains with the lawmakers and this tactic too produced some rapport.

One difference between the two Chief Executives that frequently was brought up in my interviews was that the Republican was much more willing to develop close relations with backbench legislators. Carey, as seen, did occasionally sponsor receptions for them but, on the whole, he dealt personally on a regular basis only with the leaders while keeping the rank and file at "arm's length".(79) The millionaire liked to "press flesh": in this respect, according to Marchi, the Democrat was not in his league.(80) But the importance of this difference between the two Governors can be exaggerated. Again, as Anderson and Fink stress, in New York's political culture the legislators with whom the Governor must treat most frequently are the leaders.(81) And Carey did, as indicated, have an ongoing relationship, albeit not always a happy one, with the Finks, Andersons and Steinguts of the Capitol. When the Legislature was in session, he frequently had the Democratic and Republican leaders of both houses over for breakfast negotiations at the Executive Mansion. For example, on February 20, 1980, he broke bread there at 8:30 AM with Fink, Ohrenstein, Anderson and Emery. Just one week later, same time, same place, he munched lox, bagels and toast and drank coffee with Democratic leaders such as Ohrenstein, Fink and Kremer.(82) All these men, Democrats and Republicans, actually would have been distressed had he spent too much time cultivating their backbench-

ers; they would have felt that he was undercutting their leadership.
(83)

There were some rank and file lawmakers who certainly did not
feel alienated from the Chief Executive. Black Assemblyman
Herman "Denny" Farrell, Democrat of Manhattan, thinks that it is
unfair to describe Carey as "distant" from the average legislator.
Though the Governor never invited him out for a beer, he smiled
at him every time he saw him in the Capitol. They jokingly called
one another "cousin", as Farrell has some Irish blood. One day the
New York Post had a squib mentioning that Farrell's Assembly
District co-leader had survived a challenge to her nominating
petitions and thus remained on the ballot. When the Governor saw
him later he called out "Congratulations!". It took the Assemblyman
a moment to realize that Carey was referring to that tiny
article.(84)

In short, one can overstate the extent of the quarrels between
Carey and the Legislature. But these squabbles did darken the
Albany landscape. They were due not only to the Governor's
dislike of glad-handing and to his belief, mentioned to me by one
of his aides, that the state solons were inferior to his ex-colleagues
in Congress; but also to various institutional and time-specific
factors. As his final Budget Director Mark Lawton points out, the
solons are responsive to the relatively parochial needs of their little
districts; the Governor is charged with looking out for the welfare
of the State as a whole.(85) Under a constitution that features a
separation of power there are inherent tensions between executive
and legislative institutions. In addition, the Brooklynite became
Chief Executive after the days of wine and roses had faded into a
gloomy night; and consequently there was "little money for the
increased local assistance payments.... for which legislators liked
to take credit in their districts...."(86)

Many interviewees singled out one particular reason why Carey
had so many wrangles with the lawmakers. This is that ever since
the mid-1960s the tax and other committees of both chambers had
been beefing up their professional staffs; and so they no longer
had to accept blindly the financial estimates given to them by the
Executive.(87) Fink mentions, in addition, that the Democrats who
were elected to the Assembly in 1974 enabling the Party to re-
capture control of that Chamber were relatively young people who

had been repelled by the Vietnam War and Watergate and felt that it was their mission to improve the quality of life in the State, especially, as he put it, for people "living in the shadows". This type of person, even though the Governor was a fellow partisan, was not going to lay back and grant him his every wish.(88) And Benjamin contends that "Increased pay and benefits made the position of legislator a full-time job, and attracted a new kind of member, more entrepeneurial and less amenable to taking leadership direction".(89)

Whatever the factors that distanced the Governor from the State Legislature, some of its members felt that he viewed it as "that zoo".The power struggle between him and it was at times so intense that it started "recessing" rather than "adjourning" in midsummer when its work was over to prevent him from calling it into special sessions whose agendas he would have the authority to set. However, as the fiscal crises chapters indicated, he was still able to accomplish a lot of what he set out to do. And the sections soon to follow dealing with other policy arenas will show further that he was able to get many of his ideas through the Legislature even though quite a few (albeit far from all) of its men and women had little affection for him.

Notes to Chapter 7

1. Interview with former State Democratic Chairperson Dominic Baran-ello, July 19, 1994, Patchogue, N.Y.; with Burke, Aug. 28, 1992, New York City; with Edelman, May 8, 1991, Washington.

2. Interview with (currently) Brooklyn District Attorney Charles J. Hynes, Jan. 7, 1991, Brooklyn, N.Y.

3. Auletta, Ken - Runnin' Scared, Village Voice, Feb. 16, 1976, p. 26.

4. Interview with Carey's Tax Commissioner James Tully, June 8, 1990, Albany, N.Y.

5. Baranello, interview cited n.1 supra.

6. Phone interview with Carey Appointments Officer John Burns, Dec. 30, 1992, Binghamton, N.Y.; A Frustrated Job-Seeker - 'What's Carey Doing? What the Hell Is Going On'?, Village Voice, May 5, 1975, p. 12.

7. Interview with Carey Appointments Officer Judith Hope, Sept. 25, 1991, East Hampton, N.Y.

8. Ibid.

9. Interview with Emergency Financial Control Board Executive Director Stephen Berger, Feb. 21, 1991, New York City.

10. Hynes, interview cited n.2 supra; interviews with Kahan, Nov. 21, 1990, New York City; with Lehman, July 10, 1990, New York City; with Lewis, Dec. 6, 1994, New York City; with Emergency Financial Control Board aide (later New York City Schools Chancellor) Frank Macchiarola, Aug. 31, 1991, New York City; with Ward, Nov. 16, 1991, Brooklyn, N.Y. The Governor picked Lewis over John Lennon, the boyhood friend, for the Superintendent's position. Letter dated Nov. 23, 1977 from Judith Hope to Jerry Burton, Hugh L. Carey Collection, St. John's Univ.(NY), John F. Lennon file.
    Carey's first Appointments Officer was Cortland County Democratic Chairman and Professor of Political Science at SUNY/Cortland Victor Bahou. Bahou did not desire this job and moved to the Civil Service Commission. He was succeeded by Democratic State Chairman Patrick Cunningham's protege Thomas Lynch, who left the end of 1975. Judith Hope, who took over then, had been Town Supervisor of East Hampton, a Democratic official in a traditionally Republican area. Hope, interview

cited n.7 supra; Public Papers of Governor Hugh L.Carey 1975 (Albany: State of New York Executive Chamber, 1982), p. 1690, 1692; New York Times, Dec. 27, 1975, p. 31.

11. Interview with a Carey staffer, Nov. 30, 1991.

12. See letter from K.E. Buhrmeister to Hope dated July 27, 1976, Hugh L. Carey Collection, St. John's Univ.(NY), Gubernatorial Files 1975-82 (Executive Office Files 1975-82: Issue/Project Files 1975-82 A-E) file. See also New York Times, May 2, 1976, Sec. 1, p. 62.

13. Hope, interview cited n.7 supra; A Frustrated Job-Seeker, op. cit. n.6 supra.

14. New York Times, May 2, 1976, Sec. 1, p. 62.

15. Hope, interview cited n.7 supra; interview with Carey Assistant Appointments Officer John Marino, Nov. 8, 1991, New York City.

16. Baranello, interview cited n.1 supra; New York Times, Jan. 22, 1975, p. 41.

17. Baranello, interview cited n.1 supra; Hope, interview cited n.7 supra.

18. Interview with Carey Deputy Appointments Officer William Cunningham, Dec. 30, 1991, Albany, N.Y.; interview with 1974 Carey campaign aide Professor Richard Wade, Mar. 11, 1991, New York City.

19. New York Times, Jan. 22, 1975, p. 41.

20. Marino, interview cited n.15 supra.

21. Interview with State Senator Manfred Ohrenstein, Oct. 25, 1994, New York City; Stokes, Geoffrey - Runnin' Scared, Village Voice, Oct. 20, 1975, p. 26; New York Times, Oct. 6, 1975, p. 15.

22. Hope and Marino, interviews cited n.7 and n.15 supra.

23. Marino, interview cited n.15 supra.

24. Hope, interview cited n.7 supra.

25. Burns and Hope, interviews cited n.6 and n.7 supra.

The Days of Wine and Roses Are Over

26. Auletta, Ken - Runnin' Scared, Village Voice, Nov. 22, 1976, p. 45; New York Times, May 17, 1976, p. 55.

27. Baranello, interview cited n.1 supra; Cunningham, interview cited n.18 supra; Marino, interview cited n.15 supra.

28. Auletta, Ken - Runnin' Scared, Village Voice, Mar. 1, 1976, p. 11; New York Times, Jan. 19, 1976, p. 48.

29. Marino, interview cited n.15 supra; interview with Mayor Robert Wagner, Dec. 11, 1990, New York City; New York Times, Apr. 24, 1976, p. 1; May 14, 1976, p. D17; May 17, 1976, p. 55; June 2, 1976, p. 1.

30. Burke, interview cited n.1 supra.

31. Marino, interview cited n.15 supra. Baranello, interview cited n.1 supra, admits that he, like almost all American state party chairpeople, had little input into substantive state policymaking. He saw his main task as obtaining money for a financially-strapped State Party and even convinced Senator Edward Kennedy of Massachusetts to speak at a fundraiser.
    Baranello over the years did not raise as much cash as he had hoped to, since individual legislators and the State Senate and State Assembly Democratic Campaign Committees competed with him for scarce dollars. Nonetheless, he enjoyed his tenure as State Party Chairman.

32. Burns, interview cited n.6 supra.

33. New York Daily News, Dec. 30, 1976, p. 3.

34. McElvaine, Robert - Mario Cuomo: A Biography (New York: Charles Scribner's Sons, 1988), p. 228.

35. Ibid. p. 229.

36. Interview with Mayor Abraham Beame, Dec. 27, 1990, New York City; with Carey Special Assistant Raymond Harding, July 2, 1990, New York City.

37. Interview with Governor Hugh Carey, Nov. 30, 1991, Shelter Island, N.Y. His 1974 campaign manager, Gerald Cummins, was the person who told me that had Beame opposed Carey's obtaining the 25%, he would

Carey, the Democratic Party, and the State Legislature

never have received it. Interview, Feb. 28, 1991, New York City.

38. Harding, interview cited n.36 <u>supra</u>; McElvaine, <u>op. cit</u>. n. 34 <u>supra</u>, p. 227, 229.

39. McElvaine, <u>op. cit</u>. n.34 <u>supra</u>, p. 236, pp. 242-43; Logan, Andy - <u>Around City Hall: Beyond The Pale</u>, <u>New Yorker</u>, May 30, 1977, p. 96, 97; Stokes, Geoffrey, <u>Runnin' Scared</u>, <u>Village Voice</u>, May 16, 1977, p. 18; <u>Staten Island Advance</u>, May 11, 1977, p. 3; May 20, 1977, p. 1.

40. McElvaine, <u>op. cit</u>. n.34 <u>supra</u>, p. 236.

41. <u>Staten Island Advance</u>, Aug. 15, 1977, p. 4.

42. McElvaine, <u>op. cit</u>. n.34 <u>supra</u>, p. 245.

43. <u>Staten Island Advance</u>, Sept. 27, 1977, p. 3.

44. McElvaine, <u>op. cit</u>. n.34 <u>supra</u>, p. 262, 265.

45. Interview with Beame's Corporation Counsel W. Bernard Richland, Jan. 7, 1991, Brooklyn, N.Y.

46. Benjamin, Gerald - <u>The Carey Governorship</u> at p. 235, 246 of Benjamin, Gerald and Hurd, T. Norman (eds.) - <u>Making Experience Count: Managing Modern New York In The Carey Era</u> (Albany: Nelson A. Rockefeller Institute of Government, 1985).

47. <u>Ibid</u>.; <u>New York Times</u>, Apr. 12, 1976, p. 57.

48. Weisman, Stephen - <u>The second Carey administration</u>, <u>New York Times Magazine</u>, Oct. 3, 1976, p. 18, 78.

49. <u>New York Times</u>, Apr. 12, 1976, p. 57.

50. Cummins, interview cited n.37 <u>supra</u>; interviews with Senator Anderson's Counsel Jack Haggerty, Aug. 9, 1990, Queens, N.Y.; with Lieutenant Governor Mary Anne Krupsak, Apr. 3, 1991, Albany, N.Y.

51. Lewis, interview cited n.10 <u>supra</u>; Ohrenstein, interview cited n.21 <u>supra</u>; Stokes, Geoffrey - <u>Will Hugh Carey Talk to Manfred Ohrenstein?</u>, <u>Village Voice</u>, Jan. 13, 1975, p. 31.

52. Haggerty, interview cited n.50 <u>supra</u>.

53. Burke, interview cited n.1 <u>supra</u>.

54. Interview with State Assembly Member Alan Hevesi, Sept. 15, 1990, Queens, N.Y.; <u>New York Times</u>, Mar. 13, 1976, p. 50; Apr. 12, 1976, p. 57. Burke, interview cited n.1 <u>supra</u>, mentioned that during the fiscal crisis Carey made promises to the Legislature that he later found he could not keep. Needless to say, the lawmakers were not overjoyed with what they perceived to be breaches of faith.

55. <u>Public Papers of Governor Hugh L. Carey 1979</u> (Albany: State of New York Executive Chamber, 1992), p. 688.

56. <u>Ibid.</u>, p. 395.

57. See <u>ibid.</u>, pp. 277-78, 394-97; <u>New York Times</u>, Nov. 17, 1979, p. 26.

58. <u>New York Times</u>, Nov. 21, 1979, p. A1; Nov. 22, 1979, p. A1; Nov. 25, 1979, Sec. 4, p. 6.

59. Interview with State Senator Martin Connor, Oct. 9, 1990, Staten Island, N.Y.; interview with Assembly Speaker Stanley Fink, July 12, 1990, New York City; Ohrenstein, interview cited n.21 <u>supra</u>.

60. Connelly interview, Aug. 8, 1990, Staten Island, N.Y.

61. Hevesi, interview cited n.54 <u>supra</u>; interview with Kremer, Aug. 22, 1990, Uniondale, N.Y.

62. Benjamin, <u>op. cit</u>. n.46 <u>supra</u>, p. 246.

63. Connor, interview cited n.59 <u>supra</u>.

64. Interview cited n.50 <u>supra</u>.

65. Interview with Senate Majority Leader Warren Anderson June 22, 1990, Binghamton, N.Y.; interview with Dr. Kevin Cahill, July 26, 1993, New York City.

66. Interview with Marchi, Aug. 8, 1991, Staten Island, N.Y.

67. <u>Staten Island Advance</u>, Oct. 15, 1978, p. E2.

Carey, the Democratic Party, and the State Legislature

68. Marchi, interview cited n.66 supra.

69. Interview with Duryea, June 26, 1990, Montauk, N.Y.

70. New York Times, Apr. 12, 1976, p. 57.

71. Kremer, interview cited n.61 supra.

72. Baranello, interview cited n.1 supra; Frey, phone interview Aug. 9, 1991, Rochester, N.Y.; Krupsak, interview cited n.50 supra. After the Stavisky override, Morgado and Steingut Secretary (and later Carey Director of Policy and Management) Michael Del Giudice arranged for their respective chiefs to have dinner one-on-one, which reduced the tensions between them. Interview with Del Giudice, June 28, 1994, New York City.

73. Benjamin, op. cit. n.46 supra, p. 246.

74. Underwood, James and Daniels, William - Governor Rockefeller In New York (Westport, Ct.: Greenwood Press, 1982), p. 141.

75. New York Times, July 4, 1969, p. 1.

76. Burns, interview cited n.6 supra.

77. Interview with ex-New York City Deputy Mayor Robert Wagner, Jr., Oct. 25, 1991, New York City.

78. New York Times, July 30, 1978, Sec. 1, p. 25. It should also be noted that Carey usually approved "member items". These provide funding for projects in the members' districts that the legislators believe will be popular with the voters. For example, New York State Laws of 1979, Ch. 312, provides cash for numerous programs. Among these are $68,000 for a feasibility study for a senior citizen residence facility in the Williamsburg section of Brooklyn; $123,000 for a Jewish Heritage collection at Queens College; $50,000 for the Staten Island Children's Museum; $52,000 for transportation services in the Malverne, Long Island, School District; $200,000 for support of the Schomburg Library in Harlem; $50,000 for the Rochester Urban-Suburban Program; $25,000 for a pilot program for school delinquents in Syracuse, etc., etc. These grants make the local communities involved happy and the Governor's approval of them thus cheers the legislators who have pushed vigorously

The Days of Wine and Roses Are Over

for them. A truly intransigent governor would have vetoed these bills. In fact, it was to please the legislative leaders that the Carey Administration gave them (rather than the executive agencies, as had been the case) the right to determine which items a given member received. Miller, David and Steck, Henry - Legislative Initiatives in the New York State Legislature: Pork Barrel or Public Service?, pp. 9- 10. (Unpublished paper delivered at the 1994 New York State Political Science Association Convention, Albany, N.Y.) The appropriation for the Carrier Dome, the Syracuse stadium, was to a certain extent designed to help a Democratic legislator from that city who was in political trouble. Del Giudice, interview cited n.72 supra. Had the State's financial position been more secure, Carey doubtlessly would have had more "member items" to sign.

79. Burns, interview cited n.6 supra.

80. Interview cited n.66 supra.

81. Interviews cited n.65 and n.59 supra.

82. Lewis, interview cited n.10 supra; Ohrenstein, interview cited n.21 supra; Carey Materials, New York State Archives, Albany, N.Y., Governor's Daily Scheduling Log 1978-1982. (Series 13690).

83. Cunningham, interview cited n.18 supra.

84. Interview with Farrell, Jan. 29, 1993, New York City.

85. Lawton, C. Mark - C. Mark Lawton: Director of the Budget, at p. 53, 79 of Benjamin and Hurd (eds.), op. cit. n.46 supra. Senate Minority leader Manfred Ohrenstein is in full agreement on this point. Interview cited n.21 supra.

86. Benjamin, op. cit. n.46 supra, p. 247. See also New York Times, Apr. 12, 1976, p. 57.

87. This was brought out in, e.g., the interviews with Anderson cited n.65 supra; Kremer cited n.61 supra; and Marchi cited n.66 supra.

88. Fink, interview cited n.59 supra.

89. Benjamin, op. cit. n.46 supra, p. 24.

Chapter 8
Carey Wins a Second Term

CAREY's successes in resolving the State and City financial crises and in improving relations with his county chairpeople would have led one to predict that he would cruise to victory in his 1978 reelection race. He **was** reelected; but the ride to this triumph was a surprisingly turbulent one.

In 1974, State Senator Mary Anne Krupsak from Amsterdam, west of Albany, replicated on the Lieutenant Governor level Carey's feat of beating the Party leaders' choice in the September primary. Carey had nothing to do with the Senator's victory; but from the moment of their mutual upsets they were bound together for better or for worse, since in New York the people do not cast separate ballots for Governor and Lieutenant Governor. During the general election race of September and October of 1974 she traveled throughout the north and west of the State where she was better known than he.(1) She could therefore justifiably claim some credit for their easy win over the Malcolm Wilson/Ralph Caso slate; though in that particular contest Carey probably would have come in first had he had a suspected communist as a running mate.

Any camaraderie that they may have developed on the campaign trail was soon dissipated. Part of the reason was institutional; part was due to the personalities of the Governor, the Lieutenant Governor and some of the former's aides. A Lieutenant Governor has few duties under the State Constitution: she acts as Governor while the Chief Executive is out of the State and presides over the State Senate recognizing speakers and making rulings on parliamentary procedure.(2) But her main function is the same as that of the Vice President of the United States: to wait for her "superior" to die or at least suffer from a disabling illness that will force him to resign. Robert McElvaine puts the matter bluntly but accurately in his biography of Mario Cuomo where he says that "Lieutenant governors, like vice presidents, have outlived their usefulness by the time the polls close on election night. Their only real purpose is to be there in case tragedy strikes. As long as it doesn't, they serve no discernable purpose".(3)

Some individuals might be satisfied with this role of sitting around doing not very much of anything but waiting for lightning to strike someone else. But Krupsak was not at all desirous of keeping the Lieutenant Governorship a sinecure. Both would deny it; but in many ways she and Carey are very similar. This is true not only in the superficial sense that both are Democrats and both are Catholics (he Irish, she Polish); but in the more crucial regard that both are brilliant, honest and honorable individuals who want to make this world a better place before they depart. At the time we are talking about, the mid-and late-seventies, both were highly ambitious; but it was an ambition ennobled by a vision of improving society and by a sense that there were limits beyond which one must not compromise one's integrity. She was a graduate of the elite University of Chicago Law School and by the end of 1974 had had "14 years of Albany experience as a lawyer and legislator in both houses...."(4) Also, Carey and most of his aides were ignorant of Albany when they arrived there for his 1975 inauguration.(5) So it was preordained that this "bright, outspoken woman"(6) would be more than willing to give advice to the Governor on what policies to pursue after he had unpacked his bags in the Executive Mansion.

It was almost inevitable, as well, that Carey would not pay much attention to her and that the press would soon be speaking about the "strain" between the two.(7) This "strain" was not produced by ideological differences; though Krupsak labels herself a member of the "reform" wing of the Democratic Party and deems Carey an adherent of its "regular" branch. In fact, she like he believed that state and local governments should not spend money that they did not have and that New York City had been living far beyond its means.(8) But his staff, as has been emphasized throughout, was an extremely talented one; and not only was he thus wont to rely on its members but they, in turn, felt that they knew more than the Lieutenant Governor about the problems faced by the State. This was especially true as the major policy issue of the early Carey years was the impending bankruptcy of New York City; and to solve that crisis required an intimate knowledge of the metropolis, a thorough acquaintance with the world of finance, and many contacts in a Washington, D.C. that had to be convinced to deliver the aid necessary for a rescue. On these particular matters, the Careys, Rohatyns, Burkes and Goldmarks had a leg up on the upstate lawyer-legislator who was now Lieutenant Governor. Moreover, some of her interests were not the Governor's. Reorganizing the bureaucracy to make it more productive was a major concern of hers but Carey did not lose sleep over this problem. Thus he closed his ears to most of her comments on this matter even though he at her request did once listen to a 70-year old lady describe in detail for a full hour how the State's Commerce Department should be restructured.(9) For all these reasons, Krupsak was by and large "frozen out" of the decision making process and took umbrage at this.(10)

The friction between Carey and Krupsak was aggravated by personality problems. Bright and decent both were and are -- but in the 1970s both were also moody and temperamental.(11) Thus sometimes the Governor did not want to listen even to his closest staff, let alone the Lieutenant Governor. And she, when she could not contact him because he was in one of his "blue" moods or because his Secretary Robert Morgado was digging a moat around his chief(12) or for some other reason, was understandably resentful. Some men and women might have been able to shrug off these fits of pique; but in her they accumulated. Thus by early 1978 she was fed up with Carey and some of his staff and knew that she still was being underutilized.(13) At that time, however, his first term was drawing to an end; and so she was faced with an imminent decision as to whether she would run as his loyal adjutant again.

One of the factors that in Spring of 1978 inclined her to stick with the Governor was that just before Christmas of 1977 he had placed a nice present under her Christmas tree in the form of a statement that he wanted her to be his running mate. He called her "an enormous asset" for the Democratic ticket; an endorsement that was made even more attractive by the fact that at the same time he refused to back the antiquated but respected Arthur Levitt for renomination as State Comptroller.(14) Other reasons tempting her to stick with Carey were that her record of accomplishments from 1975 through 1977 was not meager and that he had not been totally unresponsive to her. The budget he had secured for her for fiscal year 1975-76 was, despite the State's fiscal straits, twice as much as had been allotted to Wilson under Nelson Rockefeller and even she admitted that she was satisfied with it.(15) With the extra cash she was able to set up two regional offices -- one in Rochester and one in Harlem. These bureaus, plus her main one in Albany, enabled her to function as an "ombudsman", i.e., an official who makes it her goal to resolve disputes between the ordinary citizen and a governmental unit. Moreover, it was on her initiative that the Chief Executive pushed a set of bills that helped the State's wine industry.(16)

So though she certainly was not a member of the Governor's "inner circle", she had received enough respect from him to make it reasonable for her to opt to share the ticket with him once again. As late as Thursday, June 8, 1978, less than a week before the start of the Democratic State Convention that was planning to renominate them both, she had made up her mind to run with him and had met with members of her staff to discuss how she should coordinate their campaigns.(17) As of that date, he and his people also assumed that she was going to join them: media expert David Garth, for example, had filmed some television and radio commercials in which she had praised him.(18)

Then suddenly turmoil ensued. The Governor was scheduled to give a talk at a June 8th Nassau County, Long Island, Dem-ocratic dinner but could not make it. Krupsak said in her interview with me that Morgado had called asking her to go in the Governor's stead because he was "indisposed".(19) However, her memory might be incorrect on this score, for she told the Nassau guests themselves and the *New York Times* in late June of 1978 that she had been requested to grace the Long Island feast because Carey that same day had to attend two political dinners in Sullivan County in the Catskill Mountains.(20) Also present at the Nassau event was State Commerce Commissioner John Dyson, with whom she had been feuding over which one should get the glory for saving Radio City Music Hall in New York City. Both gave talks: hers was noncontroversial but Dyson's stunned the pro-labor people in the audience. The California electorate, reacting to high real estate taxes, had recently approved a Proposition 13 threatening the provision of social services in the State by strictly limiting the amount that property levies could be raised each year. Dyson felt that the Republicans in New York State were going to push for their own Proposition 13. To steal their thunder he, with the Governor's consent, flew a trial balloon at the Nassau banquet and called for a lid on the number of State employees. When Krupsak heard this proposal she was furious. Not only did the anti-labor tone of his remarks annoy her but she was galled by the fact that

Carey Wins a Second Term

he spoke at all. (According to the Commissioner, he went because he was told that neither the Governor nor the Lieutenant Governor could be present: he maintains her decision to travel to Nassau was a last-minute one that surprised him.(21))

There were other factors that increased her irritation. She was already feeling exhausted when Morgado phoned and this was the first time in quite a while that he had deigned to contact her.(22) At midnight on the 8th she got back to her Manhattan hotel from Nassau feeling even more drained than when she had started out. Her chief of staff then informed her that Carey had attended neither Sullivan County banquet: his aides said that bad weather conditions had made it impossible for him to take a helicopter there. Krupsak boiled over: as seen, she had told her suburban audience that Carey could not honor them with his presence because he was in Sullivan and his passing up the Catskill events made her, she felt, into a liar.(23)

It was now after 1AM Friday morning, June 9th. Morgado, a solid citizen, was snug in his bed in his Albany home. He heard the phone ringing, resisted a natural urge to rip the instrument off its wire, and picked up the receiver. Whom should he hear but an angry Krupsak denouncing Dyson and announcing that she might quit the ticket.(24) The threat amazed him. So Carey campaign manager John Burns was dispatched to talk with her. If anyone could have kept Krupsak in Carey's camp, it was this pleasant upstate liberal. But even he could not prevail, though he made it clear that she was still free to remain on the ticket so she could not contend that she had been shoved off.(25) As a desperation move, the Governor, at the suggestion of Morgado and Garth, phoned her on Sunday, June 11th. She was not impressed by what he said, feeling that he was basically hostile. According to her, he told her that her leaving was an "unstable act" and continued with "'One more time I'm asking you: Will you be my Lieutenant Governor? I want you to be my Lieutenant Governor'. 'No, thank you, sir,' I answered. 'So be it,' he said".(26)

As the State Convention was beginning on Wednesday June 14th, the Governor felt that he had to make a decision on a replacement immediately. Assistant Appointments Officer John Marino urged his chief Judith Hope to beg Carey to select Secretary of State Mario Cuomo. Marino felt that the highly able

The Days of Wine and Roses Are Over

Cuomo could galvanize the large Italian American vote. Somehow Hope got connected with the Chief Executive, who asked her whether she could find any woman who would support a Cuomo selection. She immediately mentioned a few.(27) However, though Hope and Marino may have influenced Carey, the swift pick of Cuomo was really his decision. He had always liked and trusted him. He knew, further, that the Queens lawyer might gain him votes not only among Italians but among liberals and upstaters who otherwise might turn to Krupsak. Thus he was genuinely satisfied with his new partner.(28)

Snubbing Carey was one thing; but running against him was another. The first move did not necessarily demand the second; but a couple of weeks after Krupsak dumped him, she decided to enter the September Democratic gubernatorial primary. She took this step though she had real qualms about it. She knew that most prominent Democrats would oppose her; and she feared that the very fact of her candidacy would give the more conservative Perry Duryea ammunition he could use to sink the Governor in November.(29) Some of her forebodings about the race proved justified. Though Congress Member Bella Abzug and City Council Member Ruth Messinger supported her, most women in the State who were prominent in politics did not. As soon as she quit the ticket, Congress Member Elizabeth Holtzman, New York City Council President Carol Bellamy, Karen Burstein (at the time a Carey appointee to the State's Public Service Commission) and Miriam Bockman, leader of "Tammany Hall" (i.e., the New York County Democratic Party), clustered around the Governor, with Bellamy pointing out that he had a good record of picking women to fill vacancies.(30) Ed Koch, then a very popular Mayor, cheered the Governor on. Even the liberal New Democratic Coalition backed Carey over her -- and she was a member. And this loss shattered her one hope of forging a coalition of upstaters and City progressives.(31)

Moreover, the issue differences just were not there. She began criticizing his support of the proposed express highway on the West Side of Manhattan known as Westway, a pet Carey scheme that was very unpopular among Greenwich Village liberals. But she had never attacked the roadway before she formally jumped off his

Carey Wins a Second Term

ship; and thus her opposition was suspect. On the emotional issues of Medicaid funding for abortions for poor women and the death penalty she was in agreement with him; favoring the first and opposing the second. It was difficult for her to criticize his record, for this included saving the City and, moreover, she had worked **with** him on this and other matters.(32) Her most trenchant and politically-successful thrust at Carey was that he was isolated and aloof.(33) The reason that this charge did not have more impact was that when the Governor began campaigning, he just did not seem "isolated" and "aloof" but projected the image of a warm, humorous man who loved the young, middle-aged and old of all races, colors and creeds.(34) She herself was usually a fine public speaker; but in this campaign she sometimes rambled or did not make much of an attempt to respond to the questions put to her.(35)

Then there was that little matter of money. As an incumbent with a creditable record, the Chief Executive had less trouble raising funds from sources other than brother Ed than he had had in 1974.(36) As of the September primary, he had garnered $1.5 million, of which he had already spent $1.1 million leaving the $400,000 as a kitty to begin his war with Duryea. On the other hand, Krupsak collected less than $100,000, totally inadequate for a statewide race in New York.(37)

There was a third candidate in the Democratic gubernatorial primary -- State Senator Jeremiah Bloom from Brooklyn, he who had backed Carey in his 1974 primary against Samuels. However, he continued to fume after his fellow Brooklynite had failed to give him much support in his unsuccessful 1975 race against Manhattan's Manfred Ohrenstein for the Minority Leadership of the State Senate.(38) Bloom at least differed with Carey on the death penalty question; but his support of the gallows obtained for him a war chest of only $150,000, a sum which was not even enough to enable him to retain his public relations adviser.(39) To compound his problems, on August 10th, the three main New York City newspapers -- the *Times*, the *Post* and the *Daily News* -- went on strike and remained shut through primary day and beyond. This could only benefit the incumbent, who was better known than his challengers (especially Bloom).

The miracle was that as late as August 20th, a few weeks before

The Days of Wine and Roses Are Over

the primary date of September 12th, Krupsak and Carey were almost even in the polls, with Bloom, a terrible campaigner, bringing up the rear.(40) In fact, she had a chance to go ahead if she had been able to outperform him in a series of debates among the three; but she was stiff and he confident and effective.(41) With a television and radio blitz that his opponents were unable to afford, Carey won the primary 52% to 34% for Krupsak and 14% for Bloom. Though she endorsed him immediately, his Republican opponent Perry Duryea had to be heartened by the results. Her one third plus slice of the vote was not only a moral victory for her, considering the odds she had to struggle against; but it also showed how politically vulnerable the individual then occupying the Executive Mansion was. Only 20% of the registered Democrats turned out, also indicating a lack of support for the winner. And Bloom's 14% was quite a bit higher than most observers had expected that he would receive, indicating that Carey's anti-death penalty stance could cause him trouble in November.(42)

Unlike Krupsak, Suffolk County's Duryea started his battle against Carey as the favorite. He should have won that race and had largely himself to blame for his loss. During 1977 the press was full of stories about the Chief Executive's spending too much time in Manhattan bars and restaurants during the wee hours of the morning. Some gossipers went so far as to say that he was drinking excessively and not attending to the State's business. Quite a few politicians and voters were annoyed by his ultimately turning his back on Cuomo in 1977. His opposition to the death penalty did not help.(43) Thus when he began his primary campaign in June, he was a fantastic 28 points down in the polls to Duryea.(44) Moreover, the Long Islander, with his tall stature and his silver hair, looked like a governor.(45) Though the premises of his lobster wholesaling establishment are modest, the enterprise had made him a millionaire. Added to his business success was a record as a legislative leader that he could use to impress various segments of the electorate. Before the Democrats took control of the State Assembly in 1975, he had been its Speaker and had helped force Rockefeller to accept some spending cuts in 1971. In 1970 he had cast the deciding vote in favor of repealing the State's anti-abortion laws.(46) And during the 1975 fiscal crisis, though he as Minority Leader had opposed the creation of the Emergency Financial Control Board and a rise in State taxes, he had lent crucial support in November to the boost in New York City imposts that was a necessary condition of federal aid.

Of course he had some problems at the start of the race. Carey, despite being held in low esteem by the public, had his City/State rescues and marvellous speaking skills. Also, the Minority Leader was relatively unknown outside Long Island at the start of the year. One has to wonder about the common sense of the men in charge of his campaign at that moment. If a politician is not familiar to voters and has a regal appearance, the obvious strategy in this television era is to get him on the tube early and keep him there. So what did the geniuses who headed his effort do? In late Spring they aired some TV clips "showing him playing with his lobsters out in Montauk (which no doubt went down well in, say, Canarsie [an Italian-Jewish neighborhood in Brooklyn])".(47) All Summer he took a siesta: "one upstate paper even ran a cartoon during the summer portraying Duryea as Rip Van Winkle".(48) Meanwhile, Carey was making maximum use of the airwaves during the warm weather spending $1,000,000 on commercials made by David Garth telling the voters every great thing he had done during the past three and a half years.(49)

However, Duryea made his major mistake in October 1978, the month before the election. The Carey campaigners knew that Duryea was considerably richer than their man and figured they could use this fact to their advantage. They did not suspect Duryea of dishonesty; and in fact none was ever revealed. However, they did have a hunch that he was taking advantage of tax loopholes and thus that he was not paying very much in the way of federal and State taxes. They also knew that if this were so, he would not want the electorate to know about it. So they asked that he make his tax returns for the last five years public as Carey was doing.(50) However, he released these documents for 1977 only.

The Governor and his aides were overjoyed at this stone-walling. They made sure that reporters covering the campaign knew about Duryea's refusal and the journalists responded brilliantly, from the Democrats' point of view, by continuing to dog the GOP nominee about it. Instead of "coming clean", he simply became testier on the issue and showed this irritation in the last few of the thirteen television debates between himself and the incumbent, including the final one where the questioner was the acerbic New York City TV commentator Gabe Pressman.(51) The Chief Executive gleefully pointed to one bit of information appearing in the 1977 tax returns. Duryea, with assets between $700,000 and one million, paid significantly **less** in overall federal and State income taxes than did Carey, who had accumulated a much more modest quantity of wealth. The Assemblyman's total federal-State income tax bill was $18,000; that of his less affluent rival was $31,000. Once again, Duryea was simply making use of "tax shelters" afforded by the relevant bits of legislation. But Joe and Jane Doe, the average New Yorker, grumbled at the sight of a rich man claiming that his tax returns were private and handing over fewer dollars to the government than a middle class politician whose financial circumstances were not too different from their own. Many of them, therefore, turned away from him. His tax "problems" (especially the nondisclosure) were probably the main reason he lost.(52)

William Haddad, an employee of Democratic Assembly Speaker Stanley Steingut, also contributed to the Republican's political demise. He got hold of some of his financial records and gave them to the Associated Press wire service and the *New York Post*. The GOP candidate on September 3, 1978 had reported **his own** assets as totalling $731,000. However, in 1976, the "purloined" documents showed, **he and his wife** had had assets of $1 million plus. The story appeared in the middle of October in the *Post* and in upstate papers such as the Albany *Times Union*.(53) The Page One headline in the *Post*, which by this time was on the streets again whereas the *Times* and *Daily News* were still on strike, read "Did Duryea hide assets or not? New $ statement dips by 300G". The banner over the continuation of the article on Page 2 was "Is Duryea hiding his real wealth?".(54) In fact, there **was** nothing illegal about what he was doing, which was for tax purposes to transfer assets to his wife and son who were in lower tax brackets. But the story implied that there was something not quite right about this activity.

The very next day after this scoop, the *Post* had another one that was even more damning to Duryea, albeit topped with a smaller headline. This streamer read "Duryea and the $8M govt. Contract".

(55) The "Haddad Papers" contained information showing that two contractors had become partners in a Duryea real estate investment in the Bahamas "while they were awaiting the results of a bid on the I-8 section of Suffolk County's Southwest Sewer District". (56) This sewer, the article continued, was supposed to cost $291 million but actually was going to come to $1.2 billion, an increase that the federal government was investigating. Moreover, the Republican candidate had secured the passage of a bill by the State Legislature keeping the project alive despite the overrun. Furthermore, the original low bidder had pulled out under rather strange circumstances giving the contract to Duryea's partners, who had orginally come in second.(57) The innuendo of the story was that Duryea had become cosy with people who were swindling the county of which he was a resident.

Both contenders must be lauded for agreeing to a large number of debates at a time during which the print media in an important corner of the State were out of action. It was Garth who wanted as many of these confrontations as possible(58): he figured rightly that the Chief Executive would come out on top in most of them. Duryea himself paid tribute to his opponent's debating skills, noting that he was well spoken and quick with a response.(59) The Governor could shake up an opponent while no rival could rattle him.(60) For example, during an exchange on statewide public television Carey put his tongue in his cheek and asked Duryea how much the State spent per capita in the latter's district. Nonplussed, the Assemblyman asked "school district or Assembly District". The Democrat retorted "either". His rival froze for about 15 seconds. Carey then gave him the answer, and the GOP standard-bearer spent the rest of the show trying to recover.(61) Luck also helped the Chief Executive in these confrontations. For example, one day he was in The Bronx watching the Yankees play in the World Series. He left during the sixth inning to get to Albany in time for another square-off with Duryea. The lawmaker had arrived very early and, when the Governor strode in, he told him he was late. Though he entered after the time the program was scheduled to start, it turned out he was not tardy. The station had decided to stay off the air until the game had ended because it knew that many who wanted to tune in Carey/Duryea would not do so until after the final out had been made.(62)

The Days of Wine and Roses Are Over

Not only was Garth, in charge of the media side of the race while the Governor's son Donald and Morgado controlled its other aspects(63), shrewd in pushing the two candidates to argue on the tube as much as possible; but he also made the best possible use of the money he had available for the incumbent's television effort. Though the Krupsak race oddly enough proved very helpful in the long run to Carey because it forced him to travel throughout the State and address the issues relatively early in the year(64), it left him short of money in mid-September. Thus Garth decided at that moment to hoard his ads for a few weeks even though Duryea was returning to the air to get himself known. When Carey's cache increased his media expert began his ad campaign again which, at least at first, emphasized only the Governor's accomplishments and completely ignored his opponent on the theory that "there's no point in doing a negative commercial about a guy nobody knows".(65) Among the successes paraded was, of course, saving New York in 1975, which later was contrasted with his opponent's votes against the City that year.

The two rivals did not differ greatly on most issues. Both held out hope for additional tax cuts and curbing the increase in State expenditures. Duryea reiterated Krupsak's theme that Carey was aloof.(66) As in the primary, the Governor's campaigning ability helped rebut that charge. And a very clever slogan coined by Mario Cuomo blunted any remaining fallout from it. Early in the Summer he was asked by the press how he could join Carey after he had double crossed him in the mayoral primary. He responded that "I don't think the Governor is much of a politician.... but I think he's a great governor".(67) The Brooklynite blew up when he heard of this comment, telling Garth that Cuomo was out to screw him by saying that he wasn't a good politician. According to the Secretary of State, Garth screamed in response: "You dummy-shut your mouth! This is the line we win with: 'He's a lousy politician, but a great governor'".(68) This catchy phrase, with which Carey soon became infatuated, proved a potent weapon.(69)

The most publicized substantive point on which they split was the death penalty, with Duryea pro and Carey con. Duryea knew that he had "the people" with him on this matter and so harped on the contrast. The Chief Executive and his strategists managed to make the impact of his opposition minimal. He and Cuomo emphasized to voters who believed that bringing back the gallows would reduce crime that both favored life without parole for murderers. His Press Secretary David Murray found for him a passage from Arthur Koestler indicating the futility of capital punishment by describing pickpockets frequenting Tyburn Hill, the locale in London where pickpockets used to be publicly hanged.(70) The same luck that got him to the TV show on time held up in the law 'n order area as well. His aides were terrified that a rash of killings just before election time would focus voters' minds on the electric chair problem; but an epidemic of this sort never materialized.(71)

Often he was able to make his audiences forget about his "soft" position on capital punishment or about his "isolated" personality by the time-honored incumbent's tricks of announcing that this or that federal or state grant had been awarded to the locality where he was speaking and of dedicating this facility here and of gracing that event there. In July he proclaimed that hundreds of thousands of dollars would be given to the Buffalo Zoo to build a tropical rainforest and a visitors' service center. The boon was announced as he was touring the facility, doubtlessly more interested in the potential voters tagging along behind him than in the tigers and elephants. In the heat of August he went to Syracuse to attend the Empire State Games, a mini-Olympics which he and the State Legislature had funded. And TV news during the midst of the press strike showed a "human" Governor with shirtsleeves rolled up stocking a lake in Central Park with catfish and then baiting fishhooks for his younger onlookers.(72) With a resigned shrug, Duryea told me that this aspect of the "incumbency advantage" worked like a charm for his rival.(73)

Only even in the polls two weeks before the race -- albeit in a much better position than he had been in June -- Carey won the November 7, 1978 election fairly easily. His majority was about 330,000, less than half of what it had been in 1974, it is true, but not bad for a man down almost 30 points five months previously. (Translated into percentages, Carey's approximately 2,400,000 votes come to almost 54% while Duryea's 2,033,000 calculate as 46%.) Duryea won each of the suburban counties of Nassau, Suffolk, Westchester and Rockland, doing especially well in his Suffolk homeland. He also took upstate, i.e., the rest of the State outside New York City. But his margin there was small; and did not compensate him for the fact that he was clobbered by more than 2-1 (or by about 440,000 votes) in New York City. Even conservative Staten Island supported his opponent. Cuomo became Lieutenant Governor; while Democrat Bob Abrams became Attorney General. However, the race for State Comptroller produced an upset triumph for Erie County's Edward (Ned) Regan, a Republican who held that office until resigning in 1993.(74)

Right after the election the jubilant Governor announced that he was going to wage a new campaign -- to get his frequent date Anne Ford Uzielli to wed him.(75) Though this race flopped, Anne's dad, auto magnate Henry Ford 2d, was one of the prominent business people giving large chunks of cash to the Carey effort, which in the primary and general together spent about $5 million. In fact about half of that sum came from rich individuals or unions. Duryea raised almost as much but, because of the absence of Rockefeller aid, he relied a lot less on a few "fat cats". (Nelson's banker brother David, however, handed him $25,000.) The list of big Carey donors or creditors included some of those who had lent him a hand in 1974, e.g., the AFL/CIO's VOTE COPE, the International Ladies Garment Workers Union, lawyer William Shea and builder Fred Trump, this time joined by son Donald. Other realtors such as Sigmund Sommer, Harry Helmsley, William Levitt and Lewis Rudin were also generous with their money. Brother Edward Carey provided "only" $75,000.(76)

The election results showed that the City that Carey saved in 1975 rescued him in 1978. However, his keeping New York from default was, as has been stressed, far from his only major policy success. What were these other triumphs?

Notes To Chapter 8

1. Interview with Lieutenant Governor Mary Anne Krupsak, Apr. 3, 1991, Albany, N.Y.

2. New York State Constitution, Art. 4, Sec. 5; Cuomo, Mario - <u>Diaries of Mario M. Cuomo</u> (New York: Random House, 1984), pp. 25-26; <u>New York Times</u>, Feb. 27, 1977, Sec. 4, p. 6.

3. McElvaine, Robert - <u>Mario Cuomo: A Biography</u> (New York: Charles Scribner's Sons, 1988), p. 269.

4. <u>New York Times</u>, Feb. 27, 1977, Sec. 4, p. 6.

5. Interview with Carey's first Secretary David Burke, Aug. 28, 1992, New York City; with Matthew Nimetz, Director of Carey's Transition Council, May 17, 1990, New York City.

6. <u>New York Times</u>, Feb. 27, 1977, Sec. 4, p. 6.

7. <u>New York Times</u>, Jan. 26, 1975, Sec. 1, p. 40.

8. Krupsak, interview cited n.1 <u>supra</u>; <u>New York Times</u>, Jan. 18, 1976, Sec. 1, p. 29.

9. Interview with Carey Executive Assistant Martha Golden, Dec. 5, 1990, Washington; Krupsak, interview cited n.1 <u>supra</u>.

10. Interview with <u>Times Union</u> (Albany) reporter Fred Dicker, June 12, 1991, Albany, N.Y.; Krupsak, interview cited n.1 <u>supra</u>; <u>New York Times</u>, Feb. 27, 1977, Sec. 4, p. 6.

11. Interviewees too many to mention described Carey this way. Purnick, Joyce - <u>Omen III: Now Krupsak, the Mercurial Mystic of '78</u>, <u>Village Voice</u>, July 10, 1978, p. 1 notes on p. 11 that "emotional" and "mercurial" were adjectives frequently applied to his Lieutenant Governor.

12. Krupsak, interview cited n.1 <u>supra</u>.

13. <u>Ibid</u>.

14. <u>New York Times</u>, Dec. 19, 1977, p. 19.

15. Interview cited n.1 <u>supra</u>; <u>New York Times</u>, Jan. 9, 1976, p. 1.

The Days of Wine and Roses Are Over

16. New York Times, Apr. 19, 1977, p. 74.

17. New York Times, June 30, 1978, p. A1.

18. Phone interview with Carey Director of State Operations Thomas Frey, Aug. 9, 1991, Rochester, N.Y.; New York Times, June 13, 1978, p. A1; Staten Island Advance, June 12, 1978, p. 1.

19. Interview cited n.1 supra.

20. New York Times, June 30, 1978, p. A1.

21. Interview with Dyson, Jan. 21, 1991, Millbrook, N.Y. Dyson and Krupsak are friends now. Krupsak, interview cited n.1 supra.

22. Krupsak, interview cited n.1 supra.

23. New York Times, June 30, 1978, p. A1.

24. Ibid.

25. Phone interview with Carey Appointments Officer John Burns, Dec. 30, 1992, Binghamton, N.Y.

26. New York Times, June 30, 1978, p. A13.

27. Interview with Hope, Sept. 25, 1991, East Hampton, N.Y.

28. Frey, interview cited n.18 supra; McElvaine, op. cit. n.3 supra, pp. 264-65.

29. Krupsak, interview cited n.1 supra.

30. Conason, Joe - Runnin' Scared, Village Voice, June 26 1978, p. 3; New York Times, June 13, 1978, p. A1.

31. Krupsak, interview cited n.1 supra; New York Times, July 9, 1978, Sec. 1, p. 1.

32. Purnick, op. cit. n.11 supra, p. 11.

33. Ibid.; New York Times, June 13, 1978, p. A1.

Carey Wins a Second Term

34. See New York Times, Aug. 7, 1978, p. B1.

35. Purnick, op. cit. n.11 supra, p. 11.

36. Interview with Carey's 1978 Reelection Campaign Treasurer Arthur Emil, Nov. 12, 1991, New York City.

37. Staten Island Advance, Sept. 13, 1978, p. 1.

38. Newsday, Nov. 8, 1978, p. 19.

39. New York Times, Aug. 9, 1978, p. B3; Staten Island Advance, Sept. 13, 1978, p. 1.

40. Purnick, op. cit. n.11 supra, p. 12; Staten Island Advance, Aug. 20, 1978, Sec. 1, p. 2; Sept. 10, 1978, p. E2.

41. Staten Island Advance, Aug. 20, 1978, Sec. 1, p. 2.

42. Staten Island Advance, Sept. 13, 1978, p. 1.

43. New York Times, Aug. 26, 1977, p. A1; Oct. 31, 1977, p. A1; Newsday, Nov. 10, 1977, p. 6.

44. Cuomo, op. cit. n.2 supra, p. 25.

45. Wall St. Journal, Oct. 20, 1978, p. 1, makes this point.

46. Stokes, Geoffrey - Duryea in Distress, Village Voice, Oct. 23, 1978, p. 1, 31; New York Times, Apr. 13, 1971, p. 43; Newsday, Oct. 17, 1978, p. 6.

47. Purnick, Joyce - How To Spot a Republican in Trouble, Village Voice, Sept. 25, 1978, p. 38.

48. Ibid.

49. Ibid.

50. Interview with Carey Deputy Appointments Officer William Cunningham, Dec. 30, 1991, Albany, N.Y.; with Carey Press Secretary David Murray, July 23, 1991, Albany, N.Y.

The Days of Wine and Roses Are Over

51. Murray, interview cited n.50 supra; interview with Carey Press Secretary Michael Patterson, Sept. 20, 1991, Northport, N.Y.

52. New York Times, Nov. 8, 1978, p. A1.

53. Times Union (Albany) Oct. 13, 1978, p. 3; New York Post, Oct. 12, 1978, p. 1.

54. New York Post, Oct. 12, 1978, p. 1, 2.

55. New York Post, Oct. 13, 1978, p. 1.

56. Ibid.

57. Ibid. See also Staten Island Advance, Oct. 14, 1978, p. 1.

58. Cunningham, interview cited n.50 supra; Patterson, interview cited n.51 supra.

59. Interview with Perry Duryea, June 26, 1990, Montauk, N.Y.

60. Cunningham, interview cited n.50 supra.

61. Ibid.

62. Ibid.

63. Burns, interview cited n.25 supra; interview with Carey Assistant Appointments Officer John Marino, Nov. 8, 1991, New York City; Murray, interview cited n.50 supra; Newsday, Nov. 8, 1978, p. 19.

64. Frey, interview cited n.18 supra; Krupsak, interview cited n.1 supra; Newsday, Nov. 8, 1978, p. 19.

65. New York Post, Nov. 8, 1978, p. 19.

66. Wall St. Journal, Oct. 20, 1978, p. 1.

67. McElvaine, op. cit. n.3 supra, pp. 266-67.

68. Ibid., p. 267.

69. Ibid.

Carey Wins a Second Term

70. Murray, interview cited n.50 supra.

71. Cunningham, interview cited n.50 supra.

72. Public Papers of Governor Hugh L. Carey 1978 (Albany: State of New York Executive Chamber, 1988), p. 1591, pp. 1593-94; Ransone, Coleman - The American Governorship (Westport, Ct.: Greenwood Press, 1982), p. 58.

73. Interview cited n.59 supra.

74. All these statistics come from New York Times, Nov. 9, 1978, p. B6.

75. Ibid., p. B4.

76. New York Times, Dec. 26, 1978, p. B1.

Chapter 9
Economic Development in the Carey Years

WHEN Carey became Governor in 1975, his first task obviously had to be to stanch the financial collapse of the State and City. But his victories here would have been in vain had they not been followed by measures designed to get the State's economy moving again. The problems faced by that economy when he moved to Albany are vividly depicted by Sarah Liebschutz. In the 1970s, when the United States population was growing, the Empire State's shrank from over 18 million to 17.6 million. "Its per capita personal income declined from 113 percent of the national average to 109 percent. And New York State's share of the nation's jobs slipped from 11% in 1963 to 7.7% in 1978."(1) It was "the only state to experience a net loss of jobs in the private sector during the decade of the 1970's"(2) -- 146,000 of these, in fact.(3) Carey's program to reverse these trends had three primary components: "[reductions in] taxes, [improvements in] infrastructure, and [encouragement of] high technology".(4) This Chapter will, accordingly, concentrate on his tax cuts, large scale building schemes, and programs to further the development of advanced technology.

To help resolve the fiscal crisis, he had, as seen, finally convinced the Legislature to pass a $600,000,000 **hike** in business taxes in December, 1975 to close a State budget deficit. However John Dyson, who had been his Agriculture Commissioner in 1975 and was made Commerce Commissioner in early 1976, began publicly taking up the cudgels on behalf of serious State tax cuts as early as February of 1976. He pointed out that New York companies, while not having to pay a high corporate tax, were confronted with big local property levies. More importantly, he went on, neighboring Connecticut and New Jersey had no personal income tax while New York had a graduated income tax with (relatively) high rates on the very rich. Consequently wealthy business people were moving out of the State and taking their firms with them after they got tired of commuting.(5) This view that hefty personal income taxes imposed on the prosperous drove entrepeneurs out of New York and were thus detrimental to its economic health became an article of faith with his chief.(6)

In January, 1977, acting in accordance with this new phil-osophy, Carey proposed, and the Legislature accepted, a $225 million reduction in the personal income tax. This was accom-plished by repealing a 2.5% surcharge, having the 15% maximum tax start at $30,000 of taxable income rather than $25,000 as had previously been the case, and by giving some tax breaks to households with an income of less than $20,000.(7) In a March, 1977 speech to the Empire State Chamber of Commerce, a major business interest group, he defended these steps by pointing out that he had listened to leaders of commerce and industry about how to jumpstart the State's economy and had heard most frequently a recommendation to "cut taxes".(8) "And what taxes? The one most often cited - not just by the individual on the street, but by business and industry leaders, was the personal income tax. We can't attract or hold the vital middle-level executive, you told us....The burden on the individual citizen in our State is the highest in the nation. That had to change we were told."(9) The 1977 decrease was followed by slashes in 1978, 1979 and 1981. In 1982, his last year in office, the lame duck Chief Executive was confronted with the prospect of a mammoth State deficit and thus did not urge new tax relief. Overall, as a result of his cuts companies and individuals had to pay $7.2 billion less in taxes from fiscal 1978 through fiscal 1983 than they would have had the reductions never found their way into the statute books.(10)

There is no huge public works project associated with Carey's name in the way that the State University of New York and the Albany Mall are linked to Nelson Rockefeller. However, a sizeable City University of New York can, as seen, be considered a magnificent tangible memento of his tenure in office even though his forcing the imposition of tuition there caused a lot of anger; and there are several major developments in New York City that were begun or largely completed when he was Governor due in part to the initiatives of himself and his aides. These were or are being constructed with the assistance of the same Urban Development Corporation (UDC -- now called Empire State Development Corp-oration) whose financial troubles in 1975 caused him so much pain and suffering and which he bailed out later that year.

After that rescue, the Corporation was quietly allowed to finish its ongoing residential projects and ended up building 33,000 units housing 150,000 persons throughout the State.(11) One would think, though, that it would have been put to sleep once the last nail was hammered into the last plank of its last housing scheme.

The number of its employees had declined from a high of 550 to 175 by 1978.(12) The remaining staff was demoralized. It was clear that a financially strapped State would not let it continue with its traditional role of erecting inexpensive residential housing no matter how much this was needed; and so at this time it had its fingers in only five projects.(13) However, it was still exempt from local zoning laws, building codes and taxes.(14) Thus structures built on its land could be erected quickly and cheaply: zoning laws and building codes often add significantly to the cost of a project and slow it up. Therefore, if it would construct, e.g., hotels, shopping centers, industrial parks and office buildings on land that it was able to acquire by condemnation, it could rent these at low rates to private or public concerns. These lessees would employ people directly. And these men and women plus the tourists and shoppers some of the new facilities would attract would spend money in the area, which in turn would lead to further job creation.

By 1977 UDC participation in a project to expand a Chrysler plant in DeWitt in upstate New York had been approved.(15) About this time, the Radio City Music Hall in Rockefeller Center in mid-Manhattan was in serious financial difficulties and there was a real fear that this world-renowned tourist attraction featuring the "Radio City Rockettes" would have to shut its doors. People were becoming unwilling to take the subway to reach it and parking in the area was expensive. Also the first-run films that it alternated with its vaudeville acts could no longer be shown by it exclusively: Hollywood studio executives insisted that they be exhibited simultaneously throughout the metropolitan area.(16) Dyson had pledged the State to keeping the Music Hall open through the use of the UDC. Carey Secretary Robert Morgado was initially not overly-happy about the idea but in the last analysis had no alternative but to allow the agency to manage the Hall temporarily and to bear $1.8 million of its short-term operating losses. Upon the recommendation of New York real estate lawyer Charles Goldstein, Morgado and Carey picked 32-year old Richard Kahan to run Radio City on its behalf. Kahan had worked for the Corporation in 1971; then had been employed by real estate developer Samuel Lefrak; but had returned to his old haunts in 1976. Despite his affiliation with the UDC, he had never met Carey or Morgado or been involved in party politics.(17) He turned out to be one of the

The Days of Wine and Roses Are Over

Governor's many outstanding appointees. Under the UDC/Kahan aegis, the Music Hall revived its fortunes to such an extent that Rockefeller Center agreed in September, 1978 to operate it again. This success had two consequences. First, Kahan was named that month to be President of the UDC (which also has a Chairman, who is less involved in its day-to-day activities). Second, it made Morgado and through him Carey more aware of how effective a tool of economic development that agency could be.(18)

A Rockefeller creation even more moribund than the UDC during the early Carey years was the Battery Park City Authority (BPCA). This had been founded in 1968 to supervise a multibillion housing and office development on landfill stretching a mile north of Battery Park in lower Manhattan. The Hudson River piers that used to dot the area were then decaying and unused; and the dirt comprising the landfill was a residue of the construction of the World Trade Center Towers nearby. By 1978 the site was still barren. The reasons for this included a glut of office space in Manhattan that surfaced as early as 1973 and the recession of 1974-75, both of which made people leery of erecting more commercial skyscrapers. In addition, Rockefeller and John Lindsay, Mayor of New York when the project was announced and through 1973, feuded not only politically but also over its architecture.(19) Everyone wanted something done about the acres of wasteland controlled by the Authority but paralysis prevailed.

Enter now Kahan and the Urban Development Corporation. Morgado suggested to him that Battery Park City be made its responsibility. This would be done, in the first place, by the UDC's taking title to the land from the City through the power of condemnation that it still retained from the Rockefeller days.(20) Second, in early 1979, Carey appointed Chairman (not President) William Hassett of the UDC to be Chairman of the BPCA as well in place of Rockefeller aide Charles Urstadt. Hassett then named Kahan President of the BPCA as well as of the UDC. With the same President and Chairman, the BPCA became, in essence, a unit of the UDC.(21)

Kahan began moving immediately to resolving the Battery Park City impasse. He had to quickly present some sort of document to

Economic Development in the Carey Years

the Legislature and Governor in order to convince them to appropriate funds to avoid default in 1980 on $200 million in bonds the BPCA had issued in 1972.(22) (A failure to satisfy these obligations was imminent because the Authority was custodian of property which was not producing any revenue). He and others were very dissatisfied with the original design for Battery Park City, which isolated it from the rest of Manhattan. So he hired the architectural firm of Cooper and Eckstut to produce a new plan within 90 days: he had read firm partner Alexander Cooper's views on urban design and liked his thesis that new developments should have regular streets, not (as originally proposed for the project) simply pedestrian skyways.(23) Cooper and Eckstut drafted a blueprint that accorded with the former's philosophy of urban planning; Carey, Kahan, City Planning Commission Chairman Robert Wagner Jr. and Mayor Ed Koch were all smitten with it; and so a consensus developed at the end of 1979 that the UDC and BPCA should transform it into reality.(24) The Chief Executive and the lawmakers came through with the money in time to avert default on the bonds.(25)

Kahan felt that the commercial part of the "new town" should be completed first. He asked various major contracting companies to bid to handle this part of the construction. The Canadian firm of Olympia and York was the winner: the reason it was selected was that it promised to erect the entire business precinct and to do so quickly and pledged a bundle of its assets in case it failed to keep its word. Losers were Kahan's old Lefrak firm and the realtor Arthur Emil, Carey's fundraising chairman in the 1978 gubernatorial election and a major contributor to the Governor. Olympia and York kept its word and did its job swiftly and well. It made money on this particular venture; though later it got into deep financial trouble because of unremunerative efforts such as Canary Wharf in London.(26)

The Olympia and York plot is in the north part of Battery Park City and the residential community is in its south. The office buildings are across West Street from the World Trade Center: they were placed there at Kahan's insistence because he believed that their proximity to the Twin Towers would make them more appealing to potential business tenants.(27) The commercial com-

The Days of Wine and Roses Are Over

plex consists mainly of four handsome office skyscrapers and a "winter garden" with stores and restaurants. About 5000 people live in the residential area; and more apartments and cooperatives are planned for the development's northern tip. Battery Park City has become a place where its inhabitants, other New Yorkers, suburbanites and tourists can come to enjoy the view of the Hudson, eat in pleasant bistros, and browse in interesting shops. It even has regular streets and just a few pedestrian skyways -- and, to boot, a new building housing Stuyvesant High School, one of the best public schools in the nation.(28)

Every major city and resort community in the United States wants to attract conventions and trade shows. For many years, the only place for trade fairs of this sort in New York City was the small Coliseum at 59th Street and Eighth Avenue. Meanwhile, municipalities like Chicago had erected modern and large convention halls for the makers and wholesalers of goods to display them to potential buyers. As a result, New York started to lose convention business during the late 1960s and early 1970s despite the fact that its night and cultural life was far superior to that of any other jurisdiction in the nation. It was obvious to State and City political leaders even before Carey took office that an exposition hall adequate to the demands of the late twentieth century had to be built in Manhattan. The State Legislature had even formed a corporation to erect one on the West Side waterfront at 44th Street. However, the 1975 fiscal crisis forced the City to back away from this project.(29)

In 1978 Carey and Koch agreed on a plan to build a convention center on a 25 acre site on West 34th Street between 11th and 12th Avenues, a location which included an unused Penn Central rail yard.(30) This was ten blocks south of the original location: the new choice was justified on the ground that it was cheaper, "further away from the residential Clinton area, and eliminated...an expensive over-the-river platform".(31) Wayne Barrett contends that one big reason for the switch was that Donald Trump, the New York City realtor who had become a major contributor to Carey, owned the 34th Street Penn Central Yards and had hired Mrs. Louise Sunshine, Finance Director of the ex-Congressman's 1974 and 1978 campaigns, to lobby with the Legislature to have the center placed there.(32) However, Barrett himself admits that there at one time had been opposition to the center from some Clinton residents and that the 34th Street locale was no worse than the others proposed.(33) The Governor tried in 1978 to get the Legislature to approve the 34th Street arrangement but could not get the proposal through the Republican State Senate, which was leery of spending $257 million on an edifice that would not benefit their upstate/suburban constitutents.(34)

In early 1979, though, he and Koch won the lawmakers over. Some believe, as seen, that the quid for this quo was his backing of State aid for the stadium in upstate Syracuse(35), even though Hassett and Carey Director of Policy and Management Michael Del Giudice deny this.(36) The act providing for the construction of the 34th Street exposition hall gave the UDC $45 million for site acquisition and planning and authorized the Triborough Bridge and Tunnel Authority to issue $375 million in bonds to finance what is now called the Jacob Javits Convention Center.(37) Note, of course, the jump of over $100 million in estimated costs in just a year: by the time it was completed during the Cuomo years in 1986 two years behind schedule, the State had spent a total of $486 million to erect it.(38) However, despite extensive inefficiency and corruption in its operations, it is now breaking even.(39)

The Times Square area of New York City (centered around 42nd Street and Broadway) needs major improvements. There are fewer pornographic bookstores and movie houses then there were in the late 1970s but menacing characters, drunks and con artists still roam these streets that border the country's most extensive legitimate theater district. The hundreds of thousands who rush through it every day on business or pleasure may be unaware that it is the object of a rehabilitation project inching along under the aegis of the UDC and first approved while Carey was still Governor and Koch was still Mayor.(40) Delayed by lawsuits brought by persons opposing the blueprint and by the recession that hit the City in the late 1980s and early 1990s, no new construction has begun yet (though renovations have commenced) and, in fact, the UDC did not start tearing down buildings until 1990.(41)

The first major segment of the Times Square renewal was supposed to have been four tall office towers located at 42nd and

Broadway.(42) However, three of the quartet have been put on hold for an indefinite period. They certainly would not have attracted many tenants during the early 1990s: even now there is a glut of office space in the neighborhood.(43) Many go as far as to contend that four towers (as opposed to just one or two) would not improve the area's current state. They lament that the 42nd Street they would dominate would be sterile, cold and homogeneous whereas, for all its crime and grime, the crossroads is now vital, diverse and attractively boisterous. Also, the tax abatements that would be granted their builders would cost the state a lot of revenue.(44) Thus the Times Square redevelopment may even in the long run simply emphasize the improvement of existing shops and theaters, some of which are now boarded up.(45) Some structures will be left as playhouses or cinemas; others will be converted into restaurants, jazz and supper clubs, intimate bars, souvenir shops, newsstands, music and book stores and other enterprises attractive to tourists. Walt Disney Enterprises plans to transform a porn palace into a theater that features Mickey and Minnie Mouse and other family entertainment; and will be a partner in a hotel, retail and entertainment complex scheduled for the seedy intersection of 42nd Street and Eighth Avenue. Madame Tussaud's may replicate its famous London wax museum on 42nd Street. A burlesque house has been reopened as a performing arts center for children.(46) Exactly how Times Square will look in a decade or so is unclear; but certainly it will be more appealing than the rot that prevailed at the time that Carey, Koch and Kahan formally decided to have the UDC give it a facelift.

It has become axiomatic that one magic wand for economic health in a jurisdiction is the burgeoning of "high technology". It was in the last year of Carey's first term and during his second four years that New York State finally followed the lead of jurisdictions such as Massachusetts and North Carolina and moved to incubate or speed the growth of high tech firms within its borders. A task force recommended to him the rejuvenation of the New York State Science and Technology Foundation (NYSSTF, now merged into the State Economic Development Department), a public body created in 1963 while Rockefeller was still Governor.(47) This had been devoting most of its efforts (which were not very energetic) to subsidizing pure research in academia.(48) Under legislation enacted in 1981(49) its mission was expanded to cover "technology transfer"; i.e., encouraging companies located in New York State to develop commercial uses for and market the innovations that were being developed in laboratories in the State and elsewhere.(50) It was mandated to obtain funds from public and private sources to carry out its duties of supporting basic research and stimulating the conversion of the findings to practical use.(51) In addition, the Program Office of State Assembly Speaker Stanley Fink convinced him of the need to establish "Centers for Advanced Technology" (CATs) at various universities in the State.(52) The idea was that these Centers would bring academics and private entrepeneurs into partnerships to develop, make and sell high technology products.

The CAT bill became law in 1982. This measure allowed the NYSSTF to designate several universities as Centers for Advanced Technology. Each Center does research for small high-tech firms that lack significant research and development capacity themselves. The firms and faculty then work together to convert laboratory findings into marketable products. Perhaps for political reasons, the CATs (the number varies) are scattered throughout the State. For example, Cornell is the CAT for agricultural biotechnology; SUNY Stony Brook for medical biotechnology; SUNY Buffalo for medical instruments; Syracuse for computer applications and software; and Rochester University for optical technology. A building at Rensselaer Polytechnic Institute houses the CAT for Automation and Robotics.(53) The Centers get some of their funding from the NYSSTF: an award from this source usually is matched by a grant from the private sector. Quite a few enterprises springing from CAT activities show promise. Thus computer firms spun off from the former Columbia information technology CAT employed 500 persons in 1992, 200 in New York.(54) (It is, admittedly, difficult to determine how much these 200 jobs cost the taxpayers.) The Stony Brook Center has helped create quite a few biotechnology enterprises in Long Island, which *in toto* have 3000 employees. For example, Curative Tech-nologies, located near the Stony Brook Campus, operates wound treatment centers as collaborative ventures with hospitals.(55)

One step taken by the NYSSTF was to establish a subsidiary known as the Corporation for Innovation Development(CID). This unit makes investments in and loans to small high tech firms in the State that cannot obtain from the private sector as much capital as they need. As early as 1985 it had stakes in 14 companies: by 1989 this number had increased to 37. One of these firms produced hardware that permitted industrial robots to carry out more tasks; a second developed a system to send X-Rays and other medical images over telephone lines; while a third invented software to speed up and make more reliable the laboratory analysis of certain scientific data. The CID, proposed in Carey's 1981 economic message to the Legislature, has received funding from the federal government as well as from the State. The firms that it assists will repay their debt to it when they are able to do so; and in addition it profits from increases in the equity it holds in them. It has, therefore, a continuing pool of money to use to subsidize new firms.(56)

CID's big hope is a company known as Regeneron Pharmaceuticals, located on a handsome campus-like setting in Tarrytown, Westchester County. The Corporation put $250,000 into it in 1988: this was very helpful in convincing it to stay in New York rather than cross the river to New Jersey. The State's backing also was influential in persuading a large Japanese pharmaceutical concern, Sumitomo, to place $10 million of its own money in the Tarrytown firm. Amgen, a major California biotech enterprise, provided it with an additional $15 million stake.(57) It is working to develop "neurotrophic agents", protein molecules that will promote the growth of nerve cells. It is hoped that these pharmaceuticals will prove useful in the treatment of degenerative maladies such as Alzheimer's, Parkinson's and Lou Gehrig's (A.L.S.) disease as well as of neurological disorders produced by diabetes. Shares in Regeneron have been marketed over the counter since 1991. Its research has not yet resulted in any sales, though clinical trials are continuing. Thus, like most biotech ventures, it is still in the red. However, it could be a big money maker and a major New York employer in future years; and has gone from four employees to

Economic Development in the Carey Years

about 200. It is erecting its major manufacturing facility in the upstate town of Rensselaer, with the UDC and the State's Job Development Authority providing the financing. And part of its Westchester plant was built by Clean Room Technology of Syracuse, another CID investment.(58)

Ironically, in the development field as in other areas of life one can be successful at times thinking little rather than big. New York during the Carey years provides an excellent example. In 1977 an employee of the State's Commerce Department asked designer Milton Glaser to produce a logo that could be publicized to attract tourists to the State. Glaser sketched out the slogan "I Love NY"(59) -- "Love" not being written out but implied by the picture of a red heart. The employee and his superiors, including Dyson, were quick to see the potential in the new catchphrase and used it to lure business as well as sightseers. The Department calculated that between 1977 and 1982 revenues from tourism attributable to the "I Love NY" campaign were over $3 billion while publicizing the slogan cost the State only about $50 million. To save money, the State halted the "I Love..." ads in the early 1990s but has now resuscitated them.(60) And as everyone knows, variations on them are seen everywhere in the world -- e.g., "I Love Soweto" (a South African ghetto) or "J'aime fromage" (cheese). But these versions surely do not hurt New York. Rather, when an American sees one in Canada, London or Zambia, the phrase "New York" is like to spring to his/her mind, as he/she may well be aware that "I Love NY" is the mother of all these boasts.

Notes To Chapter 9

1. Liebschutz, Sarah - Economic Development Policy in the State, at p. 267, 268 of Colby, Peter (ed.) - New York State Today:Politics, Government, Public Policy (Albany: SUNY Press, 1985).

2. Ibid.

3. Ibid.

4. Ibid., p. 273.

5. New York Times, Feb. 2, 1976, p. 1. Both Connecticut and New Jersey now have an income tax.

6. Interview with Carey's second Commerce Commissioner William Hassett, Sept. 26, 1990, New York City; with his Office of Development Planning head Hugh O'Neill, June 17, 1992, New York City.

7. Public Papers of Governor Hugh L. Carey 1976 (Albany: State of New York Executive Chamber, 1986), pp. 37-38, p. 1139; Public Papers of Governor Hugh L. Carey 1978 (Albany: State of New York Executive Chamber, 1988), p. 43.

8. Public Papers of Governor Hugh L. Carey 1977 (Albany: State of New York Executive Chamber, 1987), p. 805.

9. Ibid.

10. Public Papers of Governor Hugh L. Carey 1979 (Albany: State of New York Executive Chamber, 1992), p. 49, pp. 865-66; Broome, Paul - The Carey Years: 1975-1982, Empire State Report, July 1982, p. 9, pp. 9-10.

11. New York Times, Feb. 25, 1979, Sec. 8, p. 1.

12. Ibid.

13. Interview with Carey UDC/Battery Park City Authority President Richard Kahan, Nov. 21, 1990, New York City.

14. New York Times, Dec. 7, 1977, p. B12; Feb. 25, 1979, Sec. 8, p. 1.

15. Letter dated Apr. 7, 1978 from acting UDC Chairman William Hassett to Commerce Commissioner John Dyson, Hugh L. Carey Collection, St.

Economic Development in the Carey Years

John's Univ.(NY), Housing (Urban Development Corporation) file.

16. Interview with Rockefeller Center President (and former Rockefeller Secretary) Alton Marshall, Mar. 23, 1993, New York City.

17. Kahan, interview cited n.13 supra; letter from Dyson to Hassett dated April 11, 1978, Hugh L. Carey Collection, St. John's Univ.(NY), Housing (Urban Development Corporation) file; Hassett, op. cit. n.15 supra; Carey, (1978) op. cit. n.7 supra, p. 1323; Gill, Brendan - The Skyline: Battery Park City, New Yorker, Aug. 20, 1990, p. 69, 78.

18. Kahan, interview cited n.13 supra; Marshall, interview cited n.16 supra; Carey (1978) op. cit. n.7 supra, p. 1323.

19. Gill, op. cit. n.17 supra, p.72; New York Times, Dec. 9, 1979, Sec. 2, p. 39.

20. Kahan, interview cited n.13 supra.

21. Gill, op. cit. n.17 supra, p. 72.

22. New York Times, Nov. 9, 1979, p. B1.

23. Ibid.; Gill, op. cit. n.17 supra, pp. 74-75.

24. Gill, op. cit. n.17 supra, p. 74.

25. See New York State Laws of 1980, Ch. 50, p. 254.

26. Hassett, interview cited n.6 supra; Kahan, interview cited n.13 supra; O'Neill, interview cited n.6 supra; New York Times, Dec. 1, 1986, p. D1; Mar. 28, 1992, p. 38.

27. Kahan, interview cited n.13 supra.

28. New York Times, May 24, 1981, Sec. 2, p. 25; Dec. 26, 1993, Sec. 10, p. 3; Sept. 4, 1994, Sec. 9, p. 1.

29. Barrett, Wayne - Donald Trump Cuts the Cards, Village Voice, Jan. 22, 1979, p. 1, 24; Staten Island Advance, Nov. 27, 1977, Sec. 1, p. 8.

30. Carey (1978) op. cit. n.7 supra, pp. 1302-04.

The Days of Wine and Roses Are Over

31. Ibid.

32. Barrett, op. cit. n.29 supra, pp. 24-25. Sunshine had good contacts with prominent Democratic legislators. Ibid., p. 24.

33. Ibid., p. 25.

34. See New York Times, July 19, 1978, p. 22.

35. See New York Times, Mar. 4, 1979, p. A1.

36. Interview with Del Giudice, June 28, 1994, New York City; Hassett, interview cited n.6 supra. The stadium was built with the aid of the UDC. New York Times, Jan. 28, 1981, p. B1.

37. Carey, op. cit. n.10 supra, pp. 135-36.

38. New York Times, Apr. 4, 1986, p. B3.

39. New York Times, Mar. 19, 1995, Sec. 1, p. 1.

40. New York Times, Apr. 6, 1982, p. B3; Newsday, Nov. 19, 1990, p. 12.

41. New York Times, June 24, 1990, Sec. 10, p. 1; May 18, 1994, p. B1; Newsday, Nov. 19, 1990, p. 12.

42. Newsday, Apr. 22, 1991, p. 31.

43. Ibid; New York Times, Aug. 3, 1992, p. A1; Aug. 10, 1992, p. B3; May 18, 1996, p. 21.

44. See New York Times, Aug. 6, 1992, p. C15; July 20, 1994, p. B3.

45. New York Times, Aug. 3, 1992, p. A1.

46. New York Times, Aug. 3, 1992, p. A1; June 27, 1993, Sec. 10, p. 1; May 18, 1994, p. B1; Dec. 15, 1994, p. A29; Feb. 17, 1995, p. 1; May 12, 1995, p. B1; July 16, 1995, Sec. 1, p. 25; Dec. 11, 1995, p. A1. By 1981 the UDC was assisting dozens of commercial projects. It was, e.g., renovating hotels in Albany and Syracuse and an electronics manufacturing plant in Yonkers. See New York State Laws of 1981, Ch. 1041; Liebschutz, op. cit. n.1 supra, pp. 274-76.

Economic Development in the Carey Years

47. Schoolman, Morton - Solving the Dilemma of Statesmanship: Reindustrialization Through an Evolving Democratic Plan, at p. 3, 21 of Schoolman, Morton and Magid, Alvin (eds.) - Reindustrializing New York State (Albany: SUNY Press, 1986).

48. Interview with H. Graham Jones, Director, New York State Science and Technology Foundation, July 28, 1992, Albany, N.Y.; Black, Michael and Worthington, Richard - The Center For Industrial Innovation at RPI: Critical Reflections on New York's Economic Recovery, at p. 257, 260 of Schoolman and Magid (eds.), op. cit. n.47 supra.

49. New York State Laws of 1981, Ch. 197.

50. O'Neill, interview cited n.6 supra; New York State Science and Technology Foundation - 1984-85 Annual Report (Albany: NYSSTF, 1985), inside front cover.

51. NYSSTF, op. cit. n.50 supra, inside front cover.

52. Black and Worthington, op. cit. n.48 supra, p. 261.

53. Interview with Dr. Lester A. Gerhardt, Associate Dean, RPI School of Engineering, Oct. 15, 1993, Troy, N.Y.; New York State Science and Technology Foundation - 1986-87 Annual Report (Albany: NYSSTF, n.d.); Schoolman, op. cit. n.47 supra, pp. 23-24; New York Times, May 15, 1993, p. 23.

54. New York Times, Sept. 17, 1992, p. B3.

55. Forbes, May 11, 1992, pp. 186ff; New York Times, Apr. 26, 1992, Sec. 10, p. 9; Dec. 15, 1993, p. A1.

56. Corporation for Innovation Development Program - 1985 Report (Albany: NYSSTF, 1985), p. 1; NYSSTF, op. cit. n.50 supra, p. 10; Carey, Hugh - State Policy and New Enterprise Development, at p. 301, 303 of Friedman, Robert and Schweke, William (eds.) - Expanding the Opportunity to Produce: Revitalizing the American Economy Through New Enterprise Development (Washington: The Corporation For Enterprise Development, 1981); New York Post, Mar. 21, 1989, p. 38.

57. NYSSTF - Opportunity NY, June 1989, p. 8; Wall St. Journal, Sept. 6, 1990, p. B8.

58. New York Post, Mar. 21, 1989, p. 38; New York Times, Apr. 1, 1992, p. D10; June 24, 1994, p. D5; Wall St. Journal, June 27, 1995, p. B3. A good deal of the information in this paragraph was provided me by Richard Bonamo, Regeneron's former Directo of Facilities, whom I interviewed in Tarrytown, N.Y. on Sept. 24, 1993.

59. New York Times, Feb. 3, 1995, p. B11.

60. Interview with Carey Commerce Commissioner John Dyson, Jan. 21, 1991, Millbrook, N.Y.; Blossom, Laurel - Selling the State, Empire State Report, June 1985, p. 16, 17; New York Times, July 28, 1991, Sec. 4, p. 16; May 13, 1993, p. B1; Staten Island Advance, Jan. 9, 1993, p. A8.

Chapter 10
Carey and Ravitch Fix the Subways:
Transportation Initiatives During
the Carey Years

ECONOMIC development in a jurisdiction without a good system of transportation is futile. Bringing tourists and jobs into a state without giving them a means of getting from hotel to attraction or from home to job will soon drive both visitors and employees to other locales. But the Carey Administration cannot be accused of neglecting New York State's travel arteries. The New York City and suburban transportation systems owe much to his years in office. As anyone who rides the City subways, Metro-North (formerly Penn Central and then Conrail) or the Long Island Railroad knows, these networks still have their flaws. But older readers may remember the state of affairs in 1975 when Carey was sworn in: graffiti-covered subways and buses and frequent breakdowns and delays on subways and Metro-North due to antiquated rolling stock and poor track.(1) The situation got worse for the first several years of his tenure. Then, steps were taken that laid the seeds for the transformation of these networks from utter disasters to adequate means of getting around.

In the way of background, the Metropolitan Transportation Authority (MTA) is a regional body sent up during the Rockefeller years to supervise the activities of the many agencies in the New York City area responsible for transportation. On its board now sit 17 persons. Five of these and the Chair are appointed by the Governor alone; four by him on the recommendation of the New York City Mayor; and seven by him on the recommendation of various suburban public officials.(2) All these picks must be approved by the State Senate. Though it has no jurisdiction over the interstate (New York plus New Jersey) Port Authority, it is ultimately responsible for the New York City Transit Authority (TA) and the TA's buses and subways; the Long Island Railroad (LIRR); the Metro-North commuter lines; and the Triborough Bridge and Tunnel Authority (TBTA) (collecting tolls and maintaining not only the Triborough Bridge but, e.g., the Queens-Midtown Tunnel and the Bronx-Whitestone and Verrazano Bridges).

For a long time it was the politically popular course of action for the State's gubernatorial candidates and New York City's mayoral hopefuls to call for keeping the lid on subway and bus fares in the

The Days of Wine and Roses Are Over

metropolis. Carey when he ran for Governor in 1974 was but following a tried and true course of action when he pledged to hold the rate at its then-current level, i.e., $.35. Unfortunately, the country and the metropolitan area were at the time suffering from a dose of both inflation and recession. As a consequence, the costs of running the TA's fleet were increasing while ridership was declining.(3) This network itself was in terrible physical shape, partly because thanks to a generous offer by the City, many talented bus and subway repairpersons had retired early.(4) Moreover, the low fare made it difficult for the MTA to lay its hands on the net income it needed to mend things. In 1974, for example, it had a deficit of almost $400 million.(5) Gaps such as this due to the politically-set charge were among the causes of the subways' deterioration.(6)

In that year, of course, the New York City fiscal crisis appeared on the horizon. As seen, the metropolis desperately wanted federal aid but the Ford Administration viewed its government as a wastrel. Secretary of the Treasury William Simon demanded "a responsible program of fiscal reform"(7) before Washington would even contemplate granting it financial assistance. One of the examples of wasteful practice pointed to by Simon and his colleagues was the $.35 cent fare. It became apparent that political as well as economic realities demanded an increase. Consequently, effective Sept. 1, 1975, the MTA Board voted to up the cost of the subway and bus token to $.50, a figure which itself became a politically-charged symbol in future years. Largely overlooked, because it had no immediate visible impact, was the enactment in Spring, 1975 by the Legislature and Carey Administration of a crucial measure not only giving local transportation systems State operating aid but also making this assistance permanent for the first time.(8)

In 1977, Harold Fisher, a long-time confidant of the Chief Executive, was made MTA Chair. He turned down the opportunity to play this role full-time at an $80,000 salary; and took the job as a part-time position albeit one keeping him extremely busy.(9) Sadly, his dedication to his job and his connections with the Governor did not do much to improve the metropolitan region's transportation arrangements. 1978 was a gubernatorial election

Carey and Ravitch Fix the Subways

year and Carey promised to maintain the fare at $.50 through 1981. The City's new Mayor, Ed Koch, also insisted on keeping a lid on this charge. Critics continued to point out that this cap prevented the needed repair or replacement of subway cars, tracks and signal and power systems.(10) So the TA's domain kept rotting away.

In the midst of this disaster afflicting public transportation, it seemed to some as if Carey's mind was centered entirely on the construction of Westway, an expressway to replace the then-crumbling (and now torn-down) elevated West Side Highway between 42nd Street and the Brooklyn-Battery Tunnel. In 1974, he had criticized the Westway proposal but shortly after his election had become its strong supporter. In 1977 Koch when he ran for Mayor had opposed it; but after his triumph he agreed with his former Congressional colleague to set up a three person panel to study the benefits and costs of constructing the road, 90% of which was to be funded by the federal government. Carey's appointee was his second Transportation Commissioner William Hennessy, whose Department had been very influential in swinging the Governor to side with the superhighway. Hennessy himself strongly backed it. Koch's selection was his old friend David Margolis, who had earlier indicated some support for the highway; while the Governor and Mayor-elect jointly chose Fisher. The panel concluded that it would be of great benefit to the City economically, creating thousands of jobs. Even Fisher joined in the panel's judgment: he felt that the area needed both new highways and better mass transit.(11) (Those opposed to the freeway said that the federal funds that would be used to build it could be "traded-in" for subway improvements that everyone admitted were needed; that the increased traffic would pollute the adjoining areas, etc. The supporters pointed out that it was not at all certain that the State would get anything in a trade-in and any funds it did obtain would probably come to less than the federal dollars that would vanish from State/City coffers as a result of a decision to cancel the autobahn.(12) Moreover, the Governor contended, the project would actually reduce pollution on local streets by attracting traffic from them; would encourage private, job-creating investment on the West Side of Manhattan; and would replace dilapidated piers with recreational facilities including a new park which would cover the road for part of its route.(13))

In April 1978, somewhat convinced by the arguments of the panelists and of others whose opinions he respected but probably swayed even more by a Carey promise to spend $800 million extra on mass transit and to guarantee the $.50 fare at least through Jan. 1, 1982, Koch agreed to the construction of the freeway.(14) But the Mayor's about-face did not end the troubles of those who backed it. Erhard Beck, Regional Administrator of the federal Environmental Protection Agency, recommended that the Army Corps of Engineers refuse the project a "dredge and fill" permit needed to start construction on the ground that it would harm aquatic life and aggravate flooding problems in various New Jersey communities.(15) He also urged State Environmental Commissioner Peter Berle to hold back another necessary okay (this one relating to air quality) until the road's supporters demonstrated that the increased traffic it would generate would not "foul the air".(16) Carey's reaction to Beck's recommendation was to call the federal official a "lunkhead".(17) However, Berle followed Beck's advice and denied the road the license, which thus had to be issued by his successor, Robert Flacke. And the advent of the Reagan Administration in 1981 meant that the State and City never saw a penny of the federal $640 million share of the $800 million that had lured Koch.(18) Reagan was a great fan of Westway; but in 1982 a decision by Federal Judge Thomas Griesa for all intents and purposes killed it. Griesa found that the Corps of Engineers, which ultimately had accorded a permit, had acted illegally in doing so because it had not written an environmental impact statement showing that the landfill resulting from the construction of the boulevard would not reduce the Hudson's striped bass population.(19)

In 1979 Carey and the Legislature did place on the ballot a $500 million Transportation Bond issue. This paper, to be supplemented by $300 million in Triborough Bridge and Tunnel Authority Bonds (20), was cleverly designed to improve public transportation in all areas of the State. Thus to help the suburbs it pledged monies for the construction of a new railroad car storage yard for the Long Island Railroad and to buy new trains for the LIRR and the commuter lines serving Westchester and Dutchess Counties. For

Carey and Ravitch Fix the Subways

upstate, the bond proceeds were to be employed to improve freight and passenger services between Albany and Buffalo; while New York City was to get $280 million for rehabilitated and new subway cars.(21) Though Carey irritated some by saying that the success of the bond plan was a *sine qua non* of keeping the subway fare at $.50 -- a statement he later backed down from(22) -- the voters narrowly approved it. Mindful of his defeat on an Economic Development Bond issue in 1977, the Governor got Lieutenant Governor Mario Cuomo, Hennessy and Assistant Transportation Commissioner John Marino to criss-cross the state to convince chambers of commerce, editors, tv reporters and ordinary people of the bonds' benefits. Their hard work and his planning resulted in a victory that confounded some who had predicted that the scheme was doomed to defeat.(23)

Fisher left before the bond proposal passed. Though at the beginning of Carey's 1978 reelection campaign an aide to the Governor had described the transportation czar as "key on both politics and substance", by election day the Chief Executive had become "openly critical of the M.T.A.'s operations" and had decided to "reduce" Fisher's role.(24) Governors of New York State normally do not ride the subway -- Carey usually journeyed on state aircraft or in state cars -- but in 1978 he heard frequent laments from bus and subway riders and suburban commuters.(25) Despite rumors appearing in the press in 1979 that Fisher was departing, he did not resign until October of that year.(26) Even now it is unclear whether he willingly quit or was shoved.(27) He himself declared to me(28) that he went voluntarily and referred to Carey as a "fine Governor", which is some evidence that he really was glad to return to private life. However, it may well be that several Carey aides were making subtle suggestions during 1978 and 1979 that the MTA head decamp. Some felt that the Governor himself wanted him to, as he desired a stronger figure to represent the MTA and the TA in upcoming contract negotiations with the City's Transit Workers Union (TWU).(29) But he may well have been unwilling to order him out as he hated "to give bad news to anyone, particularly an old friend like Mr. Fisher".(30)

The Governor's choice to succeed his old friend was builder and

The Days of Wine and Roses Are Over

ex-Urban Development Corporation Chairman Richard Ravitch, who by chance happened to be lobbying the Chief Executive in favor of aid to public television on the day he had resolved to make the pick.(31) Whatever his lack of experience as a transit executive, Ravitch was an expert on both finances and (as a straphanger himself) on the defects of New York City's subways.(32) He also knew that public transportation in the metropolitan area faced grave fiscal problems. For example, he was aware that the MTA was looking at an operating deficit of at least $200 million for its 1981 fiscal year even without accounting for likely wage increases.(33) And everyone recognized that pay raises would have to be granted to workers on some of the MTA's subsidiaries, including the TA. The TWU contract with the TA was scheduled to expire on March 31, 1980 and the City's bus and subway drivers, who had not seen much in the way of salary growth recently, were hungry for a big hike. So a TA work stoppage began at the start of April, 1980; and Mayor Koch got favorable headlines by standing on the Brooklyn Bridge and congratulating those who were walking to work.(34) He wanted to keep a tight lid on TWU wage growth because a big jump in its members' pay packets would set a bad precedent for his negotiations with the City unions later in the year.(35) (The MTA is a State agency and thus the major burden of the negotiations with the TWU and the LIRR workers union, also on strike, had to fall on Ravitch and the Governor.)

Carey, too, was not thrilled at the prospect of a huge TWU pay gain. However he felt strongly that a prolonged walkout would cripple the City's economy and in the long run cost more than giving the union a tad above the 7% that Ravitch had initially offered.(36) Thus he had his aide Meyer Frucher communicate behind the scenes with the TWU board and started labelling the union concessions he and Ravitch hoped would be forthcoming as "buybacks" rather than "givebacks". (He believed that these concessions would be more acceptable to the rank-and-file if they were viewed not as surrenders of a right but as an exchange of that right for extra cash.(37)) The first few days of the strike were not a tremendous inconvenience for most New Yorkers because of the Easter weekend and the balmy climate.(38) Then on Wednesday, April 9th, it poured; pedestrians were soaked; major roads were flooded; and traffic moved at a crawl.(39) This put additional pressure on the Governor and Ravitch to reach some sort of settlement. On Thursday, April 10th, negotiations starring Carey, Koch, Ravitch, their aides and union representatives lasted into the morning of Friday, April 11th. Early Friday evening the union told Ravitch it could not accept Koch's "maximum" 8% a year raise but consented to 9% the first year and 8% the second with some cost of living increases thrown in. The MTA chief decided to support this counterproposal and phoned the Governor for his approval. This was forthcoming though the Mayor's definitely was not.(40) Koch lamented not only that the raise was far too high but that on Thursday he had been told by the Governor that "he was against any settlement that Mr. Koch was against ...."(41)

Though subways and buses started running Friday evening, the Governor and Ravitch were still not out of the woods. The agreement had to be approved by the then 14-member MTA Board. All of these people had been appointed by the Governor; but four of the 14 had been picked by him on the Mayor's recommendation. The latter were unanimously against the pact and two or three of the others were not overjoyed with it either. There was thus a real chance that the Board would reject it and the walkout resume. However, Carey made personal phone calls to "his" waverers, including the Emergency Financial Control Board's Stephen Berger, who was worried that the contract did not sufficiently provide for increased worker productivity. Thus the deal eventually was ratified 9-4 with Berger abstaining. He told me(42) that he really wanted to vote "nay" but sat this one out as a favor to a Governor who had been so good to him in the past.(43)

By May, 1980 the strikes on the TA and LIRR had been over for a month and the MTA deficit for the next two years was now calculated at $930 million, of which $389 million was for fiscal 1981.(44) Thus it was evident to all but the most optimistic that the $.50 fare would soon be as extinct as the dodo; and in fact it jumped to $.60 by the end of June. So evaporated Carey's promise to maintain the magical $.50 figure through 1981.(45) However, the State did increase its operating aid by enacting a controversial tax on oil companies.(46)

The Days of Wine and Roses Are Over

The end of the strike and this temporary infusion of operating assistance alloweed Ravitch to focus on much-needed capital improvements (e.g., new subways and busses). In November of 1980 he called for a $14 billion program over ten years. When this was not greeted enthusiastically by many in Albany, he scaled it down to $7 billion over five. The Governor did not bother to communicate his own position on this matter to his appointee. However, without telling him in advance, in late February of 1981 he wrote the legislative leaders (Senate Majority Leader Republican Warren Anderson; Senate Minority Leader Democrat Manfred Ohrenstein; Assembly Speaker Democrat Stanley Fink and Assembly Minority Leader Republican James Emery) asking them to support a capital transit bill based on the MTA Chair's effort and to meet with Ravitch and himself for a briefing.(47) Carey's recommendation called for $5 billion over five years. Two billion of this sum was to come from new bonding authority given to the MTA, which paper would be backed up by fares and concessions at subway stations. Five hundred million more would be produced by bonds issued by the TBTA; $2 billion by existing federal, state and local capital transit programs; and $500 million by other sources.(48)

Carey proved of little help to Ravitch in securing passage of the capital project since he had other items on his mind. He and the Republicans in the State Senate were locking horns over a proposal of his to have the state take over local Medicaid costs and he was courting and marrying Evangeline Gouletas.(49) As a result, the MTA head and not the Governor took charge of the negotiations with Anderson and Fink; the bill passed; and the Chief Executive signed it at the end of June, 1981.(50) Under the final package the MTA could issue $1.6 billion in new bonds, the TBTA $800 million and the Port Authority $200 million. To get support from suburban legislators, the LIRR and the Harlem and Hudson commuter rail line (now part of Metro-North) got some help and, to obtain the votes of upstaters, the act contained $68 million for highways and $9 million for upstate mass transit authorities.(51) Ultimately, this $5.6 billion act swelled to close to $8 billion (with $5.7 billion for the TA) thanks to some federal funds and clever manipulation by Ravitch of loopholes in the federal tax laws that permitted the MTA to sell tax deductions to private companies such as Metromedia and Topps Chewing Gum for $500 million.(52) When the five years of the measure's life elapsed, it was renewed during Cuomo's Governorship. As a consequence, $16 billion was spent during a decade to upgrade MTA's capital facilities.(53)

As any veteran subway rider is aware, they are much better than they used to be. Many cars are new and the older ones have been rehabilitated so that they break down less, air-condition more adequately in the summer, heat better in the winter and are largely graffiti-free. In 1981 they ran an average of 7,000 miles between breakdowns; the figure a decade and a half later was 58,000.(54) There are new busses on New York City's streets; and commuter lines in the suburbs have expanded routes. And this improvement in the public transportation of the metropolitan area is directly due to this 1981 Carey Administration transportation capital improvements measure -- a bill that at times no one except Richard Ravitch seemed to love.

It was always obvious that the 1980 $.10 fare boost was not the permanent solution to the MTA operating-aid problem, i.e. to the conundrum of where to find the money to pay for the annual excess of the agency's disbursements over its receipts. Assuming maintenance of the same level of service, the needed cash could come from rate hikes, tax rises to fund more ample State subsidies, or a combination of the two. By May, 1981, Ravitch was talking of a budget deficit for the TA alone of close to $400 million for fiscal year 1982 and saying that if the State did not increase its operating subsidy to the MTA, the bus/subway fare would have to become $1.(55) Perhaps as a ploy to protect himself from political criticism in the light of almost-inevitable fare and tax boosts, Carey appointed that month a blue-ribbon panel to ascertain the implications of a fare rise and recommend a satisfactory tax system to serve as the basis of state MTA operating aid. The seven-person team was headed by Kenneth Axelson of J.C. Penney Co. and included such other cab and limousine users as financier Felix Rohatyn, William Ellinghaus of American Telephone and Telegraph and Margolis. It contained just one straphanger and was attacked for this reason.(56) (When I mentioned this criticism in my interview(57) with Carey transport-

The Days of Wine and Roses Are Over

ation assistant Stanley Kramer, he retorted, not unreasonably, that the problems of the MTA were primarily economic and managerial and that most of the panel members were highly expert in business and finance.)

The panel did work hard and suggested, among other things, a $.0025 sales tax increase in the region served by the MTA to be earmarked for that agency.(58) This is why the New York City/State combined sales tax is currently a cumbersome 8.25%. It also estimated the MTA deficit for fiscal 1982 at $560 million, which is why it accepted a fare increase to $.75 on July 1, 1981.(59) Needless to say, the solons were not too thrilled with the idea of having to raise the sales tax, but Ravitch "bludgeoned"(60) them into this action by threatening to set the fare at $1. Thus after the July 4th break, the lawmakers passed and Carey signed an operating-aid law that included the sales tax hike and other revenue measures.(61)

Some felt that the Governor never gave any indication that this bill was an urgent one. Koch charged that he had "walked away" from the bargaining once it became probable that taxes were going to be raised.(62) He also contended that the resident of the Executive Mansion had "lost control" of the transit negotiations. (63) When the act was being debated, Carey was staying at the home of a cousin in Buffalo and attending a private dinner party. It is clear that the operating aid-tax package was to a considerable extent the work of Ravitch, Speaker Fink and Senator Anderson. (64) But the Governor's aides did extend themselves to round up votes for the final measure.(65) Moreover, Hennessy, Kramer and Henry Peyrebrune, another Carey transportation adviser, point out that they were significantly involved in the discussions concerning that legislation.(66)

In January 1982 the Governor decided not to run for reelection. If he thought that that resolution would free him from worries about fare hikes in the MTA region and about the MTA operating aid/tax problem, he was sadly mistaken. In the middle of the year, the Financial Control Board wanted the MTA to add $.20 more to New York City subway and bus fares. However Ravitch persuaded the MTA Board to delay any change until December: this would be after the November election when all the members of the State Assembly and State Senate could be dumped by the voters and when Koch expected he would be the gubernatorial candidate.(67) After Cuomo and not the tenant of Gracie Mansion won the Democratic gubernatorial primary and then eked out a victory over Louis Lehrman in the 1982 general election, the lame-duck Carey got the legislative leaders to call their membership out of recess to decide how to stop the fare from going up and simultaneously to close a projected MTA deficit of $300 million for fiscal 1983.(68) Right before Christmas, and about a week before he departed for private life, he signed a compromise measure that raised $225 million for the Authority via a two year surcharge on taxes on corporate profits.(69) This last-gasp effort saved the $.75 fare until January, 1984, when it ballooned to $.90.

In sum, the most important transportation decisions made by the Carey Administration were those of 1975 to make State aid to local transit systems a permanent program, of 1981 to impose levies earmarked for such State aid in order to maintain the State subvention at a significant level(70), and of 1981 to provide over $5 billion to the MTA to rebuild its aging stock. The operating-aid (i.e., tax plus subsidy) bills allowed the agency to keep the fare moderate while the capital assistance measure made it possible for it to bring its vehicles, equipment and rights-of-way into the modern world. All this legislation was necessary to make public transportation a viable option in the New York metropolitan area and thus to prevent its economic collapse. If subways and trains are cattle cars, commuters will not ride them; and if the fare is extremely high, commuters likewise will eschew them. And if everyone in this densely-populated region piles into his/her car for work or shopping, it will choke to death on its own fumes and gridlock and become a wasteland. It is unfortunate, however, that neither Carey nor his predecessors nor his successors ever pushed for the building of a freight tunnel under the Hudson River. It is now almost impossible for freight trains to enter the metropolis and its neighboring counties from the west. Thus most goods have to come by truck, which increases road congestion and hinders the State's economic development schemes by making New York City and its suburbs less attractive locales in which to do business.(71)

Notes to Chapter 10

1. Metropolitan Transportation Authority Executive Director Mortimer Downey told me in an interview in New York City on Nov. 27, 1991 that the Long Island Railroad was in better shape in 1975 than the subways and north-of-the-City commuter lines because Governor Nelson Rockefeller had carried out a promise to spend a good deal of money on it.

2. Walsh, Annmarie Hauck - Public Authorities and the Shape of Decision Making at p. 188, 191 of Bellush, Jewell and Netzer, Dick (eds.) - Urban Politics New York Style (Armonk, NY: M.E. Sharpe, 1990); The Green Book - 1994-95 (New York: Citybooks, 1995), pp. 427-28.

3. Staten Island Advance, May 5, 1975, p. 1.

4. Downey, interview cited n.1 supra, made this point about early retirement.

5. Staten Island Advance, May 5, 1975, p. 1.

6. Downey, interview cited n.1 supra. Interview with Carey's Transportation Commissioner William Hennessy, Sept. 18, 1991, Albany, N.Y.

7. Quoted p. 64 of Newfield, Jack and Du Brul, Paul - The Abuse of Power (New York: Penguin Books, 1978).

8. Public Papers of Governor Hugh L. Carey 1975 (Albany: State of New York Executive Chamber, 1982), pp. 143-45; New York Times, Apr. 24, 1975, p. 42.

9. New York Times, Oct. 6, 1979, p. 2.

10. New York Times, Apr. 14, 1978, p. A27; June 28, 1980, p. 25.

11. Hennessy, interview cited n.6 supra; New York Times, Dec. 29, 1977, p. A1.

12. New York Times, Dec. 29, 1977, p. A1.

13. See his letter of August 9, 1982 to the Army Corps of Engineers and others, Hugh L. Carey Collection, St. John's Univ.(NY), Hennessy

file.

14. Interview with Mayor Edward I. Koch, Nov. 11, 1994, New York City; Staten Island Advance, Apr. 20, 1978, p. 1.

15. Staten Island Advance, Sept. 5, 1978, p. 8.

16. New York Times, Dec. 15, 1978, p. A32.

17. Ibid.

18. Downey, interview cited n.1 supra; interview with Robert Wagner, Jr., Oct. 25, 1991, New York City; New York Times, Oct. 31, 1980, p. B1.

19. New York Times, July 1, 1982, p. A1. The cases are Action for Rational Transit v. Westside Highway, 536 F.Supp. 1225 (1982) and Sierra Club v. U.S. Army Corps of Engineers, 541 F. Supp. 1367 (1982), aff'd in pertinent part in Sierra Club v. U.S. Army Corps of Engineers, 701 F.2d 1011 (1983). Governor Cuomo and Mayor Koch in 1985 abandoned the attempt to secure federal funds for Westway and sought to "trade-in" these sums for mass-transit monies. New York Times, Sept. 20, 1985, p. A1. The City and State received over $1 billion in mass-transit capital assistance as a result of the trade-in. See p. II A-14 of the MTA Capital Program proposed in December, 1990. A ground-level boulevard is being constructed where Westway was to run. New York Times, Apr. 2, 1996, p. B1. Reagan's favorable attitude to Westway is mentioned in Carey's letter of March 6, 1981 to Environmental Protection Administrator Ann Gorsuch, Hugh L. Carey Collection, St. John's Univ.(NY), Transportation (Highways: Westway) file.

20. Staten Island Advance, Nov. 7, 1979, p. 1.

21. Carey press release, May 14, 1979, Hugh L. Carey Collection, St. John's Univ.(NY), Transportation (Bond Issue) file; also New York Times, Apr. 3, 1979, p. B3.

22. Staten Island Advance, Oct. 21, 1979, Sec. 1, p.1; see also New York Times, Sept. 25, 1979, p. B6.

23. Interview with Carey Assistant Transportation Commissioner John Marino, Nov. 8, 1991, New York City; Staten Island Advance, Oct. 21,

The Days of Wine and Roses Are Over

1979, Sec. 1, p. 1.

24. New York Times, Nov. 7, 1978, p. 52.

25. New York Times, Nov. 14, 1978, p. B8.

26. New York Times, Jan. 9, 1979, p. B1; Oct. 6, 1979, p. 25.

27. Hennessy, interview cited n.6 supra.

28. Interview with Fisher, June 13, 1990, Brooklyn, N.Y.

29. New York Times, Oct. 6, 1979, p. 25.

30. New York Times, Jan. 3, 1979, p. B2.

31. Wagner, interview cited n.18 supra; New York Times, Oct. 18, 1979, p. B3.

32. See Staten Island Advance, Oct. 18, 1979, p. 4 on Ravitch as straphanger.

33. Lardner, James - Painting the Elephant, New Yorker, June 25, 1984, pp. 41ff, p. 44.

34. Ibid., p. 45.

35. New York Times, Apr. 7, 1980, p. B1.

36. New York Times, Apr. 12, 1980, p. 1, 26.

37. Stokes, Geoffrey - The Odd Couple, Village Voice, Apr. 14, 1980, p. 1.

38. See New York Times, Apr. 7, 1980, p. B1; Apr. 8, 1980, p. B3.

39. New York Times, Apr. 10, 1980, p. A1.

40. New York Times, Apr. 12, 1980, p. 1, 26.

41. Ibid, p. 28.

42. Interview with Berger, Feb. 21, 1991, New York City.

Carey and Ravitch Fix the Subways

43. What has preceded in this paragraph is based largely on New York Times, Apr. 12, 1980, p. 1, 26, 28; Apr. 19, 1980, p. 25.

44. New York Times, May 14, 1980, p. B1; June 5, 1980, p. A1.

45. In private, Carey as early as 1980 was willing to have a fare increase of as much as $.15 if the federal government provided no additional operating subsidy. However, he was opposed to having that boost take effect before April, 1981. See an undated (but obviously from 1980), unsigned memo on his stationery summing up his transit goals. Hugh L. Carey Collection, St. John's Univ.(NY), Gubernatorial Files 1975-82 (Personal Files 1975-82) file.

46. New York Times, June 14, 1980, p. 1; June 15, 1980, Sec. 1, p. 1.

47. Carey letter to Fink, et. al., Feb. 26, 1991, Hugh L. Carey Collection, St. John's Univ.(NY), Fink file; Lardner, op. cit. n.33 supra, p. 50.

48. New York Times, Mar. 3, 1981, p. A1.

49. Lardner, op. cit. n.33 supra., p. 51.

50. Ibid., p. 57.

51. New York Times, June 24, 1981, p. A1.

52. Wagner, interview cited n.18 supra; Lardner, op. cit. n.33 supra, pp. 59-60, p. 65.

53. New York Times, Aug. 26, 1991, p. B1.

54. New York Times, Dec. 29, 1995, p. B6.

55. New York Times, May 14, 1981, p. B1.

56. Staten Island Advance, May 20, 1981, p. B4; May 21, 1981, p. A12; May 30, 1981, p. A3.

57. Interview with Kramer, May 29, 1991, New York City.

58. New York Times, June 5, 1981, p. A1.

The Days of Wine and Roses Are Over

59. Ibid.

60. Hennessy, interview cited n.6 supra; Kramer, interview cited n.57 supra.

61. Carey press release July 11, 1981, Hugh L. Carey Collection, St. John's Univ.(NY), Transportation (Mass Transit: Operating Assistance: Legislation) file breaks the revenue measure down into its various revenue components.

62. Staten Island Advance, July 9, 1981, p. A1.

63. New York Times, July 5, 1981, Sec. 4, p. 6.

64. New York Times, July 5, 1981, Sec. 4, p. 6; July 10, 1982, p. B2.

65. New York Times, July 10, 1981, p. B2.

66. Interviews with Hennessy and Kramer cited n.6 and n.57 supra; interview with Peyrebrune, June 13, 1991, Albany, N.Y.

67. New York Times, July 1, 1982, p. A1.

68. Staten Island Advance, Dec. 8, 1982, p. A1.

69. New York Times, Dec. 23, 1982, p. A1.

70. At least half the hundreds of millions in subsidies coming to the New York City Transit Authority from Washington and Albany results from State taxes earmarked for transit subsidies. New York Times, May 8, 1995, p. B1.

71. New York Times, Nov. 27, 1993, p. 1 describes how difficult it is for rail freight to cross the Hudson and the problems that this bottleneck causes.

Chapter 11
Carey's Environmental Policy:
a Balancing Act

ANY government that is bent on expanding the economy is faced with an oft-noted dilemma of balancing growth with environmental preservation. This quandary was faced by Carey, who for a short period heartily embraced the latter cause but then seemed to lean in favor of the former. However this tilt was not very pronounced and sometimes was more rhetorical than real. Moreover, on two occasions where pre-1975 violations of conservationist imperatives posed menaces to public health that emerged only after his election, he acted relatively quickly and with vigor (and without excessively straining the State's treasury) to defang the threats.

Many of New York State's environmental concerns are dealt with by the Department of Environmental Conservation ("EnCon"). Carey's first Environmental Commissioner was Ogden Reid, a Westchester resident who had served in Congress with the future Governor. In 1974, as seen, he entered the Democratic gubernatorial primary but dropped out and just before the balloting threw his support to Carey rather than to Howard Samuels, believing that the former knew much more about government than did the latter.(1) In gratitude, Carey offered Reid several posts after his 1974 election victory and he selected EnCon because of a longstanding interest in environmental issues.(2)

1975 was a scintillating year for Reid and the environmental movement in New York State. He and the Governor recommended and the Legislature passed a major piece of legislation(3) requiring that the State and its localities prepare an "environmental impact statement" (EIS) before starting a project themselves or approving an undertaking by a private party for which government sanction is needed -- if the proposed step "may have a significant effect on the environment".(4) This EIS, not necessary if one has already been done for the federal government and which the locality can require a private individual requesting a permit to draft, is to list alternatives to the proposed action and the steps the sponsor proposes to take that will mitigate the damage it will inflict on its surroundings. Nelson Rockefeller had vetoed a similar bill three years earlier.(5)

Builders and construction unions were made unhappy by this law. Consequently, Agriculture and then Commerce Commissioner John Dyson warned the Governor that he must take positions more likely to be seen as "pro-business" if he wanted to keep industry in the State. These arguments did not fall upon deaf ears and the Governor at the end of 1975 became more convinced than ever that his Administration could not be perceived as wanting to weaken the private sector if it wished companies to stay in New York.(6) Thus in early 1976 he made what one newspaper referred to an "about face"(7) and changed from an individual who claimed that "protection of the environment is not a luxury which can be put off until a happier time in our economy"(8) to one who contended that the environmental policies of New York State "must bear a reasonable relationship to the policies of the rest of the nation".(9)

Soon Reid and the newly "less-green" Carey feuded over the discharge of "polychlorinated biphenyls" (PCBs) into the Hudson River. To understand this dispute some history is necessary. General Electric (GE) had built two big plants on the Hudson north of Albany at Hudson Falls and Fort Edward, which in the mid-1970s employed 2000 people.(10) These factories, located in an area where jobs are scarce, made a product known as a capacitor. Capacitors save energy by allowing electrical devices to function at full power for much of the time that they are in operation even though they are not drawing as much current as they could. They do this by "stor[ing] and smooth[ing] out electric current so that it is more efficient".(11) As of the mid-1970s, the most effective capacitors were those whose "paper....[layers were] impregnated with PCB's".(12)

PCBs entered the river from the Fort Edward and Hudson Falls plants mixed with water used to rinse the capacitors that had been treated with them. By the time Carey took office, there were 500,000 pounds of PCBs on the bottom of the Hudson, a large chunk of this residue coming from these buildings.(13) Some of it was swallowed by fish swimming in the river. There are those who felt and still feel that this situation is nothing to worry about: they aver that the chemical does no more than produce skin rashes on those who come into contact with it for long periods.(14) Others were and are less sanguine, as laboratory experiments conducted in the 1960s and early 1970s showed large concentrations causing cancer in rats and sterility in minks and monkeys.(15) Thus scientists at the federal Environmental Protection Agency (EPA), aware that GE under federal and state permits was placing up to

30 pounds a day of PCBs into the Hudson, poked around and found fantastically high levels of the compound in river mud and fish below Fort Edward. An astounded Reid received their report in Summer of 1975 and decided he had to act. What he did was first warn the public not to eat striped bass from the river and then close it to commercial fishing.(16) He also ordered an administrative hearing to start in November to determine whether GE had violated state water-quality standards and, if the answer were in the affirmative, to ascertain what penalty it should pay.(17) The hearing was chaired by a respected law professor at Columbia University, Abraham Sofaer. Even before Sofaer produced any decision, Reid issued a "zero discharge" order commanding GE to totally cease tossing PCBs into the Hudson by September, 1976. He did this because he felt that even minimal discharges would create serious pollution and because he was furious at the company because it had a PCB substitute but was in no hurry to phase it in. Carey, however, overturned this ukase.(18)

In February, 1976 Sofaer circulated the decision that concluded the first phase of the hearing. Even though he admitted that GE had been granted federal and State permits to dump the chemical, he also found that it had violated them by pouring enough PCBs into the river to saturate its waters and mud and make its fish dangerous to consume.(19) This judgment in and of itself resolved nothing: what GE, the Governor, Dyson and Reid were as interested in was the hearing's second phase, where Sofaer would have to determine whether GE could attain a lawful level of PCB discharge, whether there existed environmentally-friendly and technologically-adequate replacements for the chemical and, perhaps most important of all, whether the company should be compelled to take the possibly-expensive step of tidying up the messes it had already made.(20) The Governor wanted a settlement that would not prove too burdensome to the firm. In public he supported a continuation of the hearings but even before Sofaer's Phase One decision was made public, he made it clear that "it will do little good if we rescue our environment at the cost of our economy. Anyone who doesn't agree with that principle won't be working in this government".(21) And he allowed Dyson to attack Reid by comments such as "If zero discharge means zero jobs and three ounces means 1,200 jobs, I say we go for three ounces".(22)

It was the zero discharge issue that got the most play in the press as the chief difference between Reid on the one hand and Carey, GE and Dyson on the other; but this was not the main problem. The EPA itself had ordered zero discharge by July 1, 1977 -- not much beyond the Reid deadline of September 1976 -- and he himself was willing to accept the federal date.(23) GE was not worried about having to cease dumping the PCBs: it had developed a process to destroy the compound without jettisoning it in the river and had, as seen, developed a substitute chemical. (24) What was angering Carey most about Reid was his feeling that the Environmental Commissioner was not negotiating in good faith with GE.(25) Reid and the manufacturer had come to a tentative agreement under which it had agreed to make a payment of $2 million to settle the case and to stop discharging PCBs by the EPA deadline of July 1, 1977. However, the settlement was never finalized because Reid, acting in response to environmentalists' demands, insisted that GE admit that it had acted wrongly in violating water quality standards. Fearing that an admission of guilt would ultimately subject it to having to pay for a costly cleanup and also believing that it had acted legally since it had received the appropriate discharge permits, the company demanded that any settlement completely exonerate it despite its willingness to make the $2 million "contribution". It asserted that the payment should be labelled as this rather than as a penalty and promised to give some of it to EnCon to conduct environmental studies.(26) As a result of Reid's insistence that GE acknowledge some wrongdoing, the agreement fell through.(27) In mid-April 1976 negotiations were at a standstill with each side blaming the other for the breakdown.(28) Carey felt that his subordinate was not responding to his pleas to continue talking and thus made up his mind that he had to go.(29) In late April of 1976, following weeks of speculation, he resigned and was replaced by another environmentalist, Peter Berle.(30)

Berle soon negotiated a settlement. The document was silent about the concern's guilt or lack of such but provided that it and the State would spend $3 million each to remove the Hudson's PCBs. GE also said it would pay another $1 million for research into the

PCB problem. It agreed to stop using the compound by the EPA's July 1, 1977 deadline and to install a treatment facility to limit its discharges to one gram a day until then.(31) Berle was willing to let it get away without acknowledging liability because it had, after all, been acting under permit.(32)

Despite the 1976 agreement, the removal of PCBs from the Hudson has just begun. When the Commissioner settled the total cost of the cleanup was estimated at $12 to $20 million.(33) By 1978 this figure had soared to $200 million and by 1990 to $280 million.(34) The problems are two: who will pay and how the river will be cleared. The State feels it cannot afford this sum and is looking for reimbursement from the federal Superfund bill of 1980. Even if the EPA does provide the cash, there is still a problem of what to do with the stuff. The most obvious solution is to dredge it out, but towns that have been suggested as its burial ground have rebelled at the idea. So in some way or another the PCBs may have to be "detoxified" on the river's bed. Though Hudson River bass are now plentiful again, though they and the river contain lower PCB levels than at the time of the Reid-GE squabble, and though the effects on human health of consuming the compound are as unclear now as they were in 1976, commercial bass fishing in the Hudson is still banned because of laboratory reports that the chemical could cause cancer in animals. It will take at least until the year 2000 before the waterway will be PCB-free.(35)

Berle himself got into trouble with the Governor because the latter saw him as too favorable to environmental concerns. The Commissioner's partial prohibition of sports fishing in ant-poison-ridden Lake Ontario had irritated the fishing buffs who ran a Syracuse newspaper; and the Chief Executive was concerned by the prospect of strong opposition from this quarter in his race for a second term. Likewise, journals in Watertown, Buffalo and Rochester had lambasted the interdiction. Some in the Governor's entourage were angry because the Commissioner had torn down ranger lookouts and cabins in the Adirondacks at the behest of environmental groups.(36) The Governor became livid about an Albany *Times Union* story to the effect that Berle had refused to allow EnCon officials to solicit campaign contributions from low-level Department employees.(37) But most important in the latter's downfall was that denial of the air-quality permit necessary to the construction of the Governor's beloved Westway.(38) Westway was a plan into which the Chief Executive had thrown himself heart and soul and which he still feels is an "environmental home run and the biggest minority employment project ever conceived of for New York".(39) There was no way that a member of the Cabinet who openly thwarted the realization of an idea dear to the heart of this boss was going to keep his job. Berle himself contends that the turndown of the permit was not an expression of opposition to the freeway but simply a statement that the State had not met its legal burden of showing that the additional traffic it would generate would not violate air pollution standards. He admits, however, that his chief might have seen the refusal as more final than this and that he did not view him as a "team player".(40)

Berle was replaced by Robert Flacke, a Lake George businessman who was head of the Adirondack Park Agency and Town Supervisor of Lake George. As Adirondack Park Agency head, he had performed the miraculous job of satisfying the wishes of both those who wanted the Park kept a wilderness and those who wanted to see its economic resources exploited.(41) As Environmental Commissioner he did, as seen, accord Westway the air quality okay.(42) Other than this, he took no steps that inflamed either environmentalists or vigorous advocates of economic growth. Rather, he concentrated on making the Department a more efficiently-managed unit.(43) A pleasant, outgoing, undogmatic individual, he got along personally with the Governor(44); and he was one of a close group of Commissioners who had considerable influence in the second Carey Administration. (The others were Social Services Commissioner Barbara Blum, Parks Commissioner Orin Lehman, Health Commissioner David Axelrod, General Services Commissioner John Egan and Transportation Commissioner William Hennessy.)(45) So he remained as head of EnCon until the ex-Congressman left office in 1982.

Certainly the most-publicized episode involving the environment that occurred in New York State during Carey's tenure was that of Love Canal. As this incident has been the subject of at least two books(46), the discussion here of the course of events will be brief. The crisis was of a sort that was novel for all concerned and many of the important players had high stakes in the outcome. Consequently it is not at all surprising that mistakes were made and tempers lost.

In the City of Niagara Falls, an unused canal (the Love Canal) and the strips of land adjacent to it were used as dumps for chemical residues. Between 1971 and 1977 very heavy rains came to the area and "A mixture of 82 identified industrial chemicals - 11 of them suspected carcinogens - bubbled to the surface, leaching into [a] school playground and seeping into basement walls".(47) Local EnCon people heard of these gripes from neighboring property owners and notified Berle. Instead of shoving the matter under the rug, he spoke to State Health Commissioner Robert Whelan (then Axelrod's superior) about the problem in Spring, 1978.(48) By August, Whelan had decided that the Love Canal situation warranted action by his agency. So at an August 2nd meeting in Albany attended by Axelrod, some Love Canal residents and himself, he declared a "health emergency" for the area. He warned the neighbors against eating food from their gardens and announced the closing of the school, at least for the interim. He then suggested that pregnant women and children under two living on the three streets closest to the dump temporarily leave their homes.(49) One of the Love Canal area people present was Lois Gibbs, a young housewife with only a high school education and no experience of politics. Gibbs, who lived two blocks away from the mess but whose six year old attended the school and was developing symptoms of asthma(50), shouted angrily that Albany was neither proposing to pay for the evacuation nor worrying about the health of the families that were going to remain.(51)

However, the Governor not only visited the Love Canal neighborhood on August 7th but announced then that the State would **buy** the homes of those living in what later came to be called Ring I (the houses on 97th and 99th Streets and Colvin Boulevard whose backyards bordered the dump) and Ring II (the houses on the other side of those thoroughfares).(52) Though Gibbs believed that Director of State Operations Thomas Frey, accompanying the Governor that night, was stunned at his superior's decision(53), in fact he was not. The Chief Executive had talked the matter over with his aides and they had convinced him the State could afford to purchase these particular residences.(54)

By early 1979 the bill for the Canal catastrophe had swollen to $25 million, including site cleanup and relocation of 239 Ring I and II families. Of this $25 million, $15 million was borne by the State (including the total $9 million cost of relocation), $6 million by the federal government and the rest by the City of Niagara Falls.(55) "Eventually the dump was covered with clay and the...homes closest to it....were demolished."(56)

The aid to the homeowners in Rings I and II did not end the crisis. There was a worry that the chemical waste problem affected not only those in these Rings but all of Niagara Falls between 93rd and 103rd Streets. These blocks minus the territory included in Rings I and II are known as Ring III or the "outer" ring. The concern over Ring III led to warfare between the Love Canal Homeowners Assocation and Gibbs on the one hand and the Governor on the other. In September 1978, Dr. Nicholas Vianna of the State Health Department asked for the cooperation of the Association in doing a health survey in Ring III. Its members handed out questionnaires and Gibbs, though not trained in techniques of epidemological research, noted that certain illnesses (e.g., migraines, epilepsy, hyperactivity, birth defects) occurred in houses which, when connected to each other by an imaginary line, formed clusters of rather strange shapes. The idea then struck her that in the outer ring the chemicals had not spread uniformly from the canal site but had proceeded along "swales", i.e., underground streams and ponds. To help test this theory, the Association enlisted the aid of a scientist, Dr. Beverly Paigen.(57) Paigen became convinced that there might be something to the swale idea and urged that the Health Department conduct further studies of the matter. The Homeowners Association members themselves felt that Gibbs's hypothesis made a great deal of sense and that the outer ring was not a healthy place to live. Thus they demanded that Albany do for the residents of Ring III what it had done for those in Rings I and II, i.e., buy them out so that they could move to more salubrious locales.(58)

The Governor and his assistants were aghast at this suggestion. The big problem was the potential expense to a State that certainly was not flush: the Budget Division had emphasized this point in discussions with him.(59) What really scared some in the Administration was that many sites similar to Love Canal might turn up elsewhere in New York: it might be able to afford to relocate all the homeowners in one city but not all those in a plethora of towns.(60) According to Carey health aide Jeffrey Sachs, some of the Chief Executive's advisers felt that there was uncertainty about how harmful the chemicals osmosing from the dump were and/or believed that the millions that would have to go to "bail out" the habitants of the Love Canal neighborhood would be better employed in Harlem where the infant mortality rate was higher.(61) At a stormy meeting in April 1979 in the Hilton Hotel, Niagara Falls, attended by Gibbs, Paigen, Carey and Axelrod among others, the Governor asked Paigen to show him her tables demonstrating health problems in the outer ring area. "He skimmed them and asked her if she had any medical or laboratory confirmation for her survey findings [i.e. whether she had had doctors or laboratories back up a neighbor's assertion that she/he had had such and such an illness on such and such a date]. She said no, that was a problem in her studies. In that case, he said, they were worthless. As he tossed her papers across the table at her, the papers scattered all over."(62) He reiterated later in the session that it would be impossible for the State to empty all of Ring III.(63)

The stalemate over relocating Ring III homeowners lasted until 1980. Relations between Carey and Gibbs deteriorated, with the Governor referring to her in private as that "b...." (64) Then the dam burst in Summer of 1980. The EPA published a study showing that 11 of 36 residents of the Love Canal area tested were found to have some chromosome damage -- a very high percentage since normally only one percent of the population is afflicted with this problem.(65) Though Carey Administration officials such as Axelrod bitterly criticized the report on the ground that it did not use a "control group", i.e., that it did not also conduct tests on individuals who lived nowhere near the Love Canal's muck, the Governor realized that it had created so much anxiety among Ring III residents that something had to be done for them.(66) He also knew that it was a Presidential election year and that Jimmy Carter was anxious to get New York's electoral votes. So he resolved to ask the President for Washington's help in relocating those of the Ring III householders who wanted to leave.(67) And in October of 1980, at a Niagara Falls ceremony also attended by Carey and New York's U.S. Senators Jacob Javits and Daniel Moynihan, Carter agreed to provide $15 million to the State -- half as grant and half as loan -- to enable it to move the Ring III residents. Carey had demanded for several tense weeks that Washington bear the entire cost. However he compromised when federal negotiators refused to budge and it was pointed out to him that the State could have done a better job of regulating the dumping. (In fact, Albany not only agreed to repay the loan but also to ante up an extra $5 million.)(68)

The Reagan Administration kept Carter's pledge and within a few years over 1100 homes were purchased by a State body known as the Love Canal Revitalization Agency. The total cost of the cleanup to Washington and Albany was $275 million. A full 2500 individuals were helped to vacate the Love Canal neighborhood though 60 families refused to go. The EPA claims that much of the Ring III territory is safe now and the Love Canal Revitalization unit is successfully selling of the abandoned homes at bargain prices. A private developer is erecting 250 dwellings there. But the Ring I and II houses have been demolished and will not be rebuilt.(69)

The most important result of the Love Canal crisis from the point of view of the nation as a whole is that the disaster sparked the federal Superfund Law of 1980 and similar state legislation (e.g., a New York law of 1982). There are thousands of toxic waste sites scattered throughout America: Carey and his aides were certainly correct in fearing that Love Canal was not unique. The country may have to spend $750 billion under these measures to sanitize these locales, though so far the work has been proceeding very slowly with only slightly over 200 sites having been cleaned up by 1994 at a cost of $15 billion.(70) So the tocsin sounded in 1978 by Lois Gibbs and her neighbors, scientists such as Dr. Paigen, and Carey aides such as Berle, Axelrod and Whalen in an unprepossessing but superficially pleasant area of the City of Niagara Falls, New York, gave birth to projects that could be among the most costly that governments and private firms throughout the land will undertake in years to come.

West Valley is a village located about 30 miles south of Buffalo and about 50 miles south southeast of Love Canal. In the early 1960s a company known as Nuclear Fuel Services built a nuclear fuel rod recycling facility there. It was welcomed both by the Rockefeller Administration and the community as a mechanism for injecting new life into the region's stagnating economy. The company acquired used fuel rods from nuclear power plants, dissolved them in a liquid and recovered their plutonium and uranium for sale to other nuclear power enterprises. It lost money and the plant was closed down in 1972. By 1976 Getty Oil Company, then the proprietor of Nuclear Fuel Services, decided to wash its hands of the whole venture and the property reverted to the ownership and control of New York State.(71)

The liquid in which the used rods were dissolved became highly radioactive as a result of this operation. It was then stored in underground stainless steel containers encased in concrete that were expected to last about 40 to 50 years.(72) In addition, radioactive solid trash produced from Nuclear Fuel Services' salvage of uranium was buried at various places on the 3000-plus acres. This included hardware and contaminated rags and clothing.(73) After the plant had been shut, it was discovered that one stainless steel tank was not quite as watertight as had originally been thought: the pan under it had a crack. This produced a demand from people in the neighborhood that the area be decontaminated: they were worried that deadly waste would seep into their farms and houses.(74) The Carey Administration asked that Washington fund the entire cost of the cleanup; and urged New York State's Senators and House delegation to take appropriate action. In the House the effort was spearheaded by Democratic Representative (later Lieutenant Governor) Stanley Lundine in whose district West Valley was located. In the Senate much of the work was done by Republican Javits, though Moynihan lent a hand as well. A bill (the Lundine-Moynihan-Javits measure) was introduced in both chambers providing that the U.S. would provide 90% of the expenditures involved in making West Valley safe again. Lundine knew that the bill was a goner in the

The Days of Wine and Roses Are Over

House if John Dingell's Energy and Commerce Committee were the first to consider it. Dingell, a choleric Michigan Democrat, was worried about the potential cost to the federal government, especially as requests for federal aid in sanitizing similar locales might well be forthcoming. Thus the New Yorker made sure that his own Science and Technology Committee initially worked on the measure. The momentum acquired as a result of its approval by this Committee helped it get through Energy and Commerce: Arizona Democrat Mo Udall was instrumental in convincing Dingell that it deserved his blessing. Carey himself gave helpful testimony before Dingell's Committee, noting that the United States was the only party that could afford the extensive improvement costs and that the tanks were designed for only forty years' use of which ten had already elapsed. In the Senate, Javits called in every chit that was owing him to get the needed votes and worked like a beaver to insure that it passed by early October of 1980. It did, and so President Carter was able to announce at the same time and place that he pledged federal support for the relocation of Love Canal's Ring III residents that the U.S. Government would pay 90% of the amount necessary for clearing up West Valley.(75)

The West Valley improvements were supposed to total $400 million and take about six to eight years to finish. But they will have an ultimate price tag of well over $2 billion and will not be completed until at least 2008 and perhaps as late as 2020. Already they have cost Washington $1 billion and the State $125 million.(76) The work on the liquid waste is proceeding well: it is being "solidified into cylinders of cement and [eventually] glass".(77) Thus its escaping from its containers soon will pose no threat to the residents of the region. But no one knows where the cylinders' permanent home will be nor what to do with the solid wastes that are buried in trenches or boxes on the site.(78) Lundine when he originally introduced his measure wanted the federal government to pledge to remove these leftovers. But he had to drop this demand or his bill would have been doomed.(79)

To sum up this chapter, after 1975 the Carey Administration favored job growth over environmental preservation but certainly did not let the State's magnificent hills and waterways become polluted by "dark, satanic mills". With respect to Love Canal, for example, Berle commented to me that this matter was handled humanely: he noted that Carey decided to buy the Ring I and II homes even though there was no clear legal authority for him to do so. In retrospect, even Lois Gibbs feels that the Governor acted quickly to assist the homeowners in these Rings.(80) When some evidence surfaced hinting that Love Canal residents suffered from a disproportionate amount of chromosome damage, he did agree, as seen, to subsidize the relocation of Ring III's inhabitants getting Washington to shoulder half the expenses. And obtaining federal aid to detoxify West Valley was another major accomplishment.

Moreover, environmentalists were overjoyed by a farewell present the Governor handed them in Summer of 1982. For several years, he had inveighed against a proposed "bottle bill", one that would require a purchaser of a soda or beer bottle or can to leave a $.05 deposit that the storekeeper is to refund when the container is returned. The sponsors of the measure believed that consumers would bring the receptacles to the shop so they could get their nickels back rather than toss them onto sidewalks, highway shoulders or vacant lots. The retailer, in turn, would ship the containers to the bottler. Brewers such as Miller's, which had a big plant in New York State, opposed the bill. So did manufacturers' associations and glass workers unions, which feared that more bottles conserved meant fewer blown and thus fewer jobs. Delicatessen and bodega owners were also suspicious of the proposal, contending that the costs of storing the returned items would squeeze their already-narrow profit margins. In 1982 a Legislature swamped by lobbyists handed Carey not one but two measures: the first the bottle bill and the second a watered-down alternative known as the "total litter control" law. Given his past position, he surprised many by selecting the first. Though Commerce Commissioner George Dempster wanted "total litter control", EnCon chief Flacke argued for the eventual winner, as did Governor Richard Lamm of Colorado, Governor William Milliken of Michigan, New York Sanitation Commissioner Norman Steisel and movie actors Paul Newman and Joanne Woodward. What may have tipped the scales was a study carried out by gubernatorial aides showing that job losses from the bottle measure would be negligible.(81) So the next time you are driving

Notes to Chapter 11

1. New York Times, Sept. 7, 1974, p. 16; interview with Reid, Aug. 21, 1990, New York City.

2. Reid, interview cited n.1 supra.

3. New York State Laws of 1975, Ch. 612.

4. Quoted from Par. 2 of Sec. 8-0109 of that law.

5. Ibid.; New York Times, June 25, 1975, p. 1.

6. Democrat and Chronicle (Rochester), Feb. 2, 1976, p. 1; Feb. 18, 1976, p. 1.

7. Democrat and Chronicle (Rochester), Feb. 18, 1976, p. 1.

8. Quoted ibid. Permission to reprint quotes granted by the Democrat and Chronicle (Rochester).

9. See Public Papers of Governor Hugh L. Carey 1976 (Albany: State of New York Executive Chamber, 1986), p. 1707.

10. Letter to Carey dated Jan. 30, 1976 from William T. Clark, President, The First National Bank of Glens Falls, Hugh L. Carey Collection, St. John's Univ.(NY), EnCon (Pollution: Water: PCB) file.

11. Hellman, Peter - For The Hudson, Bad News and Good, New York Times Magazine, Oct. 24, 1976, p. 16.

12. Ibid., p. 17.

13. Ibid.; Economist, July 14, 1990, p. 30, 34.

14. Interview with John Dyson, Carey's Commerce Commissioner, Jan. 21, 1991, Millbrook. N.Y.

15. Economist, July 14, 1990, p. 30; Hellman, op. cit. n.11 supra, p. 26.

16. Hellman, op. cit. n.11 supra, p. 32; New York Times, Apr. 28, 1976, p. 1.

17. Hellman, op. cit. n.11 supra, p. 32.

18. Reid, interview cited n.1 supra; New York Times, Feb. 6, 1976, p. 30.

19. EnCon Statement dated Feb. 10, 1976, p. 1, Hugh L. Carey Collection, St. John's Univ.(NY), EnCon (Pollution: Water: PCB) file; Hellman, op. cit. n.11 supra, p. 34.

20. EnCon Statement cited n.19 supra, p. 2

21. Quoted in New York Times, Apr. 28, 1976, p. 1.

22. Quoted Hellman, op. cit. n.11 supra, p. 38.

23. New York Times, Apr. 25, 1976, Sec. 1, p. 1.

24. Hellman, op.cit. n.11 supra, p. 20, 34.

25. Dyson, interview cited n.14 supra.

26. Reid, interview cited n.1, supra; letter to Ogden Reid dated Apr. 6, 1976 from John F. Welch, a GE Vice-President, Hugh L. Carey Collection, St. John's Univ.(NY), EnCon (Pollution: Water: PCB) file; New York Times, Apr. 25, 1976, Sec. 1, p. 1.

27. Interview with Peter Berle, Carey's second Environmental Commissioner, Mar. 7, 1991, New York City.

28. New York Times, Apr. 25, 1976, Sec. 1, p. 1.

29. Dyson, interview cited n.14 supra.

30. New York Times, Apr. 28, 1976, p. 1; Apr. 30, 1976, p. A26.

31. New York Times, Sept. 8, 1976, p. 1; Oct. 7, 1976, p. 46.

32. Berle, interview cited n.27 supra.

33. New York Times, Sept. 8, 1976, p. 1.

34. New York Times, June 28, 1978, p. A1; May 16, 1990, p. B1; Aug. 13, 1993, p. B5.

35. Wacker, Tim - City Fishers, Sea Frontiers, Mar./Apr. 1994, pp. 22ff;

Carey's Environmental Policy

New York Times, May 16, 1990, p. B1; Apr. 12, 1992, Sec. 1, p. 42; June 1, 1996, p. 19.

36. Interview with Carey's third Environmental Commissioner Robert Flacke, June 12, 1991, Lake George, N.Y.

37. Times Union (Albany), Sept. 2, 1978, p. 1.

38. New York Times, Dec. 17, 1977, p. 1.

39. New York Times, June 3, 1992, p. B6.

40. Interview cited n.27 supra; New York Times, Dec. 17, 1977, p. 1.

41. See New York Times, Dec. 23, 1978, p. 25.

42. New York Times, Oct. 31, 1980, p. B1.

43. Flacke, Robert - Robert F. Flacke: Commissioner of Environmental Protection at p. 121, pp. 121-27 of Benjamin, Gerald and Hurd, T. Norman (eds.) - Making Experience Count: Managing Modern New York In The Carey Era (Albany: The Nelson A. Rockefeller Institute of Government, 1985), pp. 121-27.

44. Flacke, interview cited n.36 supra.

45. Hennessy, William - William C. Hennessy, Commissioner of Transportation at p. 175, 192 of Benjamin and Hurd (eds.), op. cit. n.43 supra.

46. Gibbs, Lois - My Story (Albany: SUNY Press, 1982); Levine, Adeline - Love Canal: Science, Politics and People (Lexington: Lexington Books, 1982).

47. New York Times, May 21, 1980, p. B6.

48. Interview with Carey's Director of State Operations Thomas Frey by phone to Rochester, N. Y., Aug. 7, 1991.

49. Gibbs, op. cit. n.46 supra, pp. 30-31; Levine, op. cit. n.46 supra, pp. 28-29.

50. Levine, op. cit. n.46 supra, p. 30.

51. Gibbs, op. cit. n.46 supra, p. 30.

52. Levine, op. cit. n.46 supra, p. 45, pp. 52-53.

53. Gibbs, op. cit. n.46 supra, p. 45.

54. Frey, interview cited n.48 supra.

55. Levine, op. cit. n.46 supra, p. 45, 63.

56. New York Times, May 15, 1990, p. B1.

57. Gibbs, op. cit. n.46 supra, pp. 66-67; Levine, op. cit. n.46 supra, pp. 89-91.

58. Gibbs, op. cit. n.46 supra, p. 114.

59. Interview with Carey Transportation Commissioner William Hennessy, Sept. 18, 1991, Albany, N.Y.

60. Interview with Lois Gibbs, Jan. 24, 1991, Falls Church, Va.

61. Interview with Sachs, June 7, 1991, New York City.

62. Gibbs, op. cit. n.46 supra, pp. 112-13.

63. Ibid., p. 114.

64. Gibbs, interview cited n.60 supra.

65. Levine, op. cit. n.46 supra, pp. 138-40; New York Times, May 19, 1990, p. 3.

66. New York Times, May 19, 1980, p. B3; May 24, 1980, p. 25.

67. New York Times, May 24, 1980, p. 25.

68. Phone interview with Eugene Eidenberg, President Carter's Deputy Secretary for Intergovernmental Relations, Washington, Sept. 4, 1991; New York Times, Oct. 2, 1980, p. B12.

69. Christian Science Monitor, Nov. 29, 1994, p. 10; New York Times, May 15, 1990, p. B1; June 22, 1994, p. B5; Staten Island Advance, Dec. 30, 1990, p. A28; Dec. 1, 1994, p. C1.

70. Business Week, May 11, 1992, p. 32; New York Times, Sept. 6, 1993, p. 7; Jan. 31, 1994, p. A1.

71. Interview with former New York State Lieutenant Governor Stanley Lundine, Jan. 31, 1992, New York City; New York Times, Mar. 21, 1979, p. A1; Oct. 29, 1989, Sec. 1, p. 1; Staten Island Advance, Apr. 22, 1990, p. A17.

72. Lundine, interview cited n.71 supra; Staten Island Advance, Apr. 22, 1990, p. A17.

73. Lundine, interview cited n.71 supra; New York Times, Mar. 21, 1979, p. A1.

74. New York Times, Jan. 12, 1979, p. B1.

75. Lundine, interview cited n.71 supra; Carey Statement Feb. 6, 1980, Hugh L. Carey Collection, St. John's Univ.(NY), EnCon (Hazardous Waste: Radioactive: West Valley: Federal) file; Memorandum from James Larocca to Carey dated June 26, 1980, located same place; Carey Testimony on West Valley before House Commerce Committee, July 28, 1980, Public Papers of Governor Hugh L. Carey 1980 (Albany: State of New York Executive Chamber, 1993), pp. 814-20.

76. Interview with Carey's Energy Commissioner James Larocca, May 29, 1990, Commack, N.Y.; Lundine, interview cited n.71 supra; Moynihan, Senator Daniel Patrick - letter to new york (Washington: U.S. Senate, 1994), July 1, 1994, p. 3; New York Times, Oct. 29, 1989, p. 1.

77. Staten Island Advance, Apr. 22, 1990, p. A17. See also Luoma, Jon - Right in Your Own Backyard, Audubon, Nov.-Dec. 1991, p. 88, pp. 92-93.

78. Moynihan, op. cit. n.76 supra, p. 3; New York Times, Oct. 29, 1989, Sec. 1, p. 1; Staten Island Advance, Apr. 22, 1990, p. A17.

79. Interview cited n.71 supra.

80. Berle, interview cited n.27 <u>supra</u>; Gibbs, interview cited n.60 <u>supra</u>.

81. <u>New York Times</u>, June 27, 1982, Sec. 1, p. 28.

Chapter 12
Carey's Health Policies:
Medicaid, Nursing Homes, and Willowbrook

IN his 1974 race Carey "repeatedly promised to make health care the number one priority of his Administration".(1) Because of the City/State fiscal crises, he could not keep this pledge. However his years in Albany, especially his first term, did feature some important health policy innovations. In fact, Mario Cuomo says that the ex-Congressman's efforts to reform the State's health care system were as important as his saving New York City from bankruptcy.(2)

New York State's primary agency for administering its health program is its Health Department, headed by a Health Commissioner. The two Carey Health Commissioners were both highly competent individuals -- again, it is a constant of the Carey years that excellent people were appointed to head the various agencies in the Executive Branch. The first, Dr. Robert P. Whelan, remained in office until mid-1978: the second, the late Dr. David Axelrod, stayed throughout the rest of the Carey years. Axelrod, who was regarded as a model state administrator, was reappointed by Cuomo. He remained in office until 1991, when a serious stroke forced him to resign. Both were involved, as seen, in the Love Canal crisis. Other Carey aides, e.g., Richard Berman, Robert Schiffer and Dr. Jeffrey Sachs, were also highly talented and played yeoman roles in the formulation of the Governor's physical and mental health policies. Yet none of these outstanding public servants was number one in the development of these approaches. That honor easily belonged to Dr. Kevin Cahill, a specialist in tropical medicine who was and is an extremely close friend of the Governor. He was the Carey family's personal physician who cared for Helen Carey during her last illness in early 1974 just as the Congressman was beginning his gubernatorial race in earnest. From 1975 until the resignation that he submitted at the end of 1980, he was the Chief Executive's $1 a year Special Assistant for Health Affairs. He spent only one day a week in Albany but, as an intimate of Carey who frequently talked with him, had his ear on health matters more than any other individual. Moreover, coming from outside the health bureaucracy, he was able to suggest cost-cutting and other ideas that most civil servants would have been reluctant to openly advocate.(3)

Medicaid proved a major headache for the Governor. It is a fed-

The Days of Wine and Roses Are Over

eral grant-in aid program designed to provide free basic medical services to the needy (e.g., hospital care, visits to the doctor's office, prenatal advice). In New York with its high per capita income, the U.S. pays half the cost and the State the rest. Exactly how a state comes up with its share is a matter of indifference to Washington: New York when Carey was in office made New York City and the counties outside the metropolis dig into their pockets for half the State contribution. Third grade arithmetic will demonstrate that this meant that the City and the counties had to bear 25% of the Medicaid expenditures within their respective borders. However, the shape of the program within a given governmental subdivision in New York is not set locally but is determined by U.S. and State law. Washington allows the states to offer "optional" services above and beyond the "basic" ones mentioned above. Under Governor Rockefeller, in office when Medicaid was imported into New York State in 1966, it was decided to accord most of the extras, including prescription drugs, physical and occupational therapy, nursing homes, podiatry and chiropractic.(4)

Rockefeller had no idea of how much a burden Medicaid would become for Albany, the counties and New York City. His version soon became by far the most expensive program of this sort in the nation.(5) In fiscal 1976 (i.e., from April 1, 1975 to March 30, 1976) total federal, state and local Medicaid expenditures in the State were $2,815,000,000.(6) This meant, under the then-prevailing 50-25-25 formula, that the program would cost the State treasury about $700 million and the counties plus New York City the same amount. Within New York Medicaid expenses had jumped about 25% a year since the program had made its appearance.(7) The State share alone for fiscal 1976 made up a sizeable chunk (almost 7%) of its $10.6 billion budget for that year. And about 2/3 of the "local" $700 million liability had to be born by a New York City that was staring bankruptcy in the face in 1975 and 1976. If Medicaid expenses in the Empire State continued to increase at 25% per annum, the City might go under regardless of how much cash it could squeeze out of Washington.

So though Carey genuinely wanted to improve the quality of the lives of the poorest of his constituents, he knew that he had to curb the Medicaid incubus: this was a priority of his first term.(8) He and his aides decided that the Medicaid savings should come primarily through reining in reimbursement rates as opposed to cutting the services available to Medicaid clients. This meant capping the amounts Albany would pay the hospitals, doctors, nursing homes and others who took care of the men and women embraced by the program.(9) On March 30, 1976 the Governor signed a bill, Chapter 76 of the 1976 Laws of New York State, which imposed restraints of this sort (and which gave the Health Commissioner authority to close hospitals that had beds in excess of actual public need). Under a section of "76 of 76" strongly pushed by Cahill, Medicaid payments to hospitals for outpatient and emergency care were kept for a year at the amount that had been approved for 1975. Strict limits were also set on Medicaid disbursements to hospitals for other services, and to nursing homes. In fact, a freeze on increases in payments to nursing homes had been imposed as early as 1975.(10) A system of "prospective Medicaid reimbursement" for hospitals was readopted and modified under which the institutions would recover from Albany not necessarily what they had expended on a patient but a sum equal to the "reasonable costs" of treating her.(11) The Rockefeller Administration had implemented prospective reimbursement in 1970. However, its scheme had proved inadequate to contain costs because it permitted hospitals to pass on to the State any salary increases they might grant those of their workers who dealt with Medicaid clients. The Carey genre of prospective reimbursement was more successful here because it covered rises in labor costs only to the extent they were less than the rate of inflation and because it capped restitutions for, e.g., laboratory and operating room fees and X-rays.(12)

"76 of 76" did contain some service cuts as well as repayment controls. As a rule, Medicaid patients for whom surgery had been prescribed could have only one day of "pre-operative hospital care". No Medicaid patient upon whom surgery had been performed could stay in the hospital more than twenty days "per spell of illness" unless absolutely necessary to save her life or to keep her from "continuing disability". And Medicaid would no longer pay for non-prescription drugs. In a part of Chapter 76 added by the

The Days of Wine and Roses Are Over

Legislature after a study of a California program, the Health Commissioner was placed under a duty to determine, above and beyond the general limitations embodied in the statute, the need for treatments given or proposed for individual Medicaid and other patients. The Governor, his health aides, and the Commissioner eagerly put this proviso into effect. By Fall of 1977, 150 "gestapo" nurses and doctors had been placed in threescore hospitals with many Medicaid recipients. These studied discrete cases to see whether the sick person had been admitted too early, whether she could be cured as an outpatient, whether a recommended operation for her really was necessary, and whether the facility was dragging its heels in discharging her. The hospital's "native" health personnel were unhappy with this "spy system", but the Governor and Legislature continued to support it until it was replaced (against New York's wishes) by a less-effective federally-mandated method of reviewing hospital Medicaid payments.(13)

Certain other Carey-era initiatives intended directly or indirectly to cut the cost of Medicaid should be noted here. The State prevented hospitals from "overcapitalizing", i.e., from buying fancy medical equipment that cost an arm and a leg and would pressure these institutions to demand more of a subsidy from Medicaid and other insurance programs. All major acquisitions for treating patients had to be approved by Albany under the new way of doing things.(14) Since prescription drugs marketed under a brand name usually cost more than those sold under their generic label, Chapter 776 of the 1977 State Laws made it easier for pharmacists to dispense medicines described generically. Chapter 77 of the State Laws of that year relied more on service shrinkage than did "76 of 76" and excluded, e.g., podiatrists, chiropractors, and much physical and occupational therapy from eligibility for medicaid reimbursement. (In 1979, coverage was restored for all these specialties except chiropracty.)(15) And a measure pushed by Assembly Subcommittee on Health Care Chairman Alan Hevesi required "shared health facilities", more commonly known as "Medicaid mills", to register with the State and to allow State employees to inspect them. These "mills" are offices shared by several doctors who see mainly Medicaid patients. It was quite common for one of these physicians to send a client after he had finished examining, e.g., her blood pressure, to one of his colleagues for a totally unnecessary examination to look, e.g., at her ears, nose and throat. Under the measure, the registration of a "mill" may be revoked if it engages in dishonest practices.(16)

These various steps designed to cut Medicaid costs had, taken together, considerable success. Total federal/state/local payments under Medicaid in the State actually declined from $2.9 billion in 1976 to $2.7 billion in 1977. And in 1978 they grew only to $2.8 billion, still less than the 1976 level.(17) Jeffrey Sachs estimates that during the Carey Administration, $2.3 billion was saved through closing hospitals, the Medicaid reimbursement rate freezes, and the adoption of the tighter system of prospective reimbursement. That is, the State spent $2.3 billion less than it would have had these actions not been taken. He admits that Albany's health expenditures did increase during the Carey years taken as a whole, but at less than the rate of inflation.(18) And Robert Schiffer believes that without the above-noted changes in the Medicaid system, expenditures for that program would have tripled rather than doubled (as they actually did) during the Carey era.(19) (Schiffer admitted to me that the Carey health specialists were "naive" in assuming that the hospitals and nursing homes hit by the reimbursement constraints would swallow these themselves and not pass them on to their underpaid employees. As could have been predicted, they refused to grant them wage increases and, as a result, strikes broke out in the voluntary hospitals in 1976 and in nursing homes in 1978. He and Richard Berman, among others, had to intervene in the negotiations that settled these disputes with a compromise that gave the workers something of what they wanted.(20))

Surprisingly, given the great amount of cooperation on this issue during his first term, Medicaid was the cause of one of the most bitter fights between Carey and the Republicans controlling the New York State Senate during his second. In January of 1981 the Governor, under heavy pressure from Mayor Ed Koch, proposed that the State pay all non-federal Medicaid costs within its borders. In return, the cities and counties would have to reduce property taxes. This takeover was to be effected over a four year period.(21) The State Assembly was enthusiastic about this idea as it was controlled by Democrats many of whom were from a New

The Days of Wine and Roses Are Over

York City that visualized a tremendous weight lifted from its shoulders. So this chamber passed the Carey recommendation but with a seven rather than a four year phase-in.(22) Its prospects in the Senate initially seemed rosy as well, as Senate Majority Leader Warren Anderson appeared to favor it though recommending a six-year assumption period.(23) However, the Binghamtonian soon became hostile to the Chief Executive's plan. Upstate Senate Republicans, upon whose support the Majority Leader depended, did not like it. They believed that it would increase State taxes for their constituents without reducing their local imposts: many upstate communities have few Medicaid recipients and thus the program is not a drain on their treasuries. Carey stuck by his guns as long as he could, as Koch and State Senate Minority Leader Manfred Ohrenstein admit; and the upshot was a 42 day delay in enacting the State budget, until that time the longest the public had had to endure. At the end, the Governor had to give in, extracting from Anderson a meaningless promise to "study" the problem of what jurisdiction(s) should carry the Medicaid cross.(24) None-the-less, Carey's Medicaid-assumption recommendation paved the way for a 1983 Cuomo measure which by 1992 insured that Albany bore about 60% rather then 50% of the non-federal portion of Medicaid outlays in New York.(25)

Nursing homes are residences that house the elderly. Sometimes their clients are alone and are too ill to live by themselves; sometimes they are persons with family members who for one reason or another cannot take care of them at home. Many of the residents of these facilities are poor people; and the Rockefeller Administration decided in the 1960s to use Medicaid to pay for the care of the indigents they sheltered. Under that GOP Chief Executive, Medicaid at first reimbursed nursing homes for the actual costs incurred by their owners in housing Medicaid patients, at least if such costs were "reasonable". However, little effort was made by anyone check to determine the reasonableness of a particular expense. "Before the 1975 scandals, New York employed only fourteen auditors to examine the detailed reports of more than 800 facilities."(26) Consequently, as Assemblyman Andrew Stein discovered, though some homes provided excellent service, many mistreated their clients while simultaneously inflating the statement of their costs in the dossiers they submitted to the State. These untruths enabled them to receive from Albany bloated and unjustified Medicaid checks. Some placed on their payrolls family members who did no work. Some reported non-existent purchases of goods from imaginary companies. Others made phony property acquisitions at what was, on paper, a high sum. And New York handed these crooks whopping Medicaid remittances to recompense them for the no-show jobs, the products never acquired, and the fictitious and swollen real estate expenditures.

Though in 1974 candidate Carey talked very little about cleaning up the nursing home mess, soon after his election he asked Mario Cuomo, his Secretary of State-to-be, to study Stein's findings and to ascertain from appropriate federal, state and local officials what other information they had about nursing home chicanery. When he saw that his future subordinate's report accepted the Stein determinations, he decided to appoint a "Moreland Act" Commission to conduct an inquiry to see what regulatory legislation was needed.(27)

Morris B. Abram, a distinguished lawyer and former President of Brandeis University, was chosen to chair the Commission. Its chief counsel was Andrew Schaffer, who as a former United States Attorney had had an extensive background in law enforcement and investigation. Armed with subpoena power and holding televised hearings, it issued a series of reports that documented the widespread failure of Rockefeller's Health Department to enforce standards in nursing homes. It charged that the Department had never revoked a home-administrator's license nor fined an owner.(28) One of its analyses adumbrated the political influence wielded by many nursing home figures and named prominent politicians who were directly or indirectly on their payrolls. For example, Democratic Assembly Speaker Stanley Steingut's insurance company carried the insurance on six homes operated by Rabbi Bernard Bergman, one of the industry's biggest thieves. And Republican Assemblyman James Emery, later to become Minority Leader, had earned over $12,000 in insurance commissions from another proprietor.(29)

In 1975 the Commission proposed eleven reforms, which the Governor then made part of his program. These suggestions included requiring that the Health Department conduct two or more inspections of each home per year, one to be unnanounced; that all statements required by law to be submitted by a home to the Department be audited by a certified public accountant; that the State be able to recover treble damages from operators guilty of submitting swollen claims; that individuals who had been abused or inadequately treated by nursing homes be able to recover damages in individual or class actions, with the defendant possibly having to pay the plaintiffs' lawyers' fee; and (the only one not to pass) that lawyer-legislators be barred from representing clients before state agencies. The Commission, which went out of business in May of 1976, tried with Carey's help to have this proviso enacted that year; but the solons did not buy it until 1988, well into Cuomo's Administration.(30)

Lynbrook, New York, is a quiet suburban village in Long Island, just north of the Sunrise Highway. The Bronx is New York City's poorest borough. One thing these superficially dissimilar locales had in common in the mid and late 1980s was shoestores owned by one Arthur Jonas. His Bronx branch was Custom Shoe Shop, Inc; his Lynbrook enterprise had a more sophisticated label: Custom Orthotic Labs, Inc. What the shrewd Mr. Jonas did was develop a computer program to bill Medicaid for expensive orthopedic foot appliances and footwear supposedly prescribed to help poor people who were having pain in their toes, heels or arches. The program told the government that his outlets were supplying women and children with aches in these extremities with special heels and supports: what his Medicaid clients actually received were cheap shoes they could have purchased at the local five and ten. It also notified Medicaid that Jonas was selling male orthopedic patients costly shoes that his branches did not even stock. He and his enterprises were indicted in Nassau County for stealing $1.1 million by use of these tricks. In 1988 he pleaded guilty and was sentenced to a well-deserved one to three years of "cooling his heels" in prison.

The Bedford Stuyvesant neighborhood of Brooklyn has also been plagued by Medicaid cheats. Mr. Sheldon Weinberg owned a facility there called Bed-Stuy Health Care Corporation and made his sons Jay and Ronald its "coadministrators". A fantastic 400,000 of the visits to this clinic for which the Weinbergs had billed Medicaid were phony. They employed a dentist to spend all his time there forging fraudulent invoices. Later they tampered with a computer to get it to spew out claims with supporting medical charts for 12,000 fictitious patient visits a month. Tried in 1988, the three were convicted of stealing millions in Medicaid funds. Sheldon was also found guilty of not discharging his State tax liabilities on $190,000 paid him by his mill.(31)

A little known agency known as the New York State Medicaid Fraud Control Unit must be thanked for the fact that criminals such as Jonas and Weinberg have had to spend time behind bars. And this Medicaid Fraud control unit is a direct descendant of an innovation of the early Carey years. Cuomo's study of the nursing home mess recommended that the Chief Executive create not only the Moreland Commission but also a Special Prosecutor's Office to investigate and prosecute any nursing home cheating that bore signs of being a crime. The Governor accepted this idea. Upon Cuomo's advice and with the approval of Attorney General Louis J. Lefkowitz, he appointed an attorney previously unknown to him named Charles J. Hynes as the Special Prosecutor.(32) Hynes, who later became Brooklyn District Attorney, went to work on January 10, 1975, just a few days after Carey's inauguration. He immediately set up seven regional offices and, by the end of 1975, had already handed down sixteen indictments involving twenty persons and obtained four convictions.(33) As the report sent to the Governor by his office at the start of 1976 commented:

"The investigations to date....appear to confirm widespread financial skulduggery and wholesale misappropriation of taxpayer funds....The evidence suggests that the taxpayer has unwittingly subsidized personal maids, private residential landscaping expenses, personal travel expenses....personal luggage....vast quantities of liquor, interior decorating expenses....extensive vacation expenses....mink coats....personal servants, renovations to private residences....[and] theatre tickets...."(34)

In 1976 the jurisdiction of Hynes's office was extended to cover "adult" as well as nursing homes and in 1977 it was given power to recover in civil actions money stolen from any part of the Medicaid program.(35) By the end of 1976, it had brought 56 cases involving 70 defendants and 13 of these prosecutions had been completed, with the defendants pledging to give back to the State almost $4 million. The notorious Rabbi Bergman himself pleaded guilty in March 1976 and received a year in jail after he promised to cooperate fully with Hynes.(36)

New York was hardly the only state in which cheaters were living off the fatted Medicaid calf. A 1975 investigation by a subcommittee of the United States House of Representatives revealed that fraud in the program extended from sea to shining sea and that neither the federal government nor the states were doing much about it. A 1976 investigation by a United States Senate Committee documented more of the same. Thus in October 1977 Congress passed a law signed by President Carter (PL 95-142) which, to encourage the states to crack down on dishonesty in all aspects of the Medicaid system, contained a Section Seventeen providing for 90% federal funding of any Medicaid Fraud Control units they might establish.(37) In 1978 Carey certified Hynes's office as the Medicaid Fraud Control Unit for New York State, which was no surprise as this unit had been the model for the federal law.(38) The agency remains very busy to this very day rooting out Medicaid dishonesty. And in 1988 it put paid to the sordid saga of Rabbi Bergman by accepting a $1.3 million check from his estate, making a total of $3.8 million he reimbursed the State from his ill-gotten gains.(39)

Carey's record in Congress before moving to Albany would have led one to predict that his Administration would produce important gains for the mentally retarded. He was friendly with the Kennedy brothers, i.e., President John F. and Senators Robert and Edward; and this trio had a special concern for this group as one of their sisters was retarded. As a member of the House Education and Labor and Ways and Means Committees, he had helped draft a 1965 measure to provide federal funds for the education of learning-disabled children; a 1972 act mandating higher standards for residential facilities for them; and a 1973 law requiring that local school districts spend as much on them as on "normal" children as a condition of getting federal financial assistance. And in the 1974 election campaign he called for making New York State a "national model" for ending discrimination against the handicapped.(40)

Shortly after his victory in 1974 it became clear to him that he had to wage a battle on behalf of a particular group of mentally handicapped individuals, a fight which if successful could help other persons similarly situated throughout the State. He felt, however, that he had to secure the reshaping of the Department that cared for them among others before this or any other war he would conduct on their behalf could finally be won. Therefore, though reorganizations of administrative agencies often accomplish very little, this particular example must be described.

Prior to the Carey years, one large state agency, the Department of Mental Hygiene (DMH), directly operated facilities for both the retarded and mentally ill; and also provided services for alcoholics and drug addicts. Parents of the mentally handicapped believed that DMH was controlled by psychiatrists more interested in treating the unbalanced rather than the educationally subpar.(41) Carey fully understood the differences between the mentally sick and the retarded(42) and knew that one often did not need psychiatrists to care for the latter.(43) Also, some high-ranking DMH officials advocated looking mainly to the physical health rather than the developmental needs of the mentally disabled.(44) Accordingly, he was sympathetic to the demand that a separate agency be carved out of DMH for the benefit of that group. The 1974 gubernatorial election campaign saw him speaking at a dinner given by the New York State Association for the Mentally Retarded. At that banquet was Republican State Senator William Conklin of Brooklyn, a member of the Senate Committees on Finance and Mental Hygiene. Conklin himself was a strong supporter of the idea that DMH should be stripped of its power to care for the retarded and that this function should be given to a new agency. He himself had a mentally handicapped son and was one of those who felt that DMH was insensitive to the needs of the intellectually backward.(45) Carey said at the dinner that Conklin should hand him the bill creating the separate agency on a "silver platter". This was not an endorsement of the measure in so many words, but everyone at the event except the Governor himself took it as a pledge that he would sign Conklin's measure if the Legislature were to approve it.(46)

Conklin did introduce it in 1975, right after Carey became Governor; and both State Senate and State Assembly passed it by overwhelming majorities. Given the Chief Executive's campaign utterance, Albany observers felt that he was certain to okay it. However, he surprised a lot of people and angered Conklin by rejecting the bill. His veto message declared that "It is imperative to bring all medical, educational and social disciplines to bear on the problems of each [developmentally disabled] individual. The arbitrary separation of mental retardation would merely frustrate a comprehensive treatment plan and fragment the delivery of service".(47) The phraseology here is, of course, that of Cahill, who was actively involved in drafting all of his chief's health and mental health veto and approval messages through 1980. The physician felt that some retarded individuals have serious emotional as well as learning problems and that it thus makes sense to place both the mentally handicapped and the emotionally disturbed in the care of an agency which can respond to their psychological as well as their learning problems.(48)

But those who wanted to see institutions caring for the educationally below-normal free from the control of alienists were soon to have their innings. In 1977 Carey sent to the Legislature a bill providing for the creation of three autonomous agencies within DMH. One would work with the mentally ill, one with the mentally retarded, and one with drug addicts and alcoholics. The Department would remain in existence but simply be a shell to house the three new units and a forum in which they would talk to each other and coordinate their efforts.(49) Various objections to Carey's proposal were raised: e.g., persons dealing with chronic drunks felt that alcoholics should not be served by the same unit that treated drug addicts.(50) And the public employees union known as the Civil Service Employees Association (CSEA) feared that the new agencies would contract with private organizations to work with their respective clienteles.(51)

However, in July 1977 a bill containing what Carey had asked for earlier in the year was enacted.(52) It created within the existing DMH three almost-independent offices: the Office of Mental Health (OMH) (for the mentally ill); the Office of Mental Retardation and Developmental Disabilities (OMRDD) (for the retarded) and the Office of Alcoholism and Substance Abuse. OMH and OMRDD were and are headed by "Commissioners". (To keep the heavy drinkers and the drug addicts apart, there was at first no "Commissioner" of the Office of Alcoholism and Substance

Abuse but, rather, two "Directors".) The Commissioners are supposed to sit down together from time to time to insure that their services are coordinated and that those who suffer from, e.g., both mental retardation and mental illness get all the treatment they need. Carey's Mental Health Comissioner Lawrence Kolb privately opposed the DMH reorganization but loyally supported it in public even though (had he not soon resigned) it would have demoted him from being CEO of a whole department to being the head of an office (OMH) within one.(53) OMRDD and not OMH was accorded control over Staten Island's Willowbrook complex for the developmentally disabled.(54)

When I and my family moved to Staten Island in 1968, we had never heard of its huge Willowbrook Developmental Center for the retarded. Our ignorance was probably replicated by most Americans. However, within the next few years it was only the most obtuse who were totally unacquainted with this institution and its multifarious problems. In 1972, the television personality Geraldo Rivera filmed a program about it that vividly portrayed its horrors -- its overcrowding, its lackadaisical staff, its inadequate medical care, its weak educational and recreational offerings, and the dirt and nakedness of its clients. In the early 1970s, it still was jammed; though its population was somewhat less than the nearly 6000 within its walls in the mid-1960s.(55) Some of these men and women and children were of normal intelligence: they simply had been dumped in the Center by uncaring, indigent or frightened parents when they were very young. They appeared stupid simply because they never had had any decent schooling or treatment, and because many of their fellow-boarders lacked the capacity to do more than utter a few grunts. My wife and I invited a couple of these bright Willowbroook castaways to Christmas dinner in the mid 1970s, at about the time the State had decided to significantly improve the campus; and we had a fascinating conversation with them about their treatment there.

In March, 1972, frustrated parents of retarded children living at Willowbrook, aided by civil liberties lawyers, brought suit in federal district court in Brooklyn to secure an order that the State of New York and its Department of Mental Hygiene significantly improve the facility. Federal Judge Orrin Judd issued in April, 1973 a temporary injunction commanding the State to do so. In 1974 the actual trial began. In fact, the Rockefeller Administration had begun shifting patients elsewhere after the 1972 suit had been initiated so that at the time Carey moved to Albany there were "only" about 3000; staff had been added; and ill clients were being treated at Staten Island's Public Health Service (now Bayley-Seton) Hospital. Nonetheless, conditions even in 1974 were far from what they should have been.(56) During that year, lawyers for the State and for the plaintiffs worked out a consent decree but Governor Malcolm Wilson refused to initial it.(57) Shortly after his victory in November of 1974, and even before his inauguration, Carey toured the premises. This excursion made it clear to him that he had to cleanse the Willowbrook stable.(58) Accordingly, he asked Budget Director Peter Goldmark to continue the negotiations with the Willowbrook plaintiffs and their attorneys to see if some sort of agreement could be reached. (Goldmark had had some experience in dealing with institutions for the retarded when he had been Massachusetts' Commissioner of Social Services.)(59)

In April, 1975 Goldmark and the parents' lawyers drafted a consent decree -- almost immediately approved by Carey and Judd -- of over 40 single spaced, typewritten pages most of which demanded a continuing improvement in Willowbrook's ambiance but whose last page mandated that within six years, i.e., by 1981, the campus was to have only 250 residents, all from Staten Island. Among the other major provisions of the agreement were that:

1. Within a year, the state would have to transfer 200 clients to small group homes and move the rest to similar places over the subsequent five years;

2. The number of staff was to be increased from 3000 to 3800 and

3. A seven-member review panel, henceforth termed the "Willowbrook Review Panel", was to monitor the implementation of the decree.(60)

The phasing down of Willowbrook began at a disappointingly slow pace. When Carey's Assistant Counsel Clarence Sundram made phone calls nine months after the decree had been entered to see what was happening, he discovered that no one was doing much of anything to reduce the institution's population.(61) One hundred and thirty five rather than the agreed-upon 200 persons had been transferred to small community residences by the end of

1975. Six hundred were supposed to have been relocated by the end of 1976; but only 81 had been moved during the first six months of that year. Additionally, the Review Panel contended that not enough staff had been added.(62) Some observers felt that the chief bureaucrats at the Department of Mental Hygiene were responsible for the snail-like progress.(63) According to Sundram, the DMH higher-ups just did not like the decree and found "its civil liberties premises phony".(64) Kolb denies that he in any way tried to frustrate the shrinking of Willowbrook and in fact believes that the educationally subpar generally will do better in a community setting. But he confesses to having had reservations about the consent decree, contending that it created another layer of officialdom and that the small homes to which it ordered transfers made have, individually, little political clout.(65)

Carey was aware of the lack of progress; and in 1975 he appointed Thomas Coughlin as Deputy Commissioner of DMH to start the Willowbrook ball moving. Coughlin, who has a handicapped child, had been a state trooper but, at the time of his appointment, was working full time in a center for the retarded in Watertown, New York. Carey had once toured the center and was impressed by Coughlin's programs and ideas about educating its men and women. In addition, the Governor felt that as an ex-state police sergeant, he could impose his will on reluctant DMH staffers.(66)

One of the obstacles to emptying Willowbrook vanished when, as a result of the split of DMH, Coughlin became Commissioner of an autonomous OMRDD free of the control of bureaucrats sceptical about moving the retarded out of large complexes. However, other hurdles still faced him and his assistant Barbara Blum, in charge of the office (the Metropolitan Placement Unit or MPU) that was responsible for finding homelike community settings for its inmates. The Civil Service Employees Union, representing the staff of the complex, was concerned that placing them in group homes would cost its members their jobs.(67) Blum herself favored relocating the residents into houses operated by private non-profit or religious agencies. She felt that these would be cheaper and that their staff would be less rigid in the way they dealt with their clientele.(68) Nonetheless, Carey, Coughlin and Blum soon agreed that the State, too, would start to operate group homes so that the exodus from Willowbrook would mean no job loss for civil servants: any employee who was no longer needed at the Staten Island site would be offered a position at a group residence or another center. Once this concession was made to the union, more and more clients were moved from the institution.(69)

Another barrier to the implementation of the 1975 Willowbrook decree was the opposition of communities to having group homes located in their midst. To counter this hurdle, Sundram drafted and had introduced (and the Governor later signed) a measure(70) mandating community input before the Office of Mental Health or OMRDD could establish a group home in a residential area. However, the statute also provided that the agency's decision to locate this type of residence in a community need not be set aside unless its chief became convinced that the shelter would substantially alter the character of the neighborhood. This formula satisfied legislators in areas that were potential locales of small homes for "refugees" from Willowbrook and other large institutions for the mentally disabled. It also made Sundram and other advocates of neighborhood settings for them happy. They knew that the courts would give great weight to an administrator's determination that a house inhabited by the retarded would not substantially modify the nature of the district, and were thus aware that the law would not significantly slow their return to the community.(71) Certainly one located near me has not been detrimental to the area. It is well-maintained; and its habitants do not wander the streets but take the bus daily to jobs in workshops or in the private sector.

In December of 1981, Judge John Bartels, who had taken over the Willowbrook case in 1974, had paid an unannounced visit there and was shocked at the dirt still prevailing in its kitchens, bathrooms and residential areas. And by the end of April, 1982, twelve months after the April 30, 1981 deadline date by which only 250 were supposed to be left at the institution, 1300 still called it "home".(72) So he issued a long decision appointing a special master to insure that the State continued to improve this complex and the others to which its clients had been moved as a "waystation" to more intimate housing. He did, however, give the State four more years to get its "guests" into pleasant group settings as it was have real difficulty finding suitable and reasonably-priced detached homes in New York City for these men and women. Moreover, some large non-profit organizations had shown themselves reluctant to operate small facilities for the retarded.(73)

Despite these problems, there is no doubt that by 1982, Carey's final year in office, things were better for many of the 4750 who had inhabited Willowbrook in 1972 when the original suit was filed and were still alive. (Five hundred and fifty seven who had been living there in 1972 had died during the decade.) At the start of 1982 fewer than half of the 4750 (i.e., about 2350) were still at the Center or in other large complexes; and of these quite a few were in transit to residential-type houses.(74) By 1983, the total State population of sizeable institutions for the mentally handicapped was only 13,000, down from 24,500 in 1972. There were then 14,000 mentally handicapped persons (not all from Willowbrook, of course) living in 1,000 community residences: only 50 such domiciles had existed in 1975. Within a few years after Carey had left office, about 75% of Willowbroook's residents had entered group homes. In 1993, a 95-year old Judge Bartels signed papers ending the eighteen-year federal court supervision of the Center and of its former residents. Of that class, all but 150 of the survivors were by then back with their families or in group homes; and Bartels' farewell document requires that the State never move them back to gigantic dormitories.(75) Willowbrook itself presently has no retarded residents though some live in tastefully-built homes on its perimeter; the college where I teach is now located on a handsome campus on its old grounds.

There is close to unanimous feeling that Carey personally provided much of the spark for the evacuation of Willowbrook. Blum, Assembly Mental Health Chairperson Elizabeth Connelly and Coughlin all emphasized to me how genuinely devoted he was to the cause of the mentally disabled. Coughlin mentioned that he still attends masses for them.(76) Sundram pointed out that the Chief Executive could have let the consent decree sway in the wind if he had wanted to. All it required him to do was ask the Legislature for funds to implement the judgment: there was nothing that compelled him to twist the solons' arms.(77) But he took his responsibilities under the agreement seriously and pushed hard and successfully for adequate state funding of the exit from Willowbrook despite the serious fiscal crises of 1975 and 1976.(78) By May 1978, less than halfway through the Carey Administration, over $100 million had been spent to improve conditions at the complex and at other institutions to which its clients had been transferred and to move them to community settings. This was over and above the amount that would have expended on the Center anyway.(79) David and Sheila Rothman declare that Carey pushed the negotiations about the consent decree because "he....had a long and deep personal and political commitment to helping the handicapped".(80) And even in the suit that led to Judge Bartels' 1982 decree ordering further reforms on Staten Island, a Civil Liberties Union lawyer participating in the case against the State paid tribute to the Governor's "strong commitment to the mentally retarded".(81)

Unfortunately, it is impossible to laud his policies for the mentally ill, which consisted of little more than releasing them from large psychiatric hospitals without providing them with adequate care in the community. As he himself admitted in 1995, his Administration had to have priorities; and this group was way down on the list -- partly because the federal government was providing more help for the retarded than for the emotionally troubled.(82) He left it to the Cuomo Administration to finance group homes and apartments for the latter: thanks to his successor's quiet efforts, there are now more of them in these residences than in gigantic asylums.(83)

Notes to Chapter 12

1. Bulgaro, Patrick and Webb, Arthur - Federal-State Conflicts in Cost Control, Proceedings of American Academy of Political Science, Vol. 33 (1980), at p. 92, 93.

2. Cuomo, Mario - The New York Idea (New York: Crown, 1994), p. 132.

3. Interview with Cahill, July 26, 1993, New York City; New York Times, Jan. 18, 1977, p. 33. Cahill remarked that on his first day in office, Carey visited the Departments of Health and Mental Hygiene, locales which had hardly ever been honored by Nelson Rockefeller's presence. Remarks, "Carey Years" Conference, Apr. 20, 1995, New York City.

4. That part of this paragraph that describes the basic structure of the federal medicaid program comes from Cochrane, Clarke E., Mayer, Lawrence C., Carr T. R. and Cayer, N. Joseph - American Public Policy: An Introduction, 3rd ed. (New York: St. Martin's Press, 1990), pp. 279-80.

5. Staten Island Advance, July 1, 1977, p. 3.

6. Letter to Assemblyman Willis H. Stephens dated Nov. 7, 1977 from Robert Morgado, Hugh L. Carey Collection, St. John's Univ.(NY), Insurance (Medicaid) file.

7. Ibid.

8. Interview with Carey Program Associate Robert Schiffer, Apr. 22, 1991, New York City.

9. Ibid.

10. Klurfeld, Jim - Cahill: The Doctor Who Would Be King, Empire State Report, July 1976, p. 2l6, pp. 216-17; New York Times, Mar. 26, 1976, p. 68; Oct. 24, 1976, Sec. 1, p. 45. Vladek, Bruce - Unloving Care: The Nursing Home Tragedy (New York: Basic Books, 1980) notes at p. 86 the 1975 freeze on nursing home payment rates.

11. Cahill, Kevin - Health In New York State: A Progress Report (Albany: Health Education Service, 1977), p. 30.

12. Interview with Carey Deputy Director of Social Services (later head of his Office of Development Planning) Hugh O'Neill, June 17, 1992, New York City; interview with Carey Program Associate Jeffrey Sachs, June

7, 1991, New York City; Cahill, op. cit. n.11 supra, pp. 30-31.

13. Interview with William Abelow, ex-President of League of Voluntary Hospitals and Nursing Homes of New York State, Jan. 13, 1993, New York City; with Carey Office of Health Systems Management head Richard A. Berman, Aug. 5, 1991, New York City; Bulgaro and Webb, op. cit. n.1 supra, pp. 96-101; Lirtzman, Sidney and Bresnick, David - Onsite-Offsite, Empire, Feb. 1979, p. 6, pp. 6-7.

14. Abelow and Berman, interviews cited n.13 supra.

15. New York Times, June 17, 1979, p. B7; June 10, 1979, p. B2.

16. New York State Laws of 1977, Ch. 770 and 771; New York Times, Apr. 20, 1977, p. B2.

17. Bulgaro and Webb, op cit. n.1 supra, p. 108.

18. Sachs, interview cited n.12 supra.

19. Schiffer, interview cited n.8 supra.

20. Berman, interview cited n.13 supra; Schiffer, interview cited n.8 supra; New York Times, Apr. 8, 1978, p. 1. These strikes taught the State that it had to enter contract negotiations between hospitals/nursing homes and their employees at the outset of these discussions. Carey aides were involved in these sessions from the beginning in 1980 and 1982 and walkouts were thus averted in these years. Abelow, interview cited n.13 supra.

21. Letter from Carey to Senate Majority Leader Warren Anderson dated Apr. 24, 1981, Hugh L. Carey Collection, St. John's Univ.(NY), Fiscal (Budget: Yearly Budget 1981-82) file; New York Times, Feb. 11, 1981, p. B2. Koch told Carey that he would not support him for reelection unless he pushed this Medicaid takeover. Interview with Mayor Edward I. Koch, Nov. 11, 1994, New York City

22. Letter to Mayor Edward I. Koch dated Apr. 30, 1991 from Carey, Hugh L. Carey Collection, St. John's Univ.(NY), Koch file.

23. New York Times, Feb. 11, 1981, p. B2.

24. Koch, interview cited n.21 supra; interview with Ohrenstein, Oct. 25,

1994, New York City; <u>Staten Island Advance</u>, May 3, 1981, p. A26.

25. Koch, interview cited n.21 <u>supra</u>; <u>Staten Island Advance</u>, Jan. 15, 1995, p. C3.

26. Vladek, <u>op.cit</u>. n.10 <u>supra</u>, pp. 86-87.

27. <u>Public Papers of Governor Hugh L. Carey 1975</u> (Albany: State of New York Executive Chamber, 1982), p. 732, 742; Hynes, Charles J. - <u>First Annual Report to Governor Hugh L. Carey</u> (New York: Special State Prosecutor for Health and Social Services, Jan. 10, 1976), p. 1; <u>Staten Island Advance</u>, Jan. 11, 1975, p. 1. Since the State Health Department audits nursing homes, their conditions and financial practices involve a New York State agency and ergo can be probed by a Moreland Commission. (The 1907 Moreland Act gives the Governor the right to appoint a commission to investigate any problem involving a New York State agency. <u>New York Times</u>, Jan. 8, 1975, p. 26.)

28. <u>New York Times</u>, Nov. 13, 1975, p. 42.

29. <u>New York Times</u>, Feb. 26, 1976, p. 1.

30. This paragraph is based on <u>New York Times</u>, May 24, 1975, p.26; May 20, 1976, p. 65; Dec. 15, 1988, p. B7.

31. The Jonas and Weinberg episodes are described at pp. 26-27 and pp. 17-18 respectively of New York State Office of the Special Prosecutor for Medicaid Fraud Control - <u>New York State Medicaid Fraud Control Unit 1988 Annual Report</u> (New York: New York State Office of the Special Prosecutor for Medicaid Fraud Control, 1988).

32. Interview with Medicaid Special Prosecutor Charles J. Hynes, Jan. 7, 1991, Brooklyn, N.Y.; New York State Bar Association, Criminal Justice Section - <u>Report of Committee To Evaluate the Office of Special Prosecutor</u> (New York State Bar Association: 1981, no place cited), p. 16; New York State Medicaid Fraud Unit brochure (no author, place or date cited), p. 1.

33. Hynes, <u>op. cit</u>. n.27 <u>supra</u>, p. 19.

34. <u>Ibid</u>., pp. 18-19.

35. New York State Bar Association, Criminal Justice Section, <u>op. cit</u>.

n.32 supra, p. 17.

36. Hynes, Charles J. - Second Annual Report to Governor Hugh L. Carey (New York: Special State Prosecutor for Health and Social Services, Jan. 14, 1977), Appendix A, p. 1, pp. 17-18.

37. House Select Committee on Aging, 97th Cong., 2d Sess. - Medicaid Fraud: A Case History in the Failure of State Enforcement, (Washington: Government Printing Office, 1982), pp. 1-2.

38. Ibid., p. 2, pp. 14-15; Hynes, interview cited n.32 supra.

39. New York State Office of the Special Prosecutor for Medicaid Fraud Control, op. cit. n.31 supra, p. 1.

40. New York Times, Aug. 11, 1974, Sec. 1, p. 48.

41. Interview with Barbara Blum, Carey Commissioner of Social Services, July 17, 1991, New York City; Staten Island Advance, May 4, 1975, Sec. 1, p. 3.

42. Interview with State Assembly Mental Health Committee Chairperson Elizabeth Connelly, Aug. 8, 1990, Staten Island, N.Y.

43. Interview with Thomas Coughlin, Carey's first Office of Mental Retardation and Developmental Disabilities (OMRDD) (and then Corrections Commissioner), July 18, 1990, Albany, N.Y.

44. Interview with James Introne, Carey's second OMRDD Commissioner, Aug. 25, 1991, Syracuse, N.Y.

45. See Staten Island Advance, May 7, 1975, p. 2; May 14, 1975, p. 27.

46. Coughlin, interview cited n.43 supra.

47. Quoted Staten Island Advance, May 7, 1975, p. 2.

48. Cahill, interview cited n.3 supra.

49. Staten Island Advance, Jan. 6, 1977, p. 9; Mar. 2, 1977, p. 4; May 12, 1977, p. 2.

50. Staten Island Advance, Mar. 2, 1977, p. 4. Carey's first Commis-

Carey's Health Policies

sioner of Mental Health Lawrence Kolb notes that the families of alcoholics considered drug addicts as pariahs. Interview, Apr. 23, 1992, Albany, N.Y.

51. Staten Island Advance, June 29, 1977, p. 7.

52. This measure is New York State Laws of 1977, Ch. 978. This time Cahill supported the reorganization because he now thought that Kolb would function as a strong spokesperson for the mentally ill. He had been uncertain in 1975 that anyone would be their advocate in case of a Department of Mental Hygiene split -- in contrast to the mentally retarded, who had their relatives and civil liberties activists fighting for them. Cahill, interview cited n.3 supra.

53. Staten Island Advance, Mar. 2, 1977, p. 4. Kolb says that one reason he was opposed to the split was that he rejected the philosophy of some members of the State Association for the Mentally Retarded that the educationally subpar could not act anti-socially. Interview cited n.50 supra.

54. See Staten Island Advance, Jan. 6, 1977, p. 9.

55. New York Times, Feb. 2, 1972, p. 28; Feb. 26, 1977, p. 21; Staten Island Advance, May 1, 1975, p. 1.

56. Kolb, interview cited n.50 supra. See Rothman, David and Sheila - The Willowbrook Wars (New York: Harper and Row, 1984), pp. 106-12; New York Times, Apr. 11, 1973, p. 1; Oct. 7, 1974, p. 39; Feb. 26, 1977, p. 21; Staten Island Advance, Dec. 11, 1974, p. 1. Persons interested in a detailed history of the events that led to the emptying of Willowbrook should peruse the Rothmans' fine book.

57. Staten Island Advance, Dec. 6, 1974, p. 1.

58. Staten Island Advance, Dec. 11, 1974, p. 1.

59. Rothman, op. cit. n.56 supra, p. 118.

60. Interview with Christopher Hansen, a plaintiffs' attorney in the Willowbrook suit, Mar. 17, 1992, New York City; Staten Island Advance, Apr. 21, 1975, p. 1; May 1, 1975, p. 1.

The Days of Wine and Roses Are Over

61. Interview with Sundram, Nov. 1, 1991, Albany, N.Y.

62. New York Times, Nov. 14, 1976, Sec. 1, p. 55.

63. Staten Island Advance, Dec. 5, 1976, Sec. I, p. 1.

64. Interview cited n.61 supra.

65. Interview cited n.50 supra.

66. Rothman, op. cit. n.56 supra, p. 136.

67. Staten Island Advance, Mar. 22, 1978, p. 2.

68. Interview cited n.41 supra.

69. Sundram, interview cited n.61 supra; Staten Island Advance, Jan. 22, 1980, p. 1.

70. New York State Laws of 1978, Ch. 468.

71. Sundram, interview cited n.61 supra.

72. Staten Island Advance, Apr. 29, 1982, p. A1.

73. Hansen, interview cited n.60 supra; Rothman, op. cit. n.56 supra, pp. 158-64; Staten Island Advance, Apr. 29, 1982, p. 1. See also Staten Island Advance, Dec. 15, 1975, p. 1; April 26, 1981, Sec. 1, p. 1. The case in Judge Bartels' District Court is N.Y. State Association for Retarded Children v. Carey, 551 F. Supp. 1165 (E.D.N.Y. 1982).

On appeal the case has the same name and is cited 706 F.2d 956 (2d. Cir. 1983), cert. denied 464 U.S. 915 (1983). The appeals court upheld most of Bartels' decision.

74. Staten Island Advance, Apr. 29, 1982, p. 1.

75. Interview with State Budget Division staffers Robert Kerker and Alex Rollo, June 3, 1992, Albany, N.Y.; Sachs, Jeffrey - A Healthy Dose of Politics, Empire State Report, Aug. 1983, p. 10, 32; New York Times, Dec. 5, 1982, Sec. 1, p. 76; Mar. 18, 1984, p. 35; Mar. 12, 1993, p. A1.

76. Interviews cited n.41, 42, 43 supra.

77. Sundram, interview cited n.61 <u>supra</u>; see Rothman, <u>op. cit</u>. n.56 <u>supra</u>, p. 131.

78. Blum, interview cited n.41 <u>supra</u>; Coughlin, interview cited n.43 <u>supra</u>; Sundram, interview cited n.61 <u>supra</u>.

79. <u>Staten Island Advance</u>, May 1, 1978, Sec. 1, p. 1.

80. <u>Op. cit</u>. n.56 <u>supra</u>, p. 118.

81. <u>Staten Island Advance</u>, Apr. 29, 1982, p. 1.

82. The Governor made these remarks at the "Carey Years" Conference, Apr. 20, 1995, New York City.

83. <u>New York Times</u>, Oct. 14, 1995, p. 1.

Chapter 13
Carey on Courts and Criminal Justice: the Nadjari Firing, the Death Penalty, and Juvenile Crime

DURING his years in Albany, Carey fought hard and successfully for legislation under which the State assumed most local court costs and for a constitutional amendment that provided for the selection of the judges of the Court of Appeals (the State's highest court) by the Governor from a list drawn up by a Commission on Judicial Nomination. Prior to this amendment, these judges had been elected; but his Counsel Judah Gribetz and others convinced him that partisan politics should play as little a role as possible in elevating men and women to the bench. His criminal justice adviser Cyrus Vance, later U.S. Secretary of State, sold him on the principle that jurists of all courts ought to be picked by the head of the executive branch; but this idea never was adopted because both Democratic and Republican politicians view their power to put judges on the ballot as their major source of patronage.(1)

The reforms described above were geared to making the courts more efficient. Other Carey actions were aimed at making the criminal justice system more humane and took real courage to propose and implement. For instance, the most tragic episode of Governor Nelson Rockefeller's Administration was the 1971 prisoners' revolt at the maximum security Attica prison. During the rebellion and its suppression by state troopers and prison guards, 43 individuals were killed. Sixty two inmates were indicted for crimes relating to the affair and, of these, two were convicted at trial and six others pleaded guilty. After he was sworn in as Governor, Carey had two investigations conducted, one by future Court of Appeals Judge Bernard Meyer and one by former Manhattan District Attorney Alfred J. Scotti. Their reports showed that the State's behavior at the conclusion of the Attica disaster was one-sided; that its prosecutors acted primarily against inmates and largely ignored possible violations of law by guards and state police.(2) Accordingly, right after Christmas, 1976 the Chief Executive pardoned seven of the eight persons convicted of felonies committed during the uprising and commuted the sentence of the eighth, making him eligible for parole the upcoming January.(3) As he said in his statement announcing the pardons, "The Governor of the State of New York has the constitutional responsibility to...

The Days of Wine and Roses Are Over

insure equal justice for all citizens of the state....[I]t [is] irrefutably clear that the state....failed abysmally in upholding this principle in the handling of Attica investigation [sic] and prosecution in the first half of this decade. Due to [State officials'] insensitivity to their constitutional responsibilities, equal justice by way of further prosecutions is no longer possible".(4) At the same time, the Governor, to "firmly and finally close the book on this unhappy chapter of our history as a just and humane state"(5), decided not to pursue disciplinary action against 20 State Police and guards who may well have used excessive force in subduing the rioters.(6) State Corrections Commissioner Benjamin Ward and Superintendent of State Police William Connelie had reviewed the skimpy evidence against the officers and felt that it would be difficult to prosecute them.(7) Moreover, some crucial witnesses were gone and memories had dimmed, another reason why the Governor and his aides felt it desirable to have no more Attica trials.(8) The amnesty granted the inmates was a political risk: public opinion could have turned easily have turned against him for his clemency here. He was lucky and received as much praise as blame(9), perhaps in part because of his simultaneous leniency to the State employees.

Carey and Ward were determined to avoid a replay of the 1971 Attica bloodbath despite increased overcrowding in the State's prisons. The latter with Connelie devised a plan to insure that prison disturbances would not have to be suppressed at the cost of many deaths and injuries. The essence of this scheme was to have the State Police remain on the perimeter of the jail during the disturbance and to send officials of Ward's Correctional Services Department (more skilled at dealing with prisoners) into the lockup to negotiate. Its drafters vowed that the Police would never move in except *in extremis*. During Ward's tenure as Commissioner, which lasted until 1978, there were seven riots but all of these were ended without any loss of life. The Governor not only backed the Ward-Connelie plan but during a disturbance stayed on the phone continually and never pressured them to adopt a strategy different from the one they were following.(10)

Almost certainly the bravest actions of Carey's career in the capital were his vetoes of the death penalty. From 1977 through 1982, a Legislature anxious to curry favor with the electorate enacted such a measure; each time the Governor vetoed it and the veto was sustained. And he did so even though the polls showed overwhelming support for capital punishment and though his position reduced his political popularity.(11) His opposition to the penalty is fervently expressed in his 1977 veto message, in which he said the following.

> "I have spoken plainly on the penalty of death in our criminal justice system. On numerous occasions I have reiterated the arguments that stand against it-it is no proven deterrent to crime....; it leaves no room for human fallibility; it lowers all of us who abide by the law and the Judeo-Christian tradition of preserving and perfecting human life and dignity. In my view, for a government to sanction the death of a man or a woman is not only an admission of our inability to cope with the worst among us, it also admits the possibility that there are times when the government has the power to act violently and kill its own people -- a power that throughout the ages has never elevated a society or been known to protect any minority."(12)

With respect to the last clause of the quote, a former Carey aide mentioned to me that the Governor feared that the death penalty would have a disproportionate impact upon racial minorities.(13)

My interview with Ward gave me further insight into the depth of the Governor's opposition to executions. He and Ward did not know one another prior to his election but various people recommended that this black ex-police officer be appointed Corrections Commissioner. He asked Ward to come before him for a "job interview" and told him that he was worried that the electric chair would be brought back and that Ward would have to put to death the first defendant -- who would probably also be black. Ward remarked to me that the Chief Executive did not realize that he was **for** the death penalty and that, in any event, he could not throw the switch for an executioner has to have a license. On another occasion, the two were together on a State plane and the Commissioner started giving his boss some arguments for the death penalty. Carey pretended to fall asleep; as he was by then sick and tired of hearing all the debating points repeated again and again by its proponents.(14)

Many would like to lock up all narcotics dealers and users and throw away the key. Yet on two occasions Carey succeeded in getting the New York State Legislature to modify draconian laws relating to substance abuse. In 1975 he recommended the "decriminalization" of the possession of small amounts of marijuana.(15) On June 29, 1977 he signed a measure incorpor-ating that idea. (16) Under this act, the possession of small amounts of the drug was made a "violation" rather than a crime and the penalties for possession or sale of larger quantities were reduced.(17) He then immediately directed his Counsel's Office to study each individual conviction under the repealed marijuana laws.(18) And before the year was out, he had commuted the sentences of a dozen persons incarcerated under the outdated measures to the time they would have had to serve had the new law been in effect when they sold or smoked cannabis.(19)

In 1973, at Rockefeller's behest, there were enacted some of the toughest drug laws in the nation. Because of these measures, individuals who possessed even the smallest amounts of illegal narcotics could not plead guilty to a lesser offense and had to serve at least one year in jail.(20) By 1979, more than 3800 people had received sentences under these acts that bore a maximum of life imprisonment.(21) One consequence of their implementation was to cram the prisons.(22) In 1979 the Legislature at Carey's urging accepted a bill that reduced the penalties for relatively-minor drug offenses for first offenders and allowed them to plea bargain with the possibility of probation.(23) He argued strongly that the Rockefeller policy had not done much in the way of ridding the State of narcotics. At the same time, his measure increased penalties for certain repeat drug law violators.(24) Though he did not seem to have suffered serious political consequences from either the statute reducing marijuana penalties or that liberalizing the tough Rockefeller policy, there can be no doubt that these steps **could** have hurt him in the polls and thus that he showed political valor in sponsoring and signing them.

Another sort of act requiring political courage is replacing a popular law enforcement official who is not doing his/her job well. Carey did just this in 1975; and this time the result was a tornado that blew away any hopes he may have had of running for President or Vice-President in 1976. In the early 1970s a comm-ission headed by Whitman Knapp had discovered widespread police corruption in New York City and concomitant reluctance on the part of courts and prosecutors to wipe it out. Knapp recommended that a State Special Prosecutor's Office be set up to investigate and prosecute dishonesty in the criminal justice system. In September of 1972 Rockefeller formed this Office by Executive Order and appointed a Republican lawyer, Maurice Nadjari, as the Special Prosecutor. By 1973 Nadjari had over 150 people working for him. The Order gave the Prosecutor exclusive jurisdiction over probes into rot in the courts and police in New York City; its five District Attorneys (one in each borough) were deprived of the power to look into these matters.(25)

In 1975, when Carey was sworn in as Governor, Nadjari was a public hero.(26) But there were grumblings about his performance from some quarters. Civil libertarians soon began complaining about his aggressive tactics which smacked of entrapment and included smearing suspects' names over the front pages before they had had a chance to defend themselves. For example, he conducted an undercover investigation in Brooklyn in which his agents arrested a couple of shady lawyers who had asked for $25,000 to "fix" a case before able Judge Irwin Brownstein. When the grand jury started investigating this alleged bribe, Brownstein was called to testify before it. He was willing to do so but insisted that he be informed about the scope of its powers before he waived his Fifth Amendment right not to incriminate himself. Immediately Nadjari told the press that Brownstein was refusing to appear before it and this story made the front pages even though there was not a scintilla of evidence that the shysters had ever been in contact with the justice. He soon did testify; the attorneys were indicted; and he returned to the bench but a cloud remained over his name because Nadjari's aides refused to say publicly what they admitted privately, i.e., that he was not guilty of any wrong-doing.(27)

Not only was Nadjari in his zeal to root out corruption using unfair tactics; but he was not proving very successful either. "During Mr. Nadjari's four years in office, 11 judges were indicted. Charges against nine were dismissed; two were acquitted at trial."(28) Carey soon came to the conclusion that Nadjari was incompetent and had to be replaced. The Chief Executive was fed

The Days of Wine and Roses Are Over

up with the Special Prosecutor's leaks to the press to pillory his targets and with his use of dubious stratagems that frequently led higher courts to reverse his convictions.(29) On December 4, 1975, he decided to discharge him and the next day offered the position to highly-respected Manhattan District Attorney Robert Morgenthau. According to Gribetz, his decision to get rid of the much-lauded Special Prosecutor was almost as plucky as his opposition to the death penalty.(30)

The Chief Executive was acting in the best interests of the State when he sought to replace Mr. Nadjari with the more-efficient Morgenthau; but the removal was handled in a blundering way that demonstrated a poor feel for public relations and a lack of knowledge of the law and of the nature of the quarry. He dismissed the Special Prosecutor without first getting the consent of (or even informing) State Attorney General Louis Lefkowitz; and legally that official's approval was needed. It is still not clear why the Governor did not obtain the Attorney General's imprimatur before he moved. Gribetz feels that he acted on his own because he felt that he was primarily responsible for purging the criminal justice system of its sleazy elements. The Governor's Assistant Counsel Clarence Sundram told me that Carey might have feared that Lefkowitz (a Republican) would not have heeded his wishes. In hindsight, Sundram admits, it was a mistake not to have gone to Lefkowitz first. This is especially true as the reasons for Nadjari's having been fired had never been clearly explained to the public.(31)

The Special Prosecutor struck back. On December 23, 1975, Carey's reputation was at its height. He had just succeeded in getting financial aid from Washington to save New York City from bankruptcy as well as in securing the enactment of the State and City tax boosts that were the conditions of that boon. It was on that date that he announced the decision to replace Nadjari with Morgenthau. He could not have revealed his decision in early December, when it actually had been taken, for Morgenthau did not accept until December 22nd. It was unfortunate that the firing could not have been made public earlier, because around December 17th Patrick Cunningham, Carey's State Democratic Chairman, had realized that he was a target of a Nadjari investigation.(32) So the Prosecutor was able to imply to the press that Carey was discarding him because he was on the trail of the

Carey on Courts and Criminal Justice

ex-Congressman's close friend. This, of course, was nonsense as the crucial decision had been made almost two weeks before Cunningham had learned that Nadjari was tracking him; but the media put the innuendo on the front page. The Governor was seen by the citizens of the State as just another crooked politician and any Presidential/Vice Presidential ambitions he may have had for 1976 went up in smoke.(33) He received many letters and telegrams on the Nadjari affair; almost all of these were unfavorable to him. One that came from a New York City businessman declared that "Your outrageous behavior in the Nadjari dispute has caused [sic] the entire Democratic Party in New York State my vote for the foreseeable future. It is clear that Nadjari had gotten too close to the cynical corruption in high places that characterized Watergate...."(34) The Chief Executive's position that he had ousted Nadjari because the latter had been hit by a whole host of adverse court rulings(35) and because he "was not getting close enough to people high enough soon enough"(36) was greeted sceptically because, according to Nadjari, on December 7th the Governor had expressed confidence in him at a dinner both attended and on December 15th he had zealously defended him at a news conference.(37)

Carey's riposte to Nadjari's charges of a cover-up was to call for an investigation into this accusation. Lefkowitz now joined the fray actively and said that the Special Prosecutor would have six more months (i.e., until June, 1976) to complete his inquiries into the City's courts and police.(38) In early 1976, Nadjari accused Cunningham of selling judgeships in The Bronx(39), and demanded from the Governor the right to dig into all corrupt acts attributable to politicians (not limited to police officers, DAs and judges) in that borough.(40) The beleaguered tenant of the Executive Mansion had no choice but to grant Nadjari his wishes.(41) Cunningham was indicted for accepting payments to put a former City Councilman on the bench but the charge eventually was dismissed.(42)

The investigation of his reasons for sacking Nadjari that Carey had demanded was conducted by Jacob Grumet, a well-regarded former State Supreme Court Judge and a Republican himself. Grumet's report, issued in June of 1976, exonerated the Governor.

The Days of Wine and Roses Are Over

It concluded that he had sought to discharge the Special Prosecutor not because he was looking into the sale of judgeships by Cunningham but because, in his view, the public interest would be served by the removal. Grumet backed the Governor's contention that the decision to cast Nadjari aside had been taken on December 4th (i.e., before even Cunningham, to say nothing of Carey, knew that the Special Prosecutor was interested in the Bronx leader). The ex-judge continued that Carey had simply greeted Nadjari casually at that Pearl Harbor Day banquet at which he was supposed to have expressed confidence in him. He added that at the December 15th press conference the Chief Executive had merely noted that the Special Prosecutor had a tough job, which was far from the fervent defense of him that the latter claimed he had made there.(43) Lefkowitz removed Nadjari in midsummer 1976(44); but his office was not abolished until 1990.

The Governor thus strove to improve the quality of New York State's courts and took unpopular steps to protect civil liberties and make the State's criminal law less vindictive. However, he was a very pragmatic politician who knew the deep concern ordinary people harbored about crime and who was aware that it would be political suicide to ignore it. He felt, moreover, that this worry was perfectly justified and, in fact, a Park Slope residence belonging to him where he sometimes stayed when not in Albany was burgled and $4000 worth of jewelry, silverware and other items was stolen.(45) Therefore he did shepherd certain bills through the Legislature which significantly increased the possible penalties for criminal activity by certain classes of wrongdoers.

When Carey went to Albany, young people in trouble with the law were tried for "juvenile delinquency", irrespective of whether they had killed someone or stolen an apple from a streetcorner peddler. His first step in the child crime minefield was a veto of a bill extending the maximum period a young person could be held in a state "facility" from three years to four: the veto message declared that there was no evidence that locking up youngsters for longer terms would rehabilitate them.(46) This negative was delivered mid-August, 1975, just before he named Peter Edelman the Director of the State Division for Youth. (This Division operates the State's reformatories and its head is the Governor's main adviser on juvenile justice matters.) Edelman had been a legislative assistant to Senator Robert Kennedy and law clerk to U.S. Supreme Court Justice Arthur Goldberg.(47)

At the time of his appointment, the public was outraged by the escalation of juvenile thuggery. The *New York Times* had done studies indicating that juveniles who committed murder "....in New York rarely serve the full term - three years if they are 15 years old, 18 months if they are under 15. Usually....they serve about a year in a reformatory or a 'nonsecure state facility'".(48) Thus at the end of April, 1976 the Governor sent to the Legislature a bill drafted by Edelman and others that called for mandatory minimum penalties for youngsters found guilty of crimes involving force, for increasing the maximum duration of their confinement behind bars, and for a "bill of rights" for institutionalized children. However, Carey and Edelman rejected the idea, favored by quite a few legislators, that 14 and 15 year olds who commit extremely dangerous acts should be tried as adults and sentenced to real prisons, not simply reformatories.(49) The resulting Juvenile Justice Reform Act of 1976 embodied many of the Carey/Edelman ideas, and it and other measures accompanying it are still considered by Edelman and Sundram a masterpiece of dealing with the youth violence problem.(50) (The Act is Ch. 878 of the Laws of 1976.) As a result of compromises with various important legislators the mandatory minimum for the most serious crimes committed by 14 and 15 year olds was made two years and the maximum term was upped to five years and even, in a few cases, until the youth turned 21.(51) The proposed "bill of rights" was not enacted.

1978 was that election year in which the Governor initially was almost 30 points back of his Republican opponent Perry Duryea in the polls. The electorate's concern with juvenile wrongdoing had not abated and many residents of the State were miffed at Carey's opposition to the death penalty. Then on June 27th a fifteen year old named Willie Bosket was given five years for murdering two subway passengers. He had carried out his executions a few months after he had been released from a state reformatory over the objection of social workers.(52) Flying on a state plane from New York City to Rochester, the Governor read the *Daily News* spread on the Bosket verdict. After finishing the article, he amazed reporters by telling them that he was reversing his position and now favored the trial in adult court of juveniles accused of committing very serious crimes. He said that if this law was passed, hoodlums such as Bosket would "never [walk] the street again".(53) Edelman and Gribetz both opposed this proposal; but to no avail -- his political opponents were at the Governor's heels because of the death penalty issue and he felt he had to do something to show he was "tough on crime".(54) His resolve to try certain youths as adults was stiffened on July 2nd, when two young thugs brutally murdered Hugh McEvoy, a teenager preparing to enter a seminary, in the Morningside Heights neighborhood of New York City near Columbia University. Carey attended McEvoy's funeral and said there that "There will be a McEvoy program in this state. Those who choose crime will be punished. But we have to find ways to direct them away from crime".(55)

Given that 1978 was a state legislative as well as a guber-natorial election year and that neither major party wanted to be appear to be catering to Bosket and his ilk, the Governor's try-some-kids-as-adults proposal was enacted in a special session held during July.(56) As a consequence, some thirteen, fourteen and fifteen year olds can be tried in State Supreme Court for murder and jailed for relatively long terms. Fourteen and fifteen year olds can also be haled before Supreme Court (the State's major trial court) for other major transgressions. However, a judge may hand the case of any thirteen, fourteen or fifteen year old to a tribunal for children known as Family Court; and if the transfer is effected the defendant is usually faced with a maximum of five years incarceration. To further demonstrate their commitment to "fighting crime", the Legislature and the Governor added to this juvenile justice bill provisions imposing stiffer sentences for adults who had committed two or more violent felonies.(57)

In practice, only about 30% of the children who could be tried in Supreme Court as a result of the 1978 juvenile justice act are convicted there. About 40% are acquitted or see their cases dismissed. About a third are shunted to Family Court. Moreover, few of those convicted in Supreme Court are locked up for longer than five years. Juvenile crime in New York State declined between 1979 and 1987 but rose afterward.(58) Nonetheless, the act is sensible policy. There are a few juvenile psychopaths who will engage in violent activity at the drop of a hat: it is irrational to let such people walk the streets. Bosket is a good example of such an individual. He himself admitted to committing 2000 crimes between the ages of 9 and 15, including 25 stabbings. A few years after the subway murder he was jailed for another offense; and since then has had to be kept in solitary confinement as a danger to his guards.(59) Edelman, however, still opposes trying young people in Supreme Court because, among other things, children upstate get judged as adults more than do their counterparts in New York City and so on the average receive higher sentences for the same type of crime.(60)

From the time of his appointment, Edelman was anathema to some of the conservative Republicans in the State Senate. For example, the counsel to the Republican-dominated Senate Crime and Corrections Committee denounced his advocacy of the children's bill of rights and referred to him as "frankly a very nice, sentimental liberal who holds the old juvenile-delinquency-is-an-illness" idea.(61) When a youth of 17 on furlough from a minimum security facility raped and tried to electrocute a 63 year old woman, Senator Ralph Marino, head of the Crime Committee, said that "Edelman is never concerned about the safety of the people and that's why he must go".(62) (Actually, as Edelman pointed out in my interview with him and in the *New York Times*, this youngster had been furloughed not because of any order coming from the Director but because of a slip-up somewhere in the agency's chain of command.(63)) The Youth Division chief resigned after the Governor's reelection. Some think that his leaving was due to the attacks on him by the Republicans. However, actually he had asked the Chief Executive to let him depart at the end of 1977 so that he could be with his wife in Washington but had been requested to remain another year.(64)

The Rockefeller drug laws, tougher penalties for recidivists, the closing of facilities maintained by the Narcotics Addiction Control Commission and rising crime generally made prison overcrowding inevitable during Carey's tenure.(65) In early 1975, when Ward was appointed as Corrections Commissioner, there were "only"

15,000 inmates in the State's prisons.(66) By mid-1981 the figure had soared to 23,700.(67) According to his third Corrections Commissioner Thomas Coughlin (who was retained by Mario Cuomo), Carey was much more interested in helping disabled children and the retarded than in building prisons.(68) Yet to avoid other Attica disasters in the state's "secure facilities", the Governor was forced to take steps to increase cell space. He was at first somewhat reluctant to do this, but Ward got on the phone to his Secretary, David Burke; and painted a bleak picture of the dangers of penitentiaries where inmates were packed together like sardines. Burke talked to Carey and convinced him of the need to provide more cells. The Governor then gave his aides and Commissioners the go-ahead.(69)

However, some of his appointments to prison posts veered from the "jails must be dismal" approach of the average person. The State has an officer called the "Correction Commission Chairperson" who is responsible for insuring that its lockups are not so degrading that they violate their residents' due process rights. (The "Corrections Commissioner" is the functionary who, as head of the Department of Correctional Services, actually operates the prisons.) In mid-1975, after the end of the regular legislative session, the Governor appointed law professor and advocate of prisoners' rights Herman Schwartz to this post. The State Senate's Crime and Corrections Committee did not have the opportunity to hold hearings on this choice until early 1976. In the interim, Schwartz had irritated county sheriffs and law-and-order types by proposing that it become easier for prisoners in local jails to receive mail and visitors and for reporters to have access to these facilities. He also hired three ex-convicts to work for the Commission. All this led Committee Chairman Marino to refer to him as suffering from "tunnel vision with regard to inmates' rights and can't see the other side of the coin". Republican Senator Richard Schermerhorn said in the debate on Schwartz's confirmation that "Everyone is talking about prisoners' rights. *They have none.* You want the convicts to run the institutions? That's exactly what Mr. Schwartz is trying to do".(70) Attitudes such as these resulted in a stunning 35-22 defeat for the professor in the vote in the full State Senate. This loss was especially galling to Carey for it marked the first time in living memory that a gubernatorial nominee had been denied confirmation by the Upper House.(71) However, in a dramatic example of poetic justice, Schermerhorn served ten months in a federal jail for tax evasion.(72) He must then have bitterly regretted his diatribe against prisoners!

In Summer, 1978 the Governor chose the colorful Richard Hongisto to succeed Ward as Corrections Commissioner. He had been San Francisco sheriff for many years. In late 1977 he had left to become Chief of Police in Cleveland but soon was fired by Mayor Dennis Kucinich. Hongisto had a "deserved national reputation as a liberal law-enforcement man".(73) That reputation in itself was enough to anger the Republicans on the Senate Crime and Corrections Committee but his vita had specific items that were bound to annoy them further. He had hired some gays as sheriff's deputies and had received a large share of the gay vote when reelected in 1975. When a riot took place in which prisoners burnt some of the San Francisco County jail, he commented that the inmates had staged merely a "fire demonstration" to protest against poor prison conditions.(74) When after several months in the office he was finally called to testify before the Crime Committee, some Republican lawmakers asked him why he had visited Communist Russia and Cuba and why he had criticized the gay-bashing singer Anita Bryant. Marino was incensed that he had refused to enforce a court order to evict elderly people from a San Francisco hotel.(75) Ward suggested that Hongisto stop dressing like a Californian in his appearances before the Committee so as to please the Republicans there who preferred witnesses in dark suits and wide ties to those in light brown suits and string ties, but Hongisto did not fully heed this advice. Marino became convinced that Hongisto was incompetent and hounded him more and more at the hearings.(76) Still, it was unclear whether the Committee would have turned him down if the matter had come to a vote. However, he took a foolish step that forced Carey to withdraw his candidacy. Perhaps out of a feeling of panic that he would be rejected, he and his wife contributed $500 each to the Bronx Borough Presidential campaign of Democratic State Senator and Crime Committee member Joseph Galiber. When news of this

The Days of Wine and Roses Are Over

transaction reached the press, the Governor had to retract his nomination of the West Coaster even though the latter had done an excellent job preventing riots during a prison guard strike in Spring, 1979.(77) Luckily for the State, Carey's next selection, Thomas Coughlin, turned out to be a superb Corrections Commissioner.

Notes to Chapter 13

1. Interview with State Senate Minority Leader Manfred Ohrenstein, Oct. 25, 1994, New York City; with Vance Oct. 17, 1990, New York City.

2. New York Times, Dec. 22, 1975, p. 1, 34 (Meyer Report); Feb. 27, 1976, p. 1 (Scotti statement); Dec. 31, 1976, p. A1, p. A10 (Carey statement on Attica affair).

3. New York Times, Dec. 31, 1976, p. A1.

4. Public Papers of Governor Hugh L. Carey 1976 (Albany: State of New York Executive Chamber, 1986), p. 835.

5. Ibid., p. 837.

6. Ibid. See also New York Times, Feb. 27, 1976, p. 1 (Scotti Statement).

7. Interview with Benjamin Ward, Carey's first Corrections Commissioner, Nov. 6, 1991, Brooklyn, N.Y.

8. Interview with Carey Assistant Counsel Clarence Sundram, Nov. 1, 1991, Albany, N.Y.

9. Ibid. Tom Wicker, writing in New York Times, May 13, 1977, p. A27, mentions the political danger the pardon posed to Carey.

10. Ward, interview cited n.7 supra.

11. New York Times, Aug. 26, 1977, p. A1, A13.

12. Public Papers of Governor Hugh L. Carey 1977 (Albany: State of New York Executive Chamber, 1987), p. 294.

13. Sundram, interview cited n.8 supra.

14. Ward, interview cited n.7 supra.

15. Carey, op. cit. n.12 supra, pp. 989-90.

16. New York State Laws of 1977, Ch. 360.

17. Staten Island Advance, June 30, 1977, p. 6.

The Days of Wine and Roses Are Over

18. Carey, op. cit. n.12 supra, p. 1037.

19. Ibid., pp. 1773-79.

20. New York Times, Aug. 12, 1975, p. 1.

21. New York Times, Feb. 13, 1979, p. B1.

22. New York Times, Dec. 14, 1976, p. 40.

23. New York State Laws of 1979, Ch. 410. See also New York Times, July 8, 1979, Sec. 1, p. 34.

24. New York Times, July 8, 1979, Sec. 1, p. 34.

25. New York Times, Apr. 10, 1975, p. 28; Jan. 14, 1990, Sec. 1, p. 28.

26. Tracy, Phil - From Super Cop to Superflop: The Case Against Maurice Nadjari, Village Voice, March 17, 1975, p. 5.

27. Ibid., p. 6.

28. New York Times, Jan. 14, 1990, Sec. 1, p. 28.

29. Interview with Carey Counsel Judah Gribetz, Sept. 28, 1990, New York City.

30. Ibid.; New York Times, Nov. 10, 1977, p. A1.

31. The information in this paragraph is based on Gribetz, interview cited n.29 supra; Sundram, interview cited n. 8, supra; Newfield, Jack - Save the Office, Defend the Bill of Rights, Village Voice, Jan. 12, 1976, pp. 10ff; Pileggi, Nicholas - Can Nadjari Prove his Latest Charge? Can He Prove Anything?, Village Voice, May 3, 1976, pp. 25-26.

32. Newfield, op. cit. n.31 supra, p. 10.

33. See Time, Feb. 23, 1976, p. 9.

34. Telegram located in Hugh L. Carey Collection, St. John's Univ.(NY), Government (City: New York City: Special Prosecutor) file.

35. <u>Staten Island Advance</u>, Dec. 24, 1975, p. 1.

36. <u>Staten Island Advance</u>, Dec. 31, 1975, p. 1.

37. <u>New York Times</u>, June 23, 1976, p. 1.

38. <u>Staten Island Advance</u>, Dec. 31, 1975, p. 1.

39. <u>New York Times</u>, Jan. 7, 1976, p. 1.

40. <u>Staten Island Advance</u>, Jan. 10, 1976, p. 2.

41. <u>New York Times</u>, Jan. 29, 1976, p. 38.

42. <u>New York Times</u>, Dec. 23, 1976, p. 1; Mar. 4, 1977, p. A13; Apr. 27, 1977, p. D20.

43. <u>New York Times</u>, June 23, 1976, p. 1.

44. <u>New York Times</u>, June 26, 1976, p. 1.

45. See <u>New York Times</u>, Oct. 26, 1977, p. B3.

46. <u>New York Times</u>, Aug. 14, 1975, p. 1.

47. <u>New York Times</u>, Aug. 19, 1975, p. 39.

48. <u>New York Times</u>, Dec. 10, 1975, p. 1.

49. <u>New York Times</u>, Apr. 30, 1976, p. 1.

50. Interview with Peter Edelman, Carey's Director of State Division for Youth, May 8, 1991, Washington; Sundram, interview cited n.8 <u>supra</u>.

51. Edelman, Peter - <u>Justice and Juveniles</u>, <u>New York Times</u>, Feb. 26, 1977, p. A23; <u>New York Times</u>, June 29, 1976, p. 20; Feb. 6, 1977, Sec. 1, p. 26.

52. <u>New York Times</u>, June 30, 1978, p. Al.

53. <u>Ibid</u>; Butterfield, Fox - <u>All God's Children: The Bosket Family and the American Tradition of Violence</u> (New York: Knopf, 1995), pp. 226-27.

54. Edelman, interview cited n.50 <u>supra</u>.

55. <u>New York Times</u>, July 14, 1978, p. B3.

56. The measure is New York State Laws of 1978, Ch. 481. It is known as the Juvenile Offender Act of 1978.

57. See the excellent summary of the law in <u>Staten Island Advance</u>, Sept. 3, 1978, Sec. 1, p. 14. See also <u>New York Times</u>, May 15, 1989, p. B1.

58. <u>New York Times</u>, May 15, 1989, p. B1, B4; Dec. 10, 1995, Sec.1, p. 1.

59. Butterfield, <u>op. cit</u>. n.53 <u>supra</u>, p. xi.

60. Interview cited n.50 <u>supra</u>.

61. <u>New York Times</u>, Feb. 6, 1977, Sec. 1, p. 26.

62. <u>New York Times</u>, July 15, 1978, p. 1.

63. <u>Ibid</u>.; Edelman, interview cited n.50 <u>supra</u>.

64. Edelman, interview cited n.50 <u>supra</u>; <u>New York Times</u>, Dec. 14, 1978, p. B21.

65. Ward, interview cited n.7 <u>supra</u>.

66. <u>New York Times</u>, Jan. 27, 1975, p. 27.

67. <u>New York Times</u>, Aug. 2, 1981, Sec. 4, p. 6.

68. Interview with Coughlin, June 18, 1990, Albany, N.Y.

69. Ward, interview cited n.7 <u>supra</u>.

70. <u>New York Times</u>, Apr. 14, 1976, p. 56. Emphasis supplied.

71. <u>Ibid</u>.; also <u>New York Times</u>, Jan. 26, 1976, p. 45.

72. <u>New York Times</u>, Dec. 16, 1989, p. 30; July 9, 1991, p. B18.

73. Levering, Robert - <u>The Bay Sheriff Rides Again</u>, <u>Village Voice</u>, Aug.

Carey on Courts and Criminal Justice

7, 1978, p. 12.

74. Ibid.

75. New York Times, Apr. 5, 1979, p. B9.

76. Ward, interview cited n.7 supra.

77. New York Times, June 12, 1979, p. B1; Staten Island Advance, June 10, 1979, p. 8. Hongisto gave the money for delivery to Galiber to a black PhD in the Department of Correctional Services on the assumption that that person was a Democrat. However, the employee turned out to be a Republican and leaked to the press the story of the contribution. Ward, interview cited n.7 supra.

Chapter 14
Carey's Long Winter of Discontent: Fall 1980 - Fall 1981

A CHILL enveloped Hugh Carey's Governorship from Fall, 1980 to Fall, 1981. This period can justly be called the "long winter of discontent" of his stay in Albany. It consisted of a series of disasters which shredded his public image. The arctic air was introduced by the Presidential election of 1980, featuring Democrat Jimmy Carter against Republican Ronald Reagan. Carey had no love for Carter. Recall that shielded by the secrecy of the voting booth he chose the Republican Ford over the Georgian in 1976. He told me that he disliked the Southerner from the first time he met him.(1) The Governor's Secretary David Burke gave me an account of that 1976 get together. Carter had asked them to visit him in his hotel suite in New York's Plaza Hotel. Carter was delayed and so the notoriously-late Governor and his aide hung around the Plaza Bar for an hour and a half and had some drinks. They went up to the candidate's suite and found him lying propped up on his bed and speaking to them in what they thought was an offhand manner. Carey was heartily unimpressed even though the future President promised him "access".(2)

The ex-Congressman's initial dislike of the ex-Dixie Governor never dissipated. This is true even though as Burke pointed out, Carter proved to be a man of his word and always was willing to talk to the Chief Executive of the nation's second most-populous state and help it financially. During the transition period after his 1976 win, he invited Burke and the Governor to his vacation home and had a friendly conversation with them.(3) He worked hard in 1978 for the passage of the federal aid package that was still necessary to keep New York City out of insolvency and provided cash for Love Canal and West Valley. But few words of gratitude came from Albany.(4)

As of the beginning of August 1980, the month of the Democratic National Convention held in Manhattan, Carter was sure of being his Party's Presidential nominee. Carey at this moment stunned the political world by demanding an "open convention" in which the delegates would not be bound to the candidate to whom they had committed themselves in the caucus or primary but would be free to vote their consciences. He may have acted this way to get leverage to force Carter to pay for the Love Canal and West Valley cleanups; it is unlikely that at that point in time he thought he could get the nomination for himself even if the latter's delegates were to desert their leader's emblem.(5) Or it may just have been that he thought Carter the weakest Democratic candidate and was hoping against hope that the Convention would turn to a figure who had more of a chance to beat Reagan. In any event, this sudden "open convention" call infuriated the Carter camp, especially as it came from the head of the Convention's "host" state(6); and also was one of several episodes over the next year that convinced many New Yorkers that their Governor was a flake.

Later in the month he again made himself an object of ridicule, this time by poorly choosing his words. He said he was backing former Miss America Bess Myerson over former New York City Mayor John Lindsay in the Democratic primary for the United States Senate because he regarded the seat for which they were contending as a "Jewish" one.(7) Voters naively took this to mean that the Governor was saying that the seat "belonged" to Jewish voters, which is of course as absurd as saying that the one held by Senator Daniel Moynihan was the fief of the Irish. What Carey meant, obviously, was simply that many politicians considered that the seat should go to a member of the Jewish faith because its incumbent was the ailing Jewish Republican-Liberal incumbent Jacob Javits who had succeeded his co-religionist Herbert Lehman.(8) In the event, Congress Member Elizabeth Holtzman was victorious in the Democratic primary; Alfonse D'Amato won the Republican primary over Javits; and D'Amato then took the general over Holtzman and Javits running on the Liberal Party line.

Though there is no evidence that Carey jumped the Dem-ocratic ship in 1980 and voted for Reagan, he did not exert himself urging the residents of New York State to cast their ballots for the President.(9) In fact, he let slip several comments that were unhelpful to Carter's cause. At the end of September, he made a speech in drug-ridden Bryant Park in Manhattan calling for a State tax on liquor to fund a "war on heroin". He rightly added that the State could not itself produce enough cash to successfully win this struggle and therefore requested federal aid for that purpose. "[W]ithout federal support and assistance we cannot succeed. The problem goes beyond our borders."(10) So far, there was nothing in the talk that anyone except a narcotics smuggler could object to. But his inserting a clause in that address **condemning** the national Administration for cutting funding for a drug abuse program drove the Carterites wild. The last thing the Democrat, engaged in a close race with Reagan, needed at that moment was a blast from someone in his own Party who supposedly was campaigning for him. Undeterred, the Governor a few weeks afterward referred to Washington's anti-drug battle as mere "tokenism".(11) While it is probable that these attacks did not drive many voters to Reagan, it is also likely that they increased the ranks of those who felt that Carey was off in outer space.

During his eight years in office Carey ran a very honest ship. There were remarks raised in the press about his children and friends riding for free on State vehicles; but just about all these hitches were on trips that also carried a State official on public business or on the return leg of these journeys, which the car or plane would have had to make anyway.(12) *New York Times* reporter Richard Meislin commented in October, 1978 that the Chief Executive was "not known as a particularly acquisitive man".(13) But the next month he took a step which seemed at odds with Meislin's view of him, and one which further diminished his standing with the public. He got the State to seize the parcel of property next to his vacation home on Shelter Island.

This islet is located between the North and South Forks of Long Island and about 100 miles east of New York City. Carey purchased his abode there at the end of the 1960s while still a Member of Congress. It fronts on a lane called Westmoreland Drive. If one were to stand on the Drive facing it she might, around twilight, see deer bounding across the piece of property on the right to nibble on the grass of its lawn. In 1980 that parcel, which like Carey's extends from the Drive to West Neck Creek, was owned by a dentist from Scarsdale, New York, named Philip D'Arrigo.(14) In 1979 he had purchased the land for $48,000, the Chief Executive having turned down an offer to acquire it for the same price. As soon as he obtained the necessary permit, D'Arrigo began building a two and a half story house on the lot about 15 feet from the property line and over 100 feet from the Carey residence.(15) Seeing the new edifice rising, the Governor grew irritated. He asserted that the new creation threatened his safety,

The Days of Wine and Roses Are Over

especially as he was becoming outspoken on the drug issue. A sniper on the second floor of D'Arrigo's house, from which one had a clear view of his abode, might be tempted to take a shot at him or another member of his family. He therefore had his Transportation Commissioner William Hennessy refer the matter to the State Police, who certified that the rising D'Arrigo home did pose a security threat. On Thursday, November 6th, two days after the Reagan triumph, papers were served on D'Arrigo seizing (subject to the payment of just compensation) the lot on which it was standing. The plan was that the Governor's security staff would be housed in D'Arrigo's retreat and that the dentist would get first option to repurchase his former grounds once Carey was no longer Chief Executive.(16)

Newsday broke the story on Sunday, November 9th(17); and the next day it appeared all over the State. And everyone who read it thought that the move was made not to protect the Governor from a gunman but to shield him from the possible prying eyes of his neighbors. Even the spokesperson for the State Police admitted that the height of the dentist's structure would make it "difficult for any **privacy** for the Governor, although that's not the total consideration".(18) A resident of Shelter Island commented, and she was typical of those who expressed opinions on the matter, "It looks like he misused his office to protect his privacy".(19) Editorials were just as critical: for example, one in the *Staten Island Advance* was headed "Governor's 'security' claims are weak".(20)

Even the Governor's inner circle was not happy about the episode. Hennessy at Secretary Robert Morgado's urging had pleaded with him not to have the papers served. After they had been delivered, his Counsel Richard Brown, his Press Secretary Michael Patterson and Morgado all begged him to cancel the condemnation proceedings.(21) Hennessy joined in this chorus, telling him that his hope that he could convince the public that the takeover was justified was wildly optimistic.(22) These aides knew that he had a deep emotional attachment to Shelter Island -- for example, he had lost his temper when the State's Office of General Services (OGS) had bulldozed one of its shrubs to construct a gate for a security guard(23) -- but they informed him in no uncertain terms that to protect it by taking his neighbor's plot

Carey's Long Winter of Discontent

was politically disastrous. He finally saw that they were making sense and on Wednesday, November 12th, less than a week after D'Arrigo received the notice saying that he would have to surrender his land, he rescinded the takeover.(24) Shortly afterward, the State agreed to accord the dentist $6400 to recompense him for the legal fees and the higher mortgage charges that he had to pay as a result of his powerful neighbor's desire to maintain the intimacy of his holiday haven.(25) The Governor soon recognized that what he did was morally as well as politically improper. As he once said, "...I am...apologetic for ever entertaining the notion that my family's acre of land in Shelter Island would be more livable for me and my neighbor, the dentist, if he waited until I was no longer governor to build his house. Perhaps justice was served, because I got the punishment I deserved by paying in notoriety for what I tried to do in the name of privacy".(26) But the return of the plot did not prevent acerbic Albany *Times Union* columnist Barney Fowler from calling him "The Squire of Shelter Island".(27)

Fowler's blast at the Chief Executive was one of an avalanche of newspaper articles around this time that made him feel that journalists were waging a vendetta against him and ignoring the issues.(28) He traveled to the Far East in late January and early February of 1981 to convince Japanese corporations to build plants in New York State. When he returned, newspaper stories denounced him for accepting a free air flight from Pan American Airways and free hotel rooms from an insurance company.(29) About this time, columnist Jimmy Breslin wrote one of the articles in the *New York Daily News* in which he referred to him as "Society Carey".(30) His response to these criticisms that he had offers to work in the private sector for more than $2 million a year(31) did little to endear him to reporters or the electorate.

While he was touring the Orient, the normally placid city of Binghamton, New York, home of State Senate Majority Leader Warren Anderson, saw some rare excitement. There is a large State office building there, employing hundreds of people. A solution containing the chemical polychlorinated biphenyls (PCBs) was used to cool the structure's electrical transformers. On February 5, 1981 the failure of a device analogous to the ordinary home's circuit breakers caused the temperature in the room where the transformer was located to rise to 2,000 degrees Farenheit, which resulted in the release of 180 gallons of the coolant containing the compound. The coolant was transformed into vapor, which in turn mixed with soot produced by the fire caused by the heat; and the soot then spread through the entire eighteen-story building. The upshot was an entire skyscraper polluted by PCBs. OGS, the agency responsible for maintaining State buildings, sent 22 janitors to clean up. The local press denounced this effort not only because cash, food and cigarettes were stolen from the building while they were there but also because, after work, they changed their clothes in city offices next door, thus adding to the number of people exposed to the PCB-laden grime. On February 26th OGS Commissioner John Egan, after consultation with Health Commissioner David Axelrod, locked the State building, partly because dioxins, another set of toxic chemicals, had been found there.(32)

Carey could easily have shrugged the incident off as an unfortunate mishap. But on March 4th he said, at an Albany news conference called to announce the publication of a report on health problems in the State, that "I offer here and now to walk into Binghamton in any part of that building and swallow an entire glass of PCB's and run a mile afterward".(33) This offhand, spontaneous comment not only infuriated the residents of the Binghamton area, but also was widely publicized in a way that made him look foolish throughout the State.(34) For example, the Albany *Times Union* headlined its story "Carey: I'll swallow a glass of PCB'S"(35); and the next day ran a follow-up declaring that two well-known scientists had said that he would risk death if he gulped that poison down.(36) Further angering the electorate were his statements that to be in danger from PCBs, you have to take them "in quantities steadily over a long period of time, and probably be pregnant, which I don't intend to be"(37); and that with some good workers and vacuum cleaners he could make the Office Building safe. Explaining that last remark, he asserted that "I want to warn everybody in this state that we can sacrifice jobs in this state, we can interrupt the public process by not having people working if no one is willing to take a risk. But life is a risk. We'll use all the reasonable and available means that we can to clean that building. I believe that a tolerable level of dioxin should be reached, then we should move back into the building".(38) Though Lee Clarke, the author of a book describing the Binghamton episode, believes that this position made considerable sense, it did not go over well with the public.(39) For whatever reason he uttered the PCB dictum, he soon came to realize that it was hurting him politically. So in October of 1981 he visited Binghamton specifically to apologize for what he called his "flip statements" and confess that he was at fault in making them.(40)

The Governor could not have anticipated attending Reagan's inauguration on January 20, 1981, with great joy. He knew that the incoming anti-tax, anti-spending regime in Washington would cut federal aid to important State programs. But at one of the inaugural balls he met Miss Evangeline ("Angie" or "Engie" to her friends) Gouletas, whose biography said she was a "widow". By early April the press had unearthed Evangelos Metaxas, a **living** former spouse: she maintained, however, that her first had passed away. Both husbands had divorced her, she added.(41) She was the millionaire president of a real estate firm known as American Invsco, which specialized in buying apartment buildings and converting them into condominiums. At the time she was 44; Carey 61. According to the *New York Post*, he had proposed to his close friend Anne Ford Uzielli twice in January of 1981, once just before he met Miss Gouletas and then again before he left for Japan; but both times she turned him down. Immediately after his return, he began wooing Gouletas, the article said.(42) About this time too, he began to dye his hair reddish-brown. The State's newspapers could not resist discussing the Chief Executive's current flame and trendy tint. The *Staten Island Advance's* Bruce Alpert grumbled that the *Post* and *Daily News* were giving the Chief Executive's love life and the pigmentation of his sideburns more play than the fight between him and Warren Anderson over the budget that was supposed to be adopted by April 1st. While praising his own paper, the *New York Times* and *Newsday* for placing the budget gridlock story on their front pages, even he had to admit that this high-class trio had nonetheless featured the Governor's new amour and hair color in their "people" sections.(43)

One reporter definitely not amused by Carey's behavior was Breslin. The writer once had had a tremendous amount of respect for the politician but this high regard had dissipated by 1981. Thus

The Days of Wine and Roses Are Over

in a "Society Carey" column he said that:

> "Society Carey hardly does anything except fly. He is
> the governor of New York and the discoverer of the 10-
> hour workweek. When he is on the ground, most of his
> time is spent driving to or from the airport....He likes to
> fly around in the air with his girlfriend....
>
> When you look at Society Carey with his new
> auburn hair and his girlfriend and his 10-hour
> workweek, with state pilots flying him and the girlfriend
> around in the sky in state planes, with limousines
> waiting on the ground....you can see the reason why
> there is no other name in the world for Society Carey
> except....Society Carey."(44)

However exaggerated this fusillade was, it contributed to the growing perception that the object of its fire was "a bit nuts".(45)

Notwithstanding the unpleasant words from Breslin, the Gouletas - Carey wedding was set for Saturday, April 11th. Had no problems about the nuptials cropped up, the public would doubtlessly have forgotten about Shelter Island, the PCBs and "Society Carey", for Miss Gouletas was an intelligent, well-dressed woman who could charm the public. The couple could not get married in Carey's Roman Catholic Church, for she was a divorcee whose previous marriages had been terminated legally but not by the Catholic hierarchy. But the fact that the wedding had to take place in a Greek Orthodox edifice in New York City did not hurt him with the average voter, though it did upset the Governor himself.(46)

Alas, any political benefit of the nuptials to him lasted exactly one day, Sunday April 12th. On Monday the 13th the papers reported that Evangeline Gouletas-Carey (the name she took at her wedding to the State's First Citizen) had been mistaken when she had said her first husband was dead. The gentleman, who by 1981 had changed his name from Frangiskos Kallaniotis to Frank Kallos or Kallas, was very much alive and running a Greek restaurant in Los Angeles. He plaintively told the press "I am not dead. I am alive. I don't know why she would say that".(47) The next day, Tuesday April 14th, the media carried a story that, added to the fact that Kallas was alive and selling souvlaki in his diner, made the Angie-Hugh marriage a complete disaster from a public relations viewpoint. This was that she had had a **third** husband, one George Kaltezas, a Greek-born engineer whom she had divorced in 1963 and who was still on this side of the grave. Carey himself had no idea when he married Gouletas that she had ever been wed a third time: as of April 11th he and the public had been aware only of Kallas (though he thought him departed from this earth) and of Metaxas.(48) An embarrassed Governor could only comment that "I am certain in my own mind that I now possess all the relevant facts about the life and marriages of Evangeline Gouletas-Carey prior to our marriage".(49) His wife, interviewed at Buffalo Airport on their way to a budget-abbreviated honeymoon at Niagara Falls, simply said with tears in her eyes that "There's only one man in my life. That's Governor Carey".(50)

Some voters simply shrugged their shoulders at the revelations about Angie's resurrected ex-spouse and the newly-discovered husband number three. A poll in the *Staten Island Advance* taken about a fortnight after the wedding and asking "Will his marriage hurt Carey's future?" found two of the eight respondents saying "No" and agreeing that the couple's personal life was their own business. But the remaining six answered in the affirmative. One of those believing that the nuptials would be detrimental to the Chief Executive's political career reasoned this way (and she was not alone): "The whole thing is pretty strange. It makes me think twice about voting for him, because if he's dumb enough to do this, then who knows what he'll do".(51) People who shared the viewpoint of that respondent started making jokes about him, e.g., "Did you hear that there's a softball game scheduled? Gov. Carey's press secretaries are going to play Evangeline Gouletas' former husbands".(52) Nor were there many people in New York unaware of his misfortunes. The national weekly *Newsweek* and the popular television program *The Today Show* featured them, as did the major TV networks' evening news shows.(53)

The marriage hurt Carey in a way above and beyond the bad publicity about the revivified first spouse and the newfound third ex. This was that relations between Ms. Gouletas-Carey and most Carey staffers were poor, with the result that some good political advisers left. According to Albany *Times Union* reporter Fred Dicker, she was ambitious, wanted to set policy, and thus clashed with the people already on board. She once had the chutzpah to declare that Carey's government was now "our" government.(54) One of Carey's most able aides, who does not want his name mentioned, told me explicitly that he departed his entourage because she wanted him out. To this day, he hates her. She alienated the Governor's main adviser, Robert Morgado, by convincing her husband without consulting his Secretary to hire one Michael Colopy to deal with his public relations problem. Some aides went so far as to try to sabotage the newcomer by leaking unfavorable reports about him to the press.(55) To be fair, not every Carey assistant disliked Ms. Gouletas-Carey. John Burns, Appointments Officer during his second term, declared to me that she never tried to intervene in politics and that she was a pleasant lady who took great pleasure in showing off the Executive Mansion to members of the public.(56) But his view of her was distinctly the minority one among the Chief Executive's staffers. She and Carey are now divorced; and he has described their relationship as "an unfortunate alliance called a marriage".(57)

The cumulative weight of all the unfavorable newspaper and television publicity about the Chief Executive, including frank reports about a nasty feud between him and Lieutenant Governor Mario Cuomo, was seriously damaging him in public opinion surveys by the end of 1981: one leaked to the *Post* showed him down 30 points in a possible 1982 race for Governor against State Comptroller Ned Regan.(58) Nonetheless on January 15, 1982 he surprised a lot of people (including Commerce Commissioner George Dempster and State Democratic Party Chairman Dominic Baranello(59), but not Office of Employee Relations Director Meyer Frucher(60)) by announcing that he would not run for reelection.

Carey denied at the time that his terrible standing in the polls had anything to do with the matter(61); but several knowledgeable people involved in his Administration disagree. Among these individuals are Burns, Director of State Operations James Introne, Commissioner of Social Services Barbara Blum, Commerce Commissioner John Dyson and Metropolitan Transportation Authority head Richard Ravitch.(62) His Counsel Judah Gribetz believes that one important factor behind his chief's decision was that he did not want Ms. Gouletas-Carey's name dragged through the mud again.(63) He clearly was fed up with the press reports ridiculing his public and private doings.(64) More generally, he yearned for a genuinely private life which it is impossible for any governor of a major state to have -- he hated always being accompanied by state troopers, for example(65) -- and he really did want to spend more time with his family.(66) He also reckoned that he had done quite a bit in eight years(67); and he did not foresee many challenges during the next four.(68) Even during his second term, he had not been confronted with many issues that had excited him. He felt, to employ Frucher's well-chosen terminology, that the problems he had faced from 1979 to 1982 were "pedestrian" compared to the ones he had solved in 1975 and 1976.(69) Moreover, he disliked the thought of having to raise money again for a campaign; he realized that he was in good health in 1982 but might be ill in 1986 at the end of a third term; he believed that he was shaky financially and that he could better provide for his family in the private sector; and he lacked the stomach for further battles with the Legislature.(70) All the items mentioned in this paragraph played a role in his inner debate about whether to seek a third term. The ones heard most and that thus may have carried the greatest weight in his decision to be a eight-year Governor were his low poll ratings and his forecast that the years 1983 through 1986 would not present him with policy questions that intrigued him personally. Certainly he had by 1982 come to the conclusion that his friend Governor Michael Dukakis of Massachusetts was going a bit too far when he said that a governorship was the "...greatest job in the world, as most governors, I suspect, tell you".(71)

Notes to Chapter 14

1. Interview with Governor Hugh Carey, Nov. 30, 1991, Shelter Island, N.Y.

2. Interview with Burke, Aug. 28, 1992, New York City.

3. Ibid.

4. Phone interview with President Jimmy Carter's Deputy Secretary for Intergovernmental Affairs Eugene Eidenberg, Sept. 4, 1991, Washington.

5. New York Times, Aug. 5, 1980, p. B1.

6. Eidenberg, interview cited n.4 supra.

7. New York Times, Aug. 24, 1980, Sec. 1, p. 1; Aug. 25, 1980, p. B1.

8. New York Times, Aug. 24, 1980, Sec. 1, p. 1.

9. Eidenberg, interview cited n.4 supra.

10. Quoted Staten Island Advance, Oct. 1, 1980, p. 4. See also New York Times, Oct. 1, 1980, p. B1.

11. The attacks on the Carter drug cuts are described New York Daily News, Oct. 28, 1980, p. 7; New York Times, Oct. 1, 1980, p. B1. There were suggestions from time to time that Carey run for Vice President on John Anderson's third-party ticket. However, he never took this idea seriously. Interview with Special Assistant to the Governor Raymond Harding, July 2, 1990, New York City; New York Times, May 2, 1980, p. B6.

12. See Times Union (Albany), Sept. 14, 1977, p. 1; June 2, 1981, p. 1; New York Times, Feb. 2, 1978, p. B2. Unlike some prominent individuals featured in the press in the 1990s, Hugh and Helen Carey were punctilious about withholding social security taxes from the wages of their domestic employees. For example, in February of 1967 they withheld $1.79 of Ms. Almeto Jackson's $55 in wages on the 1st; $1.45 of her $40 in wages on the 8th; $1.85 of her $50 in wages on the 16th; and $1.45 of her $40 in wages on the 23rd. Hugh L. Carey Collection, St. John's Univ.(NY), Congressional Files 1961- 1974, (Personal Files 1961-74: Miscellaneous Personal Office Files: Personal Financial Records) file. (In "Social Security in 1967" notebook.)

Carey's Long Winter of Discontent

13. New York Times, Oct. 27, 1980, p. B1.

14. For an excellent map of the Carey and D'Arrigo lots, see Newsday, Nov. 11, 1980, p. 3.

15. New York Times, Nov. 10, 1980, p. B1.

16. Ibid.; Nov. 11, 1980, p. B1; Newsday, Nov. 9, 1980, p. 3.

17. On p. 3.

18. New York Times, Nov. 11, 1980, p. B1. Emphasis supplied.

19. Quoted Newsday Nov. 11, 1980, p. 3.

20. Staten Island Advance, Nov. 15, 1980, p. 8.

21. Interview with Hennessy, Sept. 18, 1991, Albany, N.Y.; interview with Patterson, July 20, 1991, Northport, N.Y.

22. Interview cited n.21 supra.

23. Interview with Carey Commissioner of General Services John Egan, Aug. 22, 1991, New York City.

24. Newsday, Nov. 13, 1980, p. 19.

25. Times Union (Albany), Feb. 6, 1981, p. 1.

26. Carey, Hugh - Hugh L. Carey: The Governor at p. 1, 24 of Benjamin, Gerald and Hurd, T. Norman (eds.) - Making Experience Count: Managing Modern New York In The Carey Era (Albany: Nelson A. Rockefeller Institute of Government, 1985).

27. Times Union (Albany), Feb. 11, 1981, p. 18. This and all other quotations from the Times Union (Albany) reprinted with the permission of that paper.

28. New York Times, Jan. 17, 1982, Sec. 1, p. 1.

29. See, e.g., Times Union (Albany), Feb. 13, 1981, p. 1; Feb. 14, 1981, p. 11.

30. New York Daily News, Feb. 10, 1981, p. 4. The article is headlined Travels with Carey, the Great Society Governor.

31. New York Times, Feb. 13, 1981, p. 3.

32. Clarke, Lee - Acceptable Risk: Making Decisions in a Toxic Environment (Berkeley: Univ. of California Press, 1989) at pp. 4-9, 14-16.

33. Times Union (Albany), Mar. 5, 1981, p. 1. The quote is from New York Times, Oct. 23, 1981, p. B1.

34. Interview with Times Union (Albany) reporter Fred Dicker June 12, 1991, Albany, N.Y.; with Carey Communications Director Charles Holcomb, Aug. 23, 1981, Lloyd Harbor, N.Y.; New York Times, Oct. 23, 1981, p. B1.

35. Times Union (Albany), Mar. 5, 1981, p. 1.

36. Times Union (Albany), Mar. 6, 1981, p. 1.

37. New York Times, Oct. 23, 1981, p. B1.

38. Clarke, op. cit. n.32 supra, pp. 122-23; Staten Island Advance, Dec. 30, 1982, p. 1.

39. Clarke, op. cit. n.32 supra, p. 123.

40. New York Times, Oct. 23, 1981, p. B1. The building reopened in 1994. Times Union (Albany), Oct. 12, 1994, p. B2; New York Times, Oct. 11, 1994, p. B1.

41. New York Daily News, Apr. 3, 1981, p. 5; New York Post, Apr. 17, 1981, p. 3; New York Times, March 25, 1981, p. B3; Mar. 28, 1981, p. 25; Staten Island Advance, Apr. 15, 1981, p. A1. The Times articles clearly indicate that even in late March the press believed that Miss Gouletas had been married only once.

42. New York Post, Apr. 10, 1981, p. 9.

43. Staten Island Advance, Mar. 29, 1981, Sec. 1, p. 13.

44. New York Daily News, Mar. 26, 1981, p. 4. The article was reprinted in Times Union (Albany), Mar. 29, 1981, p. B1.

45. Dicker, interview cited n.34 supra.

46. Staten Island Advance, Apr. 30, 1981, p. A8.

47. New York Times, Apr. 13, 1981, p. B3.

48. New York Post, Apr. 14, 1981, p. 5; New York Times, Apr. 13, 1981, p. B3; Staten Island Advance, Apr. 15, 1981, p. C5.

49. Staten Island Advance, Apr. 15, 1981, p. C5.

50. New York Post, Apr. 14, 1981, p. 5.

51. Staten Island Advance, Apr. 26, 1981, p. A6.

52. Quoted Staten Island Advance, Apr. 15, 1981, p. A1. A nastier barb referred to the Chief Executive as "fourth mate on a Greek tramp".

53. Staten Island Advance, Apr. 23, 1981, p. A3.

54. Dicker, interview cited n.34 supra.

55. Ibid.; Meislin, Richard - The Careys of Albany, New York Times Magazine, Oct. 4, 1981, p. 25, 30; New York Times, June 17, 1981, p. B6.

56. Phone interview with Burns, Dec. 30, 1992, Binghamton, N.Y.

57. New York Times, Dec. 19, 1993, Sec. 1, p.45.

58. Cuomo, Mario - Diaries of Mario M. Cuomo (New York: Random House, 1984), p. 110.

59. Interviews with Baranello, July 29, 1994, Patchogue, N.Y.; with Dempster, July 29, 1991, Woodbury, N.Y.

60. Interview with Frucher Aug. 17, 1994, New York City, Aug. 23, 1994, New York City (by phone).

61. New York Times, Jan. 17, 1982, p. A1.

62. Interview with Blum, July 17, 1991, New York City; with Burns cited n.57 <u>supra</u>; with Dyson, Jan. 21, 1991, Millbrook, N.Y.; with Introne, Aug. 15, 1991, Syracuse, N.Y.; with Ravitch, Nov. 20, 1990, New York City.

63. Interview with Gribetz, Sept. 28, 1990, New York City.

64. Interview with Carey Environmental Commissioner Robert Flacke, June 12, 1991, Lake George, N.Y.; with Carey Executive Assistant Martha Golden, Dec. 5, 1990, Washington; <u>New York Times</u>, Jan. 17, 1982, Sec. 1, p. 1.

65. Golden, interview cited n.64 <u>supra</u>.

66. Hennessy, interview cited n.21 <u>supra</u>.

67. Burns, interview cited n.56 <u>supra</u>.

68. Introne, interview cited n.62 <u>supra</u>.

69. Egan, interview cited n.23 <u>supra</u>; Frucher, interviews cited n.60 <u>supra</u>.

70. Morgado, Robert - <u>Robert Morgado: The Secretary to the Governor</u> at p. 27, pp. 47-48 of Benjamin and Hurd (eds.), <u>op. cit</u>. n.26 <u>supra</u>.

71. Quoted in Beyle, Thad, Muchmore, Lynn and Dalton, Robert - <u>Conclusion</u> at p. 206, 208 of Beyle, Thad and Muchmore, Lynn (eds.) - <u>Being Governor: The View from the Office</u> (Durham: Duke Univ. Press, 1983).

Chapter 15
Carey as Manager

AS JUST indicated, few of the questions that Carey had to wrestle with his second term positively excited him. Everyone admits that solving the fiscal crises in the first couple of years of his first watch totally engaged his mind and energies.(1) However, there are those, including some good friends of his, who feel that after the crisis he not only was not totally immersed in governing but that he was actually "bored". When this charge was put to him by *New York Times* correspondent Richard Meislin, he asserted vehemently that it was untrue(2); but several longtime colleagues agree with it. However, other veteran Carey aides such as Commerce Commissioner John Dyson and Counsel Judah Gribetz maintain that he never lost interest in what he was doing in Albany.(3) Where, then, does the truth lie?

There were some policy areas that just did not engross the Chief Executive, e.g., the plight of the mentally ill (as opposed to the mentally retarded)(4), restructuring the Executive Branch, and expanding the supply of housing built with State aid.(5) However, concerns such as cutting taxes, restraining excessive State and local spending to make this possible and encouraging business to come to and stay in New York kept beguiling him during his stay in the capital. During that much-criticized 1981 trip to the Far East, he and Commerce Commissioner William Hassett spent hours tossing ideas at each other about how the State's economic engine could be revved up.(6) And few doubted his continuing and strong commitment to Westway, the proposed expressway on the West Side of Manhattan, or to the cause of the retarded.

One particular type of event never failed to get Carey's gastric juices flowing: a crisis.(7) In Spring, 1975, as the financial fortunes of the Urban Development Corporation and of the five boroughs were unraveling, many physicians threatened to leave the State because they could no longer obtain medical malpractice insurance. One wrote "Dear Honorable Carey" that "The present situation of Malpractice Insurance and the judicial manner in which Malpractice cases are handled is intolerable and can not help but get worse - Unless, you and other members of Legislature [sic] make a determined effort to correct the condition, it can result in a rapid loss of physicians in New York State to an extent which is inconceivable. Within three to five years, New York State may have less than 50% of the present physician population".(8) So the

The Days of Wine and Roses Are Over

Governor and his chief health adviser Dr. Kevin Cahill quickly convinced the Legislature to adopt a plan creating two new groups to offer the necessary insurance.(9)

During his last six years, Carey was never faced with an earthquake of the magnitude of the New York City/State disasters but he was confronted with several emergencies nonetheless. Perhaps the most dramatic erupted when, as seen, poisonous vapors began pouring into the cellars of Love Canal homeowners in 1978. He worked hard on the issue; took several trips to the area; had meetings with community leaders; and worried both about the physical and mental health of the homeowners and about how helping them would affect the fiscal well-being of the State.(10) Corrections Commissioner Benjamin Ward notes that Carey often appeared to him to be "distracted". However, came a prison riot, and the Governor was all ears and continually on the phone.(11) In 1979 the State's prison guards went on strike for sixteen days. The Chief Executive was personally available to those of his aides who were bargaining with the recalcitrant corrections officers and made sure that someone was in his office twenty four hours a day. To keep up the morale of his negotiators, food and drinks from the finest delicatessen in Albany were constantly available to them, and not on paper plates but on china. In these ways, the dispute was resolved with only the most minor damage. (The comestibles were so tasty that he and many legislators dropped in for a snack.)(12)

In Summer of the same year gasoline all but disappeared from the State's petrol pumps, threatening its tourist business and its workaday economy. Lieutenant Governor Mario Cuomo, Carey's Secretary Robert Morgado, and his Director of Policy and Management Michael Del Giudice felt that there was no need to require that holders of odd (even) license plates be allowed to purchase their fuel on odd (even) days of the month only. But the Governor ignored their advice; issued the odd-even regulations; and soon commuters, businesspeople and visitors had little difficulty acquiring adequate quantities of the precious fuel.(13)

There are several reasons why many thought that Carey was a largely uninterested Chief Executive after the fiscal crises ended. Some point to the fact that he was very moody, swinging between periods where he would sparkle and days when he was withdrawn into himself and impossible to reach.(14) Various reasons have been adduced to account for these bouts of melancholy: the one most frequently given was that they were a delayed reaction to the death of his wife in 1974. Running for office that year and coping with the fiscal emergencies during the next two kept him from having much time for his private sorrows. Once the State and City were sailing on less choppy fiscal waters, his own private dam burst.(15) A less kindly explanation of his periods of remoteness is that his tremendous success in saving New York City infected him and his main aides with the virus of hubris, the feeling that they knew it all and that no one else was worth listening to.(16) Whatever the causes, he did have spells of deep depression; but these are not the same as chronic ennui. Periods of mental stress are perfectly compatible with retaining an interest in one's work. Therefore his on-again, off-again gloom is no proof that he found his job as Governor basically monotonous.

Another factor making some feel that the Governor was bored during his last several years in Albany is that after the passing of the fiscal storm he manifested his lack of interest in the **details** of government. During the crisis itself, he did often concern himself personally about specific items.(17) At the June 23rd gathering of the Emergency Financial Control Board, he remarked, for example, that if the City condemned property to build Westway, it could lay its hands on $77 million of federal funds to enable it to reimburse the owners of the seized land and buildings.(18) But the almost unanimous opinion of those who worked with him was that once City and State appeared to be saved from the prospect of default, he usually did not worry himself about how secondary problems were to be resolved. Morgado, who worked more closely with him his second term than did anyone else, admits that "He didn't have patience with the day-to-day administration of government".(19) An aide who often travelled around the State with Carey and who commented that the latter's late hours did not impair his effectiveness because he did not need much sleep, insists that his chief firmly believed that his commissioners should not bother him about questions such as the time at which the lights at the Rockefeller Mall should be dimmed.(20) Press Secretary Michael Patterson put it this way: he was much more interested in results than in trivia.(21) However, we cannot infer from this that he was uninterested in his job as a whole.

Moreover, the statement that the Governor was uninterested in "details" is ambiguous. It can mean that he was only vaguely aware of the nitty-gritty of what was happening in the jurisdictions for which he was responsible. This was **not** the case, for he did continually surprise people with his knowledge of the relevant facts and of narrow-gauge programs. John Defiggos of the State's Science and Technology Foundation attended meetings with the Governor on the problems of bringing high technology to New York, and was "amazed" by how *au courant* the Chief Executive was on this matter.(22) Mental Health Commissioner James Prevost came to realize that the Brooklynite's "intermittent involvement with the Office of Mental Health did not mean that he was unaware of our problems...."(23) Environmental Commissioner Robert Flacke contends that "There was not [an environmental] program that he did not understand in great minutiae".(24) So we have a paradox: a Governor who was uniformly reputed to be unconcerned with the technicalities but was cognizant of them.

The explanation lies in the fact that while he objected to having to solve minor problems, he has an excellent memory for facts. EFCB head Stephen Berger described it as "fantastic"; and Deffigos and Del Giudice referred to it as "photographic".(25) Thus not only did he remember just about every thing he was told or read; but these items remained stored in his mind for months or even years. Prevost mentions in discussing the Governor's awareness of the Office of Mental Health's programs that "Because of his amazing memory, he could pull out details in a later conversation, thus providing a current problem with prior information".(26) And Flacke says that "Anything we sent him, he knew. The governor had an unbelievably retentive memory. I would sit on an airplane with him and discuss very, very complex problems for 25 minutes, but when we'd land, it would just flow right out!".(27)

Another meaning of the assertion that the Governor was not interested in "details" is that he delegated a lot of problem solving to his aides. This was indubitably true; it is the corollary of his refusal to grapple with minor disputes. Time and time again I was told in my interviews that Carey's administrative philosophy was a

Carey as Manager

simple one: while those who "screw up" must get the boot, the emphasis should be on recruiting good people and letting them get on with the job. And he followed that prescription religiously. Dyson, Gribetz, Social Services Commissioner Barbara Blum, Corrections Commissioner Thomas Coughlin, Superintendent of Insurance Albert Lewis, Program Associate and Deputy Appointments Officer Robert Schiffer and Assistant for New York City and Community Affairs Menachem Shayovich all made this point.(28) As the Governor himself has phrased it, "I didn't 'nitpick' on administration...."(29)

Had this been all there was to the Carey philosophy of public management, no one would have given it a second thought. No President, Governor or Mayor is supposed to wrestle with every petty grumble that is brought to his/her officialdom. But in fact Carey permitted his commissioners and main assistants to make major as well as mundane decisions. First reference is to the transportation area, where he allowed Metropolitan Transportation Authority (MTA) chief Richard Ravitch and the legislative leaders in June and July of 1981 to negotiate a tax scheme to insure the continuation of State subsidies for mass transit. While Ravitch, Fink and Majority Leader Warren Anderson were in Albany adding the final clauses to the contract, the Chief Executive was, as seen, supping in Buffalo. Ravitch also shouldered the burden of lobbying the Legislature that year for the $5.6 capital assistance bill enabling the MTA to acquire new busses, subways and commuter trains and to modernize railroad stations and terminals. The agreement between the State and General Electric under which the latter was allowed to continue to empty minimal amounts of PCBs into the Hudson for a short period of time was the product of discussions between Environmental Commissioner Berle and company officials -- the Governor did not participate.(30)

Whether tenants at the huge, state-subsidized housing complex in The Bronx known as Co-op City paid a reasonable rent might on the surface of it not seem to be of great significance except to the tenants themselves, the corporation that held title to the buildings and some politicians who used to get elected by promising to keep these rents to a minimum. However, minuscule payments by those inhabiting Co-op City would have meant unsatisfactory revenues for the State Housing Finance Agency (HFA), the body which held the mortgages on this group of towers. And inadequate income for HFA might well have meant its defaulting; this in turn might well have made Municipal Assistance Corporation (MAC) bonds unsellable; this would surely have driven New York City into bankruptcy court; and all of the hard work by the Governor and many others in 1975 and 1976 would then have been in vain. Thus it was essential to the continued financial stability of New York City and State that the residents of Co-op City be compelled to bear additional burdens. So Carey housing aide Judith Frangos, after extensive consultation with HFA and Division of Housing and Community Renewal leaders, formulated a deal under which the State would agree to underwrite some of the structural repairs on the poorly built development while the tenants would have to pay higher rents or carrying charges. Neither Carey nor even Morgado participated in the discussions leading to this crucial compromise. (31)

Likewise when Richard Kahan became head of the Urban Development Corporation (UDC), he authored a plan to force owners of UDC projects who were using them as profitable tax shelters to fix them up and make their mortgage payments promptly. This ingenious *modus operandi* involved his threatening these speculators with a UDC foreclosure of their mortgages on the ground that they were delinquent in meeting their contractual obligations and in making repairs. He also hired top Wall Street lawyers to represent the Corporation in these impending actions in the hope that their very presence on the UDC's side would mean that the owners would listen to reason. They did and began paying the interest on time and refurbishing their buildings: they knew that these attorneys would whip them in any dispute that reached the courtroom. They were also aware that if the UDC successfully foreclosed, Washington might recoup the tax deductions their UDC investments had made possible for them. This scheme was charted by Kahan, not by the Governor or Morgado.(32) One more example of important policies that were shaped by Carey aides with little input from the Chief Executive was the gamut of measures designed to hold down soaring health and Medicaid costs; e.g, reducing the freedom of hospitals to acquire fancy Medical equipment and stationing nurses and doctors on a hospital floor to insure that Medicaid patients were not getting unnecessary operations. The persons who worked out these techniques were Cahill and staffers interested in health matters such as Robert Schiffer, Richard Berman and Dr. Jeffrey Sachs.(33)

However, that Carey delegated the resolution of important as well as trivial problems is not a reason in and of itself to criticize him. In fact if a Chief Executive hires fine people, he/she would be incredibly shortsighted not to allow them to have a great deal of leeway in drafting their own policies consistent with his/her own philosophy. A finger could be pointed at the Governor for having turned the solution of critical problems over to his aides if he had not been personally familiar with these issues or if he had been oblivious of what they were doing to solve them. But neither of these situations prevailed with respect to any important question that he asked his staff to answer. For example, as for Kahan's forcing investors in UDC-subsidized flats and cooperatives to contribute their fair share to the upkeep of these structures, Carey was after early 1975 as aware as anyone of the plight of that agency. Furthermore, its head's plan to hire expensive lawyers to convince the project owners to do the right thing ran up against the fact that some of these developers were political supporters of the Governor; and so Kahan could not put the economic screws on them without his express consent -- which was forthcoming.(34) The Chief Executive may have consigned to his aides the form-ulation of some crucial policies; but these went into effect only with his knowing approval, i.e., with his being well acquainted with their contents, the fields they dealt with, and the evils at which they were aimed. As Gribetz and the Director of his Office of Employee Relations Meyer Frucher agree, he might have been a "hands off" administrator; but he had a mind of his own and all the final, significant decisions during his stay in Albany were genuinely as well as formally his.(35)

Thus the position that Carey must have by and large been "bored" during his last several years is weak. It is true that his job did not obsess him the way it had during his first 18 to 24 months in office. However, throughout his eight years his attention was riveted by certain questions. His memory was chockful of details. He wrestled with broad problems. Morgado commented that his chief "always considered himself the 'idea person', which he was....He could spout ideas interminably. If accomodated, I could

The Days of Wine and Roses Are Over

have spent entire days staffing his ideas".(36) It is true that he **delegated** decision making power; but he **abdicated** it on minor issues only!

The Governor deserves plaudits not only for hiring outstanding individuals but also for following the suggestions of brilliant unpaid advisers from the private sector such as Cahill, Felix Rohatyn and Simon Rifkind. However, there **were** serious weaknesses in his ability to manage people, defects which sprang at least in part from his spells of gloom and doom. His first major failing as a supervisor, a flaw to some extent the product of the melancholia, was his inaccessibility to many of his subordinates. Many of my interviewees who held positions in his Administration admitted that they had trouble getting personal appointments with him and that they had to go Cahill (until he left) to discuss health matters and to Morgado to settle all other questions. The staffers considered Morgado in particular an insuperable barrier erected between themselves and the Governor; though Del Giudice and Frucher contend that those who really had to get through to Carey could. (For example, State Party Chairman Dominic Baranello had easy access to him.)(37) Stephen Chinlund, Chairman of the Correction Commission who emphasized to me that Carey fervently opposed the theory that jails were a good way to solve social problems, notes that he almost always had to speak to the Secretary rather than to the Chief Executive.(38) And Brad Johnson, New York State's person in Washington who had to scramble hard to get federal dollars for Albany during the Carter Presidency and to keep the Reagan Administration from taking them back, found it well nigh impossible to get Carey over the phone to ask him for guidance. He usually found himself speaking to Morgado or Cahill instead. In contrast, after he became Governor, Mario Cuomo called him just about every day after business hours and made small talk.(39) Interestingly, Del Giudice contends that the Secretary's rigid gatekeeping benefited many on the Chief Executive's staff in that it forced them to gather more evidence and to clarify their thinking before they conferred with the Governor.(40)

How did Morgado get so much power? When Carey first came to Albany, he and his major aides, Gribetz, David Burke and Peter Goldmark were all "strangers in a strange land".(41) On February 17, 1975, in an announcement that did not make any headlines, the Governor appointed Robert J. Morgado to be one of his Deputy Secretaries.(42) The new assistant had a PhD in Political Science from the State University of New York at Albany. He had worked for the State Division of the Budget and for the Assembly Ways and Means Committee under both Democrats and Republicans. So he not only could provide the Governor with necessary advice on budgetary matters that year of the State and City fiscal crises; but also could draw him and his entourage a "political map" indicating what legislators, legislative staffers, top civil servants and lobbyists had special expertise on or an interest in this or that issue. That is, he could tell them which habitants of the capital had to be stroked if they wanted to make progress on certain matters as well as inform them whether it was financially feasible to take steps in those areas. As Burke put it, he was the only one who knew the whereabouts of the "keys to the men's room".(43)

Morgado performed his dual role admirably and, as a reward, was made Director of State Operations on November 5, 1975.(44) On August 4, 1977, Burke resigned as Secretary and was replaced by the then 34-year-old Morgado.(45) The latter played a major role in Carey's 1978 reelection victory, which further firmed up his standing with his superior. It was during Carey's second term (until he resigned in mid-1982) that he was what Political Scientist Gerald Benjamin refers to as "the governor's governor".(46) "Bob Morgado's strength, in the later years, was that he controlled access to the governor, for his institutional role as secretary reinforced the close personal relationship he was able to develop with Hugh Carey."(47)

Morgado was liked by some of Carey's aides, tolerated by others and loathed by some. But no one felt that he was pulling the strings and that the Governor was a puppet simply dancing to his tune. For example, his Executive Assistant Martha Golden admitted that Morgado wielded a bundle of power in Albany after he became Secretary; but added that there was no doubt that this was exercised subject to his boss's "veto".(48) He may have been a one-man palace guard overly protective of his chief, but he never carried out a behind-the-scenes coup d'etat against him!

Carey's mercurial temperament had effects on his relations with his staff above and beyond their often finding him inaccessible. Sometimes he walked into his office in the morning and did not

300

The Days of Wine and Roses Are Over

even bother to say "good day": some were annoyed but some took it in stride.(49) If he were out of sorts or if he felt that you were not adequately performing whatever task he had set for you, he could be angry and nasty. He could be charming and affable to his retinue or he could be rude. He might focus on what you were saying or pay you no heed.(50) He could be very witty not only on the campaign trail but also when talking to his aides, reporters and visitors. Lewis loved swapping jokes with him.(51) Sometimes his humor was self-deprecating; at times it was at the expense of others. For example, his struggle against the death penalty gave him the occasion to launch a gentle barb against Republican State Senator James Donovan, a supporter of capital punishment. He told the assembled press that his "only discussions with Senator Donovan....would be on the question of the Baltimore Catechism". When a listener asked "Which catechism, Governor?", he responded "The Baltimore Catechism....It was the resurrection of Jesus Christ which began Christianity, not [as Donovan had trumpeted] his death".(52) The audience cracked up.(53)

He was notoriously hard on one type of staffer: his Press Secretaries.(54) He had six of them during his eight years in office: Robert Laird, James Vlasto, David Murray, Michael Patterson, Jill Schuker and Stephen Morello. In addition he had three Directors of Communication (a similar job(55)), Rockefeller/Wilson holdover Harry O'Donnell, Charles Holcomb and William Snyder, and was no easier on these. One trouble was that he often failed to give the Press Secretaries information about his policy on a particular matter or to fill them in on changes that he and his aides had made. Sometimes when he and others were resolving problems the Press Secretary was kept right next door and not told what decisions had been reached. As a result, the information he handed out to journalists was sometimes inaccurate, incomplete or both.(56) Sometimes, he was not even given the Governor's schedule.(57) Laird and O'Donnell were never asked how the firing of Special Prosecutor Maurice Nadjari would play in the papers. If their lord and master had bothered to consult them, they would have been able to suggest ways of ousting the Prosecutor that would not have left him looking like a Tammany Hall conniver.(58) Sometimes, he ignored the Press Secretary's advice: this is one reason why O'Donnell resigned.(59)

Carey as Manager

When the Press Secretary was given the task of helping the Governor write a speech, he and his boss often sat down together. Usually, the Brooklynite threw in a phrase. When he read the address as a whole the next day, he at times asked, glancing at his own handiwork, "who tossed in that stupid comment?"!(60) When he did not like something he remembered that they had penned, he let them know his dissatisfaction in no uncertain terms. Even the absence of a date could anger him.(61) Sometimes he wanted a talk written in a few minutes; sometimes he ignored large chunks of what had been drafted for him and added many comments extemporaneously.(62) Thanks for a job well done was not the lot of Carey's Press Secretaries. When in November of 1980 Holcomb heard on a Friday that the Shelter Island land-seizure story was going to break on the upcoming Sunday, he flew to Syracuse to warn his employer what was going to happen. He managed to get hold of him during halftime at a football game. Instead of expressing appreciation to his aide for interrupting his weekend to help him out, the Chief Executive simply grumbled.(63)

The above paragraphs depicting Carey chewing out his Press Secretaries do not entirely sum up the relations between his staffers and himself. They emphasize the worst; and ignore the fact that most of the people who worked for him liked and respected him and continue do so so. This is true even of Press Secretaries such as Patterson.(64) His usual attitude toward those who worked in the Executive Office as program associates, appointments staff, secretaries, etc. was one of "all business" as opposed to surliness (and joviality, for that matter).(65) He never flirted with secretaries and bright women never made him uncomfortable. If he liked someone, he/she could argue with him without fear of adverse consequences.(66)

Moreover, he rarely expected his assistants to devote all their evenings and weekends to his service.(67) At times he was extremely kind to a particular subordinate. After Transportation Commissioner William Hennessy had had a heart attack in Carey's office, the Governor visited him constantly in hospital.(68) When Deputy Appointments Secretary William Cunningham's father died, the Chief Executive attended the funeral without informing everyone in advance that he was going to do so. And in the midst of his feud with Democratic State Chairman Patrick Cunningham,

The Days of Wine and Roses Are Over

he took time to attend the funeral mass for Patrick's brother, an action the Chairman greatly appreciated.(69)

It is true that if someone joined the Carey Administration for the purpose of getting a pat on the back from him, she -- even if she were not a Press Secretary -- would have had to depart Albany with her hopes unfulfilled. He never, or hardly ever, praised you for a job well done.(70) As Berger phrased it, he did not "stroke" you.(71) He never thanked Johnson for putting his heart and soul into securing the passage of the 1978 federal New York City loan guarantee bill nor lauded Berle for negotiating the PCB-dumping agreement with General Electric.(72)

Though Carey would be unwilling to cheer you on for perform-ing your tasks like a professional, if you took a public position and were criticized for it, he usually would back you up.(73) He defended Youth Division Director Peter Edelman against attacks by persons such as Senate Crime Committee head Ralph Marino to the effect that he was too "soft on crime" and too sympathetic to troubled youngsters.(74) When Blum objected to a Koch Admin-istration plan under which welfare tenants living in the South Bronx would have to have their rent checks endorsed by their landlord as well as by themselves, Carey and the federal government backed her and the scheme was never put into practice. (Its purpose was to insure that welfare families would not waste their housing money on liquor and drugs.) He also stood by her when she was attacked for saying that at least one shelter for the homeless was needed in every New York City borough. Mayor Koch had called her a "crazy lady" for making this proposal, and changed that she wanted to bring "a cancer into each neighborhood".(75) On an occasion in 1981 when City politicians lambasted her plans to move computer-ized Medicaid files to Albany because welfare dossiers were al-ready in the capital, Carey's comment was "If she wants to do it, it is right". She was exceptionally grateful for this reinforcement for she felt exhausted after spending a lot of time in Washington fighting President Reagan's cuts in social service programs.(76)

Julio Martinez, a former drug addict himself, was chosen by the Chief Executive to be the Director of the Division of Drug and Substance Abuse Services. Martinez was reappointed to that position by Mario Cuomo but had a falling out with him and was

Carey as Manager

fired. To earn a living and simultaneously publicly protest the way the ex-law professor had treated him, he opened a hot dog stand right outside the Legislative Office Building in Albany, catty-corner to the Capitol whose Second Floor is occupied by the Governor and his aides.(77) I interviewed him while munching a tasty frank-furter at his stand. He feels that Carey, unlike his successor, was extremely supportive of his efforts. For example, there is an excel-lent drug treatment faciliity known as Daytop Village whose first building was located on the conservative, house-proud south shore of Staten Island. Many of the local homeowners objected to the intrusion of this alien presence into their law-abiding, middle class midst. In fact, one of their number tried to burn the shelter down. Martinez called a press conference in Albany and became so angry at what had happened that he started screaming. His chief was next door; heard him; called him in; and asked him what had set him off. When he learned the story, he had the Attorney General send one of his assistants to Staten Island to investigate. Martinez thus refers to him as the man he would most like to be stranded in a jungle with.(78)

A Carey characteristic that irritated some of his staffers as well as public officials and ordinary citizens was his continual refusal to be prompt in keeping appointments. One of those who was assigned the thankless task of scheduling him -- he sometimes blamed these individuals when he was late(79) -- attributes the chronic tardiness in part to his desire to read in the morning and to his inability to break away from a conversation that intrigued him.(80) Some of it was due to his off again-on again melancholia. Another aide declares that a portion of the problem was that the Chief Executive was also a single parent for the bulk of his stay in Albany. When he moved to the capital at the end of 1974, he brought with him six of his children as full time residents, the youngest of whom was eight. The aide stresses that he, unlike every other male governor in American history, had by himself to push his youngsters to get dressed in the morning and to go over their homework with them before their classes.(81) When one of them got into trouble at school, he was the one who phoned the teacher. At times the younger ones got out of hand and, e.g., shot water pistols at guests arriving at the Executive Mansion. (82) His offspring **were** a source of strength to him(83); but were also

The Days of Wine and Roses Are Over

a drain on his time and their problems sometimes took precedence over his schedule. On their side, they are grateful to him for making their youthful years interesting and for always being there when they needed him.(84)

Playing the role of parent is one important aspect of a private life but not the only one. As seen, Carey desired time to himself: he is less outgoing than was his wife Helen, whose very presence was said by one observer to make him positively radiant.(85) Some of his aides even think that he is basically very shy.(86) He wanted to get away from his desk for the sake of his children and for socializing with men and women friends; and also for reading, for thinking and for coping with his fits of unhappiness. As he was leaving Albany, he pointed out to reporters that during what he called his periods of "detachment", he had "found some answers to some very difficult problems".(87) As Morgado sensitively put it, his boss "was essentially a very private person....He enjoyed the governorship; he just didn't live it. There are people in public life whose lives are totally dominated by their public careers. [New York City Council President] Carol Bellamy is one. To some degree, Ed Koch is another. Hugh Carey wasn't".(88) And Golden, another person who saw quite a bit of him, certainly agrees that he wished for a personal life where neither politics nor the media intruded.(89) He did achieve some degree of seclusion; but this further reduced his accessibility to his staff and to others. As an article in the *Daily News* pointed out, "It's common for a caller to check the governor's office to find out where Carey is. 'We really don't know,' someone in the office often says truthfully. 'Whatever he is doing it is private business....'"(90)

Thus no one would call Carey a great leader of people once the fiscal crises were over. All in all, he has to be deemed just a fair-to-middling administrator. He should have lost his temper less, praised more and been easier to contact. Yet the mediocre CEO was an outstanding Governor.

Notes to Chapter 15

1. Interview with Carey Deputy Appointments Secretary William Cunningham, Dec. 30, 1991, Albany, N.Y.; with Carey Commissioner of Office of Mental Retardation and Developmental Disabilities James Introne, Aug. 15, 1991, Syracuse, N.Y.; with Carey Housing Commissioner Victor Marrero, Sept. 12, 1990, New York City; Benjamin, Gerald - The Carey Governorship at p. 235, 244 of Benjamin, Gerald and Hurd, T. Norman (eds.) - Making Experience Count: Managing Modern New York In The Carey Era (Albany: Nelson A. Rockefeller Institute of Government, 1985).

2. New York Times, Jan. 2, 1980, p. A1.

3. Interview with Dyson, Jan. 21, 1991, Millbrook, N.Y.; with Gribetz, Sept. 28, 1990, New York City.

4. See Prevost, James A. - James A. Prevost: Commissioner of Mental Health at p. 197, 205 of Benjamin and Hurd (eds.), op.cit. n.1 supra.

5. Marrero, interview cited n.1 supra; Frucher, Meyer - Meyer S. (Sandy) Frucher: Director of the Governor's Office of Employee Relations at p. 147, 171 of Benjamin and Hurd (eds.), op. cit. n.1 supra.

6. Interview with Carey Director of Policy and Management Michael Del Giudice, June 28, 1994, New York City; with Commerce Commissioner George Dempster, July 29, 1991, Woodbury, N.Y.; with Hassett, Sept. 26, 1990, New York City. Dempster succeeded Hassett.

7. Cunningham, interview cited n.1 supra; interview with Carey Corrections Commissioner Benjamin Ward, Nov. 6, 1991, Brooklyn, N.Y.

8. Letter to Carey located Hugh L. Carey Collection, St. John's Univ.(NY), Insurance (Malpractice: Legislation) file.

9. New York Times, May 20, 1975, p. 28; Apr. 26, 1981, Sec. 1, p. 54; Staten Island Advance, May 30, 1975, p. 1.

10. Interview with a Carey aide, June 5, 1992.

11. Ward, interview cited n.7 supra.

12. Cunningham, interview cited n.1 supra; interview with Director of Governor's Office of Employee Relations Meyer Frucher, Aug. 17, 1994,

306

The Days of Wine and Roses Are Over

Aug. 23, 1994 (phone), New York City. Frucher told me in these interviews that the solons enjoyed their repasts so much that they gladly reimbursed his Office for the cost of the victuals provided the negotiators

13. Del Giudice, interview cited n.6 supra.

14. See, e.g., Benjamin, op. cit. n.1 supra, p. 241.

15. See, e.g., ibid., p. 242.

16. Phone interview with John Omicinski, formerly of Gannett Newspapers Albany Bureau, Sept. 27, 1991, Washington.

17. See Benjamin, op. cit. n.1 supra, p. 242.

18. Emergency Financial Control Board June 23, 1976 Minutes.

19. Morgado, Robert - Robert Morgado: The Secretary to the Governor at p. 27, 48 of Benjamin and Hurd (eds.), op cit. n. 1 supra.

20. Interview with Carey aide cited n.10 supra.

21. Interview with Patterson, Sept. 20, 1991, Northport, N.Y.

22. Interview with Deffigos, Deputy Executive Director New York State Science and Technology Foundation, July 28, 1992, Albany, N.Y.

23. Prevost, op. cit. n.4 supra, p. 205.

24. Flacke, Robert - Robert F. Flacke: Commissioner of Environmental Conservation at p. 121, 141 of Benjamin and Hurd (eds.), op. cit. n.1 supra. Carey's State Consumer Protection Board Director Karen Burstein notes that once when she went to discuss a utility problem with him, he launched into a history of public utilities. Interview with Burstein, Mar. 22, 1995, New York City.

25. Interview with Berger, Feb. 3, 1991, New York City; with Defiggos cited n.22 supra; with Del Giudice cited n.6 supra.

26. Prevost, op. cit. n.4 supra, p. 205.

27. Flacke, op. cit. n.24 supra, p. 141.

Carey as Manager

28. Interview with Blum, July 7, 1991, New York City; with Coughlin, July 18, 1990, Albany, N.Y.; Dyson, interview cited n.3 <u>supra</u>; Gribetz, interview cited n.3 <u>supra</u>; interview with Lewis, Dec. 6, 1994, New York City; with Schiffer, April 21, 1991, New York City; with Shayovich, Apr.24, 1991, Brooklyn, N.Y.

29. Carey, Hugh - <u>Hugh L. Carey: The Governor</u> at p. 1, 16 of Benjamin and Hurd (eds.), <u>op. cit</u>. n.1 <u>supra</u>. Many modern governors shun "nitpicking" in administration and emphasize the importance of selecting an outstanding team of subordinates and delegating to them a good deal of decision-making power. See Dalton, Robert - <u>Governors' Views on Management</u> at p. 93 of Beyle, Thad and Muchmore, Lynn (eds.) - <u>Being Governor: The View from the Office</u> (Durham: Duke Univ. Press, 1983); Rosenthal, Alan - <u>Governors and Legislators: Contending Powers</u> (Washington: CQ Press, 1990), p. 170.

30. Interview with Berle, Mar. 7, 1991, New York City.

31. Interview with Frangos, June 13, 1991, Albany, N.Y.

32. Interview with Kahan, Nov. 21, 1990, New York City; <u>New York Times</u>, Nov. 6, 1979, p. B3.

33. Interview with Carey Office of Health Systems Management Director Berman, Aug. 5, 1991, New York City; with New York State Division of Budget aides Robert Kerker and Alex Rollo, June 3, 1992, Albany, N.Y.; with Carey Program Associate Sachs, June 7, 1991, New York City.

34. Kahan, interview cited n.32 <u>supra</u>.

35. Interviews cited n.3 and n.12 <u>supra</u>. Even in the health/mental health areas, where Cahill exerted so much influence on policy making, Carey had the final say. Interview with Cahill, July 26, 1993, New York City.

36. Morgado, <u>op. cit</u>. n.19 <u>supra</u>, pp. 35-36. The Director of Carey's 1974 Transition Council, Matthew Nimetz, agrees that the Governor was an "idea person". Interview May 17, 1990, New York City.

37. Interview with Baranello, July 29, 1994, Patchogue, N.Y.; Del Giudice, interview cited n.6 <u>supra</u>; Frucher, interviews cited n.12 <u>supra</u>. Sometimes Frucher went to Morgado first. However, if he was dissatisfied

The Days of Wine and Roses Are Over

with the Secretary's decision, he -- almost alone in Albany -- took advantage of the latter's offer that those who did not like his position should knock on the Governor's door, walk in and discuss the matter with Carey. Frucher interviews; Morgado, op. cit. n.19 supra, p. 37. Morgado asserts there that he made this offer to his colleagues generally

38. Interview with Chinlund, Feb. 28, 1992, New York City.

39. Interview with Johnson, July 26, 1991, Washington.

40. Interview cited n.6 supra.

41. Benjamin, op. cit. n.1 supra, p. 244.

42. Public Papers of Governor Hugh L. Carey 1975 (Albany: State of New York Executive Chamber, 1982), p. 1594.

43. Interview with Burke, Aug. 28, 1992, New York City.

44. Carey, op. cit. n.42 supra, p. 1595.

45. Public Papers of Governor Hugh L. Carey 1977 (Albany: State of New York Executive Chamber, 1982), pp. 1766-67.

46. Benjamin, op cit. n.1 supra, p. 244.

47. Ibid.

48. Interview with Golden, Dec. 5, 1990, Washington. After Morgado left Carey's employ, he joined the Time-Warner conglomerate headed by Carey contributor Steve Ross. He became a successful but controversial chief executive officer of Warner Music, a division of Time-Warner that is the largest record company in the world. For a fascinating account of his doings at Time-Warner, see Danner, Frederic - Showdown at the Hit Factory, New Yorker, Nov. 21, 1994, pp. 66ff. He was discharged in 1995 but will collect millions in severance pay. New York Times, June 7, 1995, p. D7.

49. Golden, interview cited n.48 supra.

50. Interview with former Emergency Financial Control Board Staff member Frank Macchiarola, Aug. 31, 1991, New York City; with Metro-

politan Transportation Authority Chairman Richard Ravitch, Nov. 20, 1990, New York City; with Carey Tax Commissioner James Tully, June 8, 1990, Albany, N.Y.

51. Lewis, interview cited n.28 <u>supra</u>.

52. See <u>Public Papers of Governor Hugh L. Carey 1978</u> (Albany: State of New York Executive Chamber, 1988), pp. 779-80.

53. Interview with a Carey staffer, July 23, 1991.

54. <u>New York Times</u>, Jan. 11, 1981, Sec. 1, p. 1.

55. Interview with Carey Communications Director Charles Holcomb, Aug. 23, 1991, Lloyd Harbor, N.Y.

56. Interview with <u>Times Union</u> (Albany) reporter Fred Dicker, June 12, 1991, Albany, N.Y.; Holcomb, interview cited n.55 <u>supra</u>; Beyle, Thad and Muchmore, Lynn - <u>The Governor and the Public</u> at p. 52, pp. 60-61 of Beyle, Thad and Muchmore, Lynn (eds.), <u>op. cit</u>. n.29 <u>supra</u>.

57. Holcomb, interview cited n.55 <u>supra</u>.

58. Interview with Carey Press secretary Robert Laird, May 18, 1993, New York City.

59. Holcomb, interview cited n.55 <u>supra</u>.

60. Patterson, interview cited n.21 <u>supra</u>

61. Holcomb, interview cited n.55 <u>supra</u>.

62. <u>Ibid</u>.

63. <u>Ibid</u>. James Vlasto noted that while he was Press Secretary, he on occasion had to attend policy discussions lasting until 2AM even though he had to get up at 6AM the next morning. Interview with Vlasto at "Carey Years" Conference, Apr. 20, 1995, New York City.

64. Patterson, interview cited n.21 <u>supra</u>.

65. Interview with a Carey staffer, July 23, 1991.

The Days of Wine and Roses Are Over

66. Burstein, interview cited n.24 <u>supra</u>.

67. Golden, interview cited n.48 <u>supra</u>.

68. Interview with Hennessy, Sept. 18, 1991, Albany, N.Y.

69. William Cunningham, interview cited n.1 <u>supra</u>; letter from Patrick Cunningham to Carey dated Mar. 26, 1976. This letter can be found in Hugh L. Carey Collection, St. John's Univ. (NY), Gubernatorial Files 1975-82 (Governor's Personal Correspondence 1975-78) file.

70. Ward, interview cited n.7 <u>supra</u>.

71. Interview cited n.25 <u>supra</u>.

72. Berle, interview cited n.30 <u>supra</u>; Johnson, interview cited n.39 <u>supra</u>. Johnson "forgives Carey his idiosyncracies" because of his outstanding work during the New York City financial crisis. Interview cited <u>supra</u>.

73. Coughlin, interview cited n.28 <u>supra</u>; Dempster, interview cited n.6 <u>supra</u>.

74. Interview with Edelman, May 8, 1991, Washington. See also <u>New York Times</u>, July 15, 1978, p. 1. In 1994 President Bill Clinton said he was thinking of nominating Edelman to fill a vacancy on the important United States Court of Appeals for the District of Columbia. Again, conservative Republicans condemned Edelman as "soft on crime"; again Carey rose to his defense. <u>New York Times</u>, Dec. 26, 1994, p. 39. Nonetheless, the President decided not to name him. <u>New York Times</u>, Sept. 1, 1995, p. A18.

75. Blum, Barbara - <u>Barbara B. Blum: Commissioner of Social Services</u> at p. 89, pp. 100-101 of Benjamin and Hurd (eds.), <u>op. cit</u>. n.1 <u>supra</u>.

76. Blum, interview cited n.28 <u>supra</u>.

77. See <u>Times Union</u> (Albany), July 26, 1991, p. A1.

78. Interview with Martinez, July 23, 1991, Albany, N.Y.

79. Patterson, interview cited n.21 <u>supra</u>.

80. Interview with the scheduler, Nov. 30, 1991.

81. Interview with the aide, June 5, 1992.

82. Lewis, interview cited n.28 <u>supra</u>.

83. Golden, interview cited n.48 <u>supra</u>.

84. Interviews with two of Carey's sons at "Carey Years" Conference, Apr. 20, 1995, New York City.

85. Lewis, interview cited n.28 <u>supra</u>.

86. Frangos made this point in the interview cited n.31 <u>supra</u>.

87. <u>New York Times</u>, Dec. 31, 1982, p. B1.

88. Morgado, <u>op. cit</u>. n.19 <u>supra</u>, p. 49.

89. Interview cited n.48 <u>supra</u>.

90. <u>New York Daily News</u>, Feb. 7, 1978, p. 21.

Chapter 16
Hugh Carey:
A Rolls Royce Engine in a Studebaker Body

SEVERAL chapters have not been easy on Hugh Carey. They have shown that he was not one to spend much time cajoling rank-and-file State Senators and Assemblypeople and that at times even the legislative leaders found him hard to reach. He did very little in support of his Party's Presidential candidate in the 1980 race despite all the help Mr. Carter had given New York State; and he tried to seize a neighbor's property because the house that was being built on it could reduce his own privacy. He made light of an explosion in a State office building that blew insidious PCBs into every nook and cranny of the edifice. Afflicted with moodiness, he frequently was inaccessible to his aides and to Democratic county chairpeople. At times, he was positively rude and nasty to some of his staffers. One of his aides is still very fond of him; but admits that no one could label him a "nice, sweet Governor".(1)

And yet despite his flaws, most of the men and women whom I interviewed in the course of writing this book gave Carey extremely high grades as a Governor. Social Services Commissioner Stephen Berger says that despite bizarre episodes such as Shelter Island, he never made a bad **governmental** decision and is the most brilliant of all the governors he has observed.(2) Democratic Assemblyman Arthur Kremer from Long Island, head of the Ways and Means Committee while Carey was in Albany, gives Carey "high marks" even though he was not good at day-to-day administration and could have done more in the way of scratching the backs of rank and file lawmakers. Assembly Member Elizabeth Connelly joins her colleague in according him good grades.(3) Environmental Commissioner Ogden Reid, who departed in 1976 after disagreements with the Governor about General Electric's discharge of PCBs into the Hudson, comments that Carey "was very good at what he did".(4) Housing aide Judith Frangos praises him for refusing to "compromise on matters of principle".(5) Salomon Brothers' Gedale Horowitz (who observed him during the fiscal crisis) refers to him as "unappreciated" and "underrated"; while his Director of Policy and Management Michael Del Giudice also emphasizes his "brilliance".(6) Metropolitan Transportation Authority Chairman Richard Ravitch, who became very irritated with him at times, nonetheless describes him as "fantastic" in coping with the Urban Development Corporation and

The Days of Wine and Roses Are Over

New York City fiscal crises and generally a "great" Governor.(7) Social Services Commissioner Barbara Blum and Commerce Commissioner William Hassett use the adjectives "spectacular" and "super" respectively to refer to his stewardship of the State(8); while Appointments Officer John Burns qualifies his Governorship with the labels "excellent" and "underrated".(9) Mayor Ed Koch calls him, Al Smith and Nelson Rockefeller the best Governors New York has had during the Twentieth Century. He feels that the Jacob Javits Convention Center should have been named for Carey instead, for the Governor did more than the Senator to insure that it was built.(10)

Carey gets tributes from unexpected places. Congresswoman Bella Abzug certainly has good reason to hold a grudge against her former colleague in the United States House of Representatives. As seen, the Governor did not look with favor upon her 1977 Mayoral candidacy because her perceived "radicalism" might, he thought, keep investors out of the market for City bonds and thus jeopardize the metropolis' future. But despite this bit of history, she terms him a "good public official" who made efforts for the "progressive Democratic causes" to which she is so devoted.(11) Albany *Times Union* correspondent Fred Dicker excoriated him for allowing his children and friends to take free rides on State aircraft. These articles so annoyed him that when he, out of the corner of his eye, noticed the journalist at a groundbreaking ceremony, he threw a shovelful of dirt at him. Nonetheless the newsman refers to him as "on the whole a good Governor who was not afraid to make unpopular decisions".(12) And State Assembly Minority Leader Perry Duryea, whom he beat in a come-from-behind finish in the 1978 gubernatorial contest, describes him as a "talented" man.(13)

Many of my other respondents also praised Carey highly; but it would serve no good purpose to mention all their names. There was a small minority who evidenced moderate or no respect for him. One of his staffers, who made the remark not for attribution, denounced him as a "bully". A man who worked for him for most of his eight years in Albany feels that once he had saved the City, his conduct for the rest of his tenure in Albany was basically irrational. Eugene Eidenberg, a Carter staffer who frequently dealt with Carey and his assistants, justifiably criticizes the Governor's treatment of the Carter Administration as ungrateful and unpredict-able.(14) Mayor Abe Beame is still somewhat annoyed with him, believing that it was he as much as the Governor who took the tough decisions that put the City on the right track.(15) And a businessman who is friendly with Beame feels that Carey was a much better Congressman than Chief Executive.

In our final rating, which Carey is it who is to prevail? Is it the moody, sometimes nasty Mr. Hyde who, even his Secretary Robert Morgado admits, could have worked a bit harder(16), who some-times was on a mental planet a million miles away from Albany, and whom his aides and Commissioners often could not contact? Or is it the Dr. Jekyll lauded by so many? Clearly the latter! The surliness, the remoteness, the late night stints at bar/restaurants such as P.J. Clarke's all lowered him in the eyes of the media, the Legislature and/or the public; but these characteristics cannot be allowed to detract from his extremely solid accomplishments. As Political Scientist Gerald Benjamin (a Republican, by the way) comments, he was guilty of a "disregard of public image" but "The substance was there".(17) And it is the substance that lets me join many of my interviewees in deeming him an outstanding Governor. Cardozo Law School Dean and former New York City Schools Chancellor Frank Macchiarola put it picturesquely but accurately when I interviewed him: Carey was a "Rolls Royce engine in a Studebaker body".(18)

I have described in detail the accomplishments of his Admin-istration. Regardless of how deeply he was involved in their design, and he was very active in conceiving some and left the development of others to his aides, he among others must be given the credit for them. Even when he was most "hands off", he gave them the final seal of approval after hiring the talented men and women who framed them; and he was fully aware of what they were designed to accomplish. This book was not conceived as a didactic exercise. But one lesson it does reinforce is that a chief executive who leaves the framing of many policy initiatives to gifted subordinates will still be highly successful if he, like Carey, (a) reviews their work to insure that it is consistent with his fundamental goals and (b) himself takes charge of matters in sit-uations where his aides are in the wrong (the 1979 gasoline shortage); or where the relevant publics (the Love Canal neigh-

The Days of Wine and Roses Are Over

bors the Congressional committees dealing with aid to the five boroughs) want to deal with him rather than his underlings.

Of course, it was he **in person** who did more than anyone else to save the City of New York from bankruptcy in 1975. He lobbied hard with and testified convincingly before his former colleagues in the House and his old friends in the Senate for aid to the metropolis. He organized others to overwhelm Congress with pleas for assistance and pressured Gerald Ford to support such help. He pushed through the Legislature unpopular City and State taxes that were the *sine qua non* of federal loans. The latter set of imposts also helped make it possible for the State to sell its notes and provide needed assistance to local jurisdictions. He was able to convince most of the municipal unions, some of which had worked for him in the 1974 general election, that they had to consent to a wage freeze. He won the trust of the bankers whose confidence in New York had to be restored before they and the general public would buy its bonds again. He had the Legislature pass the measure setting up the Emergency Financial Control Board (EFCB), which had the power to limit New York City's spending. He dominated the decisions of the Board in order to insure that the City, including its non-mayoral agencies, did not become too profligate. When New York needed federal loan guarantees in 1978 in order to continue to avert insolvency, he did his share of the battling.

On the crucial State level, he helped save the Urban Development Corporation from a second default. His Budget Director Peter Goldmark developed a complex and ingenious scheme to strengthen four other construction agencies (e.g., the Housing Finance Agency, the State Dormitory Authority) that were in financial straits; and Carey supported the plan 100%. That "buildout" of these units not only allowed them to finish their ongoing projects; but also enabled them to repay their debts on schedule and thus made it possible for the Municipal Assistance Corporation to continue to sell its own bonds. If MAC had not been able to dispose of these, the City would have gone under even though Carey and the EFCB were forcing it to cut costs.

Most of my interviewees felt that the New York City rescue was Carey's greatest accomplishment. They argued not unreasonably that if the metropolis had foundered, many if not all the evils he had warned about when soliciting federal assistance would have come to pass. There well might have been service cuts that were much more severe than those that did ensue. Jurisdictions throughout New York State as well as Albany itself might have been unable to borrow money; and municipalities located elsewhere might have seen the interest rates on their bonds surge. The City's prominence as a financial center might have vanished with a concomitant additional loss of jobs. Assemblyman Herman Farrell put the point to me in a colorful way: to ask what the Governor's biggest success was apart from keeping the five boroughs from sinking is analogous to asking Mrs. Lincoln what she disliked about the play at Ford's Theater apart from the killing of the President!(19)

Farrell, however, overstates his case: as these pages have repeated, many of the Chief Executive's other achievements were hardly minuscule. To take one arising out of the financial crisis, Carey's acceptance of the imposition of moderate tuition at the City University of New York; his willingness to revise the law that provided that the State could spend no more on CUNY than did the City; and his ultimate agreement to a full takeover by the State of the funding of CUNY's senior colleges made it possible for the University to continue to serve hundreds of thousands rather than just tens of thousands. New York City busses and subways and suburban commuter lines are in much better physical shape than they were due to the passage in 1981 of the Ravitch-drafted $5.5 billion capital assistance act to which the Governor gave his assent. Special taxes enacted around the same time make possible a meaningful and permanent Albany subsidy to the Metropolitan Transportation Authority to cover part of the operating expenses of the agencies under its umbrella and thus prevent subway, bus and commuter train fares from going through the roof.

He signed a consent decree providing for the emptying out of the giant Willowbrook Developmental Center for the mentally retarded and the transfer of its residents to small group homes; and then twisted legislative arms to insure sufficient funding to carry out the terms of the judgment. Many of those living in other huge State asylums for the developmentally disabled were also moved to more pleasant surroundings. He and his aides curbed runaway Medicaid costs not through curtailing crucial services, but through limiting the amounts those who cared for Medicaid patients could receive from the State as reimbursement and through insuring that Medicaid clients were not given medical care that they did not greatly need. The creation of the Medicaid Fraud Unit under Charles Hynes and tighter regulation of nursing homes to stop them from bilking Albany were additional Carey measures that slowed the rise in the Medicaid burden that was threatening to overwhelm the State, its counties and its biggest city. These steps also protected the indigent and the helpless; and the Hynes group served as a model for national legislation requiring all states to create similar agencies. In the environmental field, Carey's Administration can take credit for enacting a law requiring that plans for large private and public projects be accompanied by an environmental impact statement; for pressuring the federal government to join with it in purchasing all the homes near the Love Canal toxic chemical dumpsite; and for convincing Washington to bear most of the cost of cleaning up the nuclear waste site known as West Valley.

In the economic development arena, he and his appointees revitalized the Urban Development Corporation, using it as a tool to realize the Rockefeller Administration's Battery Park City dream and to have a modern convention hall built in midtown Manhattan. The Corporation also runs a Times Square Redevelopment Project that will ultimately be completed by another Governor. Its rejuvenation of hotels in downtown Albany and Syracuse has made these cities' cores more hospitable places to visit. (The irony is that one reason he decided not to run again in 1982 was that the State lacked money to enable him to leave it what he perceived to be a major tangible legacy.(20) It is sad that he did not recognize that Battery Park City, the Javits Convention Center, a modernized subway and commuter railroad network and the preservation of CUNY as a sizeable system constitute magnificent bequests of this nature.) And, beginning with 1977, measures proposed by him significantly reduced State business and individual taxes to make the State less unattractive to established and new enterprises. There were, not surprisingly, policy disappointments such as the inability to significantly improve the lot of the mentally ill and the failure to plan for a needed freight tunnel under the Hudson River to New York City. The "disregard of public image" that Benjamin stresses(21) was also a major weakness. As Coleman Ransone, a leading student of American state politics, puts it, "A governor is judged not only on what he does, but on the people's perception of what he does".(22) But Carey's failures are far outweighed by his successes.

Naturally, his tax cuts cannot be looked at in the abstract. If they had regularly produced deficits financial disaster would have ensued. But they did not, for Carey did his utmost to insure that they would be accompanied by restraining increases in State disbursements, that is, by adopting and implementing what many of my interviewees referred to as fiscal conservatism on the State level.(23) We saw his Administration taking successful steps to hold down the growth of Medicaid expenditures. He also line-item vetoed some of the 1980 and 1982 budgets. It is true that some of the 1980 cuts were restored and that the second set of the 1982 vetoes was overridden. But without these disapprovals spending would have been higher. For example, the initial 1982 vetoes deleted $900 million in various items while the outlays following upon the overrides totalled only $375 million.(24) Liberals such as State Senate Minority Leader Manfred Ohrenstein and conservatives such as Governor George Pataki, State Assembly Minority Leader Clarence Rappleyea and unsuccessful State Controller hopeful Herbert London all have praised Carey's efforts at lowering taxes and reining in State spending.(25) In fact, Republicans London and Rappleyea view Carey's governorship in a surprisingly favorable light. In an interview with the Assembly Minority Leader, London asserted that "When Hugh Carey was governor, I disagreed with him much of the time. Nonetheless the state was run more efficiently than it's run [under Mario Cuomo], and he [Carey] was a liberal democrat....Carey did **run** this state". (Emphasis London's.) Rappleyea responded that "He did....He might have been labeled a liberal democrat, but he was.... someone who made sure that the balance was better kept [than under Cuomo]".(26)

It is not that the State budget did not grow during Carey's eight years: in fact it went from (excluding federal grants in aid) $10.4 billion in 1975 to $17.4 billion in 1982.(27) The point is that it would have ballooned even more and tax cuts been impossible were it not for his having forced a slowing of expenditure escalations. For most of his term, the rise in State spending was less than the rate of inflation(28), not a bad effort for a Governor of a jurisdiction where rapid increases in public disbursements had been the rule. Between 1959 and 1973, the Rockefeller years, the budget grew from $2 billion to $8.77 billion.(29) Thus it swelled under the Republican by 339% in 15 years and under the Democrat by only 67% in eight. Carey's achievement is the more remarkable since the figures given here are actual numbers rather than ones adjusted for inflation; and on the whole prices rose more steeply in the Carey than in the Rockefeller era.(30)

A governor does owe it to the citizens of his/her state to lower taxes to retain and attract business and jobs. But in doing so she/he is really appealing to people's greed, to their unwillingness to part with their money to help others. Thus a public official whose main concern is slashing excises lacks vision and nobility. But Carey's political philosophy went far beyond a belief in subnational fiscal restraint. Civil libertarians will find much in his record such as the closing-down of Willowbrook, the pardoning of prisoners convicted for their role in the Attica riot and the modification of the overly-stringent Rockefeller drug laws, to justify a conclusion that he was a first-rate Chief Executive. To take a recondite example of his tendency to end up on the side of fairness and individual liberty, in 1977 the Legislature approved a bill requiring that the parent of a child absent from school obtain a doctor's note if a teacher or truant officer demanded one. As the father of fourteen, he knew very well that sometimes a young person is ill enough to keep home for a few days but not sick enough to justify calling a doctor. Accordingly, he rejected the measure on the ground that it placed an impossible burden on many parents.(31) He backed up an order issued by Meyer Frucher, the Director of his Office of Employee Relations, mandating that State workers not be reimbursed for business meals taken at clubs that discriminated on grounds of race or gender, e.g., the then-all-male Fort Orange Club. However, he did repudiate a Frucher directive, a decade ahead of its time, to the effect that sexual preference be ignored in decisions to hire and promote State employees.(32)

His most publicized civil liberties position, his death penalty vetoes, reflects not only a willingness to accept political risks but a humanism, a sense that human life is sacred and must not be taken except in extreme circumstances such as fighting against the armies of an Adolf Hitler. This instinct also helped mold his stance on the question of Northern Ireland. He feels himself Irish and is proud of being both Irish and Catholic.(33) He agrees with most Irish Catholics that the North and the South of Ireland should be made one. As he said in 1979, in a statement signed by such other Irish American politicians as Senators Edward Kennedy and Daniel Moynihan and fellow-governor Brendan Byrne of New Jersey, "The whole can be greater than the sum of its parts. A whole Ireland, with institutions that link the Protestant and Catholic communities and that protect the rights of each community, can bring greater benefits to both parts of the divided island than either part now enjoys, and enhance the two great and powerful traditions of the Irish people".(34) But he strongly desires **peaceful** reunification and thus execrated the Irish Republican Army (IRA) for its campaign of violence to end partition. In 1977 he joined with House Speaker Tip O'Neill as well as Senators Kennedy and Moynihan in denouncing IRA terrorism.(35) On a trip to Ireland in Spring of that year, he in much harsher language referred to that group as a bunch of "killers" and "Marxists" to whom Americans should not give "a nickel".(36) But it was in a lecture given in April, 1977 at the Royal College of Surgeons in Dublin that he spoke most movingly against the Republican Army and its love affair with bloodshed.

"Those fascinated by death as a political weapon are surely as sick as people can be....So I will speak to death - and its brother, violence - only to condemn it in my own land and yours.

....To what end then do the apostles of death and violence lead us? To no end, I say, worthy of human consideration.

....I believe most conficts that arise in the human experience lend themselves to the politics of accomodation, compromise and ultimate peaceful settlement. Those that do not are readily apparent to the vast majority of informed opinion and call for different acts.

The Days of Wine and Roses Are Over

But all of this is different from those who play at death and who seek to enhance themselves by these means in a society that has otherwise denied them respect and status.

They, to me, are the leaders in the politics of death. They, to me, are the most reprehensible, -- and they must be stopped."(37)

Poetic and convincing words, this Harry O'Flanagan lecture; but they and similar Carey comments infuriated some Irish Americans who from the comfort of their armchairs cheered on the terrorists and even sent them money.(38)

Consistent with the Chief Executive's humanism is that he always felt a concern for the more vulnerable members of society even when reducing taxes, cutting government spending and waltzing with the Anne Ford Uziellis and the Evangeline Gouletases(39) of the world. As recent commentators have emphasized, he, unlike the current crop of "government downsizers", did not view working people and the poor as the enemy but, rather, made a vigorous effort to get them to cooperate in implementing reforms he thought were necessary.(40) In his eyes some segments of the weak (e.g., the mentally retarded) were more attractive than others; but he was always concerned about the plight of the poor generally(41) notwithstanding Jimmy Breslin's acid remarks to the contrary in his "Society Carey" articles. On this point his health aide Jeffrey Sachs told me a revealing story. Budget Director Howard Miller and Morgado were sitting around a table having a debate about what should be the Carey Administration's priorities in an era of scarce resources. Miller wanted to emphasize education as an investment in the future while the supposedly heartless Secretary contended that expenditures on the neediest should take precedence. The Governor then came into the room and made it clear that he was on Morgado's side. Thus though there was talk of welfare cuts during the Carey years, practically nothing came of these proposals.(42) In fact, he successfully backed 1981 legislation increasing by 15% that part of the welfare grant not set aside for the payment of rent.(43)

I and my interviewees are not the first to refer to Carey as an "outstanding" Governor or apply a similar adjective to him. Political Scientist Larry Sabato labels him as one of the "Outstanding Gov-

Carey: a Rolls Royce Engine in a Studebaker Body

ernors, 1950-1975".(44) As he had been in the Executive Mansion only one year out of this 25-year period and as he had spent most of that year rescuing New York City, Sabato clearly gave him that accolade for that triumph alone.(45) In 1992 he was honored with the fifth Annual Nelson Rockefeller Public Service Award from the Rockefeller Institute of Government in Albany. The four previous recipients were Senator Mike Mansfield, Federal Reserve Board Chairman Paul Volcker and Secretaries of State George Shultz and Henry Kissinger.(46) The *New York Post*, in remarking on that event, said that Hugh Carey was "by no means out of place" in that "exalted company". Furthermore, his per-formance during the fiscal crisis "demonstrated beyond doubt that he was one of New York's **great** governors".(47) A 1982 com-mentary in the *Boston Globe* maintained that "When Gov. Hugh Carey declined to run for re-election, many New Yorkers realized how courageous and decisive a governor Carey had been".(48) But it was the *New York Times's* 1982 farewell editorial that best and most vividly sums up what this chapter has been saying more prosaically.

> "...Governor Carey's shortcomings were dwarfed by his stature as leader, his weight of character. **He brought greatness to the office** He deserves much of the credit for saving New York City from bankruptcy....
> He then turned his attention to the state's declining economy, and forced on it the recognition of limited resources, of the importance of attracting new businesses and expanding existing ones....
> As Hugh Carey's eight years as Governor dwindle down to their last hours, it is hard to imagine how anyone else could have done so well in leading the state through its hardest winter."(49)

Of course, Carey was not able to solve once and for all the State's and the City's problems. The often-violent political, social, demographic and economic tides that lash a jurisdiction do not disappear after its leader has left office, even if (as with the Governor) he or she has prevented them from wreaking too much destruction. In fact, because the U.S. economy has become more and more dependent on events abroad, they now buffet New York's shores more viciously than ever before. They leave in their wake a citizenry loathing the indigent they have beached; fearing the loss of their jobs; and hating the thought of giving their earnings to the revenue collector to fund the programs that made up the "wine and roses" of the Rockefeller years. Thus, despite the tax cuts that Carey initiated, still-relatively-high state and local imposts keep pushing established firms and the middle class out of New York and discourage corporations from locating branches within its borders.(50) Therefore the State's economy is sluggish again.(51) As one consequence of this, CUNY once more was ordered to reduce its budget for a particular fiscal year before the end of that twelvemonth and is faced with massive slashes in funding in the future.(52) Meanwhile Medicaid costs, as was the case in 1975, are soaring out of control.(53)

But even though he did not and could not convert his state into the Garden of Eden, Carey **was** a tremendous governor and would have made a fine U.S. President. Doubtlessly he, like every young person interested in politics, fantasized in his youth about sitting in the White House. But was this a dream on which he focused when he held political office? Only he himself knows the answer. He insisted both in 1976 and 1980 that he had no serious wish to become a candidate for the Presidency or Vice Presidency(54); but assertions of this sort by political leaders are routine and usually not taken too seriously. David Burke, his Secretary in 1976, still does not know whether Carey wanted to run that year: he feels that the Governor is a person who would be unwilling to admit to anyone that he had such an ambition unless he were absolutely committed in his own mind to entering the contest.(55) John Omicinski, Albany reporter for the Gannett newspaper chain, gives testimony that differs from Burke's and avers that Carey did that year talk to his aides about becoming a Presidential contender.(56) Carey Press Secretary Robert Laird said that his chief probably toyed with the idea of taking this step but was not willing to stump the country for primary victories. He hoped, Laird asserted, that the Democratic Party would come to him and thus make it unnecessary for him to criss-cross the Iowas, Oregons and Wyomings of the North American continent.(57) In any event, as seen, the public relations fiasco springing from the firing of Special Prosecutor Maurice Nadjari would have made it difficult for the Governor to convince the residents of these wide open spaces that he was anything more than a garden-variety urban machine politician. Judge Jacob Grumet's report exculpating him from any wrong-doing in the affair did not appeal until June 1976, after the primaries were history.

1980 saw Jimmy Carter in charge in Washington. He was un-popular with the American people and, as mentioned, with Carey. Yet anyone who challenges a President of one's own Party in primaries always has a tough road to hoe. Ronald Reagan found that out when he unsuccessfully tried to wrest the Republican nomination from Ford in 1976. Nonetheless in September, 1979 Carey, Morgado, David Garth and some wealthy contributors met to talk about a Carey candidacy. The Governor denied that he indicated any interest in seeking higher office; but some of the others certainly wished him to enter the lists. They felt that he should go if the better-known Senator Edward Kennedy did not. But Kennedy threw his hat into the ring and the boomlet for Carey, such as it was, died aborning.(58)

After he left the Governorship, Carey became a lawyer with the huge firm of Finley, Kumble and Wagner. When this partnership crumbled in 1987, he was hired by W.R. Grace and Company as Executive Vice President in charge of handling the various environmental problems it faced. His salary with Grace was initially $400,000 per annum, about three times as much as he would have made had he continued to reside in the Executive Mansion.(59) Over 75 now, and working for the Manhattan investment banking firm of Cambridge Partners, he almost certainly will never run for office again; but from time to time he has raised his voice on political issues. For example, in 1994 he declared that language calling for aid to the poor ought to be retained in any revised State Constitution, and added that he feared that a Constitutional Convention would adopt a "rigid, vindictive" attitude on social issues.(60) This warning is fully consistent with his philosophy of a lifetime.

Notes to Chapter 16

1. Interview with the aide, July 23, 1991.

2. Interview with Berger, Feb. 21, 1991, New York City.

3. Interview with State Assembly Mental Health Committee Chairperson Connelly, Aug. 8, 1990, Staten Island, N.Y.; with Kremer, Aug. 22, 1990, Uniondale, N.Y.

4. Interview with Reid, Aug. 21, 1990, New York City.

5. Interview with Frangos, June 13, 1991, Albany, N.Y.

6. Interview with Del Giudice, June 28, 1994, New York City; with Horowitz, Jan. 14, 1992, New York City.

7. Interview with Ravitch, Nov. 20, 1990, New York City.

8. Interview with Blum, July 27, 1991, New York City; with Hassett, Sept. 26, 1990, New York City.

9. Phone interview with Burns, Dec. 30, 1992, Binghamton, N.Y.

10. Interview with Koch, Nov. 11, 1994, New York City.

11. Phone interview with Abzug, May 10, 1991, New York City.

12. Interview with Dicker, June 12, 1991, Albany, N.Y.

13. Interview with Duryea, June 26, 1990, Montauk, N.Y.

14. Phone interview with Carter Deputy Secretary for Intergovernmental Affairs Eidenberg, Sept. 4, 1991, Washington.

15. Interview with Beame, Dec. 27, 1990, New York City.

16. Morgado, Robert - Robert Morgado: The Secretary to the Governor at p. 27, 49 of Benjamin, Gerald and Hurd, T. Norman (eds.) - Making Experience Count: Managing Modern New York In The Carey Era (Albany: Nelson A. Rockefeller Institute of Government, 1985).

17. Benjamin, Gerald - The Carey Governorship at p. 235, 251 of Benjamin and Hurd (eds.), op. cit. n.16 supra.

Carey: a Rolls Royce Engine in a Studebaker Body

18. Interview with Macchiarola, July 31, 1991, New York City.

19. Interview with Farrell, Jan. 29, 1993, New York City.

20. Interviews with the Director of his Office of Employee Relations Meyer Frucher, Aug. 17 1994 and Aug. 23, 1994 (phone), New York City.

21. Op. cit. n.17 supra, p. 251.

22. See his The American Governorship (Westport, Conn.: Greenwood Press, 1982), p. 112.

23. Connelly, interview cited n.3 supra; interview with Carey Commerce Commissioner John Dyson, Jan. 21, 1991, Millbrook, N.Y.; with New York State Comptroller Edward V. Regan, July 5, 1990, New York City.

24. See New York Times, June 16, 1982, p. B6 with Staten Island Advance, Apr. 13, 1982, p. 1; July 4, 1982, p. A12.
   In 1982 the initial set of vetoes was not challenged. To overcome these vetoes, the lawmakers passed instead a new appropriations bill of $375 million in the summer. Carey allowed about $50 million of this to become law and vetoed the remainder. It was that group of negatives that was overturned. He thus left office with a $500 million deficit; but the Legislature, not he, was to blame for this.

25. Interview with Ohrenstein, Oct. 25, 1994, New York City; London, Herbert and Rubenstein, Edwin - From the Empire State to the Vampire State: New York in a downward transition (Lanham, Md.: University Press of America, 1994), pp. 94-95; Staten Island Advance, Oct. 2, 1994, p. B3 (praise by Pataki).

26. These quotes appear on p. 95 of London and Rubenstein, op. cit. n.25 supra.

27. New York Times, Mar. 27, 1975, p. 20; Jan. 20, 1982, p. B6; Feb. 1, 1983, p. A1.

28. Rubenstein, Edwin - Albany's Empty Rhetoric of Austerity, New York Times, Mar. 5, 1990, p. A15.

29. New York Times, Mar. 12, 1959, p. 1; Mar. 29, 1973, p. 1.

The Days of Wine and Roses Are Over

30. Economic Report of the President Transmitted to the Congress February 1984 (Washington: Government Printing Office, 1984), p. 224.

31. Public Papers of Governor Hugh L. Carey 1977 (Albany: State of New York Executive Chamber, 1987), pp. 339-40.

32. Frucher, interviews cited n.20 supra.

33. Interview with Carey Tax Commissioner James Tully, June 8, 1990, Albany, N.Y.

34. Public Papers of Governor Hugh L. Carey 1979 (Albany: State of New York Executive Chamber, 1992), p. 621. The whole statement can be found at pp. 617-21 of ibid.

35. Interview with Carey Special Assistant for Health Affairs Dr. Kevin Cahill, July 26, 1993, New York City; New York Times, Apr. 23, 1977, p. 1.

36. New York Times, Apr. 23, 1977, p. 1.

37. The entire speech may be found Hugh L. Carey Collection, St. John's Univ.(NY), Gubernatorial Files 1975-82 (Personal Files 1975-82: Personal Subject Files T-Misc.) file. It is excerpted in Carey, op. cit. n.31 supra, pp. 883-86.

38. New York Times, Apr. 23, 1977, p. 1.

39. For a while, Carey dated Ethel Kennedy, widow of Senator Robert Kennedy. New York Times, Dec. 21, 1976, p. 47. How close the relationship was cannot be known until St. John's University Library makes public certain correspondence between the two. This step will not be taken until 2005 at the earliest.

40. New Yorker, May 15, 1995, p. 36; New York Times, Apr. 23, 1995, Sec. 4, p. 16.

41. Blum interview cited n.8 supra; Connelly, interview cited n.3 supra; interview with Carey Corrections Commissioner Thomas Coughlin, July 18, 1990, Albany, N.Y.; with Carey Office of Mental Retardation and Developmental Disabilities Commissioner James Introne, Aug. 15, 1991, Syracuse, N.Y.

42. Interview with Carey Office of Development Planning head Hugh O'Neill, June 17, 1992, New York City; interview with Sachs, June 7, 1991, New York City; New York Times, Dec. 10, 1975, p. 1; Feb. 10, 1977, p. 30.

43. Bernstein, Blanche - The Politics of Welfare: The New York City Experience (Cambridge, Mass.: Abt Books, 1982), pp. 30-31.

44. Sabato, Larry - Goodbye to Good-Time Charlie: The American Governorship Transformed (Lexington: D. C. Heath, 1978), p. 52.

45. Ibid., p. 54.

46. Times Union (Albany), May 20, 1992, p. B12.

47. New York Post, June 4, 1992, p. 24. Emphasis supplied.

48. Boston Globe, Feb. 26, 1982, p. 12. Permission to reprint granted by the Boston Globe.

49. New York Times, Dec. 30, 1982, p. A14. Emphasis supplied. (Copyright 1982 by The New York Times Co. Reprinted by Permission.)

50. New York's state taxes are now down to 22nd in the nation when measured as a share of personal income albeit sixth per capita. However, high local taxes within its borders make its state/local tax combination the second highest per capita in the United States. New York Times, Sept. 21, 1994, p. B1.

51. Staten Island Advance, Feb. 12, 1995, p. A1.

52. New York Times, Jan. 31, 1995, p. B4.

53. New York Times, Jan. 19, 1995, p. A1, B6.

54. Public Papers of Governor Hugh L. Carey 1975 (Albany: State of New York Executive Chamber, 1982), pp. 1119-20; New York Times, Aug. 5, 1980, p. B1.

55. Interview, Aug. 28, 1992, New York City.

56. Phone interview, Sept. 27, 1991, Washington.

57. Interview, May 18, 1993, New York City.

58. <u>New York Times</u>, Aug. 5, 1980, p. B1. Joyce Purnick, the author of the article, maintains there that Carey had "at least a passing interest in national office".

59. <u>New York Times</u>, May 22, 1988, Sec. 3, p. 1.

60. Quote from <u>Staten Island Advance</u>, May 11, 1994, p. B3.

Index

The Days of Wine and Roses Are Over

Index

338

The Days of Wine and Roses Are Over

Index